LANGDON GILKEY:
THEOLOGIAN
FOR A CULTURE
IN DECLINE

LANGDON GILKEY:

THEOLOGIAN FOR A CULTURE IN DECLINE

Brian J. Walsh

UNIVERSITY
PRESS OF
AMERICA

Lanham • New York • London

Copyright © 1991 by
University Press of America®, Inc.
4720 Boston Way
Lanham, Maryland 20706

3 Henrietta Street
London WC2E 8LU England

Co-published by arrangement with the
Institute for Christian Studies, Ontario, Canada

Library of Congress Cataloging-in-Publication Data
Walsh, Brain J., 1953-
Langdon Gilkey : Theologian for a Culture in Decline
/ Brian J. Walsh.
p. cm.
"Co-published by arrangement with the Institute
for Christian Studies, Ontario, Canada"—T.p. verso.
Revision of the author's thesis (Ph. D.)—McGill University.
Includes bibliographical references.
1. Gilkey, Langdon Brown, 1919- . I. Title.
BX4827.G55W35 1991
230' .044' 092—dc20   91-26355 CIP

ISBN 0-8191-8354-7 (cloth, alk. paper)
ISBN 0-8191-8355-5 (pbk., alk. paper)

For N. Thomas Wright
Worcester College, Oxford
colleague and friend

TABLE OF CONTENTS

PREFACE

This book addresses the relation between religion and culture or, more specifically, Christianity and modern culture. Such themes can be explored in a number of ways. A study of a particular cultural issue or a particular religious community could be the avenue to the broader issues of Christianity in the context of modernity. Or, one could address these issues by studying the thought of one representative thinker. If one chooses the latter path, as I have, then it is imperative that the scholar under consideration merit such close scrutiny.

Langdon B. Gilkey is such a scholar. His writings over the last three decades have demonstrated theological acumen and cultural insight. He is a theologian of interdisciplinary scope, and a study of his thought opens one both to the major themes in contemporary North American philosophical theology and the broad socio-cultural issues of our time. This critical study of Langdon Gilkey's thought arises out of a profound respect and admiration for him as a theologian and a person. It is in this spirit of respect and admiration that my critique is offered.

Theologies and cultures are communal. So also are books. The research and writing of this work was facilitated by various institutions and individuals. It is, therefore, appropriate that I acknowledge that assistance here. From 1983 to 1986 I held a doctoral fellowship from the Social Sciences and Humanities Research Council of Canada. That financial assistance is gratefully acknowledged. The earliest form of this manuscript was a dissertation written for the Faculty of Religious Studies of McGill University. That Faculty proved to be a most conducive place for scholarly research. The faculty and administrative staff supportively encouraged my successful completion of the doctoral program. Bursaries, teaching assistantships, summer fellowships and travel grants from both this Faculty and the Faculty of

Graduate Studies provided additional financial assistance. Finally, the library staff of the Faculty of Religious Studies (especially Jennifer Wheeler) went to great lengths to assure that I had all the materials necessary for my research.

Beyond institutional assistance there are also a number of people whom I would like to thank. My doctoral advisor, Dr. Joseph C. McLelland, has the courage to advise a wide variety of graduate students addressing very diverse topics, and the wisdom to give his students the room to develop their own thought. I have deeply appreciated his support throughout the doctoral program of study and beyond.

A number of people read parts or all of the manuscript and offered helpful comments. Professors James H. Olthuis and J. Harry Fernhout of the Institute for Christian Studies in Toronto read sections of Parts II and III. Jim Olthuis was also a valued dialogue partner during the final stages of the writing. Joseph McLelland, of course, read the complete manuscript. Dr. Robert VanderVennen offered many helpful editorial suggestions. Thanks also to Willem Hart whose artistic talent and graphic expertise turned my manuscript into a book.

A person to whom I offer special thanks, however, is Professor N. Thomas Wright of Worcester College, Oxford (formerly of McGill University). It is rare indeed to find a scholar in one field (New Testament Studies) who shows both interest and insight in another very different area. Tom Wright read the complete manuscript and offered detailed comments on both style and substance. Our friendship during our years at McGill was a constant source of mutual encouragement and intellectual stimulation. To him I gratefully dedicate this volume.

Another person to whom I would like to offer a word of thanks is the subject of this monograph himself, Langdon Gilkey. For ten days in the autumn of 1984 Professor Gilkey was my host at the University of Chicago Divinity School. In a series of interviews my understanding of his thought was clarified and my respect for the man was solidified. He was generous with his time and gave me access to a number of unpublished papers. Since then our relationship has continued to be most amicable. To Professor Gilkey I am indebted.

Finally, scholarly research occurs in a context that is broader than academic institutions and other scholars — that context includes one's family and friends. I am not going to thank these people for "suffering through" the writing of this book. I do not believe that others should have to suffer unduly so that one person can accomplish a task. Such tasks need to be approached in such a way that the broader scope of one's human interactions is not sacrificed. This has been the model I have attempted to follow. To these people I express my gratitude — you know who you are. But there is one person for whom special mention is due. When I began this project my son, Jubal, was still a baby — he is now ten years old. The intellectual and personal development that I have experienced during this time cannot compare with his growth. Life is more than scholarship. Playing road hockey, soccer, catch and golf continually reminds me of that. I am grateful for the reminder and it is Jubal more than anyone who will not let me forget it.

Toronto
Spring 1991

INTRODUCTION

1. Setting the Context

In December, 1933, Reinhold Niebuhr wrote in the Preface to his *Reflections on the End of an Era* that the basic conviction which runs through those reflections "is that the liberal culture of modernity is quite unable to give guidance and direction to a confused generation which faces the disintegration of a social system and the task of building a new one."[1] Later in the book he documents the failure of liberalism to produce either international cooperation or harmony among the classes.[2] He decries the "moral superficiality" of modern culture's easy faith that reason either had conquered or would conquer and restrain human anarchic impulses and egocentricity.[3]

Niebuhr says that an increase in knowledge will not save Western culture because "we are not dealing with a functional ill which might be corrected by a slight change in policy or program." Rather, "the sickness from which modern civilization suffers is organic and constitutional."[4] And he rejects the optimism of the "uncritical rationalism" of his day because it "assumes that men who are moved by interest are able to see the obvious facts of history and that they invariably obey the imperatives which the facts disclose." This assumption "fails to recognize with what stubborn inertia and blindness men will pursue their own interests even if these are proved to be in conflict with a more general interest."[5] Indeed, he argues that "adequate spiritual direction can come only through a more radical political orientation and a more conservative religious conviction" than are generally seen to be acceptable to the culture of his era.[6]

It was only a month earlier, on November 4, that Paul Tillich arrived with his family in New York, having been dismissed by the Nazis from his philosophy position at the University of Frankfurt earlier that year. It was at the invitation of Reinhold Niebuhr that Tillich came to teach at Union Seminary.[7] Tillich's voluntary exile from Nazi Germany came about because his attempts to relate all

1

cultural life to what he called the religious centre inevitably came into conflict with a regime that was both idolatrous and heteronomous. Tillich's first published speech was titled, "Über die Idee einer Theologie der Kultur" (On the Idea of a Theology of Culture).[8] Indeed, Tillich created the term 'theology of culture' to designate that mode of analysis and critique of society that discerns the 'style of a culture.' And, "he who can read the style of a culture can discover its ultimate concern, its religious substance."[9] In biblical language, theology of culture is concerned with 'discerning the spirits' of a culture. As such, theology of culture is not concerned with the cultural role of religion as it is narrowly conceived—religion as either a special function of the human spirit or as it is institutionally embodied. Rather, Tillich's theology of culture is concerned with religion more broadly understood as the dimension of depth of all human life and all human culture.[10] Tillich characteristically described the relation of culture and religion in terms of the relation of form and substance:

> Religion as ultimate concern is the meaning-giving substance of culture, and culture is the totality of forms in which the basic concern of religion expresses itself. In abbreviation: religion is the substance of culture, culture is the form of religion.[11]

The relation of religion and culture, specifically Christianity and secular culture, remained the centre of Tillich's interest throughout his teaching and writing career.

The coming together of Niebuhr and Tillich at Union Seminary in 1933 was to have a most profound effect on the development of theology in North America in the latter half of the twentieth century. It was into their classes that Langdon Gilkey was to come as a graduate student in theology in the 1946. The unique way that both Tillich and Niebuhr attempted to correlate the symbols of the Christian tradition with the pressing existential and socio-political issues of their day was not only to influence Gilkey's own constructive theological proposals, but, more fundamentally, it was to set the pattern for the very way in which Gilkey asked his theological questions. As Gilkey himself says in the Preface to *Reaping the Whirlwind*, the influence of Tillich and Niebuhr "is so thoroughly intertwined that I would myself find it impossible to clearly disentangle the strands." And further, "there is hardly a page of this volume that does not represent the insights of one or both of these two thinkers...."[12] One might add that what is true of

Reaping the Whirlwind is true of the whole Gilkey corpus.

In the light of the combined influence of Tillich and Niebuhr on Gilkey's thought it is not surprising that a concern for a theological interpretation and response to culture is characteristic of his work. Indeed, in one of his earliest articles Gilkey identifies as a central theological concern, the formulation of a response to what he sees as the crisis of Western culture, the spiritual breakdown of faith in progress, scientific knowledge and technical proficiency. In language which will reappear throughout his writings he says that "the creative union of reason, meaning and culture has dissipated itself before our eyes, much as in late Classical Society."[13] Niebuhr had said the same thing twenty years earlier. Gilkey would continue to say it for over thirty more years with increasing clarity. He went on in that early article to reject both theological liberalism's cultural identification (though affirming its concern for relevance) and neo-orthodox inwardness and dissociation (though affirming its concern for transcendence). Since neo-orthodoxy was the dominant movement at that time (or at least amongst readers of the periodical *Christianity and Crisis*) he focussed on the contribution of that movement to a Christian cultural response. While the emphasis on transcendence allows the Christian cultural analyst to challenge that which is idolatrous and demonic in culture, the concomitant emphasis on inwardness gives little actual basis for cultural decisions. Gilkey asks, "Does the Christian then do what others do, only with repentance?"[14] Does the inward act of repentance have no concrete cultural implication? Is the neo-orthodox God not only transcendent, but also elusive? "Is there not something more positive, more radical to the Christian witness, some clearer Christian guidance with regard to action, than a cultural pragmatism which is religiously repentant?"[15] This book is a study in the thought of Langdon Gilkey with special reference to these kind of questions.

2. Problems of Interpretation

Langdon Gilkey (b. 1919) completed his doctoral studies in 1954 with a dissertation on the doctrine of creation in relation to the metaphysical theories of F. H. Bradley's monistic idealism and A. N. Whitehead's pluralistic critical realism.[16] His advisor was Reinhold Niebuhr. From 1954 to 1963 he taught theology at the Vanderbilt University Divinity School. Since then he has taught theology at the University of Chicago Divinity School, being appointed to the Shailer Mathews chair in systematic theology in 1976.[17]

His contribution to North American theology has been in many diverse areas. They range from reformulations of the doctrines of creation and providence, proposals on theological method, philosophical analysis and defense of the meaningfulness of religious language, to phenomenological description of the dimension of ultimacy. He has discussed the relations of religion and science, the churches and culture, Christianity and world religions. In particular he has offered a theology of culture which ranges from broad descriptions and diagnoses of modernity to specific discussions of the nature of political power and the debate concerning creationism and evolution. It is, therefore, not surprising that Gilkey's colleague and friend David Tracy could say, "With the exception of Paul Tillich, it is difficult to name another twentieth century theologian who so straightforwardly addresses the major issues that the incredible history of our century forces upon our attention."[18]

Such a diverse contribution gives rise to two preliminary questions for the interpreter of his corpus. First, is there a coherent centre which unifies this diversity? And second, is there a continuity in the development of the corpus, or are there major shifts that must be accounted for?

The first question is answered best by seeing that Gilkey's forays into various issues and fields of inquiry are all guided by the same concern—to discover and explicate what he describes in *How the Church Can Minister to the World Without Losing Itself* as a "relevant transcendence."[19] In this way Gilkey brings together themes that have characterized traditional liberalism and neo-orthodoxy respectively. Such a concern for a "relevant transcendence" entails a certain understanding of the divine:

> The holy and transcendent is that which is ultimately relevant to our existence, both as a whole and in all its various facets. While finding no origin in our immediate social and natural environment, the holy is nevertheless that which alone is relevant to every relation the self can have to its whole world, for it is the basis of our relation to these environments, and it is the source and ground of *their* being and meaning as well as our own.[20]

Concomitant with this view that the holy can never be dualistically separated from the world is an understanding of the nature of the theological task. In his recent introduction to systematic theology

(*Message and Existence*), Gilkey describes theology as an inquiry with two poles. Theology is both reflection on our human existence, its character and destiny, from the perspective of Christian faith, and it is a coherent reflective explication of the contents of that faith. But these two poles form a correlated unity because "the contents of Christian faith on the one hand, its set of major symbols, are such that they interpret, illumine, and clarify the basic nature of our human existence and history—their goal, possibilities, obligations, problems and destiny. Correspondingly, the character of our human existence and history, their problems, possibilities, and hopes, is such that they can only be understood fully in the light of that content, as interpreted through these Christian symbols...."[21] As Gilkey's concern in the 1964 book referred to above was how the church can minister to the world *without losing itself*, so in *Message and Existence* the issue is to reinterpret the Christian faith in such a way that it is relevant to, but does not capitulate to, modern culture. Such a reinterpretation should be theistic, not naturalistic; Christian, not humanistic; Christological, not immanentistic; theonomous, not autonomous; and eschatological, not progressivist.[22]

> The result should be a *Christian* interpretation of *modern* experience. If it be not Christian, that is, "appropriate" and faithful to Scripture and tradition, it will bring no new message and thus no healing to modern life; if it be not an interpretation of *modern* experience, it will not touch that experience enough to have an effect.[23]

This understanding of the theological task has been constant throughout Gilkey's career and has been foundational to whatever issue he has addressed. In his first book, *Maker of Heaven and Earth*, he defines theology as a process of uniting two kinds of questions — questions about God and the divine activity, and questions about our general experience.[24] The interrelation of theology and ordinary experience is also the *raison d'etre* of Gilkey's prolegomenal work, *Naming the Whirlwind*, in which he says: "The symbols of a relevant theology must explicate and illumine our ordinary existence in the world, and conversely, our experience of being in the world must give meaning and reality to our theological discourse."[25] Consequently, theology is defined as engaging in the task, on the one hand, of thematizing the ultimate questions that existence raises, and, on the other hand, explicating conceptually the Christian answers in the light of these questions.[26] This definition is in accord with the definition offered in the *Entr'acte* of *Reaping the Whirlwind:* "Christian theology is the enterprise of understanding the totality of contemporary experience ... through the forms or in the terms of Christian symbols, as Christian faith is the effort to live one's life in the illumination and power of those symbols and the presence of the deity they mediate."[27]

This emphasis on the relevance of theology to human experience permeates Gilkey's thought.[28] The fact that this approach to theology bears striking resemblance to Tillich's celebrated 'method of correlation'[29] is something that Gilkey himself notes. Indeed, one commentator has argued that Gilkey's theology "can be most adequately understood in terms of a continuity-discontinuity framework with the explicitly apologetic wing of neo-orthodoxy." This framework is further described as a theological undertaking "which attempts to respond to current concerns but must not be absorbed by them."[30] I think that this interpretation is, largely, correct, and corroborated by the discussion above. The thread that runs through Gilkey's work is indeed an apologetic concern. But this reference to neo-orthodox apologetics forces us to address our second question: is there a continuity in the development of the Gilkey corpus, or are there significant shifts?

We have already seen that there is a coherent centre to Gilkey's understanding of the theological task.[31] But has there not also been at least one significant shift in his thought which complicates a study of his work as a whole? I refer to Gilkey's own description of *Maker of Heaven and Earth* as a 'neo-orthodox' book, combined with his later critique of neo-orthodoxy.[32] Indeed, Gilkey also describes *Maker of Heaven and Earth* as a "thoroughly Niebuhrian book."[33] That is, in this book (and to a similar degree in *How the Church*[34]) Gilkey was content to start with what he understood to be the 'biblical view' of creation and then relate that view to concrete experience, demonstrating thereby the illuminating power of the biblical view and the weaknesses in assorted alternative views (eg., naturalism, pantheism, monism, and dualism). Gilkey later came to be critical of this procedure that was characteristic of neo-orthodox apologetic reflection.[35]

Gilkey describes the fundamental form of neo-orthodox apologetics as follows: "*if* life, history and the paradoxes of human existence are to become intelligible, have meaning and be transformed, *then* the Christian symbols, derived from revelation, provide the necessary framework within which meaning, intelligibility and even transformation are to be achieved."[36] There are now, says Gilkey, two problems with the presuppositions of this approach. First, this approach assumes the meaningfulness of an 'ultimate framework of meaning.' But the philosophical movements of linguistic analysis and existentialism, and the problem of evil brings all of this into question. In an intellectual culture which denies the possibility of metaphysics (as both linguistic analysis and existentialism did), one can no longer *assume* that any ultimate frameworks are meaningful. In this present cultural mood the phrase 'God is dead' means 'all the gods are dead!' That is, "all ultimate structures of coherence, order, and value in the wider environment of man's life have vanished...."[37]

The second problem with this form of apologetics is that it assumes the presence of a set of meaningful and illuminating biblical categories. Gilkey comments: "The *cognitive* base of theology here was thus faith in response to the Word; if that slipped, then the whole logical structure of biblical theology and the potency of its apologetical forms would slip, too. The difficulty has been that it *has* slipped."[38] The evidence for this is the breakdown of the neo-orthodox distinction between the Church and the world. The Church, says Gilkey, is no longer the hearer and possessor of the Word because the Church has come to be as much qualified by 'secularity' as by 'faith.' Consequently, Gilkey comments in the opening pages of *Naming the Whirlwind* that "any current theology ... that does not recognize and seek reflectively to deal with this presence of secularity, of doubt, of skepticism, and so of a sense of meaninglessness of religious language inside the Church as well as outside, and so inside the theologian and believer, is so far irrelevant to our present situation."[39]

For this reason, the Niebuhrian apologetic method (and to a lesser degree even Tillich's approach) must be modified. In fact, what Gilkey does is turn the method on its head. Rather than ask, how do the symbols of the Christian tradition illuminate our experience in the secular world, Gilkey says we must shift the question to, "How, starting with secularity and not with faith, can one begin to do theology?"[40] In *Maker of Heaven and Earth* Gilkey related the biblical and traditional doctrine of creation to the existential issue of human contingency. The method in *Naming the Whirlwind* purports to go in the opposite direction: if we start with contingency, does that lead us to a dimension of ultimacy which in turn is illuminated by what the Christian tradition understands by creation?[41] There is, then, an apparent shift away from an apologetic neo-orthodoxy.

How, in our interpretation of Gilkey, are we to understand this shift? As we saw above, Gilkey himself sees it as important. I would only constitute this as a major shift, however, if there were clear evidence that what is at stake here is not just a change in procedure, but a shift in fundamental thought patterns, for example, in Gilkey's understanding of creation, or his fundamental ontology. But there is no such conclusive evidence. There is certainly a tendency away from Niebuhr's mythical approach to theology and towards Tillich's ontological approach. This may also entail a shift from a more dualistic orientation to a more monistic perspective but, again the evidence in the corpus is, at least to this commentator, inconclusive. The most we could say would be that while dualism was one of Gilkey's problems in the earlier work (i.e., a tendency in his thought that he had to constantly struggle with), monism is a problem in his later work.[42]

The evidence is stronger for seeing a coherent continuity throughout the Gilkey corpus and to understand this 'shift' in terms of that coherence. This is Gilkey's own understanding. In response to a critique of his thought by Peter Berger, Gilkey questions whether Berger had read his whole corpus, including the three books previous to *Naming the Whirlwind*, which is the focus of Berger's attack. Gilkey claims that there has been "no substantial deviation" in *Naming the Whirlwind* from the positions taken in those earlier books.[43] In *Reaping the Whirlwind* he refers to the position developed in *Maker of Heaven and Earth* as being from "a different theological epoch" but "representing a position that I still want to defend...."[44] Perhaps this is the key — it was written in a "different theological epoch." The neo-orthodox apologetic needs to be turned on its head because certain "problems arose in the intervening years."[45] A relevant theology must be relevant to its own time, but the times have changed. The shift, then, is not primarily a shift of overall theological orientation, and certainly not a shift in Gilkey's understanding of the fundamental task of theology to correlate message and existence. Rather, it is a shift in procedure precisely in order to accomplish that task better.[46]

This 'dynamic consistency', as we may call it, in Gilkey's thought can be illustrated by a comparison of his 1965 article in *Christian Century's* "How I am Making Up My Mind" series and his 1981 article in the same journal's "How My Mind Has Changed" series. In 1965 Gilkey wrote of a "dissolution" and "thaw" of the certainties of the earlier theological generation, and the experience of being on "shifting ice" and staring into the "rushing depths of dark water."[47] The cause of this theological dissolution was the power and pervasiveness of the secular spirit of the times. In such a culture, Gilkey asks, is theology even possible? If it is, then a reconstruction project must be embarked upon which will begin not with God and revelation, but with the ordinary experience of human beings, with anthropology. Here we have the call for a prolegomenon to theology which Gilkey then elaborates in *Naming the Whirlwind.*

Sixteen years later (1981) Gilkey was asked how his mind had changed since that earlier article. What is instructive about his response is that he does not mention any substantial change in his own thinking. Rather, he speaks about the changes in the cultural landscape which call forth new theological interpretations and responses. He speaks of his sense of "theological dislocation" as being a matter of his "*reaction* to external events, to massive and threatening cultural and historical changes that, quite against my will, force on me a different procedure, a different viewpoint, a different set of questions — a different theology."[48] I question whether the theology has changed. The procedures and questions certainly have.

What is important to notice in these two articles is that, insofar as Gilkey's theology shifts, it does so in response to the cultural issues that he perceives to be central to theological reflection at that time. Hence, there is a 'dynamic continuity.'[49] And that dynamic continuity is itself an expression of what he has always seen to be the theological task of correlating the symbols of the Christian faith and the experience of human life in the *sæculum.* He says that his intention is to "be a Christian theologian whose thought is inspired and structured by, and remains faithful to, Christian revelation and tradition."[50] And when there are socio-cultural shifts in the *sæculum* within which we all live (whether that be the secular perception of the meaninglessness of religious language in the 60's or the reappearance of the sacred in the 80's), then Gilkey's theology and his theological procedure will attempt to address that new situation.[51]

3. The Thesis and Structure of this Book

Once we have granted that there is this dynamic consistency and intentional coherence in Gilkey's work as a whole, the interpreter of his thought is faced with another question: what is the most helpful and illuminating way critically to interpret his theological contribution? In the light of the diversity of that contribution, what is the best 'point of entrance' into it? As far as I can tell, most detailed studies of Gilkey's thought have focussed on his prolegomenon to theology (i.e., his phenomenological-hermeneutical discussion of the dimension of ultimacy and the renewal of religious language).[52] This is also true of most critical articles. To date, his constructive theological proposals concerning creation and providence (and the ontological proposals found therein) and his theology of culture have not been addressed in any detailed study. And though there have been a few articles on his constructive theology (usually in the form of critical reviews of *Reaping the Whirlwind*), seldom do they address Gilkey's theology of culture.

In the light of the influence of Tillich and Niebuhr noted above, and in the light of Gilkey's understanding of the theological task in terms of a correlation of theological/symbolic message and cultural existence, I propose that we enter into his theological contribution by means of his theology of culture. I am not claiming that this is the *only* appropriate entrance into his thought, but, more modestly, that this entrance both captures the heart of Gilkey's concern for 'relevant transcendence' and best illuminates his theological project as a whole. This approach will also give us an important vantage point from which to evaluate critically Gilkey's diverse contribution.

While I have already shown that an interest in the relevance of theology to cultural issues is central to Gilkey's work, a brief survey of the corpus will serve to place that observation on firmer ground.[53] *Maker of Heaven and Earth* is both a defense of *creatio ex nihilo* against its cultured critics, and an attempt to illustrate the illuminating power and relevance of the doctrine of creation to existential questions of meaning in life and the problems of evil and suffering, scientific questions about the intelligibility of our world, and philosophical questions such as the nature of time and the possibility of Christian metaphysics. The cultural orientation of his second book is evident from its very title, *How the Church Can Minister to the World Without Losing Itself.* While this book is concerned with the secularization of the Church and its loss of a sense of transcendence, the next book addresses the need of transcendence in any secular culture. *Shantung Compound: The Story of Men and Women Under Pressure*[54] is an autobiographical account of Gilkey's two years (1943 - 1945) in a civilian internment camp during the war with Japan. In this book he does not focus on the treatment he received at the hands of his captors, but on the moral ambiguity of the internees themselves. He argued "that the liberal cultural optimism about human goodness and rationality was a false and 'unempirical' view and that only the traditional symbol of original sin could make sense out of our ordinary individual and communal behavior."[55]

Naming the Whirlwind proposes a renewal of God-language by demonstrating that in everyday secular experience a dimension of ultimacy can be disclosed which can only adequately be thematized by recourse to religious language. *Religion and the Scientific Future* begins by acknowledging that secular culture has had a profound effect on theology, but then goes on to argue both that a scientific culture is inescapably 'religious,' with its own scientific myths, and that such a culture not only falls into self-contradiction but also becomes potentially dangerous without a grounding in Christian symbols of human fallenness and God's purposes in history.

Catholicism Confronts Modernity is another book the cultural orientation of which is evident from its title. In this book Gilkey addresses the crisis that *aggiornamento* entails for the Roman Catholic Church. Arguing again for a relevant transcendence, he counsels the Roman Catholic communion to abandon the traditional nature/grace dualism and rethink priesthood, sacrament, tradition, Christian social action, the grammar of assent, and worship in terms that maintain the integrity and power of Catholicism in the context of modernity.

Reaping the Whirlwind is a reinterpretation of the doctrine of providence in response to the rise of historical consciousness in the modern era. In this book Gilkey also develops an ontology of history in relation to questions of cultural/historical change and political power. *Message and Existence* expounds the central confessional declarations of the Apostles' Creed by first offering an interpretation of a relevant dimension of ordinary cultural experience and then presenting a reinterpretation of the creed in relation to that aspect of human experience. *Society and the Sacred*[56] is presented as essays toward a theology of culture in decline. This book presents some of Gilkey's most mature cultural analysis and theological response. His latest book, *Creationism on Trial: God and Science at Little Rock*,[57] is an anecdotal account of Gilkey's participation in the American Civil Liberties Union legal case against the mandatory teaching of 'creation science' in the schools of Arkansas. In this book Gilkey not only presents his analysis of 'creation science', the creation/evolution debate, and the legal battle surrounding the controversy, but also addresses the problems of the 'establishment' of science in Western culture and the appearance of popular and pseudo-science. He also returns to the question of the relation of science and religion that has occupied his mind since the beginning of his career.

This survey should establish that questions of a theology of culture have always inspired Gilkey's thought. But this itself gives rise to another question. Where does a theology of culture come from? On what basis does a theologian interpret and respond to his or her cultural context? Recalling Gilkey's distaste in his early article for a "cultural pragmatism which is religiously repentant," what basis does Gilkey himself have to go beyond this pragmatism to a "more radical Christian witness" and "some clearer Christian guidance with regard to action"?[58]

An answer to these questions requires that we understand the place of theology of culture in Gilkey's theological project as a whole, and that requires, in the first place, an analysis of his theological method. This will be the task of Part I of this book. My thesis will be that Gilkey's theological method is appropriate and adequate for the theological enterprise in our time. Further, the criteria that he has established for the discipline of theology can be usefully applied to the evaluation of his own contribution.

In Part I we will see that Gilkey divides theology into three stages or sub-disciplines: prolegomenon, constructive theology, and theology of culture. Implicit in this theological method is an answer to the question raised above, namely, what is the basis of a theology of culture? In response to this question, my thesis is that Gilkey's theology of culture can only be fully understood, appreciated, and evaluated if his prolegomenon and constructive theology are seen to be foundational to it. This is *not* to argue that there is a simplistic efficient causality in the system whereby the prolegomenon is the cause of the constructive theology which in turn determines the nature of the theology of culture. The relationship between the three is more dynamic. There is much more interrelation and interdependence within Gilkey's thought. The whole project (not just the theology of culture) attempts to be culturally relevant. It also attempts to be conceptually coherent and faithful to the biblical and traditional sources of the Christian faith. Nevertheless, I *am* arguing that Gilkey's prolegomenal phenomenology of ultimacy, and certain important features of his constructive theology and its ontological implications, are both integral to and foundational for his theology of culture. Without a disclosure of a dimension of ultimacy constitutive of all

12

human life, a theology of culture has no cultural persuasiveness or power. Indeed, it has no 'point of contact' with secular culture. And without a clear understanding of creation, providence, sin, and redemption, it has no theological foundation.

Part II will be a detailed exposition and critical analysis of Gilkey's theology of culture. While theology of culture is methodologically the third stage of theology for Gilkey, I will, for the reasons outlined above, take this as our point of entrance into his theology and deal with the prolegomenon and constructive theology only in terms of their foundational role for the theology of culture. In this part of the book Gilkey's understanding of the 'religious substance' of culture, together with its Tillichian roots, will be discussed in terms of his theological interpretation and diagnosis of modernity. Further, I will address questions of the relation of religion and science, relativity and relativism, and freedom and determinism with reference to specific cultural issues such as the establishment of science and technology, the environmental crisis, the nuclear threat, 'creation science,' and Christianity and world religions.

Gilkey's theology of culture rests upon an anthropology that asserts that there is a dimension of ultimacy constitutive to all human life and therefore to all cultural activity. That anthropology is formulated and defended at the prolegomenal stage of his theological method. Part III will present and evaluate Gilkey's prolegomenon, especially insofar as it is the basis of his theology of culture.

A theology of culture, if it is to be adequate to its task, also needs foundational insight into issues such as the processes of cultural history and the sources of both cultural creativity and ambiguity. If it is not only to interpret and diagnose a culture to itself, but also offer hope to it, then such a theology of culture will require an understanding of providence and redemption — of that which can reconcile the ambiguous and renew the broken. Such questions will be addressed in Part IV. In that part I will discuss the relation of theological and ontological reflection in Gilkey's thought, and the foundational relevance of both for his theology of culture. Each part of the book will include evaluative conclusions that will both highlight the strengths of Gilkey's contribution and criticize its weaknesses.

The Conclusion will begin by summarizing the important points of coherence in Gilkey's theological work, with special reference to the way in which his prolegomenon and constructive theology are theoretically foundational to his theology of culture. Then I will bring together into an overall evaluation the strengths and weaknesses discussed in the evaluative conclusions of the four parts of the book.

NOTES

1 *Reflections on the End of an Era* (New York and London: Charles Scribner's Sons, 1934), p. ix.

2 Ibid, pp. 12-16.

3 Ibid, p. 16.

4 Ibid, pp. 23-24.

5 Ibid, pp. 29-30. The non-inclusive nature of the quotes that will appear throughout this work is an indication of the time in which most of the material was written.

6 Ibid, p. ix.

7 See Paul Tillich, "Autobiographical Reflections," in *The Theology of Paul Tillich*, ed. by Charles W. Kegley (rev. ed.; New York: The Pilgrim Press, 1982), p. 16.

8 In G. Radbruch and Paul Tillich, *Religionsphilosophie der Kultur* (Berlin: Kant - Gesellschaft, 1920), Philosophische Vortrage, No. 24. For a discussion of this early work see James Luther Adams, *Paul Tillich's Philosophy of Culture, Science, and Religion* (New York: Harper and Row, 1965), especially pp. 71-77. Theodor Siegried comments that this early paper proved to be "a significant prelude" to the work that was to follow in Tillich's career. "The Significance of Paul Tillich's Theology for the German Situation," in *The Theology of Paul Tillich*, p. 104.

9 Paul Tillich, *Theology of Culture* (London, Oxford, New York: Oxford University Press, 1969), pp. 42-43. Cf. Tillich's *Systematic Theology*, I (Chicago: University of Chicago Press, 1951), pp. 39-40.

10 Ibid, chapter one. We will discuss the notion of 'depth' further in part III.

11 Ibid, p. 42.

12 *Reaping the Whirlwind: A Christian Interpretation of History*, A Crossroad Book (New York: Seabury Press, 1976), p. viii. (Hereafter referred to as *Reaping*.)

13 "The Christian Response to the World Crisis," *Christianity and Crisis* XV, 14 (August 8, 1955), p. 107.

14 Ibid, p. 110.

15 Ibid, pp. 110-111.

16 *Maker of Heaven and Earth: A Thesis on the Relation Between Metaphysics and Christian Theology With Special Reference to the Problem of Creation as That Problem Appears in the Philosophies of F.H. Bradley and A.N Whitehead and the Historic Leaders of Christian Thought* (unpub. Ph.D. dissertation, New York: Columbia University, 1954). (Hereafter referred to as *MH.*)

17   The most insightful and complete account of Gilkey's life is found in his autobiographical reflections, "Introduction: A Retrospective Glance at My Work," in *The Whirlwind in Culture: Frontiers in Theology — In Honor of Langdon Gilkey*, D. W. Mussar and J. L. Price, eds. (Bloomington, IN: Meyer-Stone Books), pp. 1-35.
    For further biographical details on Gilkey see "Gilkey, Langdon B.," in *Contemporary Authors*, New Revision Series, vol. 7, ed. by Ann Evory (Detroit: Gale Research Co., 1982), pp. 183-184 and "Gilkey, Langdon B.," in *Dictionary of Christianity in America*, D. G. Reid, R. D. Linder, B. L. Shelly and H. S. Stout, eds. (Downers Grove, Ill.: InterVarsity Press, 1990): 481-482.
    R. L. Littlejohn has also discussed Gilkey's biography in *An Analysis of Langdon Gilkey's Phenomenology of Ultimacy and Its Implications for Theology and Ethics* (unpub. Ph.D. dissertation, Waco, Texas: Baylor University, 1979), pp. 9-14. (Hereafter referred to as: Littlejohn, *Gilkey's Phenomenology of Ultimacy.*)

18   David Tracy, "The Question of Criteria for Inter-Religious Dialogue," in *The Whirlwind in Culture*, p. 246.

19   *How the Church Can Minister to the World Without Losing Itself* (New York: Harper and Row, 1964), p. 3. (Hereafter referred to as *How the Church.*) Indeed, in his "Retrospective Glance" (referred to in note 17) Gilkey speaks of learning the notion of relevant transcendence from Niebuhr as his "conversion" and that "it has remained absolutely central to my life and work ever since." (p. 7)

20   Ibid, p. 52.

21   *Message and Existence: An Introduction to Christian Theology* (New York: Seabury Press, 1981), p. 8. (Hereafter referred to as *Message.*)

22   Ibid, pp. 59-60.

23   Ibid, p. 60.

24   *Maker of Heaven and Earth: A Study of the Christian Doctrine of Creation* (Garden City, N.Y.: Doubleday and Co., 1959), p. 123. (Hereafter referred to as *Maker.*) The dissertation of the same title referred to in note 16 is foundational to, but not to be confused with, this book. The dissertation is much longer (660pp), and two thirds of it is devoted to an analysis and critique of Whitehead and Bradley. The last third, however, is expanded into the contents of this 1959 book.

25   *Naming the Whirlwind: The Renewal of God-Language* (Indianapolis: Bobbs Merrill Press, 1969), pp. 250-251. (Hereafter referred to as *Naming.*)

26   Ibid, p. 452.

27   *Reaping*, p. 134.

28 The many more references in Gilkey's work are too numerous to list, but for a random sampling see: "Secularism's Impact on Contemporary Theology," *Christianity and Crisis* XXV (April 5, 1965), p. 66; "New Modes of Empirical Theology," in *The Future of Empirical Theology*, ed. by B. E. Meland; vol. VII of *Essays in Divinity*, ed. by G. L. Brauer (Chicago: University of Chicago Press, 1969), p. 366; and *Catholicism Confronts Modernity: A Protestant View*, A Crossroad Book (New York: Seabury Press, 1975), pp. 9, 11, 101, 108, 113-114, 122. (Hereafter referred to as *Catholicism.*)
     Thomas E. Hosinski has written that "the distinctiveness and enduring importance of Gilkey's contribution to Christian theology ... lies in the truly empirical character of his reflection...." "Experience and the Sacred: A Retrospective Review of Langdon Gilkey's Theology," *Religious Studies Review* 11, 3 (July 1985), p. 228.

29 Cf. Paul Tillich, *Systematic Theology*, I, pp. 8, 59-66 and *Naming*, p. 455 (including note 23). That Gilkey's approach is similar to Niebuhr's as well will become apparent as we proceed.

30 John Shea, *Religious Language in a Secular Culture: A Study in the Theology of Langdon Gilkey* (published S.T.D. dissertation, Mundelin, Illinois: University of St. Mary of the Lake, 1976), p. 7. (Hereafter referred to as: Shea, *Religious Language.*)

31 D. R. Stiver has also noted this coherence throughout the Gilkey corpus. See his, *Converging Approaches to a Natural Awareness of God in Contemporary Theology* (unpub. Ph.D. dissertation, Southern Baptist Theological Seminary), p. 120. (Hereafter referred to as: Stiver, *Converging Approaches.*) M. D. Ryan also notes this consistency in his introduction to an excerpt from *Naming* in: M. D. Ryan, ed., *The Contemporary Explosion in Theology: Ecumenical Studies in Theology* (Meutchen, N.J.: Scarecrow Press, 1975), pp. 24-25.

32 Cf. *Naming*, p. 83, n.4; *Catholicism*, p. 126 (and p. 208, n.6); and Religion and the Scientific Future (New York: Harper and Row, 1970), p. 148, n.32. (Hereafter referred to as *Religion.*)

33 Gilkey made this comment to the author in a personal interview at the University of Chicago on November 28, 1984. (Hereafter referred to as: Gilkey, "Interview.")
34 Note the decidedly neo-orthodox tone of chapter four, "Hearers of the Word" in *How the Church*.

35 In Part I we will have occasion to discuss Gilkey's critique of the kerygmatic wing of neo-orthodoxy. Our concern at this stage is his criticism and shift away from the apologetic neo-orthodoxy of Tillich and Niebuhr. That Gilkey never identified with kerygmatic neo-orthodoxy is evident in his critique of the 'revelationists' in his dissertation. *MH*, pp. 395f, 568.

36 "Trends in Protestant Apologetics," in *The Development of Fundamental Theology*, ed. by J. B. Metz; *Concilium* 46 (New York: Paulist Press, 1969), p. 141.

37 Ibid, p. 70.

38 "Trends," p. 142.

39 *Naming,* p. 10.

40 "Trends," p. 144.

41 Cf. Littlejohn, *Gilkey's Phenomenology of Ultimacy,* pp. 13-14.

42 These are Gilkey's own terms. Gilkey, "Interview," November 28, 1984.

43 "Responses to Peter Berger," *Theological Studies* 39, 3 (September 1978), pp. 488-489. Gilkey makes similar claims to continuity in reply to the criticism of Avery Dulles. See "Anathemas and Orthodoxy: A Reply to Avery Dulles," *Christian Century* 94, 36 (November 9, 1977), p. 1028.

44 *Reaping,* p. 414, n. 32. Indeed, in chapter 4 we will see how Gilkey's arguments against the 'creation scientists' are in fact in total continuity with his position taken in *Maker.*

45 "Trends," p. 141.

46 It is therefore instructive in Gilkey's recent "Retrospective Glance," that he refers to neo-orthodoxy as "still my general orientation ... but I see it now very differently." (p. 13.) Further, he says that in *Naming* he was "seeking to preserve ... the essential core of my neo-orthodoxy while giving to that core a now much needed ground or base in common experience." (p. 25.)

47 "Dissolution and Reconstruction in Theology," in *Frontline Theology,* ed. by Dean Peerman (Richmond, Va.: John Knox Press, 1967), p. 29. Reprinted from *Christian Century* 82, 5 (February 3, 1965).

48 "Theology for a Time of Troubles," *Christian Century* 98, 15 (April 29, 1981), p. 474.

49 Again, compare Gilkey's own self-understanding in his "Retrospective Glance," pp. 1-2.

50 "Responses to Peter Berger," p. 488.

51 Cf. Tillich: "The 'situation' to which theology must respond is the totality of man's creative self-interpretation in a special period." *Systematic Theology,* I, p. 4. That Niebuhr held a similar position is evident in all of his writing. A good example is found in the Preface to *Faith and History* (New York: Charles Scribner's Sons, 1949): "It is important ... for the preacher of the Gospel to understand and come to terms with, the characteristic credos of his age. It is important in our age to understand how the spiritual complacency of a culture which believed in redemption through history is now on the edge of despair." (p. viii) It is also worth noting that the very detailed index in this volume was prepared by Langdon Gilkey. When one notes the care with which that index was prepared it is not surprising that Niebuhr's thought should so permeate Gilkey's.

52 Beyond the dissertations by Littlejohn, Shea and Stiver referred to above (see notes 17, 30 and 31 respectively) other studies to be noted are: M. B. Beaugh, *The*

Development of the Concept of Meaningful Existence in the Chicago Divinity School as Represented by Shailer Mathews, Henry Nelson Wieman and Langdon Gilkey (unpub. Th.D. dissertation, Southwestern Baptist Theological Seminary, 1975); G. F. Davis, *Langdon Gilkey and Religious Language* (unpub. M.C.S. thesis, Regent College, 1979); and J. S. Marai, *The Problem of God-Language in the Theology of John Macquarrie and Langdon Gilkey* (unpub. M.A. thesis, University of St. Michael's College, 1975).

53   See Gilkey's own description of the corpus from *Maker* to *Reaping* in his "Responses to Peter Berger," p. 489.

54   (New York: Harper and Row, 1966). (Hereafter referred to as *Shantung Compound.*)

55   "Responses to Berger," p. 489.

56   A Crossroad Book (New York: Seabury Press, 1981). Hereafter referred to as *Society and the Sacred.*

57   (Minneapolis, Minn.: Winston Press, 1985). (Hereafter referred to as *Creationism.*)

58   See notes 13 and 14 above.

PART 1:
Theological Method

CHAPTER ONE:
Modernity and Theology's Method

1. The Preoccupation with Method

During periods of upheaval and flux in any given discipline, when there is no one dominant paradigm (or even two competing paradigms) that sets the agenda for fruitful research and the criteria by which theories are judged and evidence deemed admissible, it is not surprising that scholars in that discipline become preoccupied with questions of method. 'Method' seems only to become an explicit concern for a practitioner of a discipline when that discipline is in trouble. During such times of trouble the practitioner is forced to reflect on the foundational issues of the discipline, the methodological issues that previously had been only the explicit concern of philosophers of science.[1]

Since the 1960's (perhaps earlier) theology has found itself in this kind of situation. R. L. Maddox has correctly observed that "one of the safest generalizations concerning contemporary theological discussion is that problems of methodology have come to occupy a prominent role." And further that "one sometimes gets the impression that all constructive theological proposals have been put on hold, in lieu of discussion *about* doing theology."[2] Similarly, Gordon Kaufman comments on a "chaos" in the contemporary theological scene because "there appears to be no consensus on what the task of theology is or how theology is to be pursued." And he warns that "if theology is to survive as a distinctive and significant form of intellectual activity, it is essential that some order be brought into this confusion and the proper work of theology be clarified."[3]

An initial examination can detect two immediate causes for this period of self-appraisal and preoccupation with method. The first is the apparent demise of the cultural relevance and intellectual persuasiveness of neo-orthodoxy. Kaufman comments: "The breakdown of the neo-orthodox consensus in protestant theology, which made so much of the authority of 'God's revelation' as the ultimate court of

21

appeal, forced me, like others of my generation, to think through afresh the task of theology and to search for new and more adequate foundations."[4] Indeed, it has become commonplace in theological circles today to lament that there are 'no more giants' in theology. It could well be that the lack of so-called theological giants in the post world war two era is related to the increasing secularism of the modern Western world. As I commented in the Introduction, the validity and meaningfulness of both religious faith and theological reflection is no longer as self-evident as it was in an earlier era. Theology has found it increasingly difficult to flourish in the rarefied atmosphere of modernity.

The second cause of this reappraisal is directly related to this secularism, because with the increasing secularism of a culture has come a parallel secularization of its institutions of higher education. How does the discipline of theology justify its continuing presence in the academy? What are the foundations of its claim to be a discipline at all? This is a question of the 'publicness' of theological reflection. Many theologians are no longer willing to restrict theology to 'church dogmatics,' a parochial activity of interest only to special groups. Some will argue that theology should no longer be a 'normative' discipline, but should restrict itself to historical, phenomenological and linguistic 'description' of that which is religious.[5] David Tracy notes that "the choice of the title 'religious studies' rather than 'theology' for university departments often serves to indicate the distance which its proponents desire from theology's traditionally normative claims."[6] Such questions are methodological and therefore are foundational to the discipline of theology.

This preoccupation with method has given rise to numerous proposals. For example, Wolfhart Pannenberg, questioning the revelational positivism of Barth and the *Geschichte/Historie* distinction of Kähler and Bultmann, has argued that theology must develop a method which transcends and synthesizes the debates between European 'hermeneutical' philosophy and the critical rationalism of post-Popperian Anglo-American philosophy. Moreover, such a method would reinstate, in non-neo-orthodox terms, nothing less than theology as the science of God, recast in terms of the history of religions.[7] More modest was Jürgen Moltmann's early concern with developing a different ontological and epistemological foundation for theology which emphasizes discontinuity and contradiction in anticipatory knowledge in contrast with the status quo stance of a method based upon a correspondence theory of truth.[8]

Gustavo Gutiérrez and other theologians of liberation have advocated an 'epistemological break' with the Western theological tradition.[9] They argue that if theology is to be scientific it must not be disassociated from the grassroots where the 'first act' of theology takes place, viz., solidarity with the poor. Theological method must be oriented to reflection on praxis. Similarly, Rosemary Ruether and other feminist theologians advocate a retrieval and reintroduction of women's experience into contemporary theology.[10]

Totally different has been Bernard Lonergan's analysis of cognition in terms of transcendental method and the application of that analysis to the delineation of 'functional fields of specialization' in theology.[11] And David Tracy has developed a "three publics" model for a pluralist theology (viz., academy, church and society) which combines phenomenological, hermeneutical/literary critical and transcendental-metaphysical methods.[12]

Langdon Gilkey has not been immune to this preoccupation with theological method. Indeed, his methodological differentiation of prolegomenon, constructive theology and theology of culture has been a significant contribution to this discussion.[13] And this, of course, is not surprising in the light of his own concern that theology and theology's method be adequate to its times. Before we proceed to a discussion of this methodological proposal, however, we should take note of two characteristics of any methodological discussion in theology.

The first characteristic is that any discussion of theological method is inevitably circular. One's comprehension of what it is to be doing theology will itself rest upon certain theological assumptions.[14] Paul Tillich indirectly makes this point in his article, "The Two Types of Philosophy of Religion."[15] In this article Tillich contrasts what he calls the "ontological" type of philosophy of religion of Augustine, Meister Eckart and German Idealism with the "cosmological" type represented by Aquinas, Duns Scotus and most natural theological arguments. In the former type one's approach to God is an overcoming of estrangement: "man discovers *himself* when he discovers God." In the latter type, "man meets a *stranger* when he meets God." The meeting is "accidental" and essentially God and human creatures "do not belong to each other."[16] Clearly, Tillich identifies his own apologetic method of correlation with the ontological type of philosophy of religion, and it does not take too much imagination to see that he would place Barth (much to Barth's protest) in the second type. Herein is the heart of the distinction between apologetic and kerygmatic neo-orthodoxy. In the theological method of kerygmatic theology revelation is the dominant theme. Revelation is methodologically prior to human experience and rationality because of the radical discontinuity in the God/creature relationship. God is a stranger, the 'wholly Other'. Tillich's apologetic method, however, assumes a continuity between God and the creature. God is not a stranger, but the very 'ground of our being'. This conviction is foundational for the method of correlation.

My point in this excursus is not to mediate the debate between Tillich and Barth, but to use that debate to illustrate the role of primary theological assumptions at the very foundation of a discussion of theological method. These two methods conflict on the existentially prior issues of how one understands the God/creation relationship, the nature of the fall, and the meaning and process of redemption. While these questions are theologically elaborated in terms of one's theological method, they are also foundational to the very contours of that method. This is as true for Gilkey's theological method as it was for Tillich's and Barth's. Gilkey himself says that "a method is itself a part of that wider whole which is expressed in an entire philosophical or theological system...."[17]

The second characteristic of a theological method is delineated in the second half of the sentence just cited. Gilkey goes on to say that ultimately, "a method is an expression ... of that deeper vision of things which dominates a whole era of cultural experience and thought."[18] Adopting terminology from the phenomenological movement, Gilkey says that a change in the *Lebenswelt* requires a change in theological method. While I will have occasion later in this chapter to point out that Gilkey does *not* want simply to capitulate to the cultural *Geist* and does maintain that there can and should be important elements of discontinuity in the message/culture relationship, my point here is to acknowledge the relationship between changes in method and cultural changes. Gilkey says: "Philosophical and theological methods, as does all human thinking, exist in the *historical* dimension and so are relative to the *Geist* of their age...."[19] To a brief discussion of this changed *Geist* we now turn.

24

2. The Changed Cultural Context

Gilkey describes the 1960s as a period of dissolution in theology.[20] Not only did all the giants die, but theology itself seemed to be in serious trouble. The old certainties that there was a Word which could be heard in proclamation, that religious language was meaningful, that there was any meaning *per se* (with or without religious language) and most importantly that God (whether that be as ground of being, divine relativity or the origin of revelation) was a meaningful symbol, were seemingly dissolved. All of these certainties are undermined, says Gilkey by the spirit of secularism or modernity. He says,

> When we speak ... of the "spirit," "mind," "mood," or "Geist" of our culture, we refer to that deep, preconceptual attitude toward and understanding of existence which dominates and forms the cultural life of any epoch, the way men of a given time characteristically apprehend the world they live in and their place within it; their fundamental self-understanding of their being in the world.[21]

A cultural mood is pre-theoretical, pre-conceptual, even, says Gilkey, pre-linguistic. It is a fundamental vision of life or *Weltanschauung* that characterizes a culture, and within which every creative aspect of a culture's life (including theology) expresses itself.

The radical empiricist and relativist character of the secular spirit threatened not only metaphysics but also any form of thought that appealed to ultimacy. This secular spirit is both profoundly naturalistic (all there is is the world of finite things in causal interrelatedness) and thoroughly humanistic. Human beings are autonomous creatures open to and subject to no 'Word' which comes from beyond them and the finite world they inhabit. Such a cultural context of contingency, naturalism, autonomy, relativism and empiricism makes theological reflection (to say nothing of personal faith) difficult at best and impossible at worse.

In such a context neo-orthodox theology is not overly helpful. A theology of a proclaimed Word assumes that there is a hearing, believing community. That can no longer be assumed. Gilkey observes that the secular spirit does not stop at the doors of the church.[22] Nor could that spirit stop at the doors of the church, since neo-orthodoxy itself was an uneasy synthesis of modernity's insistence on naturalistic causes of all events within a space-time continuum with theological language about God's 'mighty acts in history.' The problem, however, is that "if events, viewed naturally, had an immanent explanation, what did it *mean* to say that they were God's action?"? Do not the naturalistic assumptions of neo-orthodox 'biblical theology' in fact undercut the very meaningfulness of theological affirmations about 'God's mighty acts in history'? Has not the rejection of the univocity of religious language actually resulted in equivocation?

Another problem that Gilkey has with this kind of neo-orthodoxy is that its language about God as a trans-natural reality "became more and more unreal and incredible to those who had learned to speak this language."[23] Indeed this was such an irrelevant transcendence that Gilkey observes an increasing disappearance of language about God since theological discourse was primarily viewed as a matter of human 'self-understanding.' Specifically referring to Bultmannian theology Gilkey says that "God was shoved further and further into the never-never land of sheer kerygmatic proclamation."[24] The consequence was that such language became increasingly esoteric and was reduced to "empty dogmatic signs."[25]

Nor does Gilkey find much help in the offspring of neo-orthodoxy in hermeneutical theology. Such theology cannot address the secular spirit because it continues to assume the meaningfulness of the Word, and it is precisely that assumption which is at stake. Such a theology remains a discussion within the church with little relevance to the everyday world around it. Gilkey likens it to the bishop's *Festung* at Salzburg, high above the town, of great interest to tourists, but of little relevance to the real problems that plague the townfolk.[26] Like their neo-orthodox forebears, hermeneutic theologians have a wholly other God, and as William Hamilton has said, "It is a short step, but a critical one, to move from the otherness of God to the absence of God."[27]

Indeed it is precisely in affirmation of modernity's empiricism and emphasis on human autonomy that William Hamilton, Paul van Buren and Thomas J. J. Altizer proclaimed the death of God.[28] Gilkey chose these radical theologians as his dialogue partners in the sixties because they expressed the secular mind and forced theology to deal with the primary, rather than the secondary issues. And the issue for them, and for Gilkey, is *God*. The question of God is primary because without God there *are* no theological issues. Moreover, the issue is not even what *kind* of God we can believe in, but whether *any* doctrine of God is possible for a secular age. Gilkey says,

A mere transition from metaphysical to biblical categories or the reverse; from a transcendent to an immanent view, or the reverse; from epiphany to eschatological theologies, or the reverse; from Thomistic to Hegelian to process, or the reverse, will not answer the secular challenge which, I believe, finds all of these views of the divine almost equally unintelligible and empty.[29]

The question then is, how *does* one even begin to reflect theologically in a secular age?

3. Prolegomenon

Gilkey argues that while the foundational issue before us is the doctrine of God, paradoxically, we must begin our theology in anthropology, with the doctrine of human being.[30] This is the role of a prolegomenon. The task of the prolegomenon is to provide an anthropological foundation for theology. It is, in this sense, a fundamental theology, an apologetic. Classical apologetics was divided into three steps, viz., *demonstratio religiosa, demonstratio christiana,* and *demonstratio ecclesiastica.*[31] R. L. Maddox has noted that Gilkey's prolegomenon is formally concerned with only the first step — *demonstratio religiosa.*[32] Gilkey's prolegomenon is a *demonstratio religiosa* because it attempts to establish that the religious dimension is a normal dimension of human life. But he has to establish this in the context of the secularist attack on the meaningfulness of religious language.

Any language game is deemed meaningless if there is a sense of no relation between its use and concepts and experienced actuality. This is the plight of religious discourse in a secular culture. Therefore, says Gilkey, one can justify religious discourse "only by seeking to locate within concrete experience some element, aspect, or being which calls for religious symbolization, for which religious or theological language is necessary, and in relation to which it communicates and so has 'meaning.'"[33] Such is the task of a prolegomenon to theology.

Gilkey defines his prolegomenon as

> ... a phenomenological analysis of the experience of the unconditioned since it has bracketed questions of reality, of explanation, or of validation and has sought an "eidetic" reduction of experience to certain general forms centering about our contingency, our relativity, our transience, and our freedom.[33A]

A prolegomenon functions as a philosophy of religion which is the logical, if not existential, basis for theology. Gilkey's prolegomenal method is best explicated as a *secular* analysis of *experience* which *phenomenologically* discloses the *meaningfulness* (though not necessarily the truth or *validity*) of religious discourse. Such discourse is meaningful because it thematizes and has reference to the *ultimate dimension* of even the most secular aspects of our lives, a dimension that the secular self-understanding fails to comprehend. I will consider each element of this description separately.

a) Secular Inquiry

This prolegomenon is *secular*, says Gilkey. This has led many of his reviewers to charge that either Gilkey has simply succumbed to modernity or that his argument is hopelessly circular, that is, that Gilkey is a Christian theologian looking to find a dimension of ultimacy in the *sæculum* and, of course, he finds what he is looking for. A discussion of each of these criticisms will serve to clarify what Gilkey means by describing his prolegomenon as a 'secular' inquiry.

The charge that Gilkey has simply capitulated to modernity comes from various (and sometimes surprising) quarters. Peter Berger argues that, for Gilkey, "secularity is the cognitive criterion *a priori*," and that the prescription for a secular theology proposed by Gilkey, Tracy and Ogden is nothing less than "a recipe for the self-liquidation of the Christian community."[34] G. Stanley Kane says that Gilkey accepts secular experience as normative and therefore neglects the central religious questions that have been universally and traditionally asked. Gilkey's overriding concern to develop a relevant theology has led his theology to "self-consciously and programmatically accommodate itself to the spirit of the age...." The consequence of such an accommodation, says Kane, is "that the basic form, if not the entire content, of theological doctrine would be determined by the culture rather than autonomously by theology."[35] The sharpest language, however, comes from Frederick Ferré. He accuses Gilkey of being a "conceptual huckster" trying to "sell" Christian symbols by "coming close to acceptance" of secularity. Ferré argues that Christian theology will not develop a more adequate epistemology and ontology as long as "books like *Naming the Whirlwind* seek to persuade secular common sense that 'modern empirical men' can utilize Christian symbols on their own terms, without submitting their prevailing 'mood' to radical scrutiny and probable reform."[36]

Not all of the critics agree that Gilkey has succumbed to modernity. Both Clark Williamson and Tom Driver say that Gilkey's understanding of modernity is out-dated. He has not realized that modernity is now in our cultural past and that our new reality is post-modernity.[37] Far from being too uncritical, Driver says that Gilkey's analysis of modern culture is too sober, too critical, too 'Niebuhrian.'[38] And contrary to Berger's critique of the 'loss of transcendence' in Gilkey's theology, Driver finds the whole enterprise too transcendent because it fails to stress the immanence of the divine in human life. Similarly, Helena Sheehan claims that Gilkey is offering us nothing less than a new "supernaturalism."[39]

How are we to understand the 'secular' character of Gilkey's prolegomenon? Has he capitulated to modernity as Berger, Ferré and others claim, or is he in fact offering us a new supernaturalism that is too sober vis-a-vis modern culture as Sheehan and Driver argue? The answer to this question depends, to a large degree, upon what one considers to constitute 'capitulation to modernity.' Further, one could only pass such a judgment upon Gilkey's work as a whole, not just his prolegomenon. But it is also clear that such a capitulation is not Gilkey's own understanding of what he is doing. In *Naming* he states very clearly that "the hard secularity of the present is *not* an ultimate authority to which all our thinking must bow, and any theology ... must part ways with it at some point or another."[40] Further, the whole point of the prolegomenon is to highlight a tension in the secular self-understanding. Gilkey's prolegomenal argument is that "the phenomenological evidence centered on the fundamental categories of the secular spirit refute its own self-understanding and drive to the recognition of a religious dimension in human existence."[41] The actual life of modern secular people discloses a religious dimension, replete with its own secular myths, in total contradiction with the secular self-understanding.[42] In Part II we will see that Gilkey views those myths as themselves contradictory, inadequate to human experience, and even dangerous. This is clearly a theology that does not intend to capitulate to modernity.[43]

Another reason that one misunderstands Gilkey's theology if it is viewed as a capitulation to modernity is that such an interpretation misses the apologetic thrust of his project. As we saw in the Introduction, the heart of Gilkey's apologetic is the correlation of message and

29

existence to the end of establishing a relevant transcendence. But Gilkey prefers *not* to view ordinary existence as a 'source' of Christian theology. In apparent opposition to his colleague David Tracy, Gilkey says: "If ordinary human experience and ordinary historical action were the 'sources' and thus provided the substance of Christian theology, nothing new or ultimately significant could be said to the world through the Christian message."[44] There must be both continuity and discontinuity in the relation between the Christian message and common experience. Further, when theology, in its apologetic task, analyzes ordinary experience, that analysis is not itself non-theological or neutral; rather, it is a Christian interpretation of that aspect of human experience.[45] This leads us to the question of circularity.

The charge of circularity comes at the question of the secularity of the prolegomenon from the opposite direction to the charge of capitulation. N. Schreurs asks whether a "pre-formed model of interpretation," which is itself based on religious concepts, is at the foundation of Gilkey's analysis of experience.[46] Does not Gilkey presuppose a dimension of ultimacy, and that presupposition then guides his analysis? And is not that presupposition decidedly non-secular and in fact Christian? How, then, is this a secular analysis?[47] Gilkey's answer is clear. The prolegomenon is a secular inquiry because the materials being investigated are secular, not the presuppositions from which the inquiry proceeds. He says, "This is not so much a secular inquiry as an inquiry into the character of secular experience, and that is all that we claim."[48] The argument makes no claim to neutrality because no inquiry is neutral in relation to the ultimate assumptions of the inquirer.[49] But this acknowledgement of epistemological or theological circularity does not invalidate *a priori* the results of the inquiry. If the argument is invalid it is not because of the point of view, but because it does not adequately disclose what it sets out to disclose.[50] In his response to Schreurs, Gilkey says that it cannot be required that a prolegomenon be presuppositionless. But it must be public. It must "present an analysis of the experience available to all readers, whatever their point of view on the issue in question, and that its method of procedure be articulate, consistent, and in accord with the demands of its subject matter."[51] This leads us to the next characteristic of Gilkey's prolegomenon.

b) Experience

According to Gilkey, prolegomenal analysis is analysis of experience. While he acknowledges the epistemological circle whereby all thought, including empirical thought, is theory-laden, and therefore there is no simple and direct access to empirical reality, he chooses to enter this epistemological circle from the side of experience. The purpose of the prolegomenon is to disclose those dimensions or regions of ordinary experience to which the language of religious symbols has reference, and therefore could be said to have meaning.[52] Following the reappropriation of naive experience in the 'life-world' advocated by the phenomenological movement, Gilkey maintains that "thought follows and symbolizes life, not the reverse; direct experience or awareness — and the symbols in which that is explicated — precede rationality and cannot be created by it."[53] For Gilkey, this is a foundational assumption. Further, Gilkey also agrees with the phenomenological affirmation — over against linguistic philosophy — "that an analysis of prelinguistic experience by reflection is possible."[54] Such an analysis of ordinary experience is necessary if religious discourse is to have meaning.

Concomitant with this emphasis on ordinary experience is a particular view of meaning. Again, following the phenomenological movement, Gilkey says that meaning is "most fundamentally the product of a relation of a symbol to felt or immediate experiencing as a whole, to the *Lebenswelt* in which man finds himself existing."[55] Therefore an analysis of ordinary language usage or of various language games cannot establish the meaningfulness of that language if it does not show how the language in question actually thematizes some significant, common area of human experience. One must go beyond linguistic analysis to phenomenological description.

> Meanings arise, to be sure, in a community of discourse. But at the most fundamental level they represent not only the lateral sharing of recognized usage, but also the interaction of symbols to our felt experience, the symbol providing thematic and so communicable form to the stream of experience, and *both* are essential if there is to be meaning at all.[56]

Borrowing a phrase from Eugene Gendlin, Gilkey often says that without symbols the experiential world is meaningless and blind, and without relatedness to common experience symbols are empty, rootless and without content.[57]

The question for religious discourse then is whether it is *empty* because it thematizes no dimension of ordinary human experience or *meaningful* because there are areas of experience which it and it alone thematizes and brings to clarity. This question can be best answered, according to Gilkey, by means of a phenomenological method which attempts to uncover a dimension of ultimacy in human life that has been unthematized or 'forgotten.'

c) Phenomenology

Gilkey's version of phenomenology is not Husserl's exact science of apodictic certainty which attempts to distill essential pure consciousness. Rather, he follows the 'existentialist turn' of Heidegger, Merleau-Ponty and Ricoeur to hermeneutical phenomenology which "seeks to interpret the latent *meanings*, i.e., unveil the implicit structures of man's being in the world, structures not evident to our normal self-understanding."[58] Such a method is certainly not a matter of rigorous science offering decisive proofs of its conclusions. Rather, it is a proposal for intuitive recognition.[59] Gilkey agrees with both Whitehead and Heidegger, who claim that philosophy (and the prolegomenon *is* philosophy) does not proceed in terms of proofs but in terms of disclosure. In the end all that the philosopher, or the prolegomenist, can say is, "Look, is *this* not the way things truly are?"[60]

Moreover, Gilkey's phenomenological prolegomenon (and here his project is distinct from Tillich's) is not primarily an ontological analysis of the structures of human being in the world, but a more modest 'ontic' search, "an examination of the shape of ordinary human experience in order to find the dimension of ultimacy" as this is apprehended there.[61] It is an analysis of the relation of religious discourse to lived experience rather than an analysis of the relation of symbols to the universal structures of being. Gilkey chooses to engage in this kind of ontic analysis not because he thinks that ontology is impossible but because it appears to him that ontology itself requires this kind of ontic prolegomenon. Metaphysical and ontological reflection require acceptance of the assumption that there is some form of a universal logos in existence. Modernity's preoccupation with contingency and the 'given' make it impossible to proceed on the basis of such an assumption.[62] Once an ontic prolegomenon discloses a dimension of ultimacy in human life, however, then ontological and metaphysical analysis can proceed.[63] Indeed, in *Reaping the Whirlwind*, Gilkey feels secure enough not only to reflect on the ontological implications of the Christian understanding of providence, but also to present in Part I of that book an ontological prolegomenon, that is, an ontology of historical process which is foundational to theological reflection on the doctrine of providence.

d) Meaning/Validity

In the phenomenological prolegomenon offered in *Naming the Whirlwind*, however, such ontological questions are 'bracketed out.' And with this *epoché* of ontology Gilkey also brackets out any question of the truth or validity of religious discourse. Adopting the distinction between *meaningfulness* and *validity* from language philosophy and translating that into his phenomenological method, Gilkey's purpose in his prolegomenon is only to establish the meaningfulness of religious language insofar as such language has legitimate reference to the ultimate dimension of human life, not the truth or validity of such language.[64] But only by establishing the meaningfulness of religious language, Gilkey argues, can one establish the "potentiality for validity" of such discourse.[65] The task of the prolegomenon is completed if it has established that religious discourse is a meaningful mode of discourse. Whether any particular religious discourse is true is a question for constructive theology.

e) Summary of the Prolegomenon

While I will present a more detailed discussion of the actual argument of Gilkey's prolegomenon in chapter six, a short summary of it is in order at this stage. Gilkey analyzes some of the most central dimensions of secular life and self-understanding, viz., contingency, relativity, temporality, freedom, science, and historicity, and argues that each of these dimensions raises questions that can only be described as ultimate in character. In the experiences of ultimate threat implied in contingency, meaninglessness in relativity, mortality in temporality, norms for freedom's actuality, commitment and judgment in scientific research, and the role of 'global myths' in historical and political existence, we have encountered, says Gilkey, a dimension of ultimacy in our ordinary experience. This dimension gives rise to what Stephen Toulmin calls 'limit questions.'[66] Gilkey says,

When we ask ... "Why am I?" "Who am I?" "What should I become and

33

be?" "Why should I value truth and the good?" "What is the meaning and future destiny of my life and the history in which it participates?" "How can I be whole again?" and "What is the meaning of my death?" then we are exploring or encountering that region of experience where language about the ultimate, and so the language game that is called "religious discourse" becomes useful and intelligible.[67]

Such questions are not peripheral but, rather, they are integral to all human life. They are ultimate questions that disclose a religious dimension of ultimacy in human life, a dimension that functions as the source, ground, horizon and limit of human life. Gilkey describes this dimension as follows:

> The ultimate or unconditioned element in experience is not so much the seen, but the basis of seeing; not what is known as an object so much as the basis of knowing; not an object of value as the ground of valuing; not the thing before us, but the source of all things; not the particular meanings that generate our life in the world, but the ultimate context in which these meanings necessarily subsist.[68]

If Gilkey's prolegomenon is successful in disclosing a dimension of ultimacy with something like these characteristics, then he can conclude that not only has he refuted the self-understanding of the secular spirit but, more importantly, he has established the necessity of religious language as a legitimate mode of discourse with reference to the dimension of ultimacy as a constitutive and indispensable dimension of human experience. Theology can no longer be dismissed as a meaningless enterprise because of its fundamental irrelevance to real experience.

f) Limits of the Prolegomenon

It is important to note, however, that the prolegomenon is limited. Gilkey says that it is certainly not yet theology but a "beginning before the beginning" of theology.[69]

> Such an analysis can at best be only a prolegomenon to systematic theology as a whole, establishing the meaningfulness of the general language game of theology, but not a direct part of systematic theology; it is, if you will, anthropology and not yet theology.[70]

As such, the prolegomenon only claims to establish the reality of the religious dimension of life and makes no claim concerning which set of symbols thematizes this dimension best. Utilizing the distinction between meaning and validity, Gilkey acknowledges that the prolegomenon "cannot move beyond the *meaningfulness* of religious language to that of the *validity* of particular systems of symbols."[71] The question of the *truth* of religious discourse is addressed in constructive theology. While the prolegomenon has an important function in any theology that follows upon it, there must also be a 'break' with the prolegomenon in order for theology to proceed. To this we now turn.

4. Constructive Theology

If Gilkey's prolegomenon is a *demonstratio religiosa*, then the task of *demonstratio christiana* falls upon constructive theology. The latter rests upon the former. David Tracy says that "the fundamental theologian both warrants the existence of a religious dimension and thereby warrants a further willingness to enter into the conversation of the religions, to pay attention to the claims in their classic expressions, even to risk being caught up in the reality of a classic religious tradition."[72] If the prolegomenon is sound, then constructive theology can proceed on that foundation. But they are different enterprises.

Gilkey describes the move from prolegomenon to constructive theology as a move from the generality of the religious dimension to a particular apprehension of things that makes a truth claim about what is real and of value. This move bears some resemblance to the method of correlation. By disclosing a dimension of ultimacy the prolegomenon also uncovers ultimate questions that arise in ordinary existence. Constructive theology is a reflection upon and application of received answers. But the fact that these answers are 'received' means that the theological enterprise now moves beyond the realm of description. Gilkey elaborates:

> A *break* must appear at this point in the course of the argument of our prolegomenon; a *new* and a *particular* assumption must be made, an assumption based on some special experience of the ultimate nature of things.[73]

Making such an assumption is a risk, though, rooted in the prolegomenon, it is a meaningful risk In Paul Ricoeur's terms, one must make a 'wager' and 'take a stand' somewhere.[74] Gilkey insists, on the basis of his prolegomenon, that such wagers and stances are universal in human experience. Moreover, "they found each cultural *Weltanschauung*, and within that wider matrix, they are the implicit and often unacknowledged 'points of view' in philosophy, and they are the explicit and celebrated basis for each religious community."[75] They function as revelatory answers to limit questions.

Gilkey describes the disclosure of a dimension of ultimacy in the prolegomenon in the traditional theological terms of 'general revelation' and 'common grace.' "Revelation of the sacral ground of life is thus *universal* and *general*, else there would be no life, no meaning, no thought, no valuing and no hope in human experience...."[76] Christian theology, however, is reflection upon a particular mode of apprehension of this sacred ground, and this apprehension has its source in 'special revelation.' Such an apprehension is beyond general experience, "beyond the possibility of the facts; it is given and received, because it manifests the depths of reality, its ultimate structures and tendencies...."[77] Prolegomenal analysis of general experience is a necessary, though not sufficient, element of Christian theology. One must go beyond general experience to the particularity of special revelation, and the reason that one takes a stand in relation to a particular special revelation is because "it is *here*, in *this* place, through *this* finite medium as expressive of ultimacy, and thus in *this* community, that the sacred has manifested itself."[78]

Another reason that special revelation is necessary is that limit questions are raised by the essential character of our finitude *as* finite (eg., contingency, freedom, etc.), therefore finitude cannot generate answers. Any answer to such questions would be characterized by ultimacy and unconditionedness, and this is something that no finite creature can create or possess. Therefore, any ultimate answer must be "one *from* transcendence *to* finitude, from that which in *not* sharing in these dependencies of the creature is itself *more than* creaturely."[79]

This parallel importance of transcendence and special revelation has been a constant concern in Gilkey's writings. It appears as early as his dissertation. Speaking of the possibility of a 'Christian philosophy' he says:

> There are ... vast areas of proximate coherence and proximate meaning which can be discovered in 'general' experience, but as we have found before, the ultimate coherence of things and the final meaning of his own existence cannot for the Christian, or actually upon analysis for anyone else, be found in terms of general experience. On the

36

contrary, he has found this coherence and meaning in a very specific place: in the historical events of the life of the Hebrew people and in Christ.[80]

The task of constructive theology is to reflect upon this special revelation in terms of its symbolic content. And, as we have seen, it also "addresses the question of the meaning and validity or truth of these symbols *for us,* for our time and in our world."[81] As such it has the character of a 'proposal' for interpreting life from a Christian perspective.[82] Further, in its systematic task, theology attempts to construct a total view of Christian faith, and of the world viewed in terms of that faith. "Like its half-sister philosophy, theology drives inevitably toward unity and so toward totality, toward a coherent understanding not only of its own symbols but of the totality of truth and of experience."[83]

To achieve such a coherent understanding is an awesome and risky task. It requires the development of an understanding that faithfully reinterprets the biblical message in terms that are adequate to our experience, conceptually intelligible to our modern minds, and serviceable to life in contemporary culture.[84] Consequently, Gilkey delineates four aspects of theological meaning ingredient in religious symbols that must be explicated if full theological understanding is to be achieved: the eidetic (the specialized concern of biblical and historical theology), the experiential (addressed in both prolegomenal and constructive theology), the reflective (the specifically theoretical and ontological task of constructive theology), and praxis (addressed in ethics and theology of culture).[85] I will explicate what Gilkey means by each of these separately, though praxis will be left for the next section of this chapter.

a) Eidetic Meaning

Reflection on theological symbols requires, at its foundation, an *eidetic* inquiry into the meaning of the symbols that constitute the tradition being reflected upon. This is a hermeneutical and historical task. In Gadamerian terms, the past horizon must be honoured.[86] This inquiry is 'eidetic' because it attempts to grasp the essential and original meanings of biblical and classical symbols.[87] Moreover, the theologian is concerned with an eidetic cluster of symbols that form a unified picture of God, the world, humankind and historical process. While Gilkey acknowledges that there is a plurality of meanings for each

37

biblical symbol, he nevertheless insists that "if the theologian is to make essential use of this plurality in his tradition, he must effect (and this is a creative and so risky task) some unifying synthesis of this diversity of meanings into one coherent or eidetic meaning."[88] He calls this an eidetic reduction "that brings to the coherence and unity of one perspective the wide variety of viewpoints found by the modern historical scholar in the plurality of documents in scripture and tradition."[89] Fully aware that most biblical scholars would be suspicious of this procedure, Gilkey nevertheless insists that biblical symbols can function creatively in theology only when a unity is postulated out of the diversity of the biblical witness.[90]

Consequently, a fundamental criterion by which any theological proposal must be judged is the depth of its understanding of and fidelity to the symbolic structure of the tradition under consideration. A theological statement must "be a consistent expression of the symbolic forms of the historical community within which the answers are received, experienced, and comprehended...."[91] Gilkey says further,

> However much it reinterprets, revises, or rethinks that structure — and it must — in its own contemporary terms, it must have the intentionality of re-expressing it, and not expressing some *other* structure of faith.[92]

Because the Scriptures are the primary witness to God's revelation, they remain the "ultimate source and the final norm for the life, the thought, and the practice of the continuing community."[93] The meaning of scriptural symbols "constitute the *norma non normata* of all subsequent Christian witness in teaching and Christian reflective speech."[94] This not to advocate an anachronistic copying or repeating of biblical propositions but, rather, to insist that creative reinterpretation be appropriate to the eidetic meaning of the symbols in their original locus.[95]

b) Experiential Meaning

Eidetic fidelity, however, is only a necessary, not a sufficient, condition for meaningful theological affirmations. As we have seen from the prolegomenon, symbols can only be meaningful for us if they thematize, shape and illumine our actual experience. Hence the *experiential* level of theological meaning, initially limited to the prolegomenon, is now taken up into constructive theology as an intrinsic, correlational element.[96] If secular experience calls for symbolic thematization, then the theologian must attempt to correlate Christian symbolic answers with the ultimate questions that have been disclosed. Therefore, theology is to be tested, in the second place, "by its relatedness, its relevance, its correlations of symbolic answers to the actual questions of our existence."[97] Does this interpretation adequately illumine the existential and ultimate questions of our existence? Does it provide a credible answer to these questions and provide grounds for a creative, just and healing life? In short, do these symbols and their present reinterpretation 'fit' the shape of experience that they claim adequately to thematize?[98]

c) Reflective Meaning

For a theology to be existentially adequate, however, it must also be intellectually coherent and intelligible, illuminating by means of its conceptual categories the contours of human life. One must move beyond existential relevance to an elaboration of the philosophical implications of a system of symbols in fields such as epistemology, historical understanding, and social structures.[99] Therefore, theology is also a *reflective* activity. It is "an attempt to understand in reflective categories that which is lived in religious commitment."[100] Religious symbols are subject to the criterion of universal applicability and therefore theology is led into an ontological elucidation of their meaning, an elaboration of a "Christian philosophy."[101] As a reflective enterprise theology is tested by its width of intelligibility and internal coherence. The 'symbol gives rise to thought,' and the kind of thought that it gives rise to is ontological thought.[102] Similar to Pannenberg, Gilkey says that,

> To be meaningful reflectively to us and so to articulate what is true for us, a theological concept must be systematized and related to all else that we hold to be true and so to shape reality as a whole for us.[103]

The relation between theology and philosophical ontology, however, is dialectical. Theological symbols must become concepts, doctrines and objects of reflection. To be meaningful to all else that we hold true, they must be reflectively explicated in ontological terms that make sense to our modern understandings. At one point Gilkey says that a modern ontology which is "on loan" to theology "provides the filling, the materials, and contents, to the theological symbols."[104] He goes on to say that "any religious symbols ... that we can regard as true, as relevant to and ultimately formative of *our* world, must share the contours of this modern ontology that is ours."[105] This is *not* to argue, however, that the reflective content of theological symbols is totally determined by the ontology of the day. Indeed, Gilkey says:

> The Christian symbol must rule the use we make of any modern ontology as a superior norm of expression, lest we proclaim a modern secular ontology as unequivocally Christian, and our gods be different than God. Thus no philosophical system per se, modern or Greek, can be adopted without transformation to fit the symbols of our tradition.[106]

While reflective theology requires both an ontological elucidation of its symbols and a theological transformation of ontology, it must not stop there. Gilkey follows Tillich in understanding ontology as a cognitive approach to reality that uncovers the invariant structures of reality.[107] Ontology is synchronic analysis. Consequently, ontology can never exhaust the meaning of symbols, nor can it be totally adequate to human experience. In order to account for the diachronic, the historical (which is characterized by estrangement) and meaning which transcends synchronic structure, we must go beyond ontology and, paradoxically, back to myth. With specific reference to historical understanding, Gilkey says,

> Though ontology has a vital role in the understanding of history, any comprehension of history as a whole, and so any theological understanding has the form of a global "myth" and not of a systematic ontology....[108]

In *Catholicism Confronts Modernity* he speaks of a dialectic between story and analysis. Theology must go beyond ontological analysis to mythical story because only myth can thematize God's personal intent to be engaged in human history through unique and revelatory events. Ontology cannot grasp personal intentionality, divine action and unique events. Myth can.[109] Indeed, "philosophy itself reaches its nemesis in seeking to express the transcendent and the sacred." "Thus even in the most sophisticated philosophical theology, myth returns to express the height of the divine transcendence and sacrality....."[110]

In a more recent article Gilkey argues that the relation of the synchronic and diachronic modes of reflection uncovers a basic dialectic within Christian belief which moves from the rational to the incredible to the credible.[111] For example, Gilkey argues that the Christian belief in providence is rational because a synchronic analysis of temporality can establish that the ontological structure of historical being requires some ground beyond, yet within, temporality.[112] But this very rationality is seen to be incredible when one reflects upon the actuality of historical existence as estranged from its ontological structure. This is the negative moment in the dialectic which overwhelms the positive thesis constituting the rationality of theistic providence. The next stage in the dialectic then is to establish (or 'wager') the credibility of Christian symbols not primarily because they account for the synchronic structure of historical being, but because they are a credible answer to the warping of that structure. Christianity as a total system of symbols is credible, says Gilkey, because "it can be shown that a Christian interpretation provides a clearer, more illuminative, and more complete access to the full character of personal and historical experience than any other viewpoint."[113]

In summary, constructive theology can be validated in terms of criteria such as coherence among its symbolic and reflective elements, relevance and adequacy to existential life, universal applicability in terms of elucidating categories that are reflectively illuminating for all aspects of being, and its appropriateness and fidelity to the symbolic tradition of the Christian community.

d) Truth

Criteria such as relevance, coherence and fidelity can never establish with apodictic certainty the truth of theological assertions, however. Neither is the satisfaction of these criteria a sufficient ground for faith (though it may be logically necessary). Indeed, any and all arguments for adequacy, intelligibility, and even appropriate fidelity are inevitably circular and inconclusive. The experience that we think our symbol system adequately and intelligibly thematizes is itself, to a large degree, determined "by the way we look at things, i.e., by the symbolic structure through which we interpret experience."[114]

Consequently, affirmation of a symbolic structure requires something more than ontology, more than reflective argument. Gilkey says that such affirmation requires "a religious mode of relating to the truth."[115]

On the most fundamental level, religious understanding depends

41

more on awareness of and participation in the dimension of the transcendent than it does on argument, though argument may help to lead our existence to that awareness and participation.[116]

To know the truth of the symbol is to participate in it.

Religious symbols function as religious symbols and so are known to be true only by those to whom they communicate a religious meaning, i.e., an awareness of an ultimate ground to life's passage and an ultimate answer to life's crises.[117]

While theology must be intelligible to anyone who is willing to ponder the evidence, the final validation of theology's cognitive claims must be found in an existential or participatory verification of its primary symbols. At this level, truth is "a matter of *self* evidence, that reality really is *this* way and really manifests *these* contours, as expressed in *these* fundamental symbolic forms."[118]

Such a stance, however, is not only a ground for understanding and apprehending reality, it is also a ground of value. Every mythic vision implies action and is legitimately judged in terms of its power to evoke, direct and sustain creative and healing action in the world.[119] This leads to the question of praxis, or theology of culture.

5. Theology of Culture

Gilkey agrees with John Dewey that valid concepts resolve actual life problems and transform the conditions of existence.[120] If such concepts do not effect changes in the reality of which they speak, they are dead.[121] He also agrees with Marx that the critique of religion is the beginning of the critique of society because "no social order can be challenged and refashioned unless its religious substance, the sacrality of its institutions, symbols and myths, is itself first challenged."[122]

More importantly, however, Gilkey's concern with the theology of culture is continuing the tradition of Tillich and Niebuhr. In his article on Niebuhr's theology of history Gilkey says that for Niebuhr, "one of the main criterion of theological validity is ... its effectiveness in initiating, in fact requiring, creative and transformative political action for larger justice, equality and peace."[123] If constructive theology begins with a wager that a particular traditional symbol system will prove to be illuminative for our present cultural life, then praxis calls for the practical enactment of that wager. If theology is to reinterpret faithfully the religious vision of the Christian tradition it must not only present an intelligible vision *of* life, it must also present a viable and healing vision *for* life.[124] Therefore Gilkey says that "the adequacy of our interpretation should be assessed, not only by its fidelity to the eidetic forms of the tradition, its relevance to our experience of our life-world, and its ontological coherence, but also by its power to evoke, direct and sustain Christian action for the future."[125]

Gilkey's theological project as a whole is both well-suited and structurally inclined toward a theology of culture. The phenomenological disclosure of a dimension of ultimacy in the prolegomenon coupled with the concern for existential relevance and reflective adequacy in his constructive theology, provides Gilkey with a good foundation for an analysis of what Tillich called the "religious substance" of society.

Gilkey understands 'theology of culture' to be an analysis of culture in terms of its religious dimension or substance. But this is a *theology* of culture because it is carried out from the perspective of a particular religious viewpoint: "it asks questions about the *religious* dilemmas of cultural life and so questions guided by *theological* problems and concerns."[126] Such analysis seeks to clarify the religious substance of a culture (since it is usually hidden and implicit, not explicit) and understand both the creative and demonic possibilities in that culture in terms of its religious substance. It is an analysis which asks questions of meaning and meaninglessness in history, of the ambiguity of our creativity, of the freedom and bondage of the will, of the career of good and evil, of pluralism and truth, and of the norms and goals of socio-political life. Since theology of culture requires a discerning of the 'signs of the times' it is prophetic in character. The theologian of culture makes historical judgments in his or her attempt to discern "where on the cycle of creativity and destruction the forces at work in our present find themselves...."[127]

If a culture is in crisis, as Gilkey thinks Western culture is, then a theology of culture in such an historical context is judged by its ability to illumine critically the religious roots of the cultural malaise. Moreover, if it is to be more than just prophetic critique and also be a constructive proposal, it must display a breadth of scope that is able to "comprehend, shape, and deal with *all* of those basic religious issues and their corresponding religious dilemmas which a scientific culture produces...."[128] Theology must propose an understanding of the totality of life not only to the church, but to the society as a whole.[129] Therefore, "Our task is ... not only the critical revision of the Christian theological tradition, but even more, lest it perish, a new and profounder vision of our cultural substance, reshaped and reconstituted in the light of the Kingdom."[130]

Before turning to a detailed discussion of Gilkey's theology of culture, some evaluative comments on his theological method as a whole are in order.

6. Evaluative Conclusions

Theology is a peculiar discipline. Like philosophy it seems to address life in its totality and, from its unique perspective, offer a total and integrative vision of life. Like any social science it engages in descriptive analysis both of a particular dimension of human life and of a particular historical tradition in its development. Yet its claim to be reflection upon a uniquely revelatory source and revelatory events, sets it apart from all other disciplines. To develop a coherent method for this discipline in a secular culture is a necessary, yet difficult task.

While Gilkey's methodological proposals may not totally satisfy all of the demands facing the discipline, they are, nevertheless, creative and fruitful. Theology does indeed require prolegomenal foundation in a secular culture. If it cannot be established that religion is a constitutive dimension of human life, rather than an inauthentic projection, then religious discourse has no meaning and theology cannot proceed. Moreover, I can think of no better a method than hermeneutical phenomenology in order to disclose the hidden and forgotten dimension of ultimacy.

Further, Gilkey is sober about the limits of the prolegomenon and the nature of the 'break' that must occur for constructive theology to proceed. Phenomenological analysis does not disclose God, only God does that. Nor does it disclose the answers to the ultimate questions which are raised by our being in the world. For this we need to go beyond immanence to transcendence, beyond general experience to special revelation. And, certainly the threefold criteria of fidelity to traditional sources, relevance to contemporary experience and illuminatory coherence are appropriate for theological reflection. Finally, if theology has adequately disclosed a religious dimension in the life of every human being and in every culture, and is reflection upon received answers to ultimate questions, then it is thoroughly appropriate that it apply that disclosure and those questions and answers to the broad cultural issues of its day in the form of a theology of culture.

Our acceptance of the basic contours of Gilkey's method and the proposed criteria for theological reflection also furnishes us with an immanent basis within Gilkey's own thought to evaluate both the constitutive stages of his theology and the project as a whole. We can ask whether Gilkey's formulations in his prolegomenon, constructive theology and theology of culture are in fact eidetically faithful, existentially relevant, intelligibly coherent, and serviceable for critical praxis. Further, is the project as a whole coherent? Since my concern is primarily with his theology of culture I will ask whether this stage of his project is founded upon and consistent with the prolegomenal and constructive stages. We will see that to a large degree there is coherence, but that in relation to some issues there is incoherence and in relation to other issues there is a coherence which is unfortunate because of weaknesses at either the prolegomenal or constructive stages.

While I have already addressed a number of criticisms that have been directed at Gilkey's method, there are still a few more criticisms, both my own and other's, that should be considered before proceeding further.

a) Religious Studies

Recalling my suggestion earlier in this chapter that one of the major reasons for the present preoccupation with method in theology is the ambiguous status of the discipline in the modern secular university, the first question that we could ask of Gilkey's methodological proposal is whether it can justify the place of theology within the broad discipline of religious studies. For those who believe that religious studies is primarily a descriptive discipline in which the personal faith of the theorist should play a minimal role, Gilkey's method and practice represent nothing less than a "failure of nerve."[131] Gilkey, so the argument goes, is attempting to reintroduce theological commitments and normative judgments into what should be a scientific and descriptive discipline. At issue here are two opposed and competing epistemologies. While I will address this issue more fully in chapter seven in my discussion of the religious dimension of science, some comments on Gilkey's view of religious studies are in order here.

45

Consistent with his prolegomenon, Gilkey believes that religious studies must be centred on the 'religious' as a *real*, not *epiphenomenal* dimension of human existence. The discipline, therefore, should follow a *responsive* interpretation of religious life (humans are responding to something sacred in religious life), rather than a reductionistic *projection* interpretation.[132] Indeed, without this approach, Gilkey can see no justification for the existence of a distinct discipline called religious studies. Further, Gilkey agrees with Wilfred Cantwell Smith when Smith says that "an objective study of religion leaves out the very part that counts; it analyzes the externals but misses the core of the matter."[133] Such an approach leads the observer to 'look at' religion rather than 'looking through' its symbols at the transcendent and the world. In its naturalistic extreme such an approach to religious studies becomes "sectarian," absolutizing its own social scientific method to the exclusion of all others.[134] And the practitioners of this method become mere "voyeurs" of religion.[135] According to Gilkey such an approach is neither appropriate to the subject matter nor does it advance religious understanding in a way that is relevant to the religious vacuum and uncertainty that characterizes modernity.

b) Special Experience

A second criticism comes from the opposite direction of the first. Why does Gilkey limit his prolegomenon to general experience and thereby avoid the whole question of special religious experience?[136] This is R. L. Littlejohn's question:

> If one is to understand experience to have such a wide range of application, then why not include numinous experiences also? If numinous experiences are acceptable, then Gilkey's grounds for rejecting neo-orthodoxy, the phenomenology of Rudolf Otto and the analysis of William James seems problematic.[137]

This criticism, however, is not very helpful. Gilkey's emphasis in his constructive theology on the role of special revelation and participatory verification is evidence enough of his acceptance of special, even numinous, experiences. Nor does he reject in principle the analyses of such experiences by Otto and James. His decision not to engage in such an analysis is strategic, not principial.[138] In a culture where such experiences are increasingly rare, he asks, can we nevertheless dis-

46

close a religious dimension even in the most ordinary and secular of experiences? His answer is, yes. The problem with neo-orthodoxy, from Gilkey's perspective, is not primarily its affirmation of numinous experience but the irrelevance and, hence, meaninglessness of such neo-orthodox experience in relation to contemporary life.

This question of special experience does, however, point to another problem that may be more significant, namely, the status of eidetic inquiry and faithfulness to the biblical and traditional sources in theology.

c) Eidetic Fidelity

As we have seen, Gilkey identifies the break between prolegomenal and constructive theology to occur when one moves from the generality of phenomenological description to reflection on a particular tradition which is rooted in special revelatory events. Those events are recorded in Scripture which functions as the *norma non normata* of Christian theology. All of this I affirm. But there are some questions which should be raised.

Francis Schüssler Fiorenza asks: "What if a conflict exists between fidelity to the eidetic meaning of the tradition and the conceptual consistency demanded by present reflection upon experience?"[138A] In principle, Gilkey's response would be that if the contents of Christian faith are such that "they interpret, illumine, and clarify the basic nature of our human existence and history," then the failure of theology both to be eidetically faithful to those contents and to be conceptually consistent and existentially relevant would be evidence of the failure of either the theology or the original symbols, or both.[139] One of my questions in the chapters to come will be whether this is in fact Gilkey's practice. Does he maintain that fidelity, and are his existential and conceptual formulations faithful to the original sources?

There are other questions to be asked concerning eidetic meaning. Gilkey is right when he says that biblical symbols can function creatively in theology only when a unity is postulated out of the diversity of the biblical witness. But, we might ask, what is the nature of this 'postulation' and what are the criteria that govern it? Is there an underlying unity in the biblical witness that the theologian attempts to appropriate, or is there, more fundamentally, a diversity, and any attempt at unity is a matter of creative postulation? If the latter (which appears to be Gilkey's view), then are the fundamental criteria by which this postulated unity is judged its supposed contemporary relevance and ontological intelligibility? Does this mean that, Gilkey's protests notwithstanding, his theology imposes upon the biblical tradition a meaning that is not eidetically appropriate or faithful to it, and that the horizon of present experience is in fact authoritative over the horizon of the biblical text? And if this unity is 'postulated' out of the diversity, then what role will be played by those elements of the biblical witness that were not included in the postulation? Is fidelity to eidetic meaning also necessary with reference to those excluded elements?

Further, if Gilkey is concerned with eidetic meaning, then why is there so little actual biblical exegesis in his work? Ted Peters also raises this question:

> The functional source of Christian symbols for Gilkey turns out to be the writings of Augustine and Calvin, not those of St. Paul or J, E, P, and D. But Augustine and Calvin were in fact theologians engaged in second order discourse, using the primary symbols found already in scripture.[140]

Why does Gilkey seem more concerned with analyzing and responding to the theological tradition then he does with the biblical witness? Could it be because he has too conceptual an understanding of symbol? This is the next criticism.

c) Symbols and Doctrines
In our exposition of Gilkey's method there has been an ambiguity in our use of terms. We have spoken of symbols, symbolic content, symbol systems, the biblical witness, the Christian tradition, and the contents of faith. This ambiguity in my exposition is a reflection of an ambiguity in Gilkey's writing. When Gilkey explicitly addresses the nature of symbols he basically follows Ricoeur's notion of double intentionality. A symbol points to both its own literal meaning and beyond itself to something which is *like* the literal meaning, yet transcendent to it.[141] Obvious examples of such symbols are 'stain' which points to its symbolic meaning in defilement, 'deviation' which points to sin, 'weight' which points to guilt, 'wine' which symbolizes blood, 'bread' which symbolically refers to body, etc. Such symbols, says Gilkey, "precede rationality and cannot be created by it."[142] Yet Gilkey also seems to refer to theological doctrines, which are clearly theoreti-

cal in nature, as if they were also symbols. For example, he describes historical theology as "a study of *past* ideas or beliefs, what the symbols of a tradition — its beliefs and doctrines — *meant* to the third century, the thirteenth century, the Reformation, the nineteenth century."[143] Here the terms, symbols, beliefs and doctrines are used interchangeably. In another place he refers to the following 'symbols': creation, fall, providence, revelation, incarnation, atonement, ecclesia, Word, sacrament, and eschatology.[144] While all of these terms clearly have an important role to play in a Christian interpretation of our world, it is just as clearly stretching the idea of symbol too far to include all of these doctrines. Consequently, some critics complain that Gilkey's understanding of symbol is too conceptual.[145] This is a valid criticism.

e) Truth

Thomas Ommen has documented a tension within what David Tracy calls 'revisionist theology' between Tracy and Gilkey on the question of the verification of religious truth claims.[146] According to Ommen, while both Gilkey and Tracy agree that theology can rationally establish the meaningfulness of religious discourse, they disagree concerning the establishment of the truth of such discourse. Tracy thinks that a transcendental analysis of the *a priori* conditions of existence can establish such truth. He says that metaphysical argument

> ... shows that certain basic beliefs must necessarily be maintained as basic conditions of the possibility of our understanding or existing at all. Such basic beliefs ... can be shown to be basic by demonstrating the self-contradictory character which their denial involves for any intelligent and rational ("reflective") inquirer.[147]

Specifically, Tracy believes that faith in the worthwhileness of life is basic to the fabric of all human life. Such faith requires, as its transcendental condition, the existence of God.[148]

Gilkey, however, makes a more modest claim. On one level he agrees that the satisfaction of the criteria of existential and conceptual adequacy establishes truth. He says, "A symbolic account can claim to be 'true' because it brings to coherent, systematic understanding the wide variety of relevant experiences, of 'facts' constitutive of that experience...." 'Adequacy' to experience is established by "showing how the central elements of relevant experience achieve intelligibility, coherence, and illumination within this set of symbols."[149] But, as we have seen, this is only a necessary, not a sufficient condition for the establishment of religious truth. Not as confident in the powers of transcendental argument as is Tracy, Gilkey says that religious symbols ultimately require participatory verification if they are to be true for us.

Ommen comments on the 'passivity' of Gilkey's position regarding truth. Truth is 'received' in the symbols of special revelation, not 'proven' by means of argument.[150] Religious symbols are argued *from*, not argued *to*. Ommen mentions two important implications of Gilkey's view of truth in contrast with Tracy's method. The first is that for Gilkey theology assumes the classical form of faith seeking understanding.[151] Therefore it is assumed that the theologian has faith. Tracy thinks that this is not necessary. Theology is a public scientific discipline and does not need to be practiced by people who have any specific religious commitment. This is especially true of fundamental theology.[152] This gives rise to the second implication. A truly public discipline requires a universal set of criteria by which one can measure the truth of its assertions. For Gilkey, says Ommen, such a set of criteria do not exist.[153] For Tracy, they do.

Tracy's suggestion that the fundamental theologian need not be a believer may be methodologically correct, but it is also existentially irrelevant. It is almost impossible to imagine a non-believer being interested in pursuing the apologetic task of fundamental theology simply out of academic interest. Here Gilkey's description of his prolegomenon as an analysis of secular experience open for anyone to evaluate, though written with clearly stated Christian presuppositions, seems to be a more adequate description of what actually occurs in the discipline. Concerning a universal set of criteria of ultimate truth, Ommen is right — Gilkey can find no such criteria. This is not to reduce his position to a subjectivistic fideism, however. The prolegomenon itself establishes (as Ommen acknowledges)[154] that a religious dimension and function of faith is constitutive of all human life. Moreover, any faith perspective must, as we have seen, be tested by its illuminatory power in existence. But ultimately faith is self-evident to the believer, or it does not exist at all.

This defense of Gilkey's position does not mean that his view of truth is totally without problems, however. Edward Farley asks whether Gilkey's understanding of the truth of symbols permits him to rise and make judgments.[155] In the Part II we will see that he does make judgments but that they are not always entirely consistent. If Gilkey does not have a set of universal criteria, then how does he avoid relativism? On what basis will he judge other viewpoints to be untrue?[156]

f) Discerning the Times

Any theology that formally includes in its method the criteria of contemporary relevance and adequacy needs to have discernment into the cultural context within which it finds itself. It is not surprising, then, that theologians will often disagree in their discernments. This was evident in Tom Driver's review of *Naming the Whirlwind.* Driver found Gilkey's cultural analysis too sober, not taking into account the new cultural optimism of the time. Whether Driver himself had correctly read the times is questionable. With the demise of the counter-culture, the economic recession and energy crisis of the seventies, and the nuclear anxiety of the eighties, Gilkey's 'sober' analysis in 1969 seems to have been more adequate.[157] This is not to say that his analysis has not undergone any change since that time. He freely admits that when he wrote *Naming the Whirlwind* he did not anticipate the renewal of interest in religious expression that would characterize the seventies.[158]

A more important critique of Gilkey's cultural discernment comes from Charles Winquist.[159] Indeed, Winquist's critique questions the validity of Gilkey's project as a whole. Rejecting what he sees to be Gilkey's attempt to relocate religion at the centre of societal life, Winquist applies Victor Turner's description of social drama to the present crisis in theology.[160] Theology is a discipline at the "margins" of society; it has "liminal" characteristics. Winquist explains:

> Liminality designates an experimental field where not only new ideas or images appear but also where new combinatory rules govern their dissemination. The meaning of meaning has a fluctuating signification. Disciplines of meaning such as theology float without anchor during liminal periods.[161]

Contrary to Gilkey, Winquist urges theology to engage in a self-admitted flight from the centre of societal life rather than attempt to redress the situation. Theology's relevance "will have to be a feature of its liminality. It will only have an illusory relevance if it claims to be something other than what it is."[162]

There are two questions that should be asked of Winquist's position. The first is, how does he know that theology is presently in a liminal situation? Is this a cultural discernment based on a theology of culture, or a prescription for theology based on Winquist's own deconstructionist presuppositions? Theology as a liminoid genre requires deconstruction, not reconstruction, says Winquist. And secondly, is Winquist not using Turner's categories for his own deconstructionist purposes in such a way that short-circuits Turner's own position? Winquist himself says that Turner's four phases of social drama move from a break in normal relations, to a mounting crisis, to adjustive and redressive actions, to a final reintegration.[163] Why then does Winquist limit theology to the first two phases of this process and advocate a deconstructionist stance which would controvert any redressive and reintegratory actions?

The conflict between the positions advocated by Winquist and Gilkey is fundamental. It is paradigmatic in scope. Does human life, culture and history have a centre or not? And if it does have a centre does religion occupy that centre? If Gilkey's theology in its prolegomenal, constructive and cultural stages is convincing, then Winquist's deconstructive proposals must be rejected.[164]

This brings my discussion of Gilkey's theological method to a close. Gilkey once said that "theology must cease speaking entirely about itself, i.e., about method, and begin to talk about its essential object: the historical life of men and women *coram Deo* and in community—for good or ill—with one another."[165] Following this advice, Part II will be a discussion of Gilkey's theology of culture.

NOTES

1 Thomas Kuhn documents this process in his *The Structure of Scientific Revolutions*, (rev. ed.; Chicago: University of Chicago Press, 1962). See also N. R. Hanson, *Patterns of Discovery* (Cambridge: Cambridge University Press, 1965).

2 Randy L. Maddox, *Toward an Ecumenical Fundamental Theology*, American Academy of Religion Academy Series; no. 47, ed. by C. A. Raschke (Chico, C.A.: Scholars Press, 1984), p. 1.

3 Gordon Kaufman, *An Essay on Theological Method*, American Academy of Religion Studies in Religion, no. 11; ed. by C. C. Cherry (rev. ed.; Missoula, Montana: Scholars Press, 1979), p. ix.

4 Ibid, p. x. Cf. David Tracy, *The Analogical Imagination: Christian Theology and the Culture of Pluralism* (New York: Crossroad, 1981): "The present search for a new paradigm for theology is complicated further by the relative decline in recent years of earlier neoorthodox paradigms in Protestant theology and the decline of neo-Thomism and its clear set of criteria and the genre of the 'manual' in Roman Catholic theology." (p. 19).

5 Gilkey rejects the normative/descriptive distinction as a false dichotomy. Cf. "The Roles of the 'Descriptive' or 'Historical' and the 'Normative' in Our Work," *Criterion* 20, 1 (Winter 1980), pp. 10-17.

6 *The Analogical Imagination*, p. 16.

7 Wolfhart Pannenberg, *Basic Questions in Theology*, I, trans. by G. H. Kehm (Philadelphia: Fortress Press, 1971); and *Theology and the Philosophy of Science*, trans. by F. McDonagh (Philadelphia: Westminster Press, 1976). For a critical interpretation and evaluation of Pannenberg's proposals see the present author's *Futurity and Creation: Explorations in the Eschatological Theology of Wolfhart Pannenberg* (published M.Phil. thesis, Toronto: Institute for Christian Studies, 1979); and "Pannenberg's Eschatological Ontology," *Christian Scholar's Review* XI, 3 (1982), pp. 229-249.

8 Jürgen Moltmann, *Theology of Hope* (New York: Harper and Row, 1967).

9 Gustavo Gutiérrez, *A Theology of Liberation*, trans. and ed. by Caridad Inda and John Eagleson (Maryknoll, N.Y.: Orbis Books, 1972).

10 Rosemary Ruether, *Sexism and God-talk: Toward a Feminist Theology* (Boston: Beacon Press, 1983).

11 Bernard Lonergan, *Insight: A Study of Human Understanding* (London: Longmans, 1964); and *Method in Theology* (New York: Seabury Press, 1974).

12 David Tracy, *The Analogical Imagination*; and *Blessed Rage for Order: The New Pluralism in Theology* (New York: Seabury Press, 1975).

13 Gilkey's three stages of theological reflection closely parallel Tracy's distinctions between fundamental, systematic and practical theologies. Cf. *The Analogical Imagination*, pp. 54-82. And Hans Küng credits Gilkey with having strengthened him "in the conviction that we find ourselves presently in a new paradigm shift from the modern to the post-modern period in theology." "Paradigm Change in Theology," in *The Whirlwind in Culture*, p. 67.

14 Kevin J. Sharpe makes this point in his discussion of Kaufman's method. "Theological Method and Gordon Kaufman," *Religious Studies* 15 (June 1979), p. 179.

15 *Theology of Culture*, chapter two. I am indebted to lectures by Prof. Douglas J. Hall of McGill University for the application of Tillich's views on the two types of philosophy of religion to questions of theological method.

16 Ibid, p. 10.

17 *Naming,* p. 190.

18 Ibid.

19 Ibid.

20 "Dissolution and Reconstruction in Theology," pp. 29-32.

21 *Naming,* p. 33. Gilkey's understanding of modernity will be discussed more fully in the next chapter.

22 *Naming,* pp. 9ff.

23 "Secularism's Impact," p. 65.

24 Ibid. Cf. *Naming,* p. 100; and "The Contribution of Culture to the Reign of God," in *The Future as Presence of Shared Hope,* ed. by M. Muckenheim (New York: Sheed and Ward, 1968), pp. 43-44.

25 *Naming,* p. 90.

26 *Naming,* p. 199, n.9.

27 William Hamilton, *The New Essence of Christianity* (New York: Association Press, 1961), p. 55.

28 William Hamilton, *The New Essence of Christianity;* William Hamilton and Thomas Altizer, *Radical Theology and the Death of God* (Indianapolis: Bobbs Merrill, 1966); Paul van Buren, *The Secular Meaning of the Gospel* (New York: Macmillan, 1963); and Thomas J. J. Altizer, *The Gospel of Christian Atheism* (Philadelphia: Westminster Press, 1966).

29 "New Modes of Empirical Theology," p. 351. Cf. *Naming,* pp. 11, 110f; and "Secularism's Impact," p. 66. Both Schubert Ogden and Gordon Kaufman agreed at that time that the question of God was *the* theological question. See Ogden's *The Reality of God* (New York: Harper and Row, 1966); and Kaufman's *God the Problem* (Cambridge: Harvard University Press, 1971).

30 "Dissolution and Reconstruction," pp. 33-34.

31 R. L. Maddox finds the earliest example of this three-step apologetic in P. Charron's *Les trois vérités contra les athées, les idolâtres, juifs, mohemétans, hérétiques et schismatiques* (1593). *Toward an Ecumenical Fundamental Theology,* p. 14.

32 R. L. Maddox, Ibid, pp. 70-72. Gilkey is not alone in seeing the need for an anthropological fundamental theology. Wolfhart Pannenberg has said that "theological anthropology ... has the status of a form of fundamental theology." *The Idea of God and Human Freedom,* trans. by R. A. Wilson (Philadelphia: Westminster Press, 1973), p. 90. Cf. his *Theology and the Philosophy of Science,* pp. 368, 371, 422. Pannenberg's own fundamental theology is most fully argued in his recent *Anthropology in Theological Perspective,* trans. by M. J. O'Connell (Philadelphia:

PART1: THEOLOGICAL METHOD

Westminster Press, 1984). For a critical discussion of this work see the present author's "A Critical Review of Pannenberg's *Anthropology in Theological Perspective*," *Christian Scholar's Review* XV, 3 (1986), pp. 247-259.

Other theologians who have attempted to ground theology by means of an anthropological analysis of a religious dimension of human life include: David Tracy, *Blessed Rage for Order*, Karl Rahner, *Hearers of the Word*, trans. by M. Richards (Montreal: Palm Publishers, 1969); Schubert Ogden, *The Reality of God*; Hans Küng, *Does God Exist? An Answer for Today*, trans. by E. Quinn, (Garden City, N.Y.: Doubleday, 1980); and Edward Farley, *Ecclesial Man: A Social Phenomenology of Faith and Reality* (Philadelphia: Fortress Press, 1975). D. R. Stiver's dissertation, *Converging Approaches*, is an excellent discussion of some of these recent fundamental theologies.

33   *Naming*, p. 13

33A Ibid, p. 414.

34   Peter Berger, "Secular Theology and the Rejection of the Supernatural: Reflections on Recent Trends," *Theological Studies* 38, 1 (March 1977), pp. 45, 51. Berger goes on to say that these authors surrender to the new authority of the secular spirit with such uncritical devotion that their position can be adequately described as an "assertive and arrogant secular 'fundamentalism'" (pp. 52, 55). Cf. Avery Dulles, *The Resilient Church* (New York: Doubleday, 1974), ch. 4; and John Gibbs, review of *Naming the Whirlwind*, *Journal of the American Academy of Religion* 39, 2 (June 1971), pp. 272-274. For Gilkey's responses to Berger and Dulles see, "Responses to Berger," and "Anathemas and Orthodoxy."

35   G. Stanley Kane, "God-Language and Secular Experience," *International Journal of Philosophy of Religion* 2, 1 (1971), p. 90.

36   Frederick Ferré, "A Renewal of God-Language?," *Journal of Religion* 52, 2 (July 1972), p. 303.

37   Clark Williamson, "The Divine Obituary was Premature: A Review Article," *Encounter* 31 (Autumn 1971), pp. 396-399; Tom Driver, review of *Naming the Whirlwind*, *Union Seminary Quarterly* 25, 3 (Spring 1970), pp. 361-367.

38   Driver, p. 364.

39   Helena Sheehan, review of *Naming the Whirlwind*, *Journal of Ecumenical Studies* 7 (Fall 1970), pp. 836-839.

40   *Naming*, p. 225, italics added.

41   "New Modes of Empirical Theology," p. 360.

42   Cf. *Naming*, pp. 248ff. On p. 253 Gilkey says: "A nonsecular dimension in our experience appears in the lived character of secular life, despite the fact that the forms of our modern self-understanding have no capacity for dealing with it." See also "The Problem of God: A Programmatic Essay," in *Traces of God in a Secular Culture*, ed. by G. F. McLean (New York: Alba House, 1973), pp. 9-11.

43 A similar defense of Gilkey against the charge of capitulation to modernity can

55

be found in John Shea, *Religious Language*, pp. 177-182.

44 *Message and Existence*, p. 10. Tracy identifies common human experience and language, together with Christian texts as the two principle sources for theology in *Blessed Rage for Order*, pp. 43-45.

45 *Message and Existence*, p. 12.

46 N. Schreurs, "Naar de basis van ons spreken over God: de weg van Langdon Gilkey," *Tijdschrift voor Theologie* 11, 3 (1971), p. 289.

47 Others who have offered this critique include: Ted Peters, "The Whirlwind as Yet Unnamed," *Journal of the American Academy of Religion* 42, 4 (December 1974), p. 700; John Gibbs, review of *Naming the Whirlwind*, p. 274; Paul van Buren, review of *Naming the Whirlwind, Theology Today* 27 (July 1970), p. 226; Helena Sheehan, review of *Naming the Whirlwind*, p. 839; and R. L. Littlejohn, *Gilkey's Phenomenology of Ultimacy*, p. 218.

48 *Naming*, p. 234.

49 Concerning presuppositions Gilkey comments: "Like all others, our thoughts are inescapably guided by the ultimate assumptions and attitudes of the person who thinks them, and in interpreting such a varied and rich 'object' as secular experience with regard to such imprecise though important characteristics as its 'meaning' and 'character,' such initial assumptions inevitably play a very heavy role in what is found there.... It is a *theologian* who is writing here, and the way this fact will weight the inquiry from the start is freely admitted." *Naming*, p. 233. In his response to N. Schreurs, Gilkey also says that in *Naming* he did *not* carry out "a 'neutral' examination of experience, undirected by my own fundamental view of the world." "Ervaring en interpretatie van de religieuze dimensie: een reaktie," *Tijdschrift voor Theologie* 11, 3 (1971), p. 295.

50 For other references to the theological circle see, *Naming*, p. 176; *Society and the Sacred*, pp. 39, 67, 149-150; and "Empirical Science and Theological Knowing," in *Foundations of Theology*, ed. by Philip McShane, S.J. (Notre Dame, Ind.: University of Notre Dame Press, 1972), pp. 88-89.

51 "Ervaring en interpretatie van de religieuze dimensie," p. 297.

52 *Naming*, p. 20.

53 *Naming*, p. 433. For a helpful discussion of the phenomenological understanding of the philosophical importance of the naive experience of the *Lebenswelt* (life-world), see, C. A. van Peursen, "Life-World and Structures," in *Patterns of the Life-World: Essays in Honor of John Wild*, ed. by J. M. Edie, F. H. Parker, and C. O. Schrag (Evanston: Northwestern University Press, 1970), pp. 139-153.

The following quotation from Maurice Merleau-Ponty summarizes well the phenomenological perspective that Gilkey is adopting: "If the ordinary acts of sense perception and the ordinary relations between human beings are invalid, then the simplest acts of scientific research and verification are also called into question, for

PART1: THEOLOGICAL METHOD

such validities presuppose and depend upon the validities of the life-world." "What is Phenomenology?," in *Phenomenology of Religion,* ed. by Joseph Bettis (New York: Harper and Row, 1969), p. 22.

In the light of Gilkey's ongoing interaction with Whiteheadian thought, it is also instructive to note that his concern with naive experience does not contradict Whitehead's view. Whitehead believed that "the elucidation of immediate experience is the sole justification for any thought." *Process and Reality: An Essay in Cosmology,* ed. by David Ray Griffin and Donald W. Sherburne (corrected edition; New York: The Free Press, 1978), p. 4.

54 *Naming,* p. 277. It is not surprising that Gilkey has been criticized for this affirmation by philosophers who work out of the analytic tradition. Both Daniel Noel, "God-Language Grounded: A Review Article," *Anglican Theological Review* 53, 1 (January 1971), pp. 67-70; and Paul van Buren, review of *Naming the Whirlwind,* pp. 227-228, deny that one can 'go behind language' to reality. N. Schreurs asks the same question: "Can experience, as Gilkey wants, be isolated from its linguistic expression?" "Naar de basis van ons spreken over God," p. 289.

To a large degree this is a debate between two conceptual paradigms that we cannot mediate in this book. Beyond the discussion in the text, however, there are two things that should be said.

a) Gilkey's primary concern in his prolegomenon is not to get behind language to experience, but to uncover a religious dimension of ordinary experience without reference to explicitly religious language. Cf. Gilkey's "Ervaring en interpretatie van de religieuze dimensie," p. 293.

b) Some have argued for a rapprochement between the phenomenological concern for lived experience and the analytic interest in ordinary language, language games and 'forms of life.' For example, see John Wild, "Is There a World of Ordinary Language?," *Philosophical Review* 68 (October 1958), pp. 460-476; reprinted as chapter three of Wild's *Existence and the World of Freedom* (Englewood Cliffs, N.J.: Prentice-Hall, 1963); and Eugene TeHennepe, "The Life-World and the World of Ordinary Language," in *An Invitation to Phenomenology: Studies in the Philosophy of Experience,* ed. by J. Edie (Chicago: Quadrangle Books, 1965), pp. 133-146.

55 *Naming,* p. 273. Cf. "New Modes of Empirical Theology," pp. 356, 367; *Reaping,* p. 233; and *Message and Existence,* pp. 9-10.

56 *Naming,* p. 269. In n.10 on this page Gilkey acknowledges his dependence for this view of meaning on Eugene Gendlin, John Wild and James Edie. J. Wesley Robbins' article, "Professor Gilkey and Alternative Methods of Theological Construction," *Journal of Religion* 52, 1 (1972) mistakenly identifies this theory of meaning with Bertrand Russell's referential theory. There are only four references to Russell in *Naming's* 470 pages, all inconsequential. Gilkey's theory is phenomenological, not analytic. Both George Davis, *Langdon Gilkey and Religious Language,* pp. 40-42, and John Shea, *Religious Language,* pp. 124ff, argue that Robbins has misunderstood the distinction between 'reference' and 'referent' in Gilkey's thought. Religious language is meaningful, according to Gilkey, if it has 'reference' to a general area or dimension of ordinary experience. Whether such language is not only meaningful but also true, that is, whether it has a real 'referent' (i.e., God), is another question altogether. We will discuss the meaning/truth distinction further below.

Equally confused is William Thompson's contention that linguistic analysis is Gilkey's "main tool" and "central object of concern." "Theology's Method and Linguistic Analysis in the Thought of Langdon Gilkey," *The Thomist* 36 (July 1972), pp. 367, 381. John Shea is correct when he says that Thompson's application of categories from linguistic analysis to explicate Gilkey's thought "seems alien and inappropriate." (*Religious Language*, p. 167).

57 Cf. *Naming*, pp. 270-271, 274, 306; "New Modes of Empirical Theology," p. 356; and "Modern Myth-Making and the Possibilities of Twentieth-Century Theology," in *Theology of Renewal*, ed. by L. Shook (Montreal: Palm Publishing, 1968), p. 311. The original phrase can be found in Eugene T. Gendlin, *Experiencing and the Creation of Meaning* (Glencoe, Ill.: The Free Press, 1962), pp. 5-6.

58 *Naming*, p. 280. Notes 18, 19 and 20 on pp. 278-279 document this shift with reference to Heidegger, Sartre, Merleau-Ponty, Ricoeur and Spiegelberg. For a more detailed discussion of Gilkey's use of phenomenology see, R. L. Littlejohn, *Gilkey's Phenomenology of Ultimacy*, chapters 2 and 3. Both Littlejohn (p. 76, n. 5), and Edward Farley, *Ecclesial Man*, pp. 267-268, n. 72, argue that Gilkey's understanding of Husserl seems to be limited to Husserl's *Ideas*, trans. by W. R. Boyce-Gibson (New York: Collier Books, 1967). Consequently Gilkey does not take into account the later Husserl's concern with the *Lebenswelt* in *The Crisis of European Sciences and Transcendental Phenomenology*, trans. by David Carr (Evanston: Northwestern University Press, 1970).
  While Gilkey may not have sufficiently grasped the corpus of Husserl, there seems to be little doubt that such an 'existential' or 'hermeneutical' turn has occurred in the phenomenological movement. Perhaps the greatest influence on Gilkey has been Ricoeur's shift from eidetics to hermeneutics. An eidetic analysis can disclose the fundamental structures of possibility in human life; but to arrive at the human being in his/her actuality one needs to move from eidetics to hermeneutics because, says Ricoeur, we can only have access to the *Lebenswelt* of actual experience through the enigmatic language of myths and symbols. Cf. Ricoeur's *Fallible Man: Philosophy of the Will*, trans. by Charles Kelby (Chicago: Henry Regnery Press, 1965); and *The Symbolism of Evil*, trans. by Emerson Buchanan (Boston: Beacon Press, 1967). An excellent discussion of Ricoeur's thought which grasps the shift we have been addressing is David R. Rasmussen, *Mythic - Symbolic Language: A Constructive Interpretation of the Thought of Paul Ricoeur* (The Hague: Martinus Nijhof, 1971).
  It should be noted, however, that Gilkey engages in a 'reversal' of Ricoeur's method not unlike his reversal of Tillichian and Niebuhrian apologetic method discussed in the Introduction. Ricoeur's hermeneutic is of religious symbols to see what they will disclose about actual experience. Gilkey's hermeneutic in the prolegomenon is "an examination of actual *experience* to find its latent sacred elements — and so of the possible use of religious symbols...." *Naming*, p. 281, n.23.
  For further discussion of Gilkey's appropriation of phenomenology see S. A. Sanders, *The Contribution of Phenomenology to Theology as Reflected in the Writings of Langdon Gilkey and Edward Farley* (unpub. Th.D. dissertation, New Orleans Baptist Theological Seminary, 1987).

59 Cf. *Naming*, p. 282: "... we assert the ultimate authority of intuition ...." See also pp. 242-243: Phenomenology is "based on the conviction that direct intuition is the one unquestionable basis of all certainty and so all authority in knowing."

60 *Naming*, p. 440. Cf. *Reaping*, p. 379, n. 35. The criticisms of Stanley Kane that Gilkey's procedure reverts to an argument by logical inference, "God-Language and Secular Experience," p. 83; of Frederick Ferré that there is a principle of sufficient reason at work here, "A Renewal of God-Language?," p. 300; and J. Wesley Robbins that all of this entails a "rationalistic assumption" concerning the "correlation between certain experiential states of human beings and the order of things...," "Professor Gilkey and Alternative Methods," p. 99 — *all* miss the point. John Shea, *Religious Language*, p. 150; R. L. Littlejohn, *Gilkey's Phenomenology of Ultimacy*, p. 167; and D. R. Stiver, *Converging Approaches*, pp. 153-155, have all argued correctly that Gilkey's method is not to infer a dimension of ultimacy as the logical *implication* of experience, but to disclose intuitively this dimension as an *aspect* of experience itself. The relevant question, then, is whether Gilkey's argument in fact discloses, however intuitively, what it sets out to disclose. Does the phenomenological description illuminate ordinary experience? Does it 'fit' that experience? Does it 'work?' Cf. Gilkey's "Ervaring en interpretatie van de religieuze dimensie," p. 295.

61 *Naming*, p. 306. See also p. 275.

62 Gilkey's criticisms of 'metaphysical' theology are generally directed at process theology, though they also encompass neo-Thomism. See *Naming*, pp. 44-47, 64-70, 203-227; "Secularism's Impact," p. 66; and "New Modes of Empirical Theology," pp. 352-353. For a more detailed argument see Gilkey's "A Review of John Cobb's *A Christian Natural Theology*," *Theology Today* 22, 4 (January 1966), pp. 530-544; and "Theology in Process: Schubert Ogden's Developing Theology," *Interpretation* 21 (October 1967), pp. 447-458.

63 *Naming*, p. 227.

64 For the meaning/validity distinction see, *Naming*, pp. 260-266, 416f; "Dissolution and Reconstruction in Theology," p. 36; "The Universal and Immediate Presence of God," p. 91; and "New Modes of Empirical Theology," pp. 355-356.

65 "Trends in Protestant Apologetics," p. 156.

66 Stephen Toulmin, *An Examination of the Place of Reason in Ethics* (Cambridge: Cambridge University Press, 1961), ch. 14. For a similar discussion of 'limit questions' see Tracy, *Blessed Rage for Order*, ch. 5.

67 *Naming*, p. 301. In chapter two of *The Transforming Vision: Shaping a Christian World View* (Downers Grove, Ill.: InterVarsity Press, 1984), Richard Middleton and I identify four questions that we term 'world view questions.' Functioning in the same way as Gilkey's 'limit questions,' they are: "Where am I?" "Who am I?" "What's wrong?" "What is the remedy?" Leslie Stevenson employs a similar series of questions in his *Seven Theories of Human Nature* (New York and Oxford: Oxford University Press, 1974).

68 *Naming*, p. 296.

69 "Responses to Berger," pp. 490-491. Gilkey thinks that the major interpretative mistake that both Dulles and Berger made in their criticisms of his work was that they read *Naming* as if it were a complete statement of his theology. "Interview,"

November 28, 1984. Cf. *Reaping*, p. 369, n. 2.

70 *Naming*, p. 261. Cf. pp. 301-302; and "New Modes of Empirical Theology," p. 361.

71 *Naming*, pp. 416-417, italics added. Pannenberg's understanding of the limits of a prolegomenon is similar. He says that while anthropological considerations are the first step in theological apologetics, they can take us no farther than the assertion that "when man's being is fully aware, man is conscious that he is dependent upon a reality which surpasses and sustains everything finite...." *The Idea of God and Human Freedom*, p. 95. Cf. his *Theology and the Philosophy of Science*, p. 309.

72 *The Analogical Imagination*, p. 163.

73 *Naming*, p. 450. Similarly, Gilkey speaks of the *Entr'Acte* of *Reaping* in terms of the 'break' between prolegomenon and constructive theology: "Something new is here added, a new stance, a new perspective, a new total view of things and so a new constellation of fundamental symbols which, while perhaps implied in the action of the first act, nevertheless is not clearly demonstrated as embedded within that action nor exhaustively supplied by it." (p. 117)

74 *The Symbolism of Evil*, pp. 308, 355.

75 "New Modes of Empirical Theology," p. 362. Cf. "The Problem of God", pp. 15-17.

76 Ibid, pp. 363-364. Cf. *Naming*, pp. 331, 427.

77 *Naming*, p. 429. Cf. *Catholicism*, p. 93: "If special historical events are uniquely revelatory of God, then analyses of general experience are not sufficient for a Christian theological understanding of God." He goes on: "Only in the event of Jesus as the Christ is clarity with regard to ultimacy manifest."

78 *Naming*, p. 419. Cf. "New Modes of Empirical Theology," p. 364; and *Message and Existence*, pp. 45-46.

79 *Naming*, p. 447. It is ironic that while both Berger and Dulles criticize Gilkey for neglecting transcendence and special revelation, Gilkey himself addresses the same criticisms to Wilfred Cantwell Smith and Bernard Lonergan. Concerning Smith's proposal for a 'world theology,' Gilkey complains that "there is no category of 'special revelation,' a special point in history or in consciousness where a special and decisive (if not exclusive) manifestation of 'God' is affirmed to have taken place...." "A Theological Voyage with Wilfred Cantwell Smith," *Religious Studies Review* 7, 4 (October 1981), p. 303. And against Lonergan he argues that the principles of theology are not founded upon an empirical analysis. "Rather theology, by its nature as reflection on our foundational *religious* symbols with regard to their meaning and validity for us, essentially concerns the impingement of *transcendence* (or 'God') on our existence — and hence neither an empirical inquiry into the 'facts' around us nor an analysis of our own 'immanent' powers of cognition will in and of themselves manifest the object of theology, which is the sacred or the divine." "Empirical Science and Theological Knowing," in *Foundations of Theology*, p. 98. T.

E. Hosinski also notes the importance of special revelation in Gilkey's theology. Cf. his "Experience and the Sacred," p. 233.

80 *MH*, pp. 578-579. Cf. *Naming*, p. 434: "The basis ... for any speculative ontology is the reception in experience of a 'revelation' of the ultimate order of things, a revelation which is not so much the result of speculative thought as its ground."

81 "Christian Theology," *Criterion* 13, 2 (Winter 1974), p. 12.

82 Ibid, p. 11. Gilkey also agrees with Lonergan's emphasis on the 'hypothetical' character of theology. "Empirical Science and Theological Knowing," p. 80.

83 Ibid, p. 12. Ted Peters is largely correct when he says that for Gilkey the theological task is primarily a matter of "worldview construction," attempting to put the "world of meaning" together. "The Christian Realism of Langdon Gilkey," (unpub. ms., n.d.), pp. 1, 7.

84 Cf. *Message and Existence*, p. 57; and *How the Church*, p. 96.

85 *Reaping*, pp. 140-146. Earlier formulations of the levels of theological meaning can be found in *Naming*, pp. 274-275, 458-459; "New Modes of Empirical Theology," pp. 366-367; and *Catholicism*, pp. 115-141.
  Hosinski has noted the interrelation of these stages in Gilkey's thought: "Theological interpretation ... does not form a single, progressive argument, but rather is constituted by an intertwining of analyses and a series of arguments that attempt to fit and illumine the full complexity that we experience." "Experience and the Sacred," p. 234.

86 Hans-Georg Gadamer, *Truth and Method*, trans. by G. Barden and J. Cumming, A Continuum Book (New York: Seabury Press, 1975).

87 Cf. *Naming*, p. 275; and *Reaping*, p. 240.

88 *Catholicism*, p. 120. Gilkey also speaks of the interdependence of all the symbols within a symbol system: "Each has 'internal relations' to each of the other symbols, and thus the whole forms in principle a systematic unity of meaning that shapes the character of any particular symbol." Ibid, p. 117.

89 *Reaping*, p. 143. Cf. *Naming*, p. 458.

90 It is important to add that Gilkey includes historical theology under this category of eidetics. The issue is not just the meaning of biblical symbols in their scriptural context, but also their meaning as that has been historically explicated in the Christian tradition. Cf. *Catholicism*, p. 117; *Message and Existence*, p. 54; and *Reaping*, ch. 7 and 9.

91 *Naming*, p. 460. Cf. "Responses to Berger," p. 493; "New Modes of Empirical Theology," p. 368; and "The Problem of God," p. 21.

92 *Reaping*, p. 142. Cf. *Naming*, p. 461: "... every valid theology must justify its own categorial structure of thought first of all in relation to the central symbolic content,

eidetically abstracted, through historical study, of the Biblical materials and the tradition and life of reflection which have made up the Church's history."

93 *Message and Existence,* p. 53. Cf. "The Authority of the Bible: the relation of the Bible to the Church," *Encounter* 27 (Spring 1966), pp. 112-123.

94 *Catholicism,* p. 117. In another place Gilkey says that "any creative theology ultimately draws its strength from its own sources." "Social and Intellectual Sources of Contemporary Protestant Theology in America," *Dædelus* 96, 1 (Winter 1967), p. 98.

95 Cf. *Message and Existence,* p. 56. Anthony C. Thiselton makes a similar point by using the analogy of the performance of a musical composition. Each performance is unique and requires creative imagination, not wooden repetition. "Yet," says Thiselton, "the creativity of the performer still takes place within clear limits. For without faithfulness to the score, the performer would not be a *faithful* interpreter of *that* work." "Knowledge, Myth and Corporate Memory," in *Believing in the Church: The Corporate Nature of Faith* (London: S.P.C.K., 1981), p. 74. Thiselton's hermeneutical approach is most fully developed in his *The Two Horizons: New Testament Hermeneutics and Philosophical Description* (Grand Rapids: Eerdmans, 1980). For a critical discussion of Thiselton's hermeneutic, see the present author's "Anthony Thiselton's Contribution to Biblical Hermeneutics," *Christian Scholar's Review* 14, 3 (1985), pp. 224-235.

96 "The prolegomenon is ... an essential aspect of dogmatic theology insofar as the experiential, if not the eidetic, meaning of theological symbols, expressive of the faith of the Christian community, is derived and established here. "Trends in Protestant Apologetics," p. 156.

97 *Naming,* p. 462.

98 Cf. *Catholicism,* pp. 122-123, 163; *Society and the Sacred,* p. 39; *Naming,* p. 460; and "The Problem of God," pp. 20-21.

99 Cf. *Naming,* pp. 452, 459; and "New Modes of Empirical Theology," p. 368.

100 *Reaping,* p. 144.

101 Cf. *Maker,* pp. 136ff; "Cosmology, Ontology and the Travail of Biblical Language," pp. 200-204; and *Naming,* p. 463. A preliminary elaboration of such a philosophy was also the task of Book III, part II of Gilkey's dissertation, *MH,* pp. 545-606.

102 Cf. Paul Ricoeur, *The Symbolism of Evil,* pp. 347-348, 356.

103 *Reaping,* p. 145. Cf. Pannenberg, *Theology and the Philosophy of Science,* pp. 302, 315f, 358-371. Pannenberg comments on his fundamental agreement with Gilkey concerning the need for ontological reflection in "Providence, God, and Eschatology," in *The Whirlwind in Culture,* p. 175.

104 *Catholicism,* pp. 123, 103.

105   Ibid, p. 125.

106   Ibid, p. 126. Gilkey reserves some of his sharpest criticisms for John Cobb's process theology on precisely this issue. Gilkey says that Cobb's uncritical adoption of Whiteheadian ontology has the consequence that in his theology "many Christian notions are either radically redrawn or else are dispensed with in order to fit the shape and the demands of Whitehead's system." Gilkey specifically refers to conflicts on the issues of sin and forgiveness, and the transcendence and self-sufficiency of God. "Review of John Cobb's *A Christian Natural Theology*," p. 532.

107   Cf. Tillich, *Systematic Theology*, I, pp. 18-19.

108   *Society and the Sacred*, p. 38. Cf. *Reaping*, p. 154; and *Maker*, pp. 284-293.

109   *Catholicism*, pp. 85-96. Hosinski summarizes Gilkey's position well: "In order to take into account both the essential structures of our existence and their 'warping' by and in our freedom, as well as the mysterious 'healing' that also enters into the lives of at least some, mythic speech is necessary." ("Experience and the Sacred," p. 232).

110   *Religion*, pp. 112, 116. This intellectual movement from theological symbols to ontological reflection, and then beyond that reflection to symbols in their mythical form, closely parallels the early thought of Paul Ricoeur. Believing that all thought has its origins in pre-reflective symbols, and acknowledging that the original naiveté of faith is no longer possible after the rise of modern consciousness with its belief in theoretical autonomy and its 'hermeneutic of suspicion,' Ricoeur strives for a post-critical faith, a 'second naiveté that is achieved through critical interpretation, yet lies 'beyond the wastelands of critical thought.' See his "The Hermeneutics of Symbols and Philosophic Reflection," in *The Philosophy of Paul Ricoeur: An Anthology of His Work*, ed. by C. E. Reagon and D. Stewart (Boston: Beacon Press, 1978), pp. 36ff.

111   *Society and the Sacred*, ch. 3. This dialectic will be explicated more fully in chapter eight.

112   Cf. *Reaping*, chs. 10-12.

113   *Society and the Sacred*, pp. 39-40. Cf. *Catholicism*, pp. 11, 163; *Reaping*, p. 153; and *Message and Existence*, p. 215. In *Reaping*, p. 128, Gilkey says that Christian symbols can be validated negatively by showing the inadequacy of other symbol systems to illuminate reality, and positively by their own illuminatory power. This was the primary apologetic focus of both *MH* and *Maker*, and has clear origins in Niebuhr's apologetic method. Cf. Niebuhr's *Faith and History*, ch. 10.

114   *Reaping*, p. 146. Cf. *Society and the Sacred*, p. 39.

115   Ibid, p. 147.

116   *Catholicism*, p. 167. Cf. p. 165: "Participation and involvement are as much elements of our assent to truth as is argument."

117   *Naming*, p. 464. Cf. p. 428; "New Modes of Empirical Theology," p. 369; *Society*

and the Sacred, p. 41; "The Problem of God," p. 22; and "Dissolution and Reconstruction in Theology," p. 36. That this view has Tillichian origins is clear in Gilkey's articles, "Tillich: Master of Mediation," in *The Theology of Paul Tillich,* ed. by C.W. Kegley (2nd ed.; New York: Pilgrim Press, 1980), p. 46; and "The New Being and Christology," in *The Thought of Paul Tillich,* ed. by J.L. Adams, W. Pauck and R.L. Shinn (San Francisco: Harper and Row, 1985), pp. 322-323. Both of these articles, as well as other previously published essays and some more recent essays have appeared in Gilkey's latest book, *Gilkey on Tillich* (New York, Crossroad, 1990) This book appeared when the present manuscript was at press. Consequently, the new essays that have appeared are not discussed here.

118 *Reaping,* p. 147. This foundational emphasis on the self-evidence of the truth of a certain symbolic structure to the believer is parallel to the emphasis on disclosure and intuition that we saw in the discussion of the prolegomenon. It is also a position that Gilkey has consistently held from the beginning of his career. In his dissertation he says that "the affirmation of a total view about the nature of things as true depends upon an inner intuition or apprehension about the nature of reality and of its intelligibility beyond which intuition there is no appeal." And later he adds that "the arbiter of the truth of a whole point of view is finally only the inward decision of each person when in the face of his own experience he asserts that this total view of things rings true." (*MH* pp. 16, 26).

119 Cf. *Catholicism,* pp. 129ff; and *Reaping,* p. 146.

120 Dewey's pragmatism is summarized well when he says that, "the test of ideas, of thinking generally, is found in the consequences of the acts to which the ideas lead, that is in the new arrangements of things which are brought into existence." Consequently, "ideas are worthless except as they pass into actions which rearrange and reconstruct in some way, be it little or small, the world in which we live." *Intelligence in the Modern World,* ed. by J. Ratner (New York: Random House, 1939), pp. 341, 342. Gilkey acknowledges his debt to this tradition of American philosophy in *Reaping,* pp. 138-139, 375, n. 17; and in "Events, Meanings and the Current Tasks of Theology," *Journal of the American Academy of Religion* 53, 3 (1986), pp. 728-729.

121 Gordon Kaufman is typical of many contemporary theologians, Gilkey included, when he says: "Thus a theological construct may be regarded as true — in the only sense of 'true' properly applicable here — if it in fact leads to fruitful life, in the broadest and fullest and most comprehensible sense possible." He goes on to say that these criteria are pragmatic and humanistic, not because he is committed to pragmatism and humanism, but because these are the only criteria "by which a way of life, a worldview, a perspective on the totality of things, a concept of God, may ultimately be assessed." (*An Essay on Theological Method,* p. 76).

122 *Society and the Sacred,* p. 20. Cf. Karl Marx and Friedrich Engels, *On Religion* (New York: Schocken Books, 1971), p. 41. An illuminating discussion of Marx's dictum and its relevance to a theological analysis of American culture can be found in Frederick Sontag and John K. Roth, "The Premise of all Criticism," *Andover Newton Quarterly* 17, 3 (January 1977), pp. 195-200.

123 "Reinhold Niebuhr's Theology of History," *Journal of Religion* 54, 4 (October 1974), p. 361. Cf. Niebuhr's *The Interpretation of Christian Ethics* (New York: Harper and Bros., 1935), chapters 5 and 6.

124 Cf. the present author's *The Transforming Vision*, pp. 31-32 and my more recent inaugural address, *Who Turned Out the Lights? The Light of the Gospel in a Post-Enlightenment Culture* (Toronto: Institute for Christian Studies, 1989), pp. 10-12.

125 *Reaping*, p. 146.

126 *Society and the Sacred*, p. x. Cf. "Christian Theology," p. 13.

127 *Reaping*, p. 264.

128 *Society and the Sacred*, p. 118.

129 David Tracy identifies 'society' as the primary 'public' of practical theology, or theology of culture. (*The Analogical Imagination*, pp. 6-14).

130 "Culture and Religious Belief," (unpub. ms., October 5), 1984, p. 23.

131 Cf. Donald Wiebe, "The Failure of Nerve in the Academic Study of Religion," *Studies in Religion/Sciences Religieuses* 13, 4 (1984), pp. 401-423. While Wiebe makes no reference to Gilkey in this article he did refer to Gilkey in an other version of the paper presented to the American Academy of Religion in December 1984.

132 "The Roles of the 'Descriptive' or 'Historical' and the 'Normative' in our Work," p. 17. Cf. *Creationist Controversy*, chapter 7, p. 37, n. 12.

133 Quoted by Gilkey in, "A Theological Voyage with Wilfred Cantwell Smith," p. 299.

134 Ibid, p. 302.

135 "Christian Theology," p. 13.

136 Avery Dulles raises this question with reference to David Tracy's fundamental theology. See his, "Method in Fundamental Theology: Reflections on David Tracy's *Blessed Rage for Order*," *Theological Studies* 37 (June 1976), p. 308.

137 *Gilkey's Phenomenology of Ultimacy*, p. 211. Cf. pp. 109-110. Oddly enough, Stanley Kane thinks that Gilkey *has* argued from certain experiences that he identifies as 'religious.' "God-Language and Secular Experience," pp. 86-87. Littlejohn's interpretation, however, is the correct one. Gilkey's argument in *Naming* is from universal features of all experience, not from certain 'religious' experiences.

138 In fact, there are no references in *Naming* to James at all, positive or negative. And the two references to Otto make it clear that, in Gilkey's opinion, Otto's mode of phenomenology is not an appropriate response to the "modern mood" and therefore what is required is not an outright rejection of his method, but that it be "stretched" so to include an analysis of secular experience. *Naming*, pp. 188, 246.

138A Review of Reaping the Whirlwind, Religious Studies Review, 4,4 (Oct. 1978) p. 237

139 *Message and Existence*, p. 8.

140 Ted Peters, "The Christian Realism of Langdon Gilkey," p. 11. For example, in *Reaping* the little biblical exegesis that occurs is usually relegated to the footnotes. Concerning the quotation from Peters, we might also ask whether reading the Pentateuch in terms of J, E, P, and D is not itself a second order discourse, hermeneutically once removed from the text itself.

141 Ricoeur says: "I define *symbol* as: *any structure of signification in which a direct, primary, literal meaning designates, in addition, another meaning which is indirect, secondary, and figurative and which can be apprehended only through the first.*" ("Existence and Hermeneutics," in *The Philosophy of Paul Ricoeur: An Anthology of His Work*, p. 98). It should be added that I am not saying that this view of symbol is unique to Ricoeur; others have had similar views (eg., Tillich).

142 *Naming*, p. 433.

143 "Christian Theology," p. 12.

144 *Catholicism*, p. 100.

145 Cf. Ted Peters, "The Christian Realism of Langdon Gilkey," p. 9; Helena Sheehan, review of *Naming the Whirlwind*, p. 838; and George Davis, *Langdon Gilkey and Religious Language*, p. 56. Gilkey's one reference to "conceptual symbols" (like incarnation, atonement, etc.) which somehow are not doctrines, is itself not sufficiently worked out to provide any further clarity on this issue. (*How the Church*, p. 119).

146 Thomas B. Ommen, "Verification in Theology: a Tension in Revisionist Method," *The Thomist* 43, 3 (July 1979), pp. 357-384.

147 *Blessed Rage for Order*, p. 159.

148 Both Avery Dulles, "Method in Fundamental Theology," p. 310; and Van A. Harvey, "The Pathos of Liberal Theology," *Journal of Religion* 56 (October 1976), p. 388, question whether Tracy has in fact established that all people share this common faith.

149 *Reaping*, p. 146.

150 "Verification in Theology," p. 380. Note how different this interpretation is in contrast with the critique that Gilkey does not allow enough room for special revelation and religious experience.

151 Ibid, p. 369.

152 Cf. *Blessed Rage for Order*, p. 7; *The Analogical Imagination*, p. 64; and "Modes of Theological Argument," *Theology Today* 38 (January 1977), p. 391. Tracy's assertion notwithstanding, it is instructive to note the observation of William VanderMarck: "Perhaps the most striking characteristic of contemporary fundamental theology is its explicitly Christian origin and orientation...," "Fundamental Theology: A Bibliographical and Critical Survey," *Religious Studies Review* 8, 3 (July 1982), p. 245. My only question is why this characteristic is described as 'striking.'

153 "Verification in Theology," pp. 370, 377.

154 Ibid, p. 370.

155 Edward Farley, "Review of *Reaping the Whirlwind*," *Religious Studies Review* 4, 4 (October 1978), p. 235.

156 It is not surprising that Paul van Buren finds Gilkey's view of participatory verification tautologous (Review of *Naming the Whirlwind*, p. 227). If any acknowledgment of an epistemological or theological circle is tautologous, then this is indeed a tautology. But it could also be established that the assertion, 'reflective arguments ought not to be tautologous' is itself, ultimately, a tautology. The issue here is not to eliminate all circularity in argument — that is impossible — but, rather, to have enough criteria to allow meaningful communication and evaluation, and to avoid what could be called 'vicious circularity.'

157 Tom Driver, review of *Naming the Whirlwind*, p. 363. The superficiality of Driver's analysis is evident in the rock song he uses to illustrate this cultural optimism, viz., B. J. Thomas' "Raindrops Keep Falling On My Head." Few observers of popular culture would mistake Thomas for a profound commentator on modern culture. Around the time that Driver wrote this review three other songs which use the imagery of rain and storms would have suggested a more sober and, I think, more adequate cultural analysis, viz., Bob Dylan's "A Hard Rain's Going To Fall," The Rolling Stones' "Gimme Shelter," and Creedance Clearwater's "Who'll Stop the Rain?"

158 Cf."Theology for a Time of Troubles," p. 475.

159 Charles E. Winquist, "Theology, Deconstruction, and Ritual Process," *Zygon* 18, 3 (September 1983), pp. 295-309.

160 Cf. Victor Turner, *Dramas, Fields and Metaphors: Symbolic Action in Human Society* (New York: Cornell University Press, 1974), pp. 37-42.

161 "Theology, Deconstruction, and Ritual Process," p. 299.

162 Ibid, p. 300.

163 Ibid, p. 298.

164 The radical distinction between Gilkey and Winquist has been restated by the latter in his recent article in the Gilkey festschrift. Winquist says, "The radical question about the reality of God called for by Gilkey in *Naming the Whirlwind* leads not to a renewal of God-language but to a deconstruction of God-language." "The Surface of the Deep: Deconstruction in the Study of Religion," in *The Whirlwind in Culture*, p. 64.

165 "Theology and the Future," *Andover Newton Quarterly* 17, 4 (March 1977), p.

255. Cf. "Religion and the American Future," (unpub. ms., n. d.), p. 10.

PART 2:
Theology of a Culture

CHAPTER TWO:
Theory and Analysis

1. Christianity and Culture

The relation of Christian faith and the Christian church to its cultural context is, in H. Richard Niebuhr's words, an "enduring problem."[1] In this chapter I will follow Niebuhr (and Gilkey) in defining culture in rather broad terms. At issue here, says Niebuhr, is

> ... that total process of human activity and that total result of such activity to which now the name *culture*, now the name *civilization*, is applied in common speech. Culture is the "artificial, secondary environment" which man superimposes on the natural. It comprises language, habits, ideas, beliefs, customs, social organization, inherited artifacts, technical processes, and values.[2]

As such, culture is characterized by sociality. It is also a manifestation of human achievement that flows from a world of values that are understood to be for human good. It is, therefore, both a temporal and material realization of those values and the means by which those values are conserved in their perceived depth and plurality.[3]

The 'enduring problem' for Christianity and, for that matter, any other religious tradition (witness the Iranian revolution), is how this particular faith and the community of people who adhere to this faith relate to the culture around it when that culture is a manifestation of another view of life and set of values. As I have already indicated in the Introduction, this problem becomes for Gilkey the question of giving expression to a culturally relevant transcendence without falling prey to acculturation. In *How the Church Can Minister to the World Without Losing Itself* he complains that "American churches, conservative and liberal alike, are in danger of merely reproducing in pious form the cultural world ... that surrounds them."[4] For Gilkey relevance must not mean acculturation. Indeed, in his second published article he argued in a typically (Reinhold) Niebuhrian way that Christianity can never be identified with a particular cause lest it lose its intrinsic and

71

essential purity, lest it be untrue to its Lord who refused to identify himself with the mores of his time — and so died on the cross.[5] While Gilkey's language has changed since he wrote those words in 1954, the spirit of his theology has not.

The issue of the relation of the church to culture is more complex than this, however. Just as there must be no total capitulation to any cultural *Geist*, so also no viable "form of spiritual life can be alien to its time and to the cultural life of that time."[6] Further, no religion *can* be totally alien because the "forms of religion and ecclesiastical life ... reflect the forms of the cultural existence in which they appear, and in that sense every form is dependent upon, and an expression of, its culture."[7] This, however, is also the source of two further problems. First, cultures change and therefore forms of religion that are developed at one point in cultural history seem outmoded in later stages, whether those forms be patterns of ministry and priesthood that are patriarchal, liturgy which is medieval, hymnology dating from 19th century Romanticism or theological concepts that reflect Greek substantialist ontology. Second, some cultures are less overtly religious and more explicitly and self-consciously secular than others. For the Christian church to know how to respond creatively to both of these problems it must engage in a spiritually discerning analysis of and response to that culture. This is the task of a theology of culture.

2. Theology of Culture

Theology of culture, like all theology, has two foci. First, theology of culture is an "analysis of [the] current socio-political-cultural situation with regard to its religious dimensions and issues...."[8] But insofar as this analysis is theological it is not only concerned with an analysis of the religious dimension of culture, it also presumes to offer proposals for new patterns of socio-political-cultural life.

> Every mythical and religious vision implies action of some sort. For one of the main functions of the myths and the religious symbols that structure the life of a culture is to express the vision of authentic man and woman, and thereby to make legitimate, and obligatory, the fundamental roles that people adopt in the culture's life....[9]

Socio-political-cultural meaning is not added *ab extra* to religious symbols, it is intrinsic to their eidetic meaning. They invoke action and are foundational for praxis.

Theology of culture, in both of its foci, requires some clarity concerning the fundamental dynamics of social process as its presupposition. Does change in social structure and patterns of production cause change in the 'spirit' of a society, as the materialist believes; or do changes in beliefs and ideas affect shifts in socio-economic patterns and institutions, as the idealist believes? Or, Gilkey asks, "is there a process of *interaction*, in which new attitudes make possible new sorts of institutional relations and structures, and new modes of life in turn create changes in sentiments and values?"[10] Gilkey adopts such an interactionary model. But the interaction of cultural patterns and the spirit of a society is itself founded upon a deeper unity because "every active culture represents a unity, a unity of the cognitive and meaning, of science and of its own fundamental mythical structure, of knowledge and the spiritual substance of the culture."[11] Theology of culture approaches that unity from the perspective of the religious substance of culture. To understand Gilkey's category of the religious substance of culture, however, we first need to see what he means by 'religion' in relation to 'culture.'

3. Religion and Culture

Defining religion is notoriously difficult. John Hick has observed that there is "no universally accepted definition of religion, and quite possibly there never will be."[12] The issue here is not simply whether religion should be interpreted in terms of inauthentic human projection as in the hermeneutics of suspicion (Feuerbach, Nietzsche, Freud, et al.)[13] or as a constitutive dimension of human life (Pannenberg, Gilkey, Tracy, Rahner, et al.). More fundamentally, the question has to do with the definition of religion per se. While the alternative definitions are legion, they tend to fall into one of two types. Either religion is defined narrowly in terms of certain kinds of special acts and unique concepts, or more broadly as a way of life that people engage in with their full existence and at all times.[14] An example of the narrow view is the position of anthropologist Melford Spiro. Spiro defines religion as "an institution consisting of culturally patterned interactions with culturally postulated superhuman beings."[15] This definition is narrow because it limits religion to particular cultural institutions and to a certain kind of belief. One of the most notable examples of a broad definition is the position of another anthropologist, Clifford Geertz. His definition merits quotation at some length:

73

> ... a religion is: (1) a system of symbols which acts to (2) establish
> powerful, pervasive and long-lasting moods and motivations in men by
> (3) formulating conceptions of a general order of existence and (4)
> clothing these conceptions with such an aura of factuality that (5) the
> moods and motivations seem uniquely realistic.[16]

Without attempting to explicate all of the facets of this definition, we should nevertheless note that this is a functional definition of religion. Religion is a system of symbols "which acts." It is also a broad definition because it is neither limited to any particular institution nor to any particular kinds of beliefs except that they be symbolic and related to conceptions of a general order of existence. Consequently, ideologies could be included in this definition, regardless of how secular or even atheistic they may be.

Gilkey shares Geertz's broad definition of religion.[17] His definition has three facets. (1) Religion is a "view of the nature of reality, and especially of 'ultimate reality' or reality as a whole...." (2) "Each religion has a way of life, a way or rules of behavior that are an important part of being a believer or a participant...." (3) This view and way of life is held and participated in communally.[18] Similar to Geertz, Gilkey's definition is not limited to institutions and beliefs in superhuman beings. And as a functional definition it can, and does, include secular ideologies within its scope. While Gilkey is aware that the term 'ideology' often carries with it pejorative connotations of being a false, biased rationalization of self-interest,[19] he prefers a more descriptive and functional definition.

> By 'ideology' here I mean a global system of ideas concepts or symbols
> which expresses in a unified, coherent form a vision or interpretation
> of all of reality; which orders that reality so as to express 'meaning', that
> is, the victory of good over evil in existence; which when 'adopted',
> unifies a community, giving its life, its institutions and its social roles
> shape, direction and purpose; and which is participated in — *must* be
> participated in — by intellectual assent, personal commitment, and
> responsible obedience.[20]

It is clear enough that there has been a rise of such ideologies in the modern West, that they have often claimed to replace traditional religion, and that they claim to be authoritative because they are 'scientific.'[21] It is also clear, according to Gilkey, that ideologies share many of the same functional characteristics of religion: "the claim to ultimacy, to deep relatedness to the normative, the requirement of faith or commitment, the fear of heterodoxy and apostasy, the ritual rites and mythologies...."[22] The only notable difference between religion and ideology is that most pre-modern cultures were explicit about their religious centre and motivations while the religious centre of modern society is usually implicit and hidden in its dominant ideology.

One of the common criticisms of the broad definition of religion is that since religion seems to encompass everything, it signifies nothing. Gilkey's response is that this criticism "assumes *a priori* that religion is always ... represented by definite and quite distinguishable, 'separate' elements ... in a culture...." This assumption is "historically unwarrantable." It also leaves no room for the distinction between 'religion' as the beliefs, practices and institutions of particular communities and traditions (parallel to the narrow definition of religion), and the 'religious' as an aspect or dimension of cultural life as a whole that is manifest in all of the other 'secular' aspects of culture (parallel to the broad definition).[23]

The fact that 'religion' has come to have such a narrow meaning in the modern world is certainly the major reason for the problem. Ninian Smart has recently noted that "the English language does not have a term to refer to both traditional religions and ideologies," though they have parallel functions in their respective societies. Smart proposes that the term 'worldview' is both specific and general enough to encompass both.[24] Gilkey often uses the term worldview or *Weltanschauung* to refer to the religious dimension of culture. But the phrase that he predominantly uses is Tillich's notion of the 'religious substance' of a culture. Indeed, he defines culture in terms of such a religious substance. Culture is not just a pattern of social relations, it is "a systematic network of meanings, norms, and goals that structure, guide, and justify those social relations."[25] To a discussion of Gilkey's understanding of the religious substance of culture we now turn.

4. The Religious Substance of Culture

Paul Tillich understood the religious substance of a culture as the soil out of which culture grows. "It is unconsciously present in a culture, a group, an individual, giving the passion and driving power to him who creates and the significance and power of meaning to his creations."[26] It determines the 'style' that will characterize that culture or epoch. Gilkey believes that Tillich's notion of a religious substance is supported by the sociological observation of culture from Durkheim to Parsons, Berger, Luckmann and Geertz.

> What these students of society have found — if I may give them a very hasty summary — is that any community or society is held together in sharing in, expressing and devoting themselves to, something sacred and ultimate — or a sacrality and ultimacy — that permeates their life together, holds them together, directs their common life, and makes that common life possible.[27]

Such a commitment that holds a community together is a matter of both belief and love. Gilkey quotes the cultural historian Gordon Leff: "If men govern the rest of nature in virtue of their reason and technical power, they are themselves governed by their beliefs."[28] And the philosopher of social science Peter Winch has said: "A man's social relations with his fellows are permeated with his ideas about reality. Indeed, 'permeated' is hardly a strong enough word: social relations are expressions of ideas about reality."[29] But it is not just sincere assent and commitment to ideas that forms a community, it is also a love for what those ideas stand for or point to. Gilkey quotes St. Augustine: a community is "an assemblage of reasonable beings bound together by common agreement as to the objects of their love."[30] These 'ideas' or 'beliefs' or 'objects' have a devotional or confessional character. They are religious. Consequently, Gilkey disagrees with Durkheim and other sociologists in their attempt to understand this religious dimension in a naturalistic and nonreligious way.

> To understand these data fully and coherently, however, requires, I believe, a *theological* interpretation…, namely a view of society and of the individual, of social ethos and belief, that centers its interpretation on the essential and active presence of the divine in human existence, and that interprets human being, both individual and social, in terms of its relations and responses to that presence.[31]

Such a theological interpretation begins with the religious substance of the culture. Gilkey describes such a religious substance as follows:

> Social existence involves and depends on a shared consciousness, a shared system of meanings. This shared system of meanings is structured by symbols that shape or express the understanding of reality, of space and time, of human being and its authenticity, of life and its goods, of appropriate relations, roles, customs and behavior, symbols

which together constitute the unique gestalt, the identity or uniqueness, of that social group.[32]

We can best explicate Gilkey's position by seeing that the religious substance of a culture functions as (a) a religious vision *of* the total structure and meaning of reality, expressed in terms of symbols and myths; which is also (b) a religious vision *for* reality, providing norms and direction for cultural development; and (c) calls for participatory belief and commitment from the members of the culture. Further, the religious substance is (d) generally in the background, not the foreground of the culture, and (e) it can function either to legitimate or to criticize and even undermine a culture. I will discuss each of these five dimensions of the religious substance of a culture in this order.

a) Vision of Life
In his article "On Worldviews" James Olthuis describes a worldview as "a framework or set of fundamental beliefs through which we view the world.... It is the integrative and interpretative framework by which order and disorder are judged, the standard by which reality is managed and pursued."[33] It is a vision of life.

Gilkey understands the religious substance of culture in similar terms. Opposed to both the dualistic separation of religion to a supernatural realm divorced from the sæculum, and the exhaustively secular interpretation of culture typical of both the Enlightenment and Marxism,[34] Gilkey says that a culture is 'constituted' and its ethos is determined primarily by its religious substance. He says that every society is "constituted, preserved and controlled by the symbolic world which is shared by its members."[35] This symbolic world is the perspective through which the members look at their world. It tells them what is and is not important, what can and cannot be known, what is and is not real.[36] An analysis of the religious substance of a culture penetrates and uncovers that which is unconditional in a culture,[37] what Ludwig Wittgenstein described as the end of justifications when "I have reached bedrock, and my spade is turned."[38] Similarly, Tillich spoke of the *kairos*, the revelation in time of the ground of being and meaning that is the basis of cultural life, not its result.[39]

While this unconditional worldview or vision of life contains philosophical and theorizable elements, "the structure as a whole is

77

symbolic rather than *theoretical* in linguistic form, and, however significant and full of meaning it may be, it cannot be formulated with complete coherence and precision."[40] It provides culture with a sacral form of knowledge and is, therefore, characteristically opaque and multivalent.

A vision of life or religious substance cannot be static, however, if it is to function as a creative centre and foundation for culture, which is a dynamic and historical reality. When symbols are related to historical passage they take on a story form, they become myth.

> Myth, as a form of language uses a story form, phenomenal or ontic language descriptive of events in space and time and of actors in those events, to describe or illumine structures and relations that transcend that phenomenal and that ontic manifold.[41]

Any global vision of history or total vision of reality (and, as we shall see, both Marxism and liberalism are such visions) entails a "mythical structure providing for those who are committed to it an understanding of their own role in the global history of good and evil, an ultimate norm for cultural life, and a sense of meaning and of hope for the unknown future."[42] Creative cultural formation requires a principle of historical interpretation, a vision of historical process and historical meaning. This is the role of myth: "… it tells us who we are in history and why we are here."[43] And such mythical understanding is an intrinsic component of the religious substance of a culture. This leads us to the second dimension of the religious substance of culture.

b) Vision for Life
The religious substance of a culture not only provides an interpretative framework for life in the culture, it is also the creative (or demonic) basis for the way in which the culture will grow and develop. Geertz notes that religion has a dual focus: it both tells us what is the case and what ought to be the case.[44] Or, as Olthuis comments, "a vision 'of' life and the world is simultaneously a vision 'for' life and the world."[45] In Gilkey's terms, the symbolic-mythical structure of the religious substance provides the "fundamental aims and norms of life."[46] A religious substance gives not only a 'worldview' but also a 'way of life.' It sets both the ethos and the élan of a culture.

The interrelation of a vision 'of' and a vision 'for' life is evident in Gilkey's description of political action:

> As politics cannot function without an ultimate vision of the *structure* of historical communal life, so politics cannot and does not function without a corresponding vision of an ultimate *norm* for history's life.[47]

Religion provides both an understanding of *structure* (vision of) and the ultimate *norm* (vision for) for the unfolding of that structure. Moreover, these norms and structure form an integral unity in cultural life because "no political action is possible unless what is regarded as ultimately authentic and good is also regarded as most real...." That is, "... every moral norm by which we judge the present ... is taken by us to be an aspect of the ultimate grain of history itself, to be ultimately real as well as ultimately good."[48]

c) Based in Faith

In chapter one we saw that for Gilkey any symbolic structure can only partially be justified by its internal coherence, existential adequacy and potential for a creative and healing way of life. Beyond these criteria Gilkey also appealed to participatory verification. Religious symbols are self-validating. This is also the case with the religious substance of any culture. It calls forth and elicits faith or participation from the members of a culture. "As a society is constituted by its symbolic structure, so internally *eros* toward that shared system of meanings is a fundamental factor in all social and political affairs."[49] Such eros entails belief which, "on the deepest level, means a personal participation in the life and ethos of a community and its traditions and assent to the fundamental symbolic forms of that tradition as true and as normative, that is, as directing or guiding one's own thought, goals and patterns of behavior."[50] Without such eros and participatory belief a people die inwardly, the community crumbles and the culture declines.

Having described the religious substance of a culture as a vision of life which is also a vision for life that elicits faithful participation, there still remain two further dimensions of Gilkey's position to be elucidated. They both concern the relation of the religious substance of a culture to the culture itself.

d) Foreground/Background

A theology of culture in the context of modernity addresses a series of complex relations. In the first instance it attempts to relate the particular vision of one religious tradition to a cultural whole that has

79

a relation of both historical continuity and spiritual discontinuity with the tradition in question. But secondly, that cultural whole is itself a complex relation. Each culture has, as we have seen, a religious substance, but that, of course, is not the whole of the culture. Each culture also has what Gilkey calls its own secular, instrumental elements.[51] That is, it has its patterns of economic life, family structure, scientific investigation, health care, artistic expression and so on. A metaphor that Gilkey often uses to describe this relation is that of background and foreground. The symbolic substance in its symbolic-mythical form is in the background, not the foreground of culture. It can be described as the foundation, presupposition or horizon of that which comes to concrete expression in the other 'secular' dimensions of culture.[52] That which is in the foreground undermines itself if it attempts to replace the religious substance which is in the background because, "... all these elements in the foreground of culture ... depend in the end on some participating apprehension and appropriation" of the vision of life found in the religious substance. Gilkey says further:

> From this religious center, the cognitive, normative and artistic life of the society flow; and from this center its personal vocations and political forms of life receive their meaning, their goals, and their enlivening hopes.[53]

This complex relation could be portrayed diagrammatically as follows:

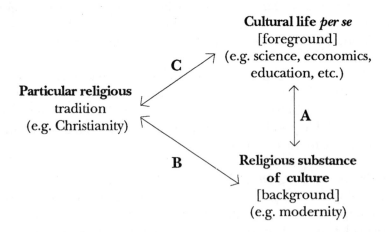

When certain patterns of cultural life come into conflict with the content of the Christian tradition (for example, waste of resources, pollution of the environment, and economic patterns that do not benefit the poor all militate against the biblical principle of steward-ship), it is tempting for the theologian simply to relate that content to the cultural issues at hand (relationship C). But this kind of theology of culture is in danger of superficiality if it overlooks the foundational role that the religious substance plays in society (relationship A).[54] Therefore a viable theology of culture must relate the vision of its religious tradition to the religious substance of the culture (relation-ship B) and in that context address the particular cultural issues of the day (both relationships C and A).[55]

It is fair to say that Gilkey's primary concern has been relationship B. As we shall see, he identifies fundamental issues in the foreground of our experience such as nuclear arms, cultural pluralism and the environmental crisis, but then relates those issues to a fundamental shift in the background of Western culture.[56] If patterns and events in our cultural life are requiring a shift in religious substance (relation-ship A), then the overriding question for the Christian theologian is: does the Christian faith offer a more creative and credible foundation (or substance) for culture than the one that is presently in crisis (relationship B)? But this is getting ahead of ourselves: there is still one more dimension of these complex relations to be addressed.

e) Legitimation/Revolution
We have seen that a religious substance has a constitutive, grounding and conserving role in social history. It legitimates the cultural forms that flow from it. But religion cannot be limited to a conservative role in history. It can also have a radical, upsetting, reconstituting and transforming role.[57] "The *criticism* of society ... as well as its *establish-ment*, expresses a religious vision."[58] Symbolic worlds "not only hold a society together, help to defend it, and so give it stability. They are also instruments in dismantling the old and initiating the new."[59] They are not merely static and conservative, they are also radical, revolutionary and prophetic. The problem is that what was once revolutionary and creative can, in time, become reactionary, preserving an oppressive status quo. Cumulative historical and cultural change makes it neces-sary to reinterpret a symbolic structure and to transform a religious substance so that it can embody new possibilities to meet new situa-tions.

81

This dual role of religion as both legitimation of culture and that which can be a revolutionary force for change in a culture presents the theologian of culture with an immediate question: what is the appropriate role of religion in this cultural context, at this point in history? Should theology advocate a constitutive or critical role for religion? To answer that question requires a theological interpretation, evaluation and judgment of the contemporary cultural context and its religious substance. To such an interpretation I now turn.

5. The Religious Substance of Modernity

Defining modernity or secularism and their concomitant, secularization, is notoriously almost as difficult as defining religion.[60] It is, however, safe to say that somewhere between 1470 (the beginning of the Italian Renaissance) and 1700 (the beginning of the Enlightenment) the modern world was born. It is also safe to say that the contours of modernity are, to a large degree, set by a reaction against Christianity.[61] Indeed, Carl Becker presents the 'faith' of the Enlightenment *philosophes* in terms of a four-article creed in which each article is clearly set against the prevailing Christian understanding of the time. His exposition merits quotation in its entirety:

> The essential articles of the religion of the Enlightenment may be stated thus: (1) man is not natively depraved; (2) the end of life is life itself, the good life on earth instead of the beatific life after death; (3) man is capable, guided solely by the light of reason and experience, of perfecting the good life on earth; and (4) the first and essential condition of the good life on earth is the freeing of men's minds from the bonds of ignorance and superstition, and of their bodies from the arbitrary oppression of the constituted social authorities.[62]

This interpretation of the Enlightenment faith (especially article 4) concurs with Immanuel Kant's description:

> Enlightenment is man's release from his self-incurred tutelage. Tutelage is man's inability to make use of his understanding without direction from another. Self-incurred is this tutelage when its cause lies not in lack of reason but in lack of resolution and courage to use it without direction from another. *Sapere aude!* "Have courage to use your reason!" — that is the motto of the Enlightenment.[63]

And, as Peter Gay has said, the consistent application of this motto results in 'disenchantment.'

> The disenchanted universe of the Enlightenment is a natural universe.... *All things are equally subject to criticism;* to say this was to move confidently in a world free — or rather, waiting to be freed — from enchantment.[64]

That which we refer to as 'modernity' is the cultural offspring of this Enlightenment faith and this Enlightenment disenchantment. Gilkey accepts the interpretations of Gay and Becker. But, while Gilkey acknowledges that modernity has roots in this intellectual movement he nevertheless insists that an understanding of modernity in terms of its religious substance requires plumbing to its pre-intellectual depths. Using the term 'secularism' to refer to what he in other places calls 'modernity,' Gilkey says:

> Secularism is not so much a philosophy, as the pre-rational basis of all potent contemporary philosophies. Like all fundamental cultural moods or historical forms of consciousness, it exists on the level of what are called presuppositions and thus are expressed *in* the variant forms of a given culture's life rather than being one of those forms.[65]

Secularism is a term which describes the *Geist* of our age, the pre-rational, pre-reflective mood or spirit that gives our culture its tone or style, and our *Lebenswelt* its determining forms.[66]

> A cultural mood, then, is the fundamental attitude toward reality, toward truth, and toward value which characterizes an epoch, and within whose terms every creative aspect of life, including a period's religion and its theology, expresses itself.[67]

Such a fundamental attitude toward reality, truth and value functions as the religious substance of a culture, its directing worldview.

Perhaps the most representative proponent of modernity in the North American context has been John Dewey. In *Reconstruction in Philosophy*, Dewey described the spirit of modern life in terms of four changes from the previous cultural-historical period. "First, there is the transfer of interest from the eternal and universal to what is changing and specific...." Rather than being preoccupied with the supernatural, modernity delights in the natural. "Secondly, there is the gradual decay of the authority of fixed institutions and class distinctions and relations, and growing belief in the power of individual minds, guided by methods of observation, experience and reflection, to attain the truths needed for the guidance of life." Third, parallel to the rejection of the authorities of the past and of tradition, modernity believes in progress. "The future rather than the past dominates the imagination. The Golden Age lies ahead of us not behind us." Indeed, "Man is capable, if he will but exercise the required courage, intelligence and effort, of shaping his own fate." And fourth, "the patient and experimental study of nature, bearing fruit in inventions which control nature and subdue her forces to social use, is the method by which progress is made."[68] Naturalism, autonomy, progress and empirical science — these are the hallmarks of Dewey's modernity.

Gilkey's theology, like that of his mentor Reinhold Niebuhr, is a Christian response to this kind of modernity. His exposition of modernity also has four points that are both related to and distinct from the four characteristics of the modern spirit found in Dewey and the four articles of Enlightenment faith explicated by Becker. Gilkey describes the characteristic features of modernity as contingency, relativity, temporality and autonomy. I will discuss these features of the modern *Geist* in this order, concluding and summarizing them all with Gilkey's description of the 'progress' motif in Western culture.[69]

a) Contingency

Modernity is preoccupied with the sense of contingency, that is, "the sense that what is — the world around us and we ourselves — is the result of causes that are neither necessary, rational, nor purposive."[70] This apprehension of our contingency restricts modernity to the immediately given. It is the heart of what Peter Gay calls our disenchantment.[71] The given is ultimately arbitrary and therefore there is "no ground, no ultimate order, no explanation, nor reason" beyond the given.[72] This loss of any sense of ultimacy, the deep sense that "existence and thought alike begin and end with the given," characterizes modern thought.[73]

On this level Gilkey detects a fundamental unity between philosophical naturalism, positivism and existentialism.

> While the naturalist understands himself as merely a part of mechanical and blind nature and hopes to use technological intelligence to better his life, and the positivist tries his best not to think at all about these things [because they are beyond empirical verification or falsification], the existentialist deliberately cuts the cord between himself and his objective environment.[74]

Whether we consider Santayana's belief that "in a contingent world, necessity is a conspiracy of accidents," Ernst Nagel's belief that while there may be causes for things there are no reasons, or Heidegger's view of Dasein's *throwness* into existence, we are faced with the same reality — radical contingency.[75]

In a contingent world, a world without ultimates, there can also be no absolutes. Hence, relativity is the second characteristic of modernity.

b) Relativity

Modernity rejects the medieval notion that society somehow reflects an ultimate and supernatural order for socio-cultural life. Consequently, no social order, institution, creed, or pattern of culture is absolute. They are all relative to one another in the passage of time.

> Nothing in nature or history, and so by implication nothing at all that is, is thus "*a se,*" an unchanging and self-sufficient substance capable of existing in and by itself and thus exhibiting an essence underived from and so unrelated to the other things that surround it.[76]

This modern understanding of relativity has had, says Gilkey, three further implications that are ontological, ethical/cultural and linguistic in character, respectively.

The ontological implication of relativity is evident in the tendency of modern thought "to emphasize change as opposed to sameness and identity, process as opposed to substance, becoming as opposed to being, and context as opposed to innate individual capacities and powers."[77]

Further, if all that exists is relative to its locus in space and time, to its past causes, present status and future destiny, then "nowhere ... in observable history is there anything permanent or of ultimate authority...."

> Any event or creative product in culture, its philosophies, religious beliefs, scriptures, laws, values or practices, is relevant and of immense significance to what surrounds it and shares its general contours: but, by the same token, any historical creation of culture becomes irrelevant to us ... as it moves away from us in space and time.[78]

Modernity knows no absolutes. Relativity gives way to relativism.

The final implication of relativity is also related to the emphasis

85

on contingency. If all that is must be understood and explained in terms of the interacting nexus of relative causes or factors, then any assertive or indicative language will be monodimensional, referent only to that finitude and its factors. Religious language, which is symbolic and multivalent, referring to an ultimate dimension within the finite, will therefore be unintelligible to this consciousness.[79]

The third characteristic of the modern *Geist* has been implicit in the first two, namely, temporality.

c) Temporality

Modernity has been suffused with a sense of process, becoming, fluidity and transitoriness. All cultures have recognized the transitoriness of being, but Gilkey says that "for moderns, time is the most fundamental structure of all experienced being. All is becoming, all is changing, all is passage out of the past and into the future...."[80]

This understanding of temporality as an essential, not accidental (as in most Greek philosophy) characteristic of being — together with the perceived advances in science, technology, economics and politics — created during the Enlightenment an explicit awareness of "a changing *social* world, of a transformation of the forms of life leading to something new...." This is the advent of historical consciousness. "We are conscious in a quite new way of being immersed in history...."[81]

Similar to Dewey's description noted above is Gilkey's view that the modern spirit "is oriented not *backward* to an essential cosmic order in which man's freedom must participate, as were ancient cultures, but *forward* to a potential existence in the open historical future which man's freedom may create."[82] Modernity entails a total denial of the myths of ancient culture that present wholeness and freedom in terms of a past golden period participated in by mythic ritual. For modernity, wholeness and freedom are future goals to be achieved by autonomous humanity, and myth represents the infancy of humanity and therefore is something to be grown out of.[83] This leads us to the fourth characteristic of modernity, viz., autonomy.

d) Autonomy

The ontological characteristics of contingency, relativity and temporality that have preoccupied modern consciousness have toppled the gods, ultimates and absolutes of the previous age. They have also, in the modern spirit, made way for a new anthropology, a new view of humanity as autonomous: *homo autonomos.* Autonomy, says Gilkey, refers to man's "innate capacity to know his own truth, to decide about his own existence, to create his own meaning, and to establish his own values." Consequently, "man was now free *in* history in a new way, on his own in a history to which he and he alone must give structure and meaning."[84]

There are two immediate implications of this view of autonomy. The first is that, as with all fundamental anthropological beliefs, it entails a soteriological meaning. Gilkey notes:

> For all forms of modern thought, salvation comes *through* the realization of freedom; it can never be salvation *from* freedom, or even a transformation from beyond ourselves *of* our freedom.[85]

If sin is the transgression of law, and autonomy is being a law unto oneself, then salvation can only be found in the complete and full expression of human autonomy.

This entails a second implication. *Where* does modern man exercise his autonomy? The answer from the Renaissance and Enlightenment has been that human autonomy is played out in the arena of a non-autonomous, law-bound nature. Nature, or the 'given,' has been disenchanted, desacralized and rendered meaningless by contingency, relativity and temporality. If nature is to have meaning, according to the modern spirit, that meaning will be found only in nature's usefulness to human autonomy.[86] For thinkers as diverse as Adam Smith, John Locke, Thomas Hobbes and Karl Marx, nature only has meaning when it is transformed by human labour. In North America John Dewey is, again, representative. According to Dewey, pre-modern conceptions of the natural world sometimes bred resignation and submission; sometimes they bred contempt and a desire to escape; and sometimes a keen aesthetic curiosity. Modernity, however, sees the natural world as material for change. Indeed, this is central to modern epistemology — one only knows the natural world by observing and experimentally creating changes in it. He explains further:

> ... in the degree in which the active conception of knowledge prevails, and the environment is regarded as something that has to be changed in order to be truly known, men are imbued with courage, with what may almost be termed an aggressive attitude toward nature. The latter

becomes plastic, something to be subjected to human uses.[87]

According to Gilkey this is an expression of the religious substance of a culture that legitimates the domination of nature.[88] Human autonomy is realized in the capability of transforming nature. He sums up modernity's faith in autonomy:

> Through the disciplined use of his reason, therefore, as evidenced in the new science and its twin offspring, technology and industrialism, man saw himself in a new way as free in history: free to reject past authority and tradition; free to accumulate new knowledge of the laws of nature; free to control nature around him through that knowledge; free to transform social structures into new forms if he understood their laws; above all, free to think what his own mind determines as the truth and his own will affirms to be right.[89]

We see in the above quotation that Gilkey considers faith in autonomy to be inseparable from the rise of modern science. *Homo autonomos* is *homo physicus*. As the medieval worldview crumbled, the clerical robes of the priest were replaced by the white laboratory coat of the scientist as the symbol of authority and sacral knowledge.[90] As medieval culture was ecclesiastical in form, dominated by religion, modern culture is scientific. Constitutive of any religious substance of a culture is a form of sacral knowledge and expertise for the gaining of such knowledge which is highly valued and lavishly rewarded. In modern culture science has this kind of religious aura because that which is ultimately real (the contingent, relative and transient 'given') can only be known by means of empirical scientific investigation.[91]

The rise of empirical science, I have said, is inseparable from the belief in autonomy. Indeed, Gilkey says that it was to a large degree the experience of the success of empirical science that "led to a new sense of human autonomy or creative freedom, of the power of informed intelligence to remake that necessitated world...."[92]

Of course the most representative proponent of this view is the person credited for 'discovering' the scientific method, Francis Bacon. Science, for Bacon, gives us knowledge, and knowledge is power. Commenting on Bacon, Gilkey says, "When men and women know the way things work then they can make those things work for them. Since science leads to far greater understanding of the dynamic causes of things, science is the secret of human control over the world."[93] The avowed purpose and ambition of Bacon's utopian society in *New Atlantis* was "the knowledge of causes and secret motions of things; and the enlarging of the bound of human empire, to the effecting of all things possible."[94] And this human empire, the "empire of man over things," Bacon claimed, "depends wholly on the arts and sciences."[95]

Since autonomy came to have soteriological significance for modernity, Gilkey does not find it surprising that science came to be seen as "*the* salvific force in history. If only, said John Dewey, we could apply the scientific method and spirit to all our problems, those problems will recede; science will serve us if only we hearken to her."[96] Again, this view has roots in the thought of Francis Bacon. Writing in his *Novum Organum* early in the seventeenth century, Bacon claimed that "man by the fall fell at the same time from his state of innocence and from his dominion over creation. Both of these losses however can even in this life be in some part repaired; the former by religion and faith, the latter by arts and sciences."[97] While Bacon still places science in the context of a generally Christian understanding of history, he is characteristically modern by granting to the arts and sciences a salvific status. Recognizing the contrast between Bacon's view and a Christian worldview, John Passmore comments on the above quote: "What sin had shattered, science could in large part repair: man could become not only the titular but the actual lord of nature."[98]

An understanding of science as salvific and as the dispensary of sacral knowledge is, according to Gilkey, a faith which is foundational to the religious substance of modernity and concomitant to modernity's faith in autonomy. Such a faith can also be described as scientism; the belief that natural science is "*the* method according to which all other *Wissenschaften* must remake themselves or be excluded from the academic court..., [and] *the* form of knowledge to which every other mode of knowing had to conform or be banned from serious consideration."[99] Science replaced theology as the queen of the sciences and the church as the institutional source of sacral knowledge.

The role of scientism in the secular worldview is, moreover, teleological. Indeed, we have seen that for Bacon it was no less than utopian. The vision *for* life of modernity offers a scientistic hope which Gilkey describes as follows: "... a New Day will dawn when men through science will become the intelligent and virtuous beings they undoubtedly can be, and will take their own destiny into their hands

89

and mold for themselves a new self and a new world."[100] The religious substance of modernity may be characterized by contingency, relativity, temporality and autonomy. It may be scientistic in outlook. But the one word that captures the dynamic force of all of these characteristics combined is, *progress*. To this we now turn.

e) Progress

A question which is inherent in the religious substance of modernity, and which, consequently, is repeatedly raised, is the question of the meaningfulness or meaninglessness of human experience in the world. If reality is characterized by radical contingency, the relativity of all social and religious forms, and by complete temporal flux, then can there be any ultimate meaning in the midst of this contingent and relative temporality? If cultural forms come and go then what meaning is there in our cultural labour? And if our fragmentary meanings have no ultimate context of meaning, are they not, in the end, meaningless? These questions are inherent in the religious substance of modernity. But modernity also has an answer to them. The process of relative, contingent and temporal change which characterizes reality is meaningful because it follows its own innate law which leads that change in a progressive direction.

> Change is, therefore, change for the better; the old is, to be sure, lost, and our present values and meanings are therefore precarious. But those to come will cumulatively build upon, not destroy or overturn, the real values achieved by past change.[101]

Post-Enlightenment liberal culture solved the problem of the potential relativity, fragmentariness and meaninglessness of its most cherished cultural forms by means of a belief in progress. Such a belief sets all that we do "into an ultimate context which was built into the very grain of things and so which could not pass away."[102] Progress is modernity's one ultimate and absolute in a sea of relativity and flux. It is that which guarantees that the sequence of relative forms in historical life is not a random or meaningless sequence, but a teleological development which leads to the goal of ultimate fulfillment of the potentials of humankind.[103]

'Progress' has been long recognized as "one of the ruling ideas in the Western thought of the last hundred and fifty or two hundred years."[104] It has been "the working faith of our civilization,"[105] and *the*

90

"dominant cultural motif in western society."[106] Indeed, "belief in progress is an act of faith."[107] While the philosophers of the Enlightenment gave different expression to this belief, it is fair to say that faith in progress functioned for them as "a unified cultural mood."[108]

Gilkey is, of course, aware of the numerous studies that have been written on the progress ideal of Western culture. But it is, predictably, Niebuhr's analysis that seems to have had the greatest impact on his own perspective. We do well to quote from Niebuhr's *Faith and History* at some length:

> A single article of faith has given diverse forms of modern culture the unity of a shared belief. Modern men of all shades of opinion agreed in the belief that historical development is a redemptive process.
>
> The dominant note in modern culture is not so much confidence in reason as faith in history. The conception of a redemptive history informs the most diverse forms of modern culture.[109]

Gilkey could not concur with his former teacher more. The 'a-religious' and 'wholly secular' self-understanding of modernity is a facade.

> Despite all its positivism and empiricism ... at the deepest level modernity has been founded on a new philosophy of history, a philosophy built on faith in knowledge and its power to control, on the triumph through knowledge of human purposes over blind fate, and on the confidence that change, if guided by intelligence informed by inquiry, can realize human fulfillment in this life.

This is "the implicit religion of the West."[110]

This religion, like the Christianity it rejects, is a historical religion. In modernity, however, the Christian notion of providence is replaced by the belief in progress. Providence is no longer necessary if autonomous man can 'provide for himself.'[111] What remains necessary, however, is an envisioning of a pattern to history and a role for Western culture in that pattern, a role which gives this culture its identity, task and value.[112] Such an 'envisioning' is constitutive of any worldview or religious substance of a culture as a vision *for* life. Modernity shows its Judeo-Christian heritage in the historical character of its fundamental mythos. The progress ideal is nothing less than a secularized *Heilsgeschichte*, an autonomous, progressive salvation history. It has its own understanding of the fall and sin (ignorance, superstition, ecclesiastical authorities), redemption (scientific and technological mastery in a free democratic society) and eschatological hope (*le perfectionnement de l'homme*). It also has its prophets (Descartes, Bacon, Newton, etc.).

Gilkey has described this myth in various ways and in numerous writings. In a typical passage he describes the myth of progress, which

> ... sees history, beginning way back with Egypt and Greece, as a story of cumulative development leading up to modern times temporally, and to Western culture, and especially America, spatially. Here and now, with us, the goal towards which this story has led, and so the goal in which it culminates, is represented by our culture. Thus, in terms of this story, do we know who we are, what we are to do, and what we can count on. This story has been one of cumulative learning and cumulative techniques, leading up to the scientific and technological world we so clearly represent.

This myth is engraved in our grade-school textbooks, the lifestyle portrayed in the popular media and in the attitudes we have towards the so-called 'underdeveloped' world. It is a myth that governs our common existence.

> It helps us determine what is creative and what is not in the world, and what our own priorities are or should be. It tells us what to defend and why we defend it. It gives meaning to our work, confidence in the midst of failure, and hope in the face of tragedy or of temporary discouragement. It helps us to distinguish good from evil forces in the world around us, and gives us confidence in the ultimate victory of good over evil in history. Above all, it tells us who we are in history and why we are here. It forms the ultimate set of presuppositions for most of our aims and so our patterns of education.[113]

Who are we? Where are we? What is our task? Where are we going? What's wrong? What is the remedy? These are all 'limit' questions or 'worldview' questions that receive an ultimate, faith-based answer in the historical myth of progress. The progress ideal brings together all the other dimensions of the religious substance of modernity (contingency, relativity, temporality, autonomy). Progress is both the foundation and utopian vision of modernity. But, says Gilkey, the foundation is structurally flawed, the vision is myopic and the religious substance is in crisis. I will begin the next chapter with this crisis.

NOTES

1 H. Richard Niebuhr, *Christ and Culture* (New York: Harper and Row, 1951), chapter one. Niebuhr's book remains a classic treatment of this subject. Using Niebuhr's categories James H. Olthuis offers a perceptive analysis in his article, "Must the Church Become Secular," in J. H. Olthuis et. al., *Out of Concern for the Church* (Toronto: Wedge Publishing Foundation, 1970), chapter 5.

For a critical discussion of Niebuhr see Charles Scriven, *The Transformation of Culture: Christian Social Ethics After H. Richard Niebuhr* (Scottdale, Penn.: Herald Press, 1988), esp. chs. 1 and 2. For my critique of this book see my *"The Transformation of Culture:* A Review Article," *Conrad Grebel Review* (1990).

2 Ibid, p. 32.

3 Ibid, pp. 32-39. Cf. Paul Tillich, *Systematic Theology,* III (1963), p. 57: "Culture, *cultura,* is that which takes care of something, keeps it alive, and makes it grow."

4 *How the Church,* p. 3. Gilkey goes on to say that both evangelical individualism and the liberal reinterpretation of Christian faith in terms of the dominant norms and concepts of the culture are more susceptible to acculturation than is American Catholicism (pp. 32-55).

For a similar analysis and critique of North American evangelicalism see the present author's *The Transforming Vision,* chapter 6; as well as my *Subversive Christianity* (Bristol, U.K.: Regius Press, 1991); and Os Guiness, *The Gravedigger File: Papers on the Subversion of the Modern Church* (Downers Grove, Ill: InterVarsity Press, 1983).

5 "Morality and the Cross," *Christianity and Crisis* 14, 5 (April 5, 1954), p. 36.

6 *Catholicism,* p. 9.

7 Ibid, p. 32. Cf. *Message and Existence,* pp. 173, 236; *Reaping,* p. 209; *Naming,* p. 36; and "The Role of the Theologian in Contemporary Theology," in *The Thought of Paul Tillich,* ed. by J. L. Adams (New York: Harper and Row, 1985), p. 344. Tillich, of course, often noted that religion actualizes itself in cultural forms. Cf. *The Theology of Culture,* pp. 47-49; and *The Protestant Era,* trans. by J. L. Adams (abridged ed.; Chicago: University of Chicago Press, 1957), p. 57.

8 "Theology of Culture and Christian Ethics," *The Annual of the Society of Christian Ethics* (1984), p. 351.

9 *Catholicism,* p. 131.

10 "Secularization," (unpub. ms., April 1981), p. 2.

11 "Theology of Culture and Christian Ethics," p. 349. Cf. "Culture and Religious Belief,' (unpub. paper presented at Marquette University, October 5-6, 1984), p. 16; and "The New Global Context for Missions," (unpub. paper presented to The World Missions Institute, April 12, 1984), p. 9. In *Creationism* Gilkey says that the unity of culture is not just a presupposition, it is also a task: "Perhaps, then, the major philosophical and theological task of our time is represented by this question, as old as the tradition of reflection itself: How are the many diverse ways of thought in a

culture — its technical and scientific thought, its social and political thinking, its artistic and moral experience and reflection, and its deepest or religious convictions — to find unity, that is, together to achieve coherence, mutual credibility and effectiveness?" (pp. 207-208).

12 John Hick, *Philosophy of Religion* (Englewood Cliffs, N.J.: Prentice Hall, 1963), p. 3. Wilfred Cantwell Smith has made a similar observation in *The Meaning and End of Religion* (Toronto: Mentor Books, 1964), p. 21.

13 The phrase "hermeneutics of suspicion" was first coined by Paul Ricoeur in *Freud and Philosophy: An Essay on Interpretation,* trans. by D. Savage (New Haven and London: Yale University Press, 1970), pp. 32-36; and *The Conflict of Interpretations,* trans. by C. Freilich and ed. by Don Ihde (Evanston: Northwestern University Press, 1974), pp. 148-150.

14 I am indebted here to two unpublished papers. One is by James H. Olthuis, "On the Nature of Religion: Faith, Vision of Life and Praxis," (Toronto: Institute for Christian Studies, n.d.); and the other by Paul Nathanson, "Religion and Secularity: A Methodological Inquiry," (Montreal: McGill University Faculty of Religious Studies, 1986).

15 M. Spiro, "Religion: Problems of Definition and Explanation," in *Anthropological Approaches to the Study of Religion,* ed. by M. Banton. (London: Tavistock Publications, 1966), p. 96.

16 Clifford Geertz, "Religion as a Cultural System," in *Reader in Comparative Religion: An Anthropological Approach,* ed by W. A. Lessa and E.Z. Vogt (3rd ed.; New York: Harper and Row, 1972), p. 168. For a more complete explication of Geertz's position see his *The Interpretation of Cultures* (New York: Basic Books, 1973), Part II, chapters 4, 5.

17 Cf. *Reaping,* p. 329, n. 36.

18 *Creationism,* p. 99.

19 Cf. *Message and Existence,* p. 31.

20 "Secularization," p. 44.

21 Indeed, the term 'ideology' was first used in the French Revolution to describe that world of ideas that would provide the intellectual grounding of a new society, a grounding that would replace the religion of the *ancien régime.* Cf. Alvin Gouldner, *The Dialectic of Ideology and Technology: The Origins, Grammar and Future of Ideology,* A Continuum Book (New York: Seabury Press, 1976), pp. 11-13; and Bob Goudzwaard, *Idols of our Time,* trans. by M. VanderVennen (Downers Grove, Ill.: InterVarsity Press, 1984), pp. 17-18.

22 *Society and the Sacred,* p. 107. Cf. "The Role of the Theologian in Contemporary Society," p. 343; and "The AAR and the Anxiety of Nonbeing: An Analysis of our Present Cultural Situation," *Journal of the American Academy of Religion* 48, 1 (March 1980), pp. 13-14.

23 *Creationism,* pp. 250-252, note 6.

24 Ninian Smart, *Worldviews: Crosscultural Explorations of Human Beliefs* (New York: Charles Scribner's Sons, 1983), pp. 1-2. Cf. James H. Olthuis, "On Worldviews," *Christian Scholar's Review* XIV, 2 (1985), pp. 153-164; Arthur F. Holmes, *Contours of a Worldview* (Grand Rapids: Eerdmans, 1983), esp. chapter one; and the present author's *The Transforming Vision,* Part One; and *Who Turned Out the Lights?*
For a nuanced discussion of the historical use of the term see Al Wolters, "On the Idea of Worldview and its Relation to Philosophy," in *Stained Glass: Worldviews and Social Science,* ed. by P. Marshall, S. Griffioen and R. Mouw, Christian Studies Today Series (Lanham, MD: University Press of America, 1989), pp. 14-25.

25 *Message and Existence,* p. 206.

26 Paul Tillich, *Systematic Theology,* III, p. 60.

27 *Society and the Sacred,* p. 19.

28 Quoted in *Reaping,* p. 17, from *History and Social Theory* (Garden City: Doubleday, 1971), p. 141.

29 Ibid, from *The Idea of Social Science and its Relation to Philosophy* (London: Routledge and Kegan Paul, 1971), p. 23.

30 Ibid, p. 346, n. 56, from *City of God,* bk. XIX, chapter XXIV.

31 *Message and Existence,* p. 32. In our discussion of Christianity and other religions below we will see that Gilkey's formulation here is somewhat problematic.

32 *Society and the Sacred,* p. 43.

33 J. Olthuis, "On Worldviews," p. 155.

34 Cf. *Society and the Sacred,* p. 147.

35 *Reaping,* p. 17. Cf. p. 41. Peter Berger and Thomas Luckmann speak similarly of the "nomic" or "ordering" character of "symbolic universes." See their coauthored work, *The Social Construction of Reality: a Treatise in the Sociology of Knowledge* (Garden City, Doubleday, 1966), pp. 90-96.

36 Cf. *Message and Existence,* p. 27.

37 Cf. "Tillich: Master of Mediation," p. 37; and "Culture and Religious Belief," p. 8.

38 Ludwig Wittgenstein, *Philosophical Investigations* (Oxford: Blackwells, 1967), ¶ 217.

39 Cf. Paul Tillich, *The Protestant Era,* chapter III; *Systematic Theology,* III, pp. 369-372; and Gilkey, "Tillich: Master of Mediation," pp. 39-40.

40 *Message and Existence,* p. 27. Arthur Holmes says that "the genesis of a worldview

is at the prephilosophical level" (*Contours of a Worldview,* p. 31). Herman Dooyeweerd also understands worldviews to be pre-theoretic or pre-scientific in character. See his *A New Critique of Theoretical Thought,* vol. 1, trans. by D.H. Freeman and W.S. Young (Philadelphia: Presbyterian and Reformed, 1953), pp. 38-59; and *In The Twilight of Western Thought* (Nutley, N.J.: The Craig Press, 1972), pp. 1-60.

41 *Reaping,* p. 150. Gilkey's understanding of the relation of symbol to myth is similar to Ricoeur's for whom myth translates (and therefore interprets) symbol into narration, thereby giving the symbol concrete actuality and a temporal orientation. *Symbolism of Evil,* pp. 161-163, 237. Cf. Gilkey, "Modern Myth-Making and the Possibilities of Twentieth-Century Theology," pp. 283-286.

42 *Society and the Sacred,* pp. 61-62. Herman Dooyeweerd made a similar observation when he said, "Cultural disclosure in history is led by faith." More specifically, he argued that behind every culture there is a "religious ground motive" [*religieuze grondmotief*]: "It is a spiritual force that acts as the absolutely central mainspring of human society. It governs all of life's temporal expressions from the religious centre of life, directing them to the true or supposed origin of existence. It thus not only places an indelible stamp on the culture, science, and social structure of a given period but determines profoundly one's whole world view" (*Roots of Western Culture,* trans. by J. Kraay, ed. by M. VanderVennen and B. Zylstra (Toronto: Wedge Publishing, 1979), pp. 99, 9).

43 Ibid, p. 24. Cf. *Religion,* pp. 66-67, 102-104.

44 Cf. C. Geertz, *The Interpretation of Cultures,* p. 93.

45 J. Olthuis, "On Worldviews," p. 156.

46 "The Creationist Issue: A Theologian's View," in *Cosmology and Theology,* ed. by D. Tracy and N. Lasch, vol. 166 of *Concilium* (New York: Seabury Press, 1983), p. 68.

47 *Reaping,* p. 67.

48 Ibid.

49 Ibid, p. 60.

50 *Message and Existence,* p. 27. Cf. p. 25: "'Belief' on the deepest level has reference to the symbolic forms that structure the perspectives, the norms, and thus the life of objective historical communities." In "Modern Myth-Making," Gilkey says that a myth represents "a vision affirmed and upheld by involved participation in the spiritual ethos and the ethical structures of the community formed by the myth" (p. 297).
For similar descriptions of faith and belief see, Wilfred Cantwell Smith, *Faith and Belief* (Princeton: Princeton University Press, 1979), chapters 5 and 6; Paul Tillich, *The Dynamics of Faith,* chapter 1; James Olthuis, "On Worldviews," pp. 156-158; and A. C. Thiselton, "Knowledge, Myth and Corporate Memory," pp. 74-75, and *The Two Horizons,* p. 384. For Gilkey's discussion of Smith's view of faith see his, "A Theological Voyage with Wilfred Cantwell Smith," p. 300.

51 Cf. "Culture and Religious Belief," p. 20.

52 Cf. *Society and the Sacred*, p. 116.

53 Ibid, p. 118. Cf. pp. 144-149; and *Creationism*, pp. 213-214.

54 It is also in danger of heteronomously dictating cultural patterns. As we shall see in the next chapter, Gilkey adopts Tillich's notion of theonomy.

55 It is important to add that relationships C and B are not, for Gilkey, unidirectional. The culture per se influences the particular religious tradition in its expression and communication (e.g., the use of radio, television, methods of education, etc.), and the religious tradition is never immune from the influence of certain elements of the religious substance (e.g., the Greek ontological basis for early creedal formulations and the present influence of Marxist thought in liberation theology). What Gilkey calls for is a 'critical correlation' in these relationships. Cf. "Culture and Religious Belief," p. 21. Nor is relationship A unidirectional. The religious substance is foundational for cultural life per se, but crises in that culture can also be the occasion for shifts in that substance.

56 Cf. "Theology of Culture and Christian Ethics," p. 343.

57 Cf. *Society and the Sacred*, p. 22; and *Message and Existence* p. 214. Charles Scriven also notes this relation in his exposition of Gilkey. (*The Transformation of Culture*, pp. 69-70).

58 *Creationism*, p. 220.

59 *Reaping*, p. 19. Cf. pp. 61-62, 290-291. Robert Nisbett makes the same point in *The Sociological Tradition* (New York: Basic Books, 1966), pp. 229-230.

60 For an excellent discussion of the debate in recent sociological and anthropological literature see David Lyon, "Secularization: the fate of faith in modern society," *Themelios* 10, 1 (September 1984), pp. 14-22.

61 Cf. the following observation of Bernard Zylstra: "As to the content of what it posits, modernity cannot be understood apart from the content of what it negates. To put it differently, modernity is an inversion of Christianity. In nearly every one of its tenets, modernity is linked to the Christian view of things, but in an inverted manner" ("Modernity and the American Empire," *International Reformed Bulletin* 68 (1977), p. 5). Cf. Eric Voegelin, "The Religion of Humanity and the French Revolution," in *From Enlightenment to Revolution*, ed. by J. H. Hallowell (Durham: Duke University Press, 1975), pp. 160-194. Allan Bloom also comments on the anti-Christian character of the Enlightenment in *The Closing of the American Mind* (New York: Simon and Schuster, 1987), p. 258.

62 Carl Lotus Becker, *The Heavenly City of the Eighteenth-Century Philosophers* (New Haven: Yale University Press, 1932), pp. 102-103.

63 Immanuel Kant, "What is Enlightenment?" in *On History*, ed. by L.W. Beck, trans. by L.W. Beck, R.E. Anchor and E.L. Fackenheim, The Library of Liberal Arts (New York: Bobbs-Merrill, 1963), p. 3.

64 Peter Gay, *The Enlightenment: An Interpretation* (New York: Alfred A. Knopf,

1967), vol. 1, pp. 148, 150.

65 "Secularism's Impact on Contemporary Theology," p. 64. Cf. "Dissolution and Reconstruction in Theology," pp. 30-31.

66 Cf. *Reaping*, p. 136. In *The Transforming Vision*, Middleton and I develop a similar perspective: "... we use *secularism* to mean a world view — that pre-theoretical, committed vision which has shaped the dominant institutions of the modern Western world since the Renaissance. The world view of secular*ism* is inevitably incarnated in the progressive secular*ization* of culture" (p. 118).

67 *Naming*, p. 34.

68 John Dewey, *Reconstruction in Philosophy* (New York: Henry Holt and Co., 1929), pp. 47-49.

69 Anthony Campolo models his apologetic defense of Christianity in the modern world on Gilkey's description of modernity in his *A Reasonable Faith: Responding to Secularism* (Waco, Texas: Word Books, 1983).

70 *Naming*, p. 40. Cf. *Reaping*, p. 242; and *Religion*, p. 68.

71 Cf. "Biblical Symbols in a Scientific Age," p. 77.

72 *Naming*, pp. 40-41.

73 Ibid, p. 41.

74 Ibid, p. 69.

75 Ibid, p. 43.

76 Ibid, p. 48. Cf. *Reaping*, p. 243.

77 Ibid, p. 49. Cf. *Society and the Sacred*, p. 94. In another context I have described this ontological shift as a move away from 'structuralist' ontologies (preoccupied with abiding and universal structures of being) to 'geneticist' ontologies (preoccupied with flux and process.) See the present author's , "Pannenberg's Eschatological Ontology," *Christian Scholar's Review* XI, 3 (1982), pp. 234-237; and "A Critical Review of Pannenberg's *Anthropology in Theological Perspective*," *Christian Scholar's Review* XV, 3 (1986), pp. 255-257.

78 Ibid, pp. 50-51. It is precisely this temporally conditioned relativity that is at the ontological roots of Allan Bloom's Platonic dis-ease with modernity in *The Closing of the American Mind*.

79 Ibid, p. 52. Ricoeur says that this narrowly instrumentalist and monodimensional approach to language characteristic of modernity, causes us to be 'embarrassed' by mythic discourse and 'forgetful' of the meaning that only myth can disclose. Cf. *Symbolism of Evil*, pp. 161, 349; "The Hermeneutics of Symbols and Philosophical Reflection," in *The Philosophy of Paul Ricoeur*, p. 37; and "The Hermeneutics of Symbols and Philosophical Reflection: II," in *The Conflict of Interpretations: Essays in*

Hermeneutics, p. 328.

80   *Naming*, p. 51. Cf. *Reaping*, pp. 5, 243, 245.

81   *Society and the Sacred*, pp. 93-94

82   *Religion*, p. 69.

83   Cf. *Religion*, p. 70; and "Modern Myth-Making," pp. 288-289.

84   *Naming*, p. 58.

85   Ibid, p. 60.

86   Cf. *Creationism*, p. 233; *Religion*, p. 76; and "Modern Myth-Making," p. 300.
Dooyeweerd has a similar perspective: "Proudly conscious of his own autonomy and
freedom, modern man saw 'nature' as an expansive arena for the explorations of
his free personality, as a field of infinite possibilities in which the sovereignty of
human personality must be revealed by a complete *mastery* of the phenomena of
nature" (*Roots of Western Culture*, p. 150). See also John Passmore's interpretation
in *Man's Responsibility for Nature: Ecological Problems and Western Traditions* (London:
Gerald Duckworth, 1974), ch. 1. A classic Renaissance statement of this man/
nature dualism is Giovanni Pico della Mirandola's *Oration on the Dignity of Man*, trans.
by A.R. Caponigni (Chicago: Henry Regnery Co., 1965).

87   *Reconstruction in Philosophy*, p. 116. Cf. pp. 54-74.

88   Cf. *Society and the Sacred*, p. 130; and *Religion*, p. 68. For a discussion of the socio-
cultural and economic implications of the modern belief in autonomy, see Robert
Heilbroner, *The Worldly Philosophers* (rev. ed.; New York: Simon and Schuster, 1961),
especially ch. 2; and his *The Making of Economic Society* (rev. ed.; Englewood Cliffs,
N.J.: Prentice-Hall, 1968), ch. 2 & 3; and Bob Goudzwaard, *Capitalism and Progress:
A Diagnosis of Western Society*, trans. and ed. by Josina Van Nuis Zylstra (Toronto:
Wedge, and Grand Rapids: Eerdmans, 1979), ch. 1-6, 22.

89   *Reaping*, p. 194.

90   Gilkey often uses this metaphor. In *Society and the Sacred* he writes of the value
and reverence that society bestows on its 'knowers,' religious or scientific; "... the
priest's robes and the scientist's white coat signifying much the same social role
of the knower of significant secrets and so the doer of all-important deeds" (p. 76).
Cf. *Religion*, p. 79.
      Karl Löwith has made a similar observation: "Because of the incredible
advances made possible by scientific progress, the physicist has taken the place of
the theologian; planned progress has taken over the function of providence" ("The
Fate of Progress," in *Nature, History and Existentialism*, ed. by Arnold Levison (Evanston,
Ill.: Northwestern University Press, 1966), p. 157).

91   Cf. *Society and the Sacred*, pp. 77-78; and *Creationism* p. 173.

92   "Secularization," p. 7.

99

93 *Society and the Sacred,* p. 91.

94 Francis Bacon, "New Atlantis," in *Ideal Commonwealths,* ed. by H. Morley (rev. ed.; New York: Colonial Press, 1901), p. 129.

95 Francis Bacon, *The New Organon and Related Writings,* ed. by F. H. Anderson (New York: The Liberal Arts Press, 1960), pp. 118-119. For further discussion of Bacon's scientism see Frank E. Manuel and Fritzie P. Manuel, *Utopian Thought in the Western World* (Cambridge: Belknop Press of Harvard University Press, 1979), pp. 254, 260.

96 *Society and the Sacred,* p. 77.

97 *The New Organon and Related Writings,* p. 267.

98 *Man's Responsibility for Nature,* p. 19.

99 *Society and the Sacred,* p. 78. Cf. *Creationism,* p. 178.

100 "Theology in the Seventies," *Theology Today* 27 (October 1970), p. 298.

101 "Theology and the Future," p. 251.

102 *Naming,* p. 343.

103 Cf. *Reaping,* p. 192.

104 John Baillie, *The Belief in Progress* (New York: Charles Scribner's Sons: 1951), p. 1.

105 Christopher Dawson, *Progress and Religion: An Historical Inquiry* (New York: Sheed and Ward, 1938), p. 3.

106 Bob Goudzwaard, *Capitalism and Progress,* p. xxiii.

107 J. B. Bury, *The Idea of Progress: An Inquiry into its Origin and Growth* (London: Macmillan, 1920), p. 4. Cf. W. R. Inge, *The Idea of Progress* (Oxford: Clarendon Press, 1920).
    In a discussion of Condorcet's belief in the *perfectionnement* of humanity articulated in his 1793 work, *Outlines of an Historical View of the Progress of the Human Mind,* Karl Löwith notes that "Condorcet's hopes for the future perfection of men were not the result of scientific inference and evidence but a conjecture, the root of which was hope and faith" (*Meaning in History* (Chicago: University of Chicago Press, 1949), p. 96).

108 Reinhold Niebuhr, *The Nature and Destiny of Man,* II (New York: Charles Scribner's Sons, 1943), p. 164.

109 *Faith and History,* pp. 1-3.

110 *Society and the Sacred,* pp. 94-95.

111 Cf. Bob Goudzwaard, *Capitalism and Progress,* ch. 3; and Karl Löwith, *Meaning*

in History, ch. 4.

112   Cf. *Society and the Sacred*, p. 113.

113   Ibid, pp. 23-24.

CHAPTER THREE
Modernity in Decline

1. A "Time of Troubles"

I have suggested in the preceding chapter that John Dewey is one of the most representative North American proponents of the faith of modernity in this century. He encapsulated the belief in progress well when he contrasted the 'savage' with the 'civilized' man in his book, *Reconstruction in Philosophy*.

> Suppose the two are living in a wilderness. With the savage there is the maximum of accommodation to given conditions; the minimum of what we may call hitting back. The savage takes things "as they are," and by using caves and roots and occasional pools leads a meagre and precarious existence. The civilized man goes to distant mountains and dams streams. He builds reservoirs, digs channels, and conducts the waters to what had been a desert. He searches the world to find plants and animals that will thrive. He takes native plants and by selection and cross-fertilization improves them. He introduces machinery to till the soil and care for the harvest. By such means he may succeed in making the wilderness blossom like the rose.[1]

Dewey's faith in the 'civilized man' is a secularization of the prophetic vision of Isaiah: "The wilderness and the dry land shall be glad, the desert shall rejoice and blossom." (35:1) But Gilkey wonders whether the visionary application of scientific knowledge has not more often "turned the natural garden into a human desert."

> Instead of making life more secure, the unstoppable accumulation of technological skills seems, in the end, to endanger that life. Instead of being the paradigm of survival, "homo faber" , now armed with technology seems to be engineering ..., through some fatal flaw, his own extinction. Our most creative talents — certainly to modern times — namely, our scientific and technological abilities, seem at present to represent our principal present danger and so strangely our greatest liabilities.[2]

103

Indeed, the victory over fate that scientific intelligence promised seems now to have led us to a submission to a new, self-created fate, "represented by a quite uncontrollable technological advance into new and ever more menacing human powers."[3] In *Reaping the Whirlwind* Gilkey speaks of this 'fate of modernity.'

> What threatens us all as a terrifying fate is the consequence of human concupiscence exacerbated by the genius, the superficialities and the lures of a technological and commercial culture into a demonic and hardly controllable force that has partly despoiled and now promises to devour the earth.[4]

In a similar way, Karl Löwith has aptly described this situation as the "fate of progress." He notes that "an uncanny coincidence of fatalism and a will to progress presently characterizes all contemporary thinking about the future course of history. Progress now threatens us, it has become our fate."[5]

While Gilkey's reference above to the sin of concupiscence with reference to modern technology displays a Tillichian influence on his theology of culture,[6] it is fair to say that his critique of modernity and its faith in progress has more decidedly Niebuhrian roots. According to Niebuhr the decisive flaw of modernity is that it overlooks the ambiguity of the human subject and the ambiguity of the history shaped by such subjects. In *The Nature and Destiny of Man* he says that the modernist vision of the Renaissance and Enlightenment "assumes that all development means the advancement of the good," and therefore, "does not recognize that every heightened potency of human existence may also represent the possibility of evil."[7] And in his earlier *Reflections on the End of an Era* he says:

> The moral superficiality of modern culture betrayed it into an easy faith that reason had conquered or could conquer and restrain the anarchic impulses which express themselves in man-as-nature. It had not realized that reason may be used much more easily to justify impulse and to invent instruments for its efficacious expression than to check and restrain impulse. That was a fatal mistake because it permitted a more unrestrained expressing of impulse than ever before in history.[8]

Such an awareness of human ambiguity or fallenness and the almost unlimited ability of modern humans to use critical intelligence and technology in service of self-interested impulses permeates Gilkey's theology of culture. Biographically such convictions had their birth for Gilkey during his imprisonment in a civilian internment camp from 1943 to 1945 in the Shantung province of China. While initially impressed by the internees' ability to develop rapidly the technical instruments of civilization, he soon came to see that the problem with his own optimistic humanism was "its rather naive and unrealistic faith in the rationality and goodness of the men who wield these instruments." Commenting on a time when the tensions in the camp were especially high because the American internees felt that they need not share the contents of the newly arrived American Red Cross parcels with the non-American internees, Gilkey says, "Staring at those symbols of our material advance, I suddenly realized that Western culture's dream of material progress as the answer to every ill was no more than a dream. Here was evidence before my eyes that wealth and progress have demonic consequences if misused."[9] What was learned experientially at the Shantung compound was deepened and expanded at the level of theory by studying under Reinhold Niebuhr. A culture that is not cognizant of its own profound ambiguity is ripe for demonic corruption and ultimate fall. That, both Niebuhr and Gilkey say, is the present condition of Western modernity.

As I noted in the Introduction, Gilkey followed his mentor's critique of the progress ideal in one of his earliest articles. In 1955 Gilkey wrote of the spiritual breakdown of the faith in progress, scientific knowledge and technical proficiency.[10] Perhaps one would wonder whether his predictions of cultural decline thirty years ago might not require some modification or softening today. The beliefs that he said were in spiritual crisis then are still very much with us. Indeed, it can safely be said that they are still the dominant convictions in Western culture. Yet Gilkey is not surprised by the persistence of these beliefs. The religious substance of a culture is, as we have seen, the very foundation of a culture. Such foundations are not shaken easily, nor are they changed in a short compass of time. Cultural epoches shift slowly, something like the seasons only on a much larger time frame. Using the analogy of the seasons Gilkey says that there is "an autumnal chill in the air; its similarity to the chill in other periods of cultural decline is undeniable." Of course it is only possible to say with certainty that a cultural epoch has ended after the fact, with historical hindsight. Yet Gilkey thinks that we can at least say that "it *feels* as if we are reaching the end of a historical era...."[11]

Gilkey also often uses Arnold Toynbee's notion of a "time of troubles" to describe the present cultural situation.[12] Following

Toynbee, Gilkey refers to a 'time of troubles' not as a fated necessity, but as a "period when the *possibility* of collapse or of radical decline appears for the first time on the scene."[13] Cultures wax and wane, and the culture of modernity appears to be waning. In this situation,

> The institutions, customs and beliefs which in the waxing of its life had been creative in developing the culture's power, security and well-being, now appear to change their character and their role and to become destructive, creating new dilemmas and new contradictions that threaten to pull the society's life apart....[14]

Modernity is in crisis because the promise of the Enlightenment to control the natural forces that threaten human life, end poverty through economic abundance, and eradicate religious superstition by establishing rational and moral political structures in history, has not been fulfilled. "What was promised has either not in fact occurred, or, if it has occurred, new problems, even contradictions, even lethal dilemmas have resulted." We are witnessing, therefore, "an ending of the Enlightenment" because "the Enlightenment dream has been falsified."[15] This ending necessarily entails, says Gilkey, an end to unlimited technological expansion, the domination of science, unfettered human autonomy, and confidence that humankind can realize earthly blessedness through its own progress. "All of these beliefs in man and his vast potentialities in history through knowledge and the control it brings that characterize the 'modernity' created by the Enlightenment have been proved to the hilt not to have established and secured human life on earth — as had been promised."[16]

When modern culture openly faces these broken promises it not only loses faith in the wisdom of scientific intelligence and the benevolence of liberal moral institutions, it loses faith in itself. As a result, "the 'world' in which people live a meaningful life begins to fall apart, and so their identity and role, their 'place' in their world, seem to be vanishing," and "the very ground on which one stands breaks apart."[17] Its progressive vision *for* history shaken, modernity begins to experience the future more as menace than promise.[18] And when a culture is in this situation where it is losing confidence in its own cultural ideals it is not surprising that widespread cultural anxiety arises. Moreover, it is precisely at this time that a declining culture is most dangerous. Gilkey notes that "an old culture, like an old bear, can suddenly whiff the dank odor of its own mortality; and then it is tempted, and tempted deeply, to sacrifice its ideals for the preservation of its life — and thus to hasten the very demise in history that it fears so much."[19]

There are, of course, those who still believe that we are in the age of progress and that such talk of cultural decline simply represents the pessimistic neuroses of the 'prophets of doom.' For example, futurist Frank Feather confidently claimed in 1980 that the "potential of our collective brains is probably infinite."[20] Similarly, Herman Kahn and John Phelps confidently predict that we are simply in the transition period from a super-industrial to post-industrial society and that "this problem-prone, super-industrial period will be marked by rising living standards and less rather than more sacrifice."[21] Other futurists, however, are more sober. Ruben Nelson's analysis echoes Gilkey's: "The thought is occurring among more and more of us that our problem is not that we lack able administration, but that we have no common purpose, no vision to guide us as we venture into the wilderness."[22]

The crisis of modernity is multifaceted. It is political, social, economic and environmental. But at heart it is a failure of vision. It is a crisis of the religious substance, the mythos of modernity. This has even been recognized by secular social analysts like Daniel Bell. Writing in *The Cultural Contradictions of Capitalism*, Bell says that "the real problem of *modernity* is the problem of belief. To use an unfashionable term, it is a spiritual crisis, since the new anchorages have proved illusory and the old ones have become submerged."[23] Gilkey would respond that it is precisely because the crisis is spiritual in character that an analysis and response limited to political science, economics and sociology is insufficient. The very nature of the crisis makes a *theology* of culture mandatory.

The question that has not been addressed in our discussion of the decline of modernity thus far, however, is whether there is sufficient evidence to speak of such a decline. Gilkey (and others) think that the evidence makes such a historical judgment necessary. He usually lists that evidence in terms of four cultural shifts, and while the content of his lists sometimes varies, his argument can be usefully summarized in the following way. The religious substance of modernity can be said to be in decline because, a) there is an increasing realization that western science and technological industrialism are inherently ambiguous. This ambiguity is especially evident in b) the ecological crisis and, c) the apparent loss of both Western influence in the world and

107

the weakening of the influence of the dominant symbols of modernity in the West itself. And, finally, d) this weakening of influence also entails a necessary abandonment of the belief in the supremacy of Western religion and an acknowledgement of what Gilkey describes as a 'rough parity' of the religions of the world. I will address each of these cultural shifts in this order.

2. The Ambiguity of Science and Technological Industrialism

We have seen above that Gilkey's theology of culture analyzes modernity in terms of the myth of progress, and that foundational to that myth is faith in science and its technological application in industrialism. Modernity believes that with the advent of modern science we now know how to know and that "with that sacral tool we can change the character of the natural environment that surrounds us, of the sociohistorical context in which we live, and even of our own weak, temporal, and recalcitrant nature."[24] Science provides sacral knowledge and its technological application effects salvation in history. Science functions in modernity as theology functioned in the ecclesiastically dominated medieval period. But as theology was once dethroned as the queen of the sciences, so now, Gilkey argues, we are witnessing the "gradual dethronement of the most recent queen."[25]

The evidence for this shift in cultural sensibility includes the rise of interest in the occult, Eastern religions, mysticism and the 'New Age Consciousness' movement, and the general disillusionment with and fear of technology. Both of these developments "bespeak a deep questioning of applied science as the answer to human problems." But the deeper cause of this uneasiness about science seems to lie in the same profound fault that was evidenced in the career of the medieval queen, viz., religion.

> There we saw that religion "fell" from sovereignty because, although it is an essential and very creative aspect of human existence, it made itself absolute, predominating over the other aspects of life, and the sole source of knowledge and of healing. I believe the same has been true of science, which is also, let me repeat, essential to life and a creative power of human being; and precisely because of that creativity has it been tempted to its fall.[26]

Gilkey's critique of modernity and his discernment of its decline and gradual fall is rooted in the biblical notion of idolatry. He once noted that "if the true Lord of history is not reflectively disclosed and preached, then false lords will be."[27] Idolatry is always a temptation in history. An idol is any dimension or aspect of creation that has been absolutized. This is what modernity has done with science and technology. By absolutizing these creative human powers, their creativity becomes demonic. Science becomes scientism, the limitation of true and authentic knowledge to that which can be quantifiably ascertained by the 'scientific method.' Technology becomes technicism. Such a technicism comes to clear expression in the words of Victor Ferkiss: "The race's only salvation is in the creation of technological man."[28]

In Part three of this book we will see that a significant step in the argument of Gilkey's prolegomenon is the phenomenological and historical claim that science and technology are, in fact, more religious in nature than the secular self-understanding could ever acknowledge. For the purposes of this chapter, however, we need to discuss Gilkey's argument that scientism and technicism manifest internal contradictions that sow the seeds of their own decline. I will begin with scientism and then proceed to the ambiguities of technicism.

The fundamental question to be addressed to scientism is whether it is, as it claims, the *sole* cognitive avenue to the real. Upon closer examination, Gilkey concludes that not only is modern science not the sole avenue to the real, but that it itself manifests a profound contradiction. This contradiction could be described alternately as the contradiction between object and subject; or the contradiction between science as inquiry and the scientific inquirer; or, simply, the freedom/determinism problem. Let me explain.

As we have seen, modernity is suffused with the sense of freedom, of autonomy. One of the ways in which modern culture has experienced this freedom most intensely is in the experience of scientifically knowing and manipulating nature for human benefit. But it is precisely here that a profound and incessant contradiction arises. Modern science assumes that its objects can be exhaustively understood within the terms of the causal nexus. Consequently, such objects are understood as determined beings, not free. But this determinism of science as inquiry contradicts the experience and self-understanding of the scientist as inquirer. Gilkey explains:

> For scientific method knows only an *object*, never a self-transcending, free, committed, and creative *subject*. When science through its method speaks "officially" of human being, it can find no shred of evidence of

such a creative, autonomous self. It finds only a complex, natural organism constituted in all it does by the various factors: genetic, physical, chemical, biological, psychological, and social, which have made it what it is and which, for objective inquiry, determines its subsequent career.[29]

The autonomous subject who is a scientific inquirer and who believes that he or she can freely apply the results of that inquiry for the betterment of humanity is, in fact, lost in the inquiry itself. This is the dilemma of rationality in modernity. Such an objectivist rationality seems to self-destruct.

A further dimension of this problem is that the scientist as inquirer experientially (or 'naively') knows himself or herself as in some way transcending the categories of their own inquiry. The inquiry is, therefore, experienced as narrow and restricting. Clearly influenced by Tillich's view of the "controlling" character of "technical" or "instrumental" reason,[30] Gilkey says that when reason is limited to "making contingent affirmations about what lies objectively around us," to "analysis of abstract concepts and their interrelations," and to "the creation, organization and critique of systems of technical processes," then the result will be that "the intuitive, imaginative, moral, political, aesthetic and religious aspects of creative spirit are separated from the rational" and relegated to the realm of the irrational. Such a narrowly scientistic understanding of reason ultimately results in "the *reduction* and *dismemberment* of the creative powers of the human spirit...."[31]

This narrowness and internal tension within the scientism that is so central to the religious substance of modernity, points to an even more fatal problem, however. Even if we reject the narrowness of scientism by affirming the freedom of the human beings who engage in scientific inquiry and use scientific knowledge, we must still face and come to terms with the ambiguity of that very human freedom. The 'free' use of scientific knowledge is, as history has repeatedly shown, fraught with dangers. Knowledge does indeed give power and the potential of greater control, "but new power, even power through knowledge, by no means guarantees the virtue or wisdom of the controller, the *self*-control of the man who can wield the power." Moreover, "the great increase in man's ability to control what is outside of him through technology has not led to any corresponding increase either in man's control over himself or over his historical fate."[32] There is no clear parallel between the increase in *scientia* or *techné* and a concurrent increase in *sapientia* or *sophia*.[33] Consequently, greater scientific knowledge and technological power can, if not coupled with increased virtue and wisdom, magnify human ambiguity and the lethal potential of that ambiguity for both human culture itself and the broader eco-system. Gilkey's point is that science and technology, like anything else human, can be misused, and therefore "they are not omnicompetent unambiguous saving forces in history." [34] Nowhere has this been more evident than in the career of modern technological industrialism.

Gilkey senses a growing feeling in the latter stages of modernity that a technological society produces as many problems as it solves. Undoubtedly, socio-economic problems like simultaneous inflation and structural unemployment, the spread and decay of cities, with its concomitant depletion of agricultural land, class and racial tensions, and tensions between the industrialized and 'third' worlds, are all related to the very structure and spiritual character of technological industrialism.[35]

Gilkey acknowledges that all of these problems are constitutive elements of modernity's decline. But, in his theology of culture, he more often comments on the dehumanizing character of a technological society. Addressing students at the Art Institute of Chicago, he observed that "a technical culture is voracious, devouring; it consumes all the other nontechnical aspects of culture in its maw by turning everything else into a skill, a knowledge of how to do it, a means."[36] Like the scientism which is its origin, technicism narrowly limits human life and culture. Following Jacques Ellul's understanding of *techné*, Gilkey describes modernity's commitment to 'efficiency' as evidenced in its rationalized bureaucracies, subdivisions of identical homes, and mega-corporations. Such organization, has, of course, its benefits. But Gilkey says that it also has drastic negative consequences as well; the most important of which is the loss of 'personness' or individuality:

> As every advanced technological society has discovered, human beings are now not so much masters as the servants of the organizations they have created, servants in the sense that they find themselves "caught" and rendered inwardly helpless within the system....

By becoming "parts of a machine" we sacrifice our inwardness and the system

111

... rewards and satisfies us only externally by giving us things to consume or watch. After all, such things are all that efficient organization can produce. Having dampened our creative activity in the world into the rote work expected of a mere part of a system, it now smothers the intensity of our private enjoyments by offering us the passive pleasures of mere consumption.[37]

In Niebuhr's sense of the term, there is something deeply 'ironic' about this state of affairs.[38] The very modernity that affirms autonomous individuality as foundational to its whole cultural project is now seen to theoretically deny that autonomy in its scientific method and to existentially threaten individuality in its technological system. Gilkey explains:

Technological society promised to free the individual from crushing work, from scarcity, disease and want, to free him or her to become him or herself by dispensing with these external fates. In many ways, on the contrary, it has — or threatens to do so — emptied rather than freed the self by placing each person in a homogeneous environment, setting him or her as a replaceable part within an organized system, and satisfying external wants rather than energizing creative powers. Thus appears the first paradox: the organization of modern society necessary to the survival and well-being of the race seems now to menace the humanity, the inwardness, and creativity of the race.[39]

The promise of technicism, like the promise of scientism, has failed. Moreover, not only has individual autonomy been threatened in technological society, so also has human freedom to direct and shape history been threatened. Indeed, the very technology that promised to liberate us from fate has now itself "become one of the fates that haunt modern man, mocking his control over himself and even over nature." Technology has taken on the character of fate because "the *fact* of the development or further expansion of technology cannot be stopped and is thus quite beyond human control." Further, "the *shape* or *direction* of this unstoppable expansion is also not under any measure of rational determination or control."[40] This technological 'frolic' seems mysteriously to have a life of its own as if there were a 'technological imperative' in history quite out of human control; an imperative to which, in fact, human freedom and human culture is subject.[41]

This fateful character of modern technology is clearly evident in the nuclear arms race. Not only does the development of nuclear arms appear to have a life of its own, so also does it seem that a nuclear holocaust and its consequent 'nuclear winter' is, in Jonathan Schell's terms, "the fate of the earth."[42] According to Schell, Enlightenment freedom has created a fate that it cannot control. In a discussion of Schell's book, Gilkey comments "that this is a strange end to the Enlightenment expectation of what freedom and rationality could bring."[43] Indeed, it is again ironic that while the unplanned evolution of blind nature has led to the increase of life, our own planned progress has led to an increase in death (a fact that should silence all confident cultural evolutionists!). In the nuclear arms race we see an extreme example of how the Enlightenment belief that absolutized applied science would free us from fate was not only an erroneous myth, it was also a mortally dangerous myth.

The fact that the nuclear threat is a threat to the very habitability of the earth itself makes it a "transcendental threat." It is a threat to the very conditions and possibility of life. It is, therefore, "unthinkable." A nuclear holocaust represents "absolute evil" because all value is dependent upon life — without life there is no value. Therefore, no values or purposes, regardless of how lofty (e.g., 'freedom,' 'democracy,' 'socialism,' 'national security,' etc.) could justify this absolute evil. Moreover, the "normal" pattern of modern history whereby nation states defend their sovereignty by weapons and war now appears, to Gilkey, to be insane. Consequently, he says, "Normal history has become madness; normality has become pathology."[44]

In summary, modernity is in decline, says Gilkey, because of profound contradictions within its own religious substance. The ambiguity of human autonomy is demonstrated in the careers of Enlightenment science and technology and in its transfiguration into its antithesis, fate. The nuclear threat demonstrates both this ambiguity and fatedness. However, while a nuclear holocaust would be the ultimate refutation of modernity's faith in progress, it is still only a threat. As we shall see in the next chapter, Gilkey insists that freedom, not fate, has the final word in history, and therefore as long as a nuclear holocaust has not happened it is possible to avert that disaster.

There is, however, another threat already in process in history that also demonstrates the ambiguity of science and technology, and evidences the decline of modernity. It is a process that can potentially be as fatal as a nuclear holocaust and is, perhaps, more difficult to avert. The process I refer to is the ecological crisis. This is the second cultural shift that Gilkey addresses.

3. The Ecological Crisis

In our discussion above of the religious substance of modernity we have already noted that the Renaissance and Enlightenment view of human autonomy established a man/nature polarity that was potentially devastating for nature. That potentiality is increasingly becoming a reality. Modernity is, by virtue of its religious substance, always expansionistic. In Daniel Bell's words, the "self-infinitizing radical self" of modernity knows no limits.[45] By transforming the natural order into a technical order, modernity seeks both to secure itself from the threats of nature and, even more, to wrest from nature her riches in order to enjoy unceasing economic growth. Indeed, Bell says that "economic growth has become the secular religion of advancing industrial societies: the source of individual motivation, the basis of our political solidarity, the ground for the mobilization of society for a common purpose."[46]

Growth and expansion are the stuff that progress is made of. Heilbroner notes that "expansion has always been considered as inseparable from capitalism," and "conversely, a 'stationary,' non-expanding capitalism has always been considered either as a prelude to its collapse or as a betrayal of its historic purpose."[47] But it is precisely such a collapse and betrayal that now seems to loom on the historical horizon. Modernity's self-infinitizing self and expansionist culture is coming to an end (say Bell, Heilbroner, Gilkey, and others) because we are now facing a new reality, the reality of limits. Heilbroner's view is representative: "... there is an absolute limit to the ability of the earth to support or tolerate the process of industrial activity, and there is reason to believe that we are now moving toward that limit very rapidly."[48]

In his extensive discussions of Heilbroner's *An Inquiry into the Human Prospect,* Gilkey notes that the situation is made even more impossible by the existence of two problems that are cataclysmic in proportion and that are on a collision course with each other. On the one hand the present rate of population growth in the world is going to require an even greater expansion of agricultural and industrial production in order to feed, house and employ these masses of people. But, simultaneously, the depletion of the earth's resources, the pollution of the environment, and especially the danger of overreaching the thermal limits of the atmosphere, all seem to require a world-wide industrial slowdown. Therefore, we find our-

114

selves in the impossible situation whereby "the expansion on which our existence depends threatens our existence."[49]

Like the nuclear threat, the ecological crisis is something new in history, a unique product of Enlightenment culture. This is not to say that humans have not polluted the environment before. Nevertheless, Gilkey notes that "for the first time, our freedom in history menaces not only our fellow humans but nature as well," because "now civilization and history have become so dominant in their power that they threaten to engulf nature in their own ambiguity."[50] Human freedom in history has always been ambiguous but the expansionism entailed in modernity's self-infinitizing self raises that ambiguity to new and more lethally dangerous heights. While the self may be self-infinitizing and expansionist, the nature which is the arena for that expansion is itself finite and limited. The combination of the finitude of nature and the infinity of human greed has, as we are now witnessing, disastrous consequences.

To understand this dynamic of modern culture Gilkey employs Tillich's reinterpretation of the sin of "concupiscence."[51] When concupiscence is understood as the infinite greed which seeks to "take the world into itself," it is appropriately seen to be "the key 'sin' of our technical, commercial culture."[52]

The ecological crisis also manifests the same kind of internal tension or contradiction in the religious substance of modernity that we have already seen in science and technology. Gilkey describes this contradiction within modernity as a contradiction between modernity's "ground of being (nature) and its ground of hope (man as dominant over nature)."[53] Not only has modern science (especially evolutionary science) emphasized the embeddedness of human being in the processes of nature (indeed, as a complex *part* of nature), but the very economic growth that animates the life of modern culture is also clearly dependent upon natural resources. Yet the ground of human hope in modernity, especially with its technological imperative and economic expectations, both denies that very embeddedness and proceeds wantonly to deplete and pollute those resources. Again, the category of 'irony' is appropriate.

The ... irony or ambiguity of a scientific culture is that its most obvious creativity, its technical dominance over nature, has become a threat to its life — for even this culture remains human and creaturely, contingent, and for all its power, utterly dependent on the nature that gave it birth and that sustains its precarious life.[54]

The contradiction and its ironic implications go even deeper than this, however. In a world faced with the limits of the environment to withstand further pollution and the limits of natural resources, the powerful and affluent nations of the world will be required, in order to avert disaster, to exercise "an extraordinary self-restraint in the use of their power," and "a willingness for the sacrifice of their affluence lest they be tempted to use their power to grab all that is left for the sake of that affluence."[55] However, as Heilbroner has said, "the voluntary abandonment of the industrial mode of production would require a degree of self-abnegation on the part of its beneficiaries — managers and consumers alike — that would be without parallel in history."[56]

Consequently, Heilbroner argues, and Gilkey largely agrees, that in the foreseeable future a vast increase in authoritarian governmental control is unavoidable. Such authoritarian governments will be necessary, in the first place, to control the intense domestic and international unrest that will result from the economic contraction that will be forced upon the world by the ecological crisis. Secondly, governments will need to exercise more authority in order to implement difficult socio-political options in this situation. In the best scenario such authority will be used to redistribute resources (especially food) evenly to the nations of the world and to ration the world's decreasing supplies. In the worse scenario such authority will be used to retain, by violence and oppression, the present inequities between classes and nations. Whatever the scenario, the future will see less, not more, freedom coupled with less, not more, affluence. Herein is the deeper irony:

> The long-term results of science and technology seem ironically to be bringing about anything but the individualistic, creative, secure world they originally promised. In fact, this progressive, dynamic, innovative civilization seems to be in the process of generating its own antithesis: a stable, even stagnant society with an iron structure of rationality and authority, with a minimum of goods, of self-determination, of intellectual and personal freedom.
>
> Strangely, now *Homo Faber*, as technologist supreme, seems himself to be alienated from "reality," bringing about through his technology his own self-destruction and showing himself to be the primary danger to the survival of his race. No more startling contradiction to the spirit of modernity from the Enlightenment to the present could be con-

116

ceived.[57]

It is, therefore, no wonder that the spirit of modernity and the culture it has spawned should now be experiencing a marked decline of influence both in the broader world context and within its own civilizational boundaries.

4. The Demise of Western Influence

The third cultural shift that marks the decline of modernity is geo-political in nature. Enlightenment culture could afford to believe in progress with some degree of confidence so long as it exercised economic, military and political dominance in the world at large. That clear cultural and political domination has now dissipated. Gilkey asks us to consider the following:

> From 1456 (when the Turks last challenged Vienna) to 1940 — five hundred years! — no non-Western power could threaten a major European power, and certainly not all of the latter together (no wonder they thought history was progress!). Now *no* European power is a major power, and only one of the present four is "Western" in inheritance, that is, a culture formed by the Enlightenment — a dramatic collapse of relative power that will be increasingly evident in subsequent historical events.[58]

This demise of Western influence is not primarily because the West has lost access to real political, economic and military power (such power is still, to a great degree, in Western hands), but rather, because the power of Western symbols has been lost. A people have cultural power, says Gilkey, when "their symbols grasp others, when their goals and intentions are shared and supported by other wills."[59] That is no longer the case with the social ideals of the Enlightenment. Indeed, such ideals as individual rights, political freedom and democratic processes now appear suspect to a growing segment of the world community, "as ideologies that are covers for special privileges and for selfish materialism — an assessment that is hard to argue with."[60]

Apart from the geo-political implications of this cultural shift (consider the way in which the Western voice is often drowned out in the United Nations by the third world), there are at least two other consequences within Western culture itself. The first is discernible in a profound change in the Western historical consciousness from a preoccupation with progress and conquest to an almost neurotic concern with survival.

> One notes that few of the conservative leaders (that is, social and political adherents of Adam Smith and of John Locke) now speak of the progress and expansion of their cherished world. It is rather a matter of "holding the line," of "retaining and preserving" their sacred values, of "defending our kind of world" against aggressors. The salvation history of progress seems to have disintegrated as *future progress* into a quest for historical survival, for ways of avoiding historical extinction. Implicit here is a quite different vision of history's career.[61]

Such a shift of historical vision is, of course, deeply disturbing for a culture that was once so self-confident. But it is also (as I have noted above) a shift that produces an anxiety that can potentially present a dangerous threat to the rest of the world community. When a dominant people senses that they are losing power and influence, "they are tempted by the onset of new insecurities to defend their slipping power and dominance [and], to shore up the vassals that support them."[62] This is a situation where the possibilities of armed conflict are heightened, especially civil conflict within the vassal states between those who want to continue to support the declining culture and those who want a new socio-cultural and economic reality.

The second consequence of the loss of the cultural power of Enlightenment symbols is the reappearance of the 'religious' within Western culture itself. Gilkey acknowledges that this reappearance is not something that he anticipated when he wrote *Naming the Whirlwind* in 1969. What is surprising and culturally significant in this phenomenon is that what we are witnessing is *not* a resurgence of the mainline, liberal and 'modern' religion which was self-consciously designed to be intelligible to and appropriate for a secular world. Rather, we are witnessing a reappearance of religions and religious expressions that are decidedly antithetical to a secular world, from right-wing fundamentalism, to the occult, to the esoteric and mystical religions of the East. Such a reappearance is certainly the last thing that Enlightenment culture, with its predictions of the ultimate eradication of religion, could have anticipated.[63]

This reappearance of religion is understandable if one appreciates the constitutive role of the religious dimension in human life, and of the religious substance of culture. When a culture is in decline, the very ground and basis of human life and culture begins to shake and disintegrate, and a new openness to the religious appears.

For when assumed values and certainties are radically questioned, when social structures are shaken, when customary styles of life seem more treacherous and destructive than beneficial and creative — *then* the need for some other base for existence is urgent indeed. And eyes and ears are opened for a religious message, a religious technique or program, and a religious promise unneeded, unwanted, and thus previously unheeded.[64]

Again it is ironic that it is precisely out of the ambiguities and anxieties of an advanced scientific culture that the need for religion has arisen.

The demise of Western influence, the radical questioning of the religious substance of modernity, and the reappearance of the religious (especially in the form of non-Western religions) all contribute to the fourth cultural shift that Gilkey addresses.

5. The Parity of Religions
In our discussion of the religious substance of modernity we saw that relativity was one of the hallmarks of the post-Enlightenment worldview. That relativity undermined and relativized the absolutist claims of Christianity. It did not, however, totally undermine the belief in the superiority of the Christian religion in relation to other religions. In fact, liberal theologians such as Schleiermacher, Troeltsch, Ritschl and Harnack all assumed Christian superiority, though not on the basis of dogmatic and exclusivist soteriological claims. Gilkey notes that "liberal Christianity interpreted itself in Enlightenment categories and viewed itself as the 'culmination' of religions largely because the culture of which it was the religious expression was clearly the culmination of civilization."[65]

It is one of the curious contradictions of modernity that while Western consciousness has introduced relativity to the rest of the world, there is one important element of this consciousness that "has consistently escaped this relativizing process, namely the Western consciousness itself." Indeed, "this consciousness has been taken ... to be universal, a consciousness that can, and ultimately will, include and transform the plurality of viewpoints of the world's other cultures and transmute them into itself."[66] As long as this consciousness seemed credible, Christianity could, if sufficiently reinterpreted and accommodated to modernity, maintain its sense of superiority. But this consciousness is no longer credible. Gilkey argues that in the light of the decline of modernity, all "claims of the Western scientific and humanistic consciousness to represent the apogee of human and cultural consciousness seem as bizarre as do the earlier claims of the universality of Christianity." We are now aware of an "imminent deconstruction of the centrality, universality and permanence of the Western consciousness and so of the universal validity of its varied forms...."[67]

While the place of Christianity among world religions may at first seem to be primarily an issue of theology or comparative religion, Gilkey discerns in this problem a matter of broad cultural significance. In this new cultural situation we must acknowledge, he argues, *both* the relativity of Western consciousness as representing only one limited, finite and partial perspective on the whole of life, *and* that other religious consciousnesses embody genuine alternatives to our consciousness which clearly manifest a truth, grace and spiritual power that is not found in either the Western consciousness or Christianity. For Gilkey, the demise of the superiority of the Western worldview and the unavoidable acceptance of the essential equality or 'parity' of the religions are parallel phenomena.[68] Other religions and cultures represent "genuine alternatives to Western metaphysics and Western ethics as much as they represent alternatives to Western theological doctrines."[69] In a context where there is no universal standpoint, each particular standpoint must reinterpret itself in the light of pluralism. For a culture that has enjoyed political, economic and cultural dominance in the world, this is a situation that necessarily entails the end of that epoch of superiority and domination and ushers in a new, and often frightening, cultural reality.

A theology of culture requires both a discerning of the times and a creative response. In this section we have seen that Gilkey's theological and historico-cultural discernment leads him to conclude that modernity is in decline. We are coming to the end of a historical epoch. Such an 'ending' brings with it dangers and temptations as well as new opportunities. How Gilkey's theology of culture attempts to respond creatively to these dangers, temptations and opportunities is the topic of the next chapter.

NOTES

1 *Reconstruction in Philosophy*, p. 85.

2 "Secularization," p. 38.

3 Ibid

4 *Reaping,* p. 263.

5 *Nature, History, and Existentialism,* p. 159.

6 Cf. Tillich, *Systematic Theology,* II, pp. 51-62.

7 *Nature and Destiny of Man,* II, p. 166. Cf. pp. 206, 240.

8 *Reflections on the End of an Era,* p. 16.

9 *Shantung Compound,* pp. 75, 105.

10 Cf. "The Christian Response to the World Crisis."

11 *Society and the Sacred,* pp. xi, 3. Such 'feelings,' of course, cannot be totally verified by means of any social scientific method. Gilkey would agree with Robert Heilbroner when Heilbroner openly acknowledges that much of his socio-cultural analysis "must rest on generalizations for which there exist no objective data at all" (*An Inquiry into the Human Prospect* (New York: W. W. Norton and Co., 1974), p. 24). The data for such an analysis is not 'hard' and quantifiable. Indeed, Gilkey (and, I suspect, Heilbroner) would present his historical analysis to us in similar terms to how he presents his prolegomenon, viz., on the model of 'disclosure,' as a proposal for 'intuitive recognition.' Cf. chapter one, 3 (c) above.

12 Cf. Arnold Toynbee, *A Study of History* (London: Oxford University Press),I (1934), p. 53; and IV (1939), pp. 1-5.

13 "Theology of Culture and Christian Ethics," p. 351. Cf. "Secularization," p. 41; "The New Global Context for Missions," p. 11; "Theology for a Time of Troubles," pp. 167f; and "Theological Frontiers: Implications for Bioethics," in *Theology and Bioethics,* ed. by E. E. Phelp (Dordrecht, The Netherlands: D. Reidel Publishing, 1985), pp. 118f.

14 Ibid, p. 352. Cf. "Culture and Religious Belief," p. 6: "The absolutes of one powerful age ... can appear oppressive and empty relics to another subsequent age."

15 *Society and the Sacred,* pp. 4-5. Similar to Gilkey's analysis of a 'time of troubles,' Heilbroner describes the present cultural mood as a "civilizational malaise," in which "the values of an industrial civilization, which has for two centuries given us not only material advance but also a sense of *élan* and purpose, now seem to be losing their self-evident justification" (*An Inquiry into the Human Prospect,* p. 21). I have offered a similar analysis in *The Transforming Vision,* ch. 9; *Who Turned Out the Lights?;* and *Subversive Christianity.*

16 "Robert Heilbroner's Vision of History," *Zygon* 10, 3 (September 1975), p. 218.

17 *Reaping,* p. 18. Cf. "Secularization," p. 24. Olthuis describes this state of affairs in terms of "a gap between vision and reality." Such a gap, if too great, creates a worldview crisis, and "if the crisis involves the dominant visions of society — as is the reality today — the whole society is prone to massive breakdown" ("On Worldviews," p. 161).

121

18   Cf. "Secularization," p. 41; *Society and the Sacred*, p. 24; and "Religion and the American Future," pp. 5-6.

19   "Theology for a Time of Troubles," p. 478. Cf. "The Role of the Theologian in Contemporary Society," p. 348; "Religion and the American Future," pp. 6-7; and *Society and the Sacred*, p. 95.
    Jeremy Rifkin has also noted the rise of this kind of cultural *Angst* and relates it to the breakdown of the worldview of modernity: "When a particular world view begins to break down, when it can no longer adequately answer the basic questions to the satisfaction of its adherents, faith is broken, uncertainty and confusion set in, and the individual and the masses are cast adrift — exposed, unprotected and above all frightened" (*The Emerging Order: God in the Age of Scarcity* (New York: G. P. Putnam's Sons, 1979), p. 212). Clifford Geertz describes this as "the gravest sort of anxiety" (*The Interpretation of Cultures*, p. 99).

20   Frank Feather, "Transition to Harmonic Globalism," in *Through the 80's: Thinking Globally, Acting Locally*, ed. by Frank Feather (Washington, D. C.: World Futures Society, 1980), p. 7.

21   Herman Kahn and John Phelps, "The Economic Future," in *Through the 80's*, p. 208.

22   Ruben Nelson, "The Exhaustion of Liberalism," Ibid, p. 27.

23   Daniel Bell, *The Cultural Contradictions of Capitalism* (2nd ed.; London: Heinman, 1979), p. 29. On the next page Bell goes on to ask, "What holds one to reality if one's secular system of meanings proves to be an illusion? I will risk an unfashionable answer — the return in Western society to some form of religion" (p. 30).

24   *Religion*, p. 80.

25   *Society and the Sacred*, p. 79. Needless to say, when Gilkey presented this analogy of medieval theology and modern science before an audience of Nobel Laureates in science, the response was overwhelmingly negative. Cf. the response and discussion to Gilkey's paper, "Future of Science," in *The Future of Science*, ed. by T. C. L. Robinson (New York: John Wiley and Sons, 1977).

26   Ibid, pp. 79-80.

27   "Theology and the Future," p. 257.

28   Quoted by Gilkey in *Religion*, p. 170, n.26; from Victor Ferkiss, *Technological Man: The Myth and the Reality* (New York: George Braziler, 1969), p. 245. Later Ferkiss says, "Technological man, by definition will be possessed by the world view of science and technology, which will themselves provide a standard of value for future civilization" (p. 247.)
    Insightful critique of this technicism can be found in Egbert Schuurman, *Reflections on the Technological Society* trans. by H. Van Dyke and L. Teneyenhuis (Toronto: Wedge, 1977); Jacques Ellul, *The Technological Society*, trans. by J. Wilkinson (New York: Knopf, 1964); and George Grant, *Technology and Empire: Perspectives on North America* (Toronto: Anansi, 1969).

29 *Society and the Sacred*, p. 80. Cf. *Religion*, pp. 81-85; and "Evolutionary Science and the Dilemma of Freedom and Determinism," *Christian Century* 84, 11 (March 15, 1967), pp. 340-341.

Herman Dooyeweerd has a similar observation. Writing on what he alternately describes as the tension between the "personality ideal" and the "science ideal," or the "freedom/nature dialectic" inherent in the modern "ground motive" he says: "When it became apparent that science *determined* all of reality as a flawless chain of cause and effect, it was clear that nothing in reality offered a place for human *freedom*. Human willing, thinking, and acting required the same mechanical explanation as did the motions of a machine. For if man himself belongs to *nature*, then he cannot possibly be *free* and *autonomous*. Nature and freedom, science ideal and personality ideal — they became enemies" (*Roots of Western Culture*, p. 153). See also his, *The Secularization of Science*, trans. by R. Knudsen (Memphis: Christian Studies Center, 1954), pp. 18-20.

30 Cf. Tillich, *Systematic Theology*, I, pp. 72-74, 97; and *Dynamics of Faith* (New York: Harper and Row, 1957), pp. 80-83. Cf. also, "Tillich: Master of Mediation," p. 38.

31 "Secularization," pp. 28-29. Cf. *Society and the Sacred*, p. 6. Lesslie Newbigin also gives eloquent expression to the same argument in *Foolishness to the Greeks: The Gospel and Western Culture* (Grand Rapids, Mich.: Eerdmans, 1986), ch. 5.

32 *Religion*, pp. 90, 92. Cf. *Reaping*, pp. 259-260.

33 Cf. "Biblical Symbols in a Scientific Culture," pp. 85-90; *Creationism*, p. 201; "Evolutionary Science and the Dilemma of Freedom and Determinism," pp. 342-343; and "Theology of Culture and Christian Ethics," p. 358. Commenting on this ambiguity, Gilkey has said, "It is the bondage of our will, not our ignorance or lack of power that threatens our historical existence as a race." *Society and the Sacred*, p. 84.

34 *Society and the Sacred*, p. 84.

35 Cf. "Religion and the American Future," p. 7; and "Theology and the Future," p. 254.

36 "Can Art Fill the Vacuum?," *Criterion* 20, 3 (Autumn 1981), p. 8.

37 *Society and the Sacred*, p. 97. Cf. *Reaping*, pp. 11-14.

38 Cf. Reinhold Niebuhr, *The Irony of American History* (London: Nisbet and Co., 1952). Niebuhr says that irony "consists of apparently fortuitous incongruities in life which are discovered, upon closer examination, to be not merely fortuitous" (p. x). The irony of American history is that it is precisely the original pretensions of liberal virtue, wisdom and power that are the nation's nemesis. Gilkey's critique of modernity follows the same line of argument.

39 *Society and the Sacred*, p. 98. An extreme example of this dehumanizing loss of freedom in a technological society is the possibility of genetic manipulation in socio-biology, and the advocation of its widespread use by cultural evolutionists. In *Catholicism* Gilkey said: "Understood merely as an objective mechanism, men can appropriately be controlled and refashioned, as is nature in traditional technology,

according to the will of the technologist, and ultimately, therefore, according to the will of the latter's political bosses" (p. 139). For Gilkey's critique of cultural evolution, cf. *Religion,* pp. 163-171; and *Reaping,* pp. 71-73, 351-353 (notes 5, 7, 10). For a similar critique of genetic engineering see Bob Goudzwaard, *Capitalism and Progress,* pp. 178-181.

40 *Religion,* pp. 93-94. Cf. "Biblical Symbols in a Scientific Culture," pp. 92-93. Commenting on the fatalism of the phrase, 'You can't stop progress!', Jeremy Rifkin describes the apparent powerlessness of modernity in terms of riding on a train that has gone out of control: "frozen and immobilized, unable to act" we place our destiny in the hands of forces which are beyond our reach or control. *The Emerging Order,* p. 94.

41 Robert Heilbroner makes a similar observation: "industrial production ... confronts men with machines that embody 'imperatives' if they are to be used at all, and these imperatives lead easily to the organization of work, of life, even of thought, in ways that accommodate men to machines rather than the much more difficult alternative" (*An Inquiry into the Human Prospect,* p. 78). This self-contradiction in the worldview of modernity is also noted by Bob Goudzwaard: "Such a culture seems at first to raise man to the position of a sovereign master of his own fate — one who calls forth these economic and technical processes and determines their direction. But in the final analysis such a culture quickly relegates this 'master' to the position of utter dependence on the powers of development which he himself has enthroned. He ends by being an object, an extension of his own creations" (*Capitalism and Progress,* p. 69). (See also chapter 15: "The Dialectic of Progress.")

42 Jonathan Schell, *The Fate of the Earth* (New York: Alfred Knopf, 1982).

43 "On Thinking About the Unthinkable," *The University of Chicago Magazine* 76, 1 (Fall 1983), p. 7.

44 Ibid.

45 Bell, *Cultural Contradictions of Capitalism,* p. xxix.

46 Ibid, pp. 237-238. Similarly, John Kenneth Galbraith has said that "a rising standard of living has the aspect of a faith in our culture" (*The New Industrial State* (Boston: Houghton Mifflin Co., 1967), p. 164).

47 *An Inquiry into the Human Prospect,* p. 83.

48 Ibid, p. 47.

49 "Robert Heilbroner's Morality Play," p. 52. Cf. "Religion and the Technological Future," p. 12; and "Robert Heilbroner's Vision of History," pp. 220-221. In "Theology of Culture and Christian Ethics" Gilkey makes a similar observation: "Without science, technology and industrial growth, we perish; but with them, it also seems we perish" (p. 353).

50 *Society and the Sacred,* p. 99. Cf. "Theology and the Future," p. 255; "Theology for a Time of Troubles," p. 477; "Religion and the American Future," pp. 9-10; and

"The AAR and the Anxiety of Nonbeing: An Analysis of Our Present Cultural Situation," pp. 9-10.

51 Cf. Tillich, *Systematic Theology*, I, pp. 51-55.

52 "The Role of the Theologian in Contemporary Theology," pp. 338-339. Cf. *Message and Existence*, p. 152.

53 *Reaping*, p. 31.

54 *Society and the Sacred*, p. 114.

55 Ibid, p. 99.

56 *An Inquiry into the Human Prospect*, p. 135. Similarly, Bell says that "Western society lacks both *civitas*, the spontaneous willingness to make sacrifices for some public good, and a political philosophy that justifies the normative rules of priorities and allocations in society" (*Cultural Contradictions of Capitalism*, p. 25).

57 *Society and the Sacred*, pp. 100-101.

58 Ibid, p. 6. While the rhetorical point that Gilkey is making here about the demise of Western influence is, I think, well taken, it does need to be corrected on two points. First, Gilkey says in the quoted passage that the Turks last challenged Vienna in 1456. In "Theology of Culture and Christian Ethics" (p. 356), Gilkey cites the date of 1520. I suspect that he really has the 1529 siege of Vienna in mind, though the Turks also besieged Vienna again in 1683. Second, the four powers that he refers to are the U.S.A., the U.S.S.R., Japan and China. While the U.S.S.R. is not a 'Western' power, the argument could be made (and is made by Gilkey himself) that the U.S.S.R. is a culture that has been formed, to a very large degree, by the Enlightenment. My purpose in raising these two historical corrections is only for the sake of accuracy. I do not think that either comment appreciably takes away from Gilkey's cultural observation.

59 *Reaping*, p. 25.

60 *Society and the Sacred*, p. 7.

61 Ibid, p. 11. Another dimension of the different vision of history's career that Gilkey does not comment on, but which reinforces his argument, is the shift of apocalyptic imagery in the American consciousness. When America was 'waxing,' the dominant apocalyptic vision was an optimistic 'post-millennialism.' The kingdom of God, or the New Israel, was now being established (in the late eighteenth century) in North America. That kind of post-millennialism no longer finds a sure foothold in the American cultural consciousness. In its place we see a more pessimistic 'pre-millennialism' receiving greater cultural acceptance. The kingdom of God is *not* being established in history. Rather, history is coming to a cataclysmic end (probably in a nuclear world war), and only after this disastrous end will Christ return (with his previously raptured saints!) to establish his millennial kingdom. Such a vision of history is, of course, appealing to a culture in decline. Its mentality is that if the kingdom cannot be established in American history, then it cannot be established in history at all. Cf. the present author's "End-times

125

Theology Offers No Hope," *Catalyst* 9, 7 (June/July 1986), p. 7.

62 "Theology and the Future," p. 254. An interesting qualification that Gilkey makes to his comments on the loss of the power of Enlightenment symbols is to note that such symbols still have revolutionary power for those who are seen as dissidents in their respective cultures, whether that be in the U.S.S.R, the U.S.A., Latin America, or even China. Cf. *Society and the Sacred,* p. 11. The historical events in China in the spring of 1989 (Tianamen Square) and in Eastern Europe during the winter of 1989/90 demonstrate the constructive power of those symbols in a way that Gilkey certainly did not anticipate when writing the essays that appear in *Naming.*

63 Cf. "Theology for a Time of Troubles," pp. 475-476; "The Role of the Theologian in Contemporary Society," p. 339; and "The AAR and the Anxiety of Nonbeing," pp. 10-12.

64 *Creationism,* pp. 201-202.

65 *Society and the Sacred,* p. 13.

66 "Events, Meanings and the Current Tasks of Theology," p. 726. Cf. "The New Global Context for Missions," p. 23.

67 Ibid, pp. 726-727.

68 Cf. "Theology of Culture and Christian Ethics," pp. 360-362; "The Role of the Theologian in Contemporary Society," p. 349; "Theology for a Time of Troubles," p. 479; and "The AAR and the Anxiety of Nonbeing," pp. 14-15.

69 "Theology of Culture and Christian Ethics," p. 362.

CHAPTER FOUR:
Gilkey's Cultural Proposals

1. The General Tenor of Gilkey's Cultural Proposals

We have seen in the preceding chapter that Gilkey's analysis of the decline of Western modernity leads him to conclude that this crisis is spiritual in nature. It is a crisis of confidence in the very Enlightenment worldview that has formed the religious substance of this culture. It is, therefore, not surprising that Gilkey's cultural proposals are, largely, directed at that religious substance and call for radical reform of that substance. But there is another dominant motif in his cultural perspective that is intimately intertwined with this call for religious reform, namely, an insistence upon freedom in history in contrast to any fatalistic understanding of our present cultural malaise. It is on this issue that Gilkey decisively parts company with the analysis of Robert Heilbroner. We can, therefore, adequately describe the 'tenor' of Gilkey's cultural proposals in terms of these two foci — the need for reform of the religious substance of modernity, coupled with the insistence that freedom in history remain an integral element of that reformed religious substance.

a) The Need for Religious Reform

Modernity is not in decline because its mythic structure is without power. Rather, it is in crisis because its unrealistically progressive worldview failed to see the ambiguous potential of that power. While most profound religions have understood the fundamental problems of human life and culture as coming from inside the self in its pride, disloyalty and greed, modernity is characterized by an externalization of evil.

> For most moderns, our ills have come not from inside ourselves but from threats from the outside: from our weakness and our ignorance, from our subjection to external forces beyond our present control, from our inability — in being ignorant of these forces and how they work — to control them.[1]

127

The problem with such an understanding, says Gilkey, is that it does not recognize the deep ambiguity of the human subject. By external-izing evil this myth self-confidently proclaimed that an increase in scientific knowledge and technological control would set us free from the evils that impose themselves on us from the outside. Gilkey notes, however, that "all an increment in knowledge can do is to increase the scope and power of [human] freedom, and thus to increase the ambiguity that opens out in his future use of these powers."[2]

Indeed, the career of modernity clearly demonstrates that the fundamental problem of human culture is not the lack of scientific knowledge, but the bondage of the will. The question is not so much whether we have intelligence and freedom, but how we *use* both. Paradoxically, "we seem to need rescue not so much from our ignorance and our weakness as from our own creative strength — not so that either our creativity or intelligence is lost, but so that their self-destructive power is gone."[3] What Gilkey's cultural analysis has dem-onstrated is that fundamentally religious issues are raised not so much *against* science and technology as *by* them. "The vast new powers of science do not, in the end, make religious commitment and faith irrelevant; they make them more necessary than ever."[4]

The essential thrust of Gilkey's cultural perspective, then, is a concern for a religious answer to the crisis of modernity. In rather harsh terms, he says that our overwhelming need is for "a credible myth that does not lie to us about ourselves and our future."[5] Modernity lied to us about ourselves by externalizing evil and it lied about our future by promising progress.

The need is for a new myth, or a new religious vision because what is at stake is not simply a matter of changing the modes of modern science and technology (though we shall see that that too is necessary) but a changing of the very humans who engage in science and technology. Gilkey argues that it is from religion alone that we can find the norms to "prevent manipulation of people and dehumanization of society." From religion alone "can come the vision or conception of the human that can creatively guide social policy." "And from religion alone can come a new understanding of the unity of nature, history and humankind," that can creatively respond to the ecological crisis.[6]

A change in the religious substance of modernity will, however, entail changes in our understanding of science and technology by virtue of the role that they have been given in modernity. The religious

128

'background' does not, however, simply replace or rule from the outside that which is in the socio-cultural foreground. Rather, the symbols of the background provide the ultimate principles that guide a culture's scientific and technological life from the spiritual centre of that culture. With reference to science, a shift in the religious substance should have, according to Gilkey, at least three immediate consequences. The first is that the idolatry of scientism must be abandoned. Science is not the absolute source of omnipotent knowledge. Rather, "as a human and cultural activity, science is *relative* to its historical context, expressing through its own spiritual categories many of the economic, political, social, psychological, philosophical, and even religious presuppositions that have determined that environment...."[7] Secondly, the reductionism inherent in this scientism must also be abandoned. Rejecting the narrowness of an absolutized 'scientific method,' Gilkey calls for a more multidimensional approach to knowing that complements scientific knowing with other modes of knowing such as the artistic, literary, speculative and religious.

> Science must, therefore, see itself as only one aspect—to be sure, a most important and valuable aspect — of human cognition and creativity, and thus one supplemented by and dependent upon other aspects, if it is to take its rightful and not dominating role in our cultural life.[8]

In terms of the division of the sciences common in Western universities there needs to be a greater rapprochement between the natural and social sciences and the humanities.[9]

The third required change in modernity's approach to science has already been noted above, namely, that we must acknowledge that scientific knowledge is an instrument of the human will "and thus subject to all the distortions of which that will is capable."[10] Science must, therefore, be recognized as ambiguous.

Rejecting scientism, advocating multidimensionality and accepting the ambiguity of modernity's most cherished institution all require a new religious vision. But which religious vision should replace the declining religious substance of modernity? Which kind of faith is the most creative? What criteria are applicable to choosing from among the plethora of religious options available? Gilkey suggests three requirements that must be met by a faith that can be creative in our present cultural crisis. The first is the requirement or criterion of breadth. A creative faith in a scientific age "must be able to comprehend, shape and deal with *all* of those basic religious issues and their corresponding religious dilemmas which a scientific culture produces...." [11] It must provide creative answers to social questions of power and justice, to the metaphysical questions of the meaning of history and nature, and the existential questions of estrangement and mortality. The greater the breadth of the religious vision the more adequate it is.

The second requirement is taken from Tillich's distinction between autonomy, theonomy and heteronomy. Gilkey says that "a creative faith must undergird and not constrict, repress or oppress our autonomous intellect, our autonomous decisions, our own artistic creativity and our legal/political structures and actions: it must be *theonomous* and not *heteronomous*." [12] Following Tillich, Gilkey rejects a purely autonomous culture because it cuts itself off from its divine ground, is unaware of its religious substance and therefore loses touch with what Tillich called the 'Catholic substance.' A heteronomous culture, however, allows its religious substance to become absolute and therefore has no ability for self-critique—it has lost the 'Protestant principle.' The goal is to strive for a theonomous culture which is "at once autonomously creative and yet dependent upon, and so affirmative of, its unconditional ground, its religious substance." [13] Only a theonomous religious vision will be a creative one.

The third criterion goes significantly beyond the first two and raises an issue that is characteristically religious, though not raised in our earlier discussion of the role of a religious substance in culture. A creative faith must not only have breadth and be theonomous, and it must not only tell us the truth about our own ambiguity and evil, but also be able to address that ambiguity redemptively. A creative faith must be able to criticize even our highest cultural achievements, recognizing their demonic potentialities; moreover, "it must offer a grace that can transmute these demonic potentialities into actions genuinely creative of higher community." [14] A credible myth that will tell us the truth about ourselves can be creative only if it can also lead us beyond the truth of our estrangement to reconciliation. We need a myth that includes forgiveness.

> In every epoch of our history, then, we need to discover not only moral standards by which we may judge ourselves and the social world we live in, but also forgiveness somewhere for what we and our world

> are, an assurance of the ability to accept ourselves and our world, even
> in the ambiguity that we know to characterize them when we are aware
> of the truth. For only thus are we enabled to go on with our worldly work
> for a better and juster world than we now have.[15]

One of the implications of this third requirement is that a creative
religion must not only foster the theonomous transformation of
social institutions (though this is essential), it must also redeem the
human freedom that continually creates such oppressive institutions.
Gilkey draws on the distinction between sin or estrangement which is
warped human freedom, and the political and economic consequences of that sin in society. As fallen freedom is sin, the historical
consequence of that sin is the transformation of historical freedom
(or destiny) into fate. "Social transformation deals with the consequences of estrangement and alienation, not with its deeper causes."[16]
A creative religion must be able to deal with the problem of sin as well
as with fate.

The question of sin and fate leads us to the second dominant
motif in Gilkey's cultural proposal, namely, the importance of freedom in history.

b) Freedom in History: Gilkey versus Heilbroner
While modernity's religious substance is suffused with a concern for
human autonomy, it is, nevertheless, a mythic structure that cannot
comprehend the mystery of human freedom. We have seen in
chapter three that modernity's preoccupation with autonomy has in
fact turned in on itself and become fate. And in our discussions of
human ambiguity we have seen that the externalization of evil has
blinded modernity to the truth that an increase in human freedom
does not necessarily entail a freedom *from* evil — it could just as easily
be an increased freedom *for* evil.[17]

The inability of modernity to comprehend the mystery of freedom in both its creative and ambiguous dimensions is one of the
constitutive reasons for modernity's present decline. Perhaps one of
the most burning questions in this cultural context is what happens
to freedom when the age of autonomy comes to an end. We have seen
that Robert Heilbroner predicts that there will be less, not more,
freedom in Western culture as authoritarian regimes take more and
more control of the life of a civilization in crisis. The kind of voluntary
submission to authority which will, in the near future, be necessary in

131

order to reduce standards of living, control pollution and population, and redistribute resources seems to be inconceivable as a possible political action. Heilbroner believes that the future will be brought in by external force because a radically self-limiting social contract is simply a historical impossibility. Commenting on Heilbroner's *An Inquiry into the Human Prospect,* Gilkey says that "the dream that free will can create its own kind of future through its creative powers has entirely faded."[18] Indeed Heilbroner envisions a static, rigidly controlled heteronomous society which will shun the new, innovative and unorthodox.[19] He insists, however, that his is not a 'doomsday' futurism. "The human prospect is not an irrevocable death sentence." Rather, he offers a "contingent life sentence — one that will permit the continuation of human society, but only on a basis very different from that of the present...."[20] Consequently, our freedom in history is drastically limited. Survival requires a control of technology and pollution, reduced economic growth, and forced redistribution of resources; and all of these necessarily entail authoritarian governments, frugality of lifestyles and a more corporate (less individualistic) social existence. To these we are 'fated.'

Gilkey largely agrees with Heilbroner's analysis but is uncomfortable with its fatalistic overtones. Heilbroner does not sufficiently acknowledge, says Gilkey, that freedom and contingency characterize history. While we do have to suffer the consequences of our past history, the future is still open. "No determined future is the truth," because "no 'force' or dynamic factor in history operates other than through human beings and through their common behavior — and thus contingency and freedom enter into each interstice of historical life."[21]

The contrast between the tenor of Gilkey's and Heilbroner's cultural perspectives is clearly seen in their different interpretations of the Prometheus myth. For Heilbroner, the Enlightenment is characterized by the Promethean spirit. It is this spirit of intellectual daring that has "enabled [modern man] to work miracles, above all to subjugate nature to his will, and to create societies designed to free man from his animal bondage." But the Prometheus myth is tragic, the hero's creativity ultimately leaves him in chains. Promethean man, says Heilbroner, can only regard the future with anger and dismay. "If after so much effort, so little is accomplished ... then let the drama proceed to its finale, let mankind suffer the end it deserves." Such an attitude condemns future generations to nonexistence by refusing present sacrifice for their sake. Therefore the Promethean myth of conquest and aspiration is no longer appropriate for us. Instead, Heilbroner points us to Atlas, "bearing with endless perseverance the weight of the heavens in his hands." "It is the example of Atlas, resolutely bearing his burden, that provides the strength we seek."[22] In the image of Atlas we can find the grim determination and fortitude to preserve humanity.

Gilkey disagrees with Heilbroner for two reasons. In the first instance Heilbroner understands myths to be merely moral ideals or imaginative projections. They are judged simply in terms of their utility as inspirational and exemplary stories. Gilkey counters, however, that religious myth is not primarily a matter of utility, but of truth. In the traditional understanding, the purpose of myth "was not primarily moral inspiration — though that was part of its role — but truth about the nature of things and so about the human role in the cosmic order and in history."[23] Myths communicate, in a non-theoretical way, ontological and anthropological perspectives that are taken to be true by those who believe the myth.

Heilbroner's view of myth allows him simply to reject the Promethean myth as no longer exemplary in our present cultural context and to look to Atlas for his inspiration. Gilkey not only thinks that Heilbroner's interpretation of the Prometheus myth is too facile, but in *Reaping the Whirlwind* suggests that Heilbroner's own analysis of the malaise of modernity implicitly suggests another interpretation. This is his second, and more important, disagreement with Heilbroner. In the Promethean myth the "titanic creativity of mankind ... has, by the logic of its own expansive dynamic in relation to the implacable character of the finite cosmos, inexorably resulted in condemning men and women to future chains." This 'fate' is no arbitrary punishment. Zeus is neither our own neurotic subjectivity, nor the restrictive presence of the church in Western history. Rather, "Zeus is now an objective symbol referent to the way external reality has revealed itself to be in relation to us." Therefore, Prometheus's punishment is not the result of a threatened tyrant's whim, "but the inevitable consequence of his transgression of grim, objective limits."[24] By showing us how human creativity can in fact result in the fatedness of history, the Prometheus myth reveals to us the ambiguity of our own creativity.

Moreover, the problem is not primarily our creativity itself, but the transgression of objective limits by that creativity in its ambiguity.

In another place Gilkey explains that it is "the pride, the greed, and the lust for gain and security which accompany that creativity in historical life that lead to the enchainment on the rocks, the descent into the cave of bare survival and authority." He continues:

> Our creativity has not in itself caused our dilemma; it is, rather, our insatiable gluttony in our use of the earth, our unwillingness to share, our resistance to equitable distribution, our frantic use of power to grasp and to maintain security that will in the end destroy us if we are destroyed.[25]

This vision of our future also vindicates the Christian tendency to see in Prometheus the figures of Lucifer and Adam — "he who in being creative and daring *also* grasped power, rule and reward to himself and his own, and *thus* destroys himself."[26]

The issue then is a 'taint' in our creativity. We are not fated to a doomed future precisely because the calamities of the present and future are, in fact, calamities of our own making. Consequently, there is no fate because "contingency is the name of history."[27] The openness of the future means that there continue to be opportunities for creativity as well as opportunities for sin. "A new constellation of all the significant factors in historical process is always possible." Moreover, as a Christian, Gilkey believes that within every tragic situation of captivity, a new covenant in history is always possible. The providence of God continues to promise new possibilities in history, and "such faith in a nonfated future, in the continuity of open possibility and in the divine completion of our every abortive creation, is now more necessary than ever."[28]

We can sum up our discussion of the tenor of Gilkey's cultural perspective by saying that he calls for a radical transformation of the religious substance of modernity. Further, that transformation must be neither heteronomous nor autonomous, but must rather be theonomous, insisting on human freedom in history, even in these times that seem so fated.

While this is the 'tenor' of Gilkey's cultural proposal, it is fair to say that, as a theologian, Gilkey seldom goes beyond this broad cultural perspective to detailed proposals concerning specific areas of cultural life. There are, however, two issues that he has addressed in some detail; they are the question of religious pluralism and the issue of creationism in the context of the rise of the religious right wing in

America. These two sets of problems raise the questions of relativism and absolutism respectively. To these we now turn.

2. Christianity and World Religions: The Problem of Relativism

We have seen above that Gilkey cites the increasing sense of a parity of all religions as evidence pointing to the decline of Western modernity. Indeed, he says that this parity poses the most interesting set of problems facing theologians today. It is a veritable uncharted sea.[29] It is no longer possible, says Gilkey to deny that all viewpoints that make universal claims, including the worldviews of both modernity and Christianity, are in fact relative, each representing only one limited and finite perspective. This is now a foundational assumption. Moreover, pluralism is no longer merely a matter of cultural tolerance — it has profound epistemological, cosmological and even soteriological implications. If no one religion represents universal truth, then each particular viewpoint must reinterpret itself in the light of pluralism.

Such an acknowledgement of relativity raises serious problems both for theological reflection and for the very manner in which religious dialogue in the context of pluralism will take place. In the first instance, once we grant that there are no absolute, universal and unchanging statements about faith (or, for that matter, morals) because all such statements are relative to their cultural and historical context, then we are forced to ask about what relation there might be between our partial and relative theological formulations and ethical principles to the divine truth and divine norms.[30]

The second question is more relevant to Gilkey's theology of culture, however. Simply stated, the question is: what happens when one acknowledges the truth, beauty and even grace of other religions, and the relativity of one's own faith? This is not a question limited only to proponents of particular 'official' religions, but is relevant to anyone who has recognized the limitedness and partiality of the Western view of life. To put the question differently: can one, without contradiction, affirm both the truth of one's own tradition and the equal truth of another? Some answer to this question is necessary if we are creatively to face the perils of the future by embracing and learning from other traditions.

Gilkey's answer to this question is not, however, totally clear. In one place he says that the truth of other religions *can* be affirmed without contradiction, yet earlier in the same book he says that such a dual

135

affirmation requires an attitude that is personally creative, though theoretically contradictory.[31] It would seem that the best way to interpret Gilkey would be to say that such a dual affirmation is not a contradiction but is better described by another word that he often employs in this respect, viz., paradox. It is paradoxical, though not contradictory, to fully affirm the truth of two (seemingly opposed and clearly divergent) religious perspectives.[32]

One is forced into a paradoxical position because an acknowledgment of the relativity of one's own position must not become a total relativity: "standing nowhere, affirming nothing to be real or of worth, embracing no ultimate principle of criticism, renewal or hope."[33] Relativity need not imply relativism. Even the typically pantheist answer that there are many ways to speak truly yet relatively of the Ultimate and participate in salvation, inevitably assumes "an unmovable standpoint or core of interpretation ... that is not relative and that becomes the hermeneutical principle for assessing the relative truth and efficacy of other faiths."[34] There is a need, therefore, to have both a relation "to some stable and assumed ... absolute standpoint..."and "a deep apprehension and recognition of the relativity of our standpoint." This entails, continues Gilkey, "a dialectic or paradox combining one part of absoluteness and two parts relativity, a *relative absoluteness*...."[35] In another place he says that "in a Time of Troubles it is precisely this mixture of the relative and the absolute, of criticism and affirmation, of humility and courage that we are called to embody."[36] In a pluralist context it is essential that one takes a stand somewhere, committed yet humble, certain and sure yet open. Without such committed stances true dialogue between contrasting positions and the possibility of authentic and mutual learning and growth between partners in the dialogue is impossible. We must embody relatively our unconditional affirmations, a relative absoluteness.

In such a context religious exclusivism, with its religious imperialism, can have, according to Gilkey, no place. Rather, he advocates the model of 'covenant' as appropriate for our present context. Reminiscent of the patristic notion of a 'covenant with the Greeks' prior to Christian revelation that legitimated a synthesis of Christian revelation with Hellenistic culture, Gilkey says that in our age similar covenants with both modernity and other religions are creative and inevitable. Christianity has always found it necessary to establish some form of a 'covenant' with the culture in which it seeks to live. Gilkey says that since this model has been creative in both the Hellenistic formulations of the faith and in the modern era, it could now creatively be applied to the relation of Christianity to other religions. He explains:

> As the situation of modernity has uncovered for us elements of the gospel unseen before, so the situation created by Buddhist, Hindu, or Islamic religion and culture — the questions they ask, the emphases they make, the answers they find — may uncover elements of the final truth — of Christ, if you will — unseen before through the spectacles of our limited tradition.[37]

This proposal of a covenant with other religious traditions is itself founded on Gilkey's understanding of the religious substance of a culture. In *Society and the Sacred* Gilkey advances two interrelated arguments concerning the divine ground of all religions. The first is taken from the Old Testament view of three stages of historical passage, viz., divine constitution, alienation and judgment, and prophetic promise of renewal. Of relevance to our present discussion is the first stage. Noting that Israel's culture was "one explicitly with a 'religious substance,' one founded directly by God and one preserved and ruled by the divine actions in history," Gilkey says that "it is not inappropriate, therefore, to regard as 'biblical' the viewpoint that each creative culture, insofar as it lives on a religious substance, is established in and through the presence of the divine, apprehended or received, to be sure, in different ways than this, but nonetheless grounded here."[38] If this is the case then a 'covenant' model, as described above, would also be appropriate.

There are, however, a number of problems with Gilkey's argument. In the first instance it is somewhat spurious to argue *from* an ancient Hebrew understanding *to* a position that would clearly be rejected within that understanding. While there may be some evidence that Israel 'borrowed' elements from the religious perspectives of neighboring nations, the overwhelming perspective of the Hebrew scriptures is that the gods of foreign nations are idols and, therefore, are to be rejected. Israel resolutely refused to grant the validity of other religious substances. And how could it be 'biblical' (at least in the Old Testament sense) to counsel 'covenants' with other religions when this was clearly prohibited in the Hebrew worldview, especially in the first two commandments of the Decalogue and in the prophetic literature?[39]

Another problem is that Gilkey says that "a *creative* culture, *insofar* as it lives on a religious substance, is established in and through the presence of the divine...." This is confusing. Gilkey seems to be saying that a *creative* culture is one which lives on a religious substance, and it is *this* kind of culture (not others?) that is established in and through divine presence. But Gilkey has already established that *all* cultures live on a religious substance, even those that he deems uncreative (i.e., modernity). What, then, are the criteria by which he judges a culture to be creative? Are non-creative cultures also established through divine presence? At certain times Israel was certainly non-creative, and it is interesting to note that in her own self-understanding these 'demonic' times are *always* attributed to making false covenants with the gods of other nations. I will return to these problems in my evaluative conclusions below.

Gilkey's second argument concerning the universal presence of the divine in all 'creative' cultures goes further than the first. He begins by saying that the notion of general revelation which claims that God is active and present in all creation and history is implied by almost all Christian symbols. This general revelation accounts for the religious substance of all cultures. Therefore, each culture is a response to the presence of God, and truth can be recognized in all cultures. But alienation and estrangement are also universally present in all cultures. Does this have implications for our understanding and evaluation of the salvific nature of other cultures and their religions? Gilkey thinks it does.

> Now, it appears to me unquestionable that not only is the creative and providential activity of God present and manifested throughout nature and history, but also the *redemptive* work of God that culminates (for us) in the Christ is universally present, as alienation and sin are universally present.[40]

If God is redemptively active throughout the religious traditions, then the truth of these traditions can be affirmed without contradiction.

The implication of this argument for Christian theological reflection is, of course, immediately evident: the traditional and eschatological 'dual' destiny of our race into the damned and the saved was a theological mistake.[41] Not only do all religions approximate a truth that lies beyond them, they also all reflect what Tillich called the New Being, and are, therefore, salvific.[42] Soteriological universalism is the necessary consequence of this line of reasoning.

This argument also has some problems. Gilkey's argument could be summarized in terms of a series of propositions and conclusions drawn from those propositions. He seems to be saying that (a) the Christian affirmation of general revelation and (b) the manifestation of a religious substance in every culture lead to the conclusions that (c) each culture is a response to God and (d) truth can be recognized in all cultures. While (c) and (d) do seem to follow from (a) and (b), they may need some modification. That each culture is a response to the presence of God (c) does not necessarily mean that each culture is a positive or appropriate response to God. Does Gilkey's analysis sufficiently account for the ambiguity or estrangement of human culture from its divine source? Given Gilkey's own Niebuhrian emphasis on ambiguity, it should, but I will suggest in the evaluative conclusions to this section of the book that perhaps it does not.

Ambiguity does, however, come into his argument. Recall that he also argued that since (e) sin and estrangement are universal, one must conclude that (f) the redemptive presence of God is also universally present and thus (g) both the truth and redemptive power of other religions can be affirmed. The problem here is that while (e) seems to be empirically justified, (f) and (g) do not logically follow either (e) or the series of (a) through (d). At best one could say that half of (g) (viz., that the truth of other religions can be affirmed) follows from the series of (a) through (d). But the key conclusion for Gilkey is the universalism of conclusion (f). If this conclusion does not follow in the logic of his argument, but rather stands as an unargued affirmation, then what basis does it really have?

There are at least two places where Gilkey presents grounds for universalism. The first comes later in the article in which the argument under discussion is found. Here he offers four grounds for universalism in contrast with the traditional view which would deny salvation to those 'outside' of Christ. The first is Christological. Christ is seen to "*manifest* rather than to *effect*, cause, or even to 'free' the loving and saving will of God." Reminiscent of the Anselm/Abelard debate, Gilkey says that since Christ is the *manifestation* of the will of God, it is still possible that that will is *effected* elsewhere in God's free grace. Secondly, what is manifest is *agape*, "a redemptive love whose essence ... is that it recognizes no barriers to its coming...." Thirdly, recognizing that salvation is by grace, we must not restrict that grace to our own inadequate and relative tradition. Indeed, the symbol of the Last Judgment teaches us "that it is God and not we who finally look into the hearts of each and determine the mode of our relationship to God and to one another, and so the final extent of salvation...." And finally, the divine victory "is a *redemptive* rather than a *retributive* one."⁴³

While all of these grounds have some compelling force, they are not without their problems. Perhaps the most important ground is the first. In part four I will evaluate Gilkey's Christology more fully. The other arguments are weaker. While *agape* certainly recognizes no barriers in the sense that it is clearly open to all, it still seems that different responses to that *agape* can, themselves, create barriers. It is curious that even though the most famous *agape* passage in the New Testament (John 3:16) is followed by the statement, "For God did not send the Son into the world to judge the world" (3:17), the passage then goes on to say that he who does not believe in this manifestation of *agape* is judged, "because he has not believed in the name of the only begotten Son of God" (3:18). Indeed, this judgment is connected to another love, viz., the love of darkness over light (3:19). If John is the apostle of *agape*, then he certainly has no difficulty with an *agape* that includes judgment. Nor does the apocalyptic literature of the New Testament (or the Old) seem to set up a redemptive/retributive dichotomy as Gilkey does. Further, Gilkey is, of course, right when he says that it is God, not us, who will do the judging, but even in saying this he implicitly acknowledges that some form of eschatological judgment is in store. And Gilkey is also probably right when he says that the extent of salvation is wider than we can dream. But how wide? Can it include, based on the biblical testimony, all people? Can a universalism of this kind be faithful to the eidetic meaning of the primary and authoritative texts? This leads us to Gilkey's second defense of universalism.

In a passage in *Reaping the Whirlwind* in which Gilkey is discussing the important criterion of eidetic fidelity to the symbolic structure of the Christian tradition, he says that while such fidelity is crucial if what is distinctive in a religion is to be maintained, it is not crucial for creative relations to God or salvation. He explains that "creative relations to God, ourselves and salvation can, I think, be found through any form of religion, thanks to the universality of the divine presence and the promised width of grace."⁴⁴ But can one say this and maintain the very fidelity that Gilkey says is essential for any theological reflection that wants to call itself Christian? In a footnote, later in *Reaping the Whirlwind*, he tries to do just this. Acknowledging that there is "no question that the theme of a dual destiny for mankind has firm scriptural warrant," Gilkey then says that there "*are* passages that indicate a universalist motif in the New Testament...."[45] He lists five such passages: Rom. 5:15, 11:32; 1 Cor. 15: 27-29; Phil. 2: 9-11; John 10:16; and Eph. 1:10.

If any of these texts actually made the universalist point that Gilkey is here advocating, then emphasizing them overagainst other non-universalist sentiments in the biblical texts could well be justified.[46] The problem is that *none* of them can legitimately be used to make such a point. Romans 5:15 contrasts the one and the many. Through one many died, through one many will receive grace. The point of the text is not *how many* will receive grace, but of the centrality of the Christ as that one through whom grace is offered—the New Adam. Romans 11:32 says that "God has shut up all disobedience so that he might show mercy to all." But this statement comes at the end of a long discourse on the opening of the gospel beyond Israel and the implications that has for a Christian understanding of Israel (ch. 9-11). This issue is universalism only in the sense of the universal availability of mercy in Christ. By "all?" Paul means "Jew and Gentile alike."

The affirmations of all things being subject to Christ, summed up in Christ, and every knee bowing before Christ in 1 Corinthians 15:27-29, Ephesians 1:10 and Philippians 2:9-11 respectively, are all proclamations of the Lordship of the risen Christ over all creation, not statements of universal salvation. Indeed, all of these passages could more easily be used to justify a religious exclusivism because this Lordship entails sovereignty over all other gods as well.

The final passage cited attributes to Jesus the words, "And I have other sheep, which are not of this fold?" (John 10:16). To see in this a statement of universalism necessarily requires one to ignore the proclamation earlier in the same pericope that Jesus is the door (10:7, 9), an image that has more exclusivist overtones. The statement is better understood as a reference to the opening of the Kingdom beyond the Jews to include Gentiles as well. There is also a rather dubious selectivity in Gilkey's use of *this* passage concerning the image of Jesus and sheep when he cavalierly rejects another passage that probably has (at least in terms of contemporary biblical scholarship) a greater chance of authenticity. I am referring to the image of a dual destiny for sheep and goats recorded in Matthew 25: 31-46. With clear reference to this passage Gilkey says that there is "no ultimate division between persons who are sheep and persons who are goats...."[47] My argument has been that one cannot make such a statement, nor advocate a covenant with other religions with the universalism that is entailed therein, *and* meet Gilkey's own criterion of eidetic fidelity to what he himself acknowledges to be a theme with "firm scriptural warrant."

Gilkey is right in seeing the increased sense of a parity of religions as a threat to both the religious substance of modernity and to the traditional understandings of the Christian faith. He is also right in attempting to articulate a position which acknowledges relativity but avoids relativism. I am not sure that the covenant model and universalism adequately get him off of the horns of this dilemma, however. Perhaps the fundamental question remains the appropriate criteria for evaluating the relative strengths and weaknesses of various religious traditions. I will return to this question in my evaluative conclusions below.

The surprising appearance of non-Western religions and the concomitant problem of relativism is not the only phenomenon on the cultural landscape that has attracted Gilkey's attention, however. Another, and according to Gilkey, perhaps more dangerous phenomenon has been the recent resurgence of the religious right in America. This development raises a problem that is the polar opposite of relativism, viz., absolutism.

3. Creation Science and the Fundamentalist Right: The Problem of Absolutism

In a rather insightful passage in the first volume of his *Systematic Theology*, Paul Tillich distinguishes between the static and dynamic elements of reason. When the theonomous unity of these two elements is ignored they generate two opposing cultural attitudes, viz., absolutism and relativism. Tillich then goes on to distinguish between two different kinds of absolutisms and relativisms.

> The static element of reason appears in two forms of absolutism — the absolutism of tradition and the absolutism of revolution. The dynamic element of reason appears in two forms of relativism — positivistic relativism and cynical relativism.[48]

The absolutism of tradition is a conservatism which rejects any dynamic change in reason or in society at large. The absolutism of revolution is equally static, but rather than conserving static traditions of the past it heteronomously rules society on the basis of a vision of a static utopian society. Positivistic relativism insists that the best we can do is simply take what is 'given' reality without applying any absolute criteria to its valuation. Cynical relativism goes a step further than positivism because, noting the meaninglessness of a positivist acquiescence to the given, yet finding no absolute criteria for actually subjecting the given to any critical valuation, it takes "an attitude of superiority over, or indifference toward, any rational structure, whether static or dynamic. Cynical relativism uses reason only for the sake of denying reason—a self-contradiction which is 'cynically' accepted."[49]

While this discussion of various forms of absolutism and relativism is itself helpful, it is Tillich's understanding of their dynamic (and dialectical) interrelation that is most interesting in our present cultural context, and most relevant to our discussion of Gilkey's theology of culture. As we have seen from Gilkey's analysis, modernity is characterized by positivistic relativism. Tillich notes that "it is the tragedy of this positivism that it either transforms itself into a conservative absolutism or into the cynical type of relativism." And, writing in the late 1940's, he goes on to observe that "only in countries where the remnants of former absolutism are still powerful enough to delay such developments are the self-destructive implications of positivism hidden (England, the United States)."[50] Implicit in this observation is a prediction that the self-destructive implications of positivism will not remain hidden, in either the United States or Great Britain, forever. Recent cultural developments have proven Tillich right. With specific reference to American culture, the emergence of two extreme movements that are in polar tension with each other perfectly illustrates Tillich's point. I refer to the cynical relativism of deconstructionist philosophy, cultural analysis, literary theory and theology, and the conservative absolutism of fundamentalism and the 'New Right.'[51]

While Gilkey has not, as yet, published a critical response to deconstructionism, we have seen in the above discussion of religious pluralism that he has addressed the problem of relativism. But relativism can only be fully addressed if one also grapples with the problem of absolutism. The present mood in America also places absolutism on the agenda of Gilkey's theology.

Gilkey's discussion of relativism and absolutism, like almost everything he addresses, does not just display his Tillichian roots. There is also a decidedly Niebuhrian tone to his analysis. A 'time of troubles' is a time when new symbols are required to give direction to new social policies and new distributions of power. Such a loss of power, combined with "the loss of a symbolic world where one feels at home, identified and placed, and the appearance of a new symbolic world in which one is a stranger produces anxiety...."[52] In Niebuhrian terms it is precisely such anxiety which gives the temptation to sin: "to panic, to fanatical self-defense, to renewed aggression, to oppression of rival points of view...."[53] The temptation in a time of troubles is to become more firmly entrenched in one's position, rather than creatively seeking to change. Idolatry stalks the terrain that anxiety has inhabited. It is precisely such an idolatry, rooted in fanatical self-defense, that Gilkey sees in the recent emergence of the fundamentalist right wing movement of the United States.

Gilkey views fundamentalism as a reaction both to the uncertainties and doubts of modernity, and to the relativism that is entailed in those uncertainties. It offers its adherents the certainty of unchanging absolutes.[54] In the place of modern liberalism (in both the political-economic and theological senses of the term) fundamentalism projects a "Christian America," a *theocracy* where evangelical Christians will run the country according to 'scriptural principles.' If we follow Tillich we will see that the rise of this kind of absolutism was called forth dialectically to replace the former positivistic relativism. Relativism breeds absolutism. And just as Gilkey argued against Heilbroner's vision of a static and authoritarian future, so also is he horrified at the prospects of a heteronomous and absolutistic Christian America.

The question that the emergence of the New Right poses is: how does a relativistic culture combat this kind of absolutism? While it is not helpful to fight one heteronomy with another, heteronomy must, nevertheless, be fought. But, in order "to combat what one takes to be a virulent false truth, some approximation to and possession of a healthier truth ... is necessary as a basis for disengagement, for protest, and for dissident political action...." Idolatrous faith must be countered by an equally unswerving faith. Therefore, "a transcendent point of criticism, of judgment and certainty, of hope of renewal is necessary in political action and in political theorizing as well as in theological reflection on events, whenever idolatry in abroad in the land."[55] To oppose the possible heteronomy of the Religious Right, one needs a clear commitment to an alternative view of the meaning of human life, the nature of justice and the state, and the relation of individual and community. Creative praxis in response to an oppressive ideology requires some form of a centred vision.

The question, however, is, where does one find such a centre in our unyieldingly centreless (because relativistic) age which does not simply parrot the idolatrous absolutism that is threatening us? Convinced that centreless relativism is toothless before a demonic absolutism, Gilkey turns to John Dewey's notion of *intelligent practice* as a way through this impasse. Creative and liberating praxis requires a "wager?" which is enacted. Faced with an oppressive ideology, we must act, but that action requires a centre which one wagers will be healthier and more liberating for human culture. By wagering we take a "stan?" somewhere. That stand provides us with "a ground for the apprehension and understanding of reality," "criteria for judgments," and "priorities in value."[56] Such a stand, or wager, must, however, also relativize itself in order to remain healthy.

Hence, we return to the notion of a 'relative absolute' discussed in the preceding section. While such a notion is intellectually contradictory, it is, to praxis, a workable dialectic. "A dialectic or paradox combining and interweaving both one part of absoluteness and two parts relativity, *a relative absoluteness*, represents a posture essential to public and political praxis...."[57] Only by embodying relatively our unconditional affirmation can we avoid both relativism and absolutism.

While Gilkey proposes this dialectic as an appropriate and creative way to respond to the New Right as a cultural phenomenon, he has also applied it specifically to the issue of 'creation science.' Apart from his theological and scientific objections to 'creationism;' Gilkey also opposes creationism because it is a threat to the health of a free society. Legislation such as Act 590 in Arkansas which requires the teaching of 'creationism' to balance the teaching of evolution in public school biology classes imposes, says Gilkey, a religious view on students. While creationists should have the right to teach and preach their religious views in freedom, legislating the mandatory teaching of those views in schools violates that very principle of freedom.

> Freedom of religion in society, especially in any modern diversified culture, invariably means plurality of religious viewpoints and even of religions within society; and so it entails widely diverse opinions regarding all sorts of issues important to each set of religious beliefs.[58]

Moreover, such legislation would also be a disaster for academic freedom. By legislating curricular content, free inquiry is inhibited.[59]

Gilkey argues that creation science, like the fundamentalism of which it is a part, is a threat to society because it fails to acknowledge the relativity of its committed stance. It is a form of absolutism and, therefore, is a demonic, not creative cultural force. As the New Right is a reaction to the relativism and liberalism of modernity, creation science is a reaction to the scientism of modernity which has elevated the scientific method from being the rule for scientific inquiry to a metaphysical and religious understanding that claims to give a total explanation of reality. Both scientism and creationism inhibit real pluralism. Gilkey views scientism as science infringing upon religion, and creationism as religion infringing upon science. Religion and science are, however, distinct. Therefore, if there is to be a real pluralism in education, then it must be with reference to things that are genuinely alternatives to each other. The biblical view of creation is an alternative to other mythical understandings and should be taught in a comparative mythology course. Gradualism and punctuated equilibrium theories are genuine alternatives in biology. Creation is not an alternative in biology, says Gilkey, because it is a religious, not scientific, theory.[60]

Whether Gilkey's arguments concerning religion and science, and the specific issues surrounding creation science, are cogent, we will leave for a later discussion. What is important for our purposes here is to see that Gilkey's theology of culture is as opposed to absolutism in religion as it is to the loss of freedom and contingency in history. While religion should be a source of healing in culture, it can also be a destructive and demonic force in history when religious communities claim ultimacy to themselves.[61] This is the threat of both fundamentalism and its offshoot, creation science. Religions can avoid this danger if they claim only to *point* to the ultimate in their own particular and relative way. Absolutism must be combatted, then, by an affirmation of a relative absolute. Only in this way can one find a centre from which to criticize competing absolutisms and relativisms. Whether Gilkey's dialectic of absoluteness and relativity is a successful answer to the problem of absolutism and relativism will be discussed in the evaluative conclusions in the next chapter.

NOTES

1 *Society and the Sacred*, p. 92.

2 *Religion*, p. 99.

3 *Society and the Sacred*, p. 101.

4 *Religion*, p. 98. Cf. *Catholicism*, pp. 128-129: "Perhaps the deepest irony of our time is that precisely when modernity had eradicated (or sought to eradicate) the symbols of ultimacy, that is, religious symbols, it has found itself most desperately in need of them."

5 Ibid, p. 97. Cf. "Biblical Symbols in a Scientific Culture," p. 90.

6 *Society and the Sacred*, pp. 102-103.

7 Ibid, p. 85. Cf. *Creationism*, pp. 182-185.

8 Ibid, p. 86. Cf. *Creationism*, p. 179: "The confinement of knowledge and of rationality to the scientific and technological enterprises alone is the dark harbinger of historical chaos, not of increased social enlightenment."

9 Cf. "Religion and the Secular University," pp. 114- 115; and "Can Art Fill the Vacuum?," pp. 7-9.

10 *Society and the Sacred*, p. 87.

11 Ibid, p. 118.

12 Ibid, p. 119. Cf. Tillich, *Systematic Theology*, I, pp. 83-94; and *The Protestant Era*, ch. 3, 4 and 9.

13 "The New Being and Christology," p. 313. Cf. "Tillich: Master of Mediation," pp. 30-31.

14 *Society and the Sacred*, p. 119.

15 *Religion*, p. 97.

16 *Society and the Sacred*, p. 152.

17 Cf. "Modern Myth-Making," pp. 300-303.

18 "Heilbroner's Vision of History," p. 224. Cf. *Reaping*, p. 83.

19 *An Inquiry into the Human Prospect*, pp. 138-142. Heilbroner's future heteronomous society bears striking resemblances to his description of pre-capitalist medieval society in his *The Worldly Philosophers*, ch. 2.

20 Ibid, p. 138.

21 "Heilbroner's Vision of History," pp. 231-232. Cf. "Heilbroner's Morality Play," p. 54.

22 All of the quotes in this paragraph are from *An Inquiry into the Human Prospect*, pp. 142-144.

23 "Heilbroner's Vision of History," pp. 229. Cf. "Heilbroner's Morality Play," p. 54; and *Reaping*, p. 88.

24 *Reaping*, p. 88.

25 "Heilbroner's Vision of History," p. 231.

26 *Reaping*, p. 89.

27 Ibid.

28 Ibid, pp. 89-90.
29 Cf. "The New Global Context for Missions," p. 22; "Theology for a Time of Troubles," p. 479; and "A Theological Voyage with Wilfred Cantwell Smith," p. 298.

30 Cf. "The Spirit and the Discovery of Truth Through Dialogue," in *Experience of the Sacred*, ed. by P. Huizing and W. Bassett, vol. 99 of *Concilium* (N.Y.: Seabury Press, 1974), p. 60.

31 Cf. *Society and the Sacred*, pp. 164 and 14.

32 The distinction between paradox and contradiction has been common in contemporary theology since Tillich. Cf. his *Systematic Theology*, I, pp. 56-57.

33 "Theology of Culture and Christian Ethics," p. 363.

34 *Society and the Sacred*, p. 162. Gilkey goes on to say: "A particular standpoint on religious truth is maintained as the logical ground for the assertion of 'truth' in other faiths, as the criterion for the more or less of that truth, and as the basis for an understanding of the salvation all seek."

35 "Events, Meanings and the Current Tasks of Theology," pp. 729-730. Cf. pp. 723-724.

36 "Theology of Culture and Christian Ethics," p. 364. Cf. "The New Global Context for Missions," p. 23; "Theology for a Time of Troubles," p. 479; and *Catholicism*, pp. 21-22.

37 *Society and the Sacred*, p. 166. Cf. pp. 123, 139-142; *Message and Existence*, pp. 62-63; and "Toward a Religious Criterion of Religion," in *Understanding the New Religions*, ed. by J. Needleman and G. Baker (N.Y.: Seabury Press, 1978), pp. 136-137.

38 Ibid, p. 68. Cf. *Message and Existence*, p. 33.

39 Cf. Exodus 20: 2-6; Deut. 5: 6-10; 1 Kings 18: 20-38; Ps. 115; Jer. 10: 1-11; Is. 40: 18-26.

40 *Society and the Sacred*, p. 163.

41   Cf. Gilkey's "The Christian Understanding of Suffering," (unpub. paper presented at a Conference on Buddhist/Christian Dialogue, Honolulu, January, 1983), p. 32; *Message and Existence*, p. 254; and *Reaping*, p. 298.

42   Cf. "The Role of the Theologian in Contemporary Society," p. 349.

43   All of the references in this paragraph are from *Society and the Sacred*, pp. 168-170.

44   *Reaping*, p. 142.

45   Ibid, p. 429, n. 56.

46   An example of this kind of a procedure that I consider legitimate is the present retrieval of female images used with reference to God in Scripture. Such references may be few but they *are* there and should, in our present cultural context, be retrieved.

47   *Reaping*, p. 298.

48   Tillich, *Systematic Theology*, I, p. 86.

49   Ibid, p. 88.

50   Ibid.

51   Perhaps the parallel cultural contrast in Great Britain is between the 'punk rockers' and Margaret Thatcher.

52   "Religion and the Technological Future," p. 11.

53   "The New Global Context for Missions," p. 19. Cf. "Reinhold Niebuhr's Theology of History," p. 369; and Niebuhr, *Nature and Destiny of Man*, I, pp. 182-186.

54   Cf. *Creationism*, p. 170; and "Events, Meanings and the Current Tasks of Theology," p. 725.

55   "Events, Meanings and the Current Tasks of Theology," p. 722.

56   Ibid, pp. 728-729. The notion of a wager is, of course, borrowed from Paul Ricoeur. See his, *The Symbolism of Evil*, pp. 308, 355.

57   Ibid, p. 730.

58   *Creationism*, p. 11.

59   Cf. Ibid, p. 14. This is not, however, a very strong argument. *Any* public school system necessarily entails the determining of curricular content by the department or ministry of education, both in terms of the specific material for each course and the overall 'public' worldview assumed by the educators. While North American public education claims to be religiously neutral it is, in fact, an agent of the

American 'civil religion' and indoctrinates children in the ways of that religion. With reference to this dimension of American education see Jonathon Kozol, *The Night is Dark and I am Far From Home* (Boston: Houghton Mifflin Co., 1975); and Samuel Bowles and Herbert Gintis, *Schooling in Capitalist America* (New York: Basic Books, 1976). With reference to Canadian (specifically, Ontario) education, see Tom Malcolm and Harry Fernhout, *Education and the Public Purpose* (Toronto: Curriculum Development Centre, 1979).

60 Cf. Ibid, pp. 61-65, 124-125, 164-165; and "Theology of Culture and Christian Ethics," p. 348.

61 Cf. Ibid, pp. 202-204.

CHAPTER FIVE:
Evaluative Conclusions

No exposition of another person's thought is totally objective and neutral. It is not possible to present the thought of another without, in the very tone of the exposition, also offering some form of an evaluation of that thought. That I am critical of Gilkey's approach to the relation of Christianity and other religions is clearly evident in my exposition of his thought on this matter. Indeed, the tone of the exposition changed drastically when I embarked on this topic. The more positive tone of my exposition of Gilkey's theoretical foundations for his theology of culture, his description of modernity and its decline, and the general tenor of his cultural proposals, is indicative of my overall evaluation of his contribution.[1] In these evaluative conclusions I will begin by briefly highlighting some of the strengths of Gilkey's theology of culture as I perceive them, and then proceed to a discussion of some of its weaknesses.

1. The Strengths of Gilkey's Contribution
a) Homo Religiosus
Paul Tillich said that theology of culture recognizes "that in every cultural creation — a picture, a system, a law, a political movement (however secular it may appear) — an ultimate concern is expressed, and that it is possible to recognize the unconscious theological character of it."[2] Gilkey's theology of culture demonstrates the enduring value of this perspective. To understand cultural patterns, institutions and history simply in terms of sociological, economic, historical or political analyses does not sufficiently plumb the depths of those realities. An analysis of the religious substance of a culture goes beyond both the Lockean, liberal view which relegates religion to 'personal' beliefs that have no legitimate role in public life and the Marxian, materialist view which understands religion to be a part of a cultural superstructure that legitimates an economic substructure.

Indeed, Gilkey's theology of culture can lead us to a new interpretation of Marx's dictum, "the criticism of religion is the premise of all criticism."[3] The role of religion in movements of liberation throughout history is evidence enough that interpreting this dictum in terms of the orthodox Marxist notion of religion as the 'opiate' of the people is not warranted.[4] As we noted in chapter two, religion can both legitimate and undermine a dominant culture, it can both conserve and protest. A Tillichian/Gilkeyian reinterpretation of Marx's dictum would point to the ultimate concerns of all cultural movements, whether they be conservative or liberationist. Cultures are formed by people with beliefs and values. Those beliefs and values are religious in nature. Therefore the critique of religion is the premise of all critique because religion has a founding, grounding and leading function in human life.[5]

We have seen that Gilkey's understanding of religion is both broad and functional. By rejecting a narrow and institutional definition of religion as concerned with beliefs in superhuman beings, he is able to see the religious, committed or ultimate nature of powerful secular ideologies. Both the Marxist materialist dialectic and the liberal belief in progress function, therefore, as religions, guiding the lives of their cultures, determining orthodoxy and heresy, and holding forth an eschatological hope.

This approach to culture assumes, of course, a particular anthropology. Human being cannot be reductionistically understood in either Marxist terms as *homo faber* or in capitalist terms as *homo economicus*. Theology of culture must assume a multidimensional anthropology which does not absolutize but does, nevertheless, recognize the leading role of the religious in human life. Theology of culture assumes human being to be *homo religiosus*. Whether that assumption is well founded will be the question for part three of this book.

b) Analysis of Modernity

The theory behind Gilkey's theology of culture is only as good as the analysis that it facilitates, however. And, again, I find his description of modernity in terms of its religious substance to be most compelling. The historical career and destiny of modernity is best understood in terms of the rise and fall of a religious vision of life. The testimony of non-theological scholars such as Daniel Bell, Robert Heilbroner and others, gives further credence to the argument that the crisis of modernity is a spiritual crisis, a crisis of confidence and of both the *ethos* and *élan* of a culture, and so calls forth a theological/spiritual

152

response.

Another strength of Gilkey's cultural analysis is its dialectical character.[6] The cherished and absolutized ideals of modernity invariably call forth their own antitheses or negations. The autonomous subject who is the creative agent in scientific research finds himself or herself lost in the midst of that very research when the scientific method is absolutized. And even more tragically, the very technological domination over nature that was supposed to serve our lives and guarantee increased freedom has now been shown to be a threat to that very life of freedom. It is no wonder that Gilkey finds Niebuhr's notion of 'irony' so appropriate to a description of modernity. Moreover, it is also Niebuhr's emphasis on the fall and human ambiguity that Gilkey has adopted to explain the root cause of this dialectic. Gilkey's contention that Christian theology is itself inherently dialectical is foundational to the dialectical nature of his theology of culture. I will address this issue further in part four below.

Perhaps one criticism of Gilkey's analysis of modernity would be that it is lacking in a sufficient understanding of the role of economics, and especially of the goal of economic growth in western culture.[7] Gilkey has admirably uncovered the scientism and technicism of modernity. But more attention could be paid to the fundamental motive that lies beneath (or ahead of) both of these. While scientism promises omniscience, and technicism promises omnipotence, the cultural motif of economism promises an age of material prosperity and leisure. This is the vision of secular salvation that both scientism and technicism serve. Walter Wink has rightly said that "our economic system appears to be wholly secular, but it bears the marks of a priestly religion."[8] While Gilkey is not unaware of this economism (he often refers to the same phenomenon under the term 'industrialism') it could have been more developed in his interpretation of modernity's religious substance.[9]

c) Modernity in Decline

Some might find Gilkey's analysis of the decline of modernity to be too pessimistic. For example, Jean Bethke Elshtain says that "there is an aura of *fin de siécle* weariness in much of what he has to say."[10] Are not the predictions of the end of an era growing a little thin? As I noted in chapter three, Gilkey does not make these predictions as if western culture is going to collapse in the next one or two decades. Rather, his observations are on a much broader scale. When we speak of the end of an era we are speaking in terms of centuries, not decades. Gilkey is also not making any fatalistic predictions. We must remember that for him freedom is what characterizes history. It is, therefore, not inconceivable that western culture could again experience a renewal of vitality and creativity.

Gilkey's diagnosis of the crisis of modernity is, fundamentally, a matter of spiritual discernment. Such discernment is never certain, especially while one is in the midst of convulsive changes. Only afterwards can a historical commentator really say that one epoch has ended and another has begun. Gilkey says that in making such judgments in the midst of the historical transition we must "settle for the fact that it *feels* as if we were reaching the end of a historical era, and that reflection on the elements that make up that feeling tends to substantiate it."[11] Of course, if one judges such 'feelings' by the canons of social science they appear to be hopelessly subjective. But, as we have seen in chapter three, any statements about general cultural shifts, any 'discernment of the times' must rest on generalizations and feelings that cannot be 'scientifically verified.'[12] Such discernments are presented for intuitive recognition, and to engage in such analysis requires both courage and creativity. Gilkey's thought displays both. I also find his 'feelings' and the reflective critique of modernity that accompanies those feelings to be compelling.

d) Relativism/Absolutism
Another aspect of Gilkey's theology of culture that I appreciate is his attempt to avoid certain extremes. Displaying the influence of Tillich he wants to steer clear of both secularistic autonomy and any form of political or religious heteronomy. Politically and economically this means that he rejects both liberal, capitalist autonomy and the heteronomy of Soviet communism. Moreover, he strives to find a position that transcends the polarity of relativism and absolutism. While I affirm this *attempt*, however, in the next section I will argue that Gilkey has not been altogether successful in his project.

e) Social/Individual
An area where Gilkey's theology shows more success is in overcoming the traditional dichotomy of the social and individual. While my exposition did not focus on Gilkey's view of the individual/social relationship, some comment on this is in order in the light of another criticism of his theology of culture from Elshtain. Elshtain is worried

that Gilkey's emphasis on the unity of Christianity as a religion of personal salvation and of social liberation will result in massive social idolatry. He explains that, "in this idolatrous order, history may be declared redeemed but individuals may well be lost." And he adds: "Absorbed within the social order totally, we would lose the spark and flame of the self."[13]

This is, however, an alarmist response to Gilkey's actual view.[14] Gilkey *does* reject the traditional individual/social dichotomy. Human being is, indeed, social being, and we experience our individuality only in the context of community. But this does not entail a loss of individuality. The relation between individual and society is dynamic and runs both ways: "the content and tone of the individual's experience is continually qualified and shaped by the structure and by the shared experiences of the group, and the social reality in which he or she lives is constituted by the shared consciousness of that society's individuals."[15] Individual and society are as interwoven as belief and tradition. Belief entails affirming a particular tradition and entering into the world of that tradition. Yet such affirmation also requires personal assent and the experience of the truth of this tradition.[16] Moreover, Gilkey's argument that social transformation only deals with the consequences of estrangement and alienation, not the deeper causes, is further evidence that the individual is not lost in his analysis. We must remember that he says that a creative religion must be able to redeem the human freedom that continually creates demonic social structures. This redemption of the individual subject is inseparable from social transformation.

These then are some of the strengths of Gilkey's theology of culture. To some of the weaknesses of Gilkey's contribution I will now turn.

2. Problems in Gilkey's Theology of Culture

My critique of Gilkey's contribution is threefold. First, more needs to be said about the religious substance of modernity. Second, Gilkey's cultural proposals lack specificity. And third, his approach to the problem of relativism and absolutism, together with the question of the relation of Christianity to other religions is inadequate. After discussing these three sets of problems I will conclude this section with a series of questions that can only be answered through further exposition of Gilkey's prolegomenon and constructive theology.

a) *Oppression and the Religious Substance of Modernity*

While Gilkey's analysis of the religious substance of modernity is profound, some would argue that there are other elements that need to be seen as integral to the Western vision of life. For example, liberationist, black and feminist theologies point to the classist, racist and sexist dimensions of the religious substance of the West (though they might not use the term, 'religious substance'). Gilkey is, of course, opposed to classism, racism, and sexism, though none of these receives extensive treatment in his theology of culture. And none of these are identified with the religious substance of modernity. The question is, should they? For example, is the man/nature dichotomy which is so admirably described by Gilkey, not only dualistic, and exploitive of nature but also inherently patriarchal? Rosemary Radford Ruether combines the concerns of feminist, black and liberation theologies when she addresses this question of the man/nature dichotomy. She writes:

> 'Man's' dominion of nature has never meant humans in general, but ruling-class males. The hidden link in their domination of nature has always been the dominated bodies, the dominated labor of women, slaves, peasants and workers. It is not surprising, then, that it is these dominated persons who are seen as 'closer' to nature, more a part of nature, partaking more of the bodily and sensual 'nature' than ruling class males, who view themselves as having a higher intellectual nature, being closer to mind and spirit and, ultimately, closer to God than these dominated 'nature-people.'[17]

Ruether's observation is, of course, historically sound. The cultural ideal of "man's domination of nature" has never been without its sexist, racist and classist implications. When we apply her observation to Gilkey's theology of culture it becomes necessary to ask whether these are merely 'implications' of a cultural ideal, or whether they are themselves cultural ideals. In terms of the diagram I presented in chapter two, should we locate the domination of women, labour and racial groups in the *foreground* of culture or in the very *background* of culture? Is such domination the understandable, though lamentable, consequences of a particular religious vision or is it inherent in the vision itself?

To some degree this question cannot be answered. No clear distinction between background and foreground, or religious substance and the cultural manifestation of that substance, is possible. A 'vision' of life and a 'way' of life are always intertwined precisely because a vision *of* life is always a vision *for* life, a vision to be incarnated in life. Yet, some placing of these phenomena is necessary and will set the tone both for one's theological analysis of culture and one's cultural proposals. If racism, sexism and classism *are* constitutive of the religious substance of the West, then one's analysis is not sufficiently radical until these issues are addressed and transformed.

The fact that Gilkey does not, except in passing, address these issues can be taken to be indicative of his position. It would appear that he views these kind of issues as important questions of the foreground of culture, not the background. The *weltanschauunglich* issue is the *human* subjection of nature. Therefore, the concomitant subjection of labourers, women and blacks is an understandable, though not necessary, implication of this man/nature dichotomy.

One can, on the basis of the observations of Ruether and other liberation theologians, raise some serious objections to this dimension of Gilkey's theology of culture. In the first instance, even if questions of racism, sexism and classism are properly understood as 'foreground', not 'background' questions, why is there almost no reference to these issues in Gilkey's analysis? Does his preoccupation with the ambiguous power of the scientific and technological dimensions of modernity display an implicit and unacknowledged bias for the white, male, ruling class? Gilkey would, of course, be horrified at this suggestion, but his silence concerning the oppression of women, blacks and labourers in Western culture makes it necessary to raise it — at least as a question.

The more fundamental question, however, is whether he has erred in not including such oppression within the very religious substance, or background, of our culture. We have seen that Gilkey says that a religious substance provides ultimate answers to ultimate, or 'limit' questions. One such question is: Who are we? That is, every worldview includes a pre-theoretical anthropology. But doesn't the 'Who are we?' question also entail questions like: Who are we as male and female, as peoples of different races and as co-labourers? If these are also ultimate questions, then the oppressive sexist, racist and classist answers that these questions have received in Western history must be seen to be essential elements of the Western worldview. I conclude, therefore, that this is a considerable weakness in Gilkey's theology of culture. With more attention to these issues his theology of culture would be more radical and more relevant to contemporary cultural movements that are clearly reshaping our world.

b) Cultural Proposals and Specificity
Gilkey's failure to address the issues raised above is endemic of a general problem with his cultural proposals — they lack specificity. While his overall call for religious reform which maintains freedom in history has been applied to issues such as science and technology, and the problems of relativism and absolutism, Gilkey has not addressed a myriad of other pressing cultural issues. His comments on the environmental crisis, third world tensions, the nuclear arms race and the dehumanization of labour seldom go beyond the general diagnosis of the problems in terms of the dynamics of the religious substance, to concrete proposals. Socio-economic issues such as unemployment, inflation, poverty, social welfare programs, agricultural policy, health care and the decay of urban life are scarcely mentioned. It is, of course, legitimate that a *theologian* of culture, as theologian, would focus on the broad cultural issues and not presume to speak on these kind of specific issues with any authority. But it is difficult to evaluate Gilkey's broad proposals without, at least, a greater sense of their concrete applications.

The problem of specificity is not limited to the lack of concrete proposals in diverse areas of cultural life, however. Gilkey also lacks specificity with regard to his proposals concerning the religious substance of culture. Albert C. Outler pointed to this problem in his review of *Society and the Sacred.* "But for all their incidental wisdom, these lectures offer muted answers to the obvious question: with what faith and hope are we to face the 'encircling gloom?'"[18]

Recalling again my diagram from chapter two which depicts the dynamic relation between a particular religious tradition, the religious substance of a culture, and the cultural life *per se* (or the foreground of culture) we can raise Outler's question in different terms, viz., what is the ideal relation of the religious faith of the Christian community to the religious centre of a modern, secular culture?[19] Does Gilkey want the particular worldview of Christianity to suffuse, or perhaps even replace the religious substance of culture? His answer to this question has not been totally clear. For example, in *Reaping the Whirlwind* he speaks of the need for any culture to live out of a 'global myth' that will guide it in history. He then says that the Christian interpretation of history is such a myth and that it is validated "as the *most coherent and adequate* mode of interpreting our common experience of historical passage...."[20]

The religious substance of a culture, if it is to be creative, must also be able to comprehend and deal with the ambiguity of history. It is, therefore, instructive to note that later in *Reaping the Whirlwind* Gilkey proclaims that "only a theological understanding of history, structured in the categories of Christian faith, is, we have argued, adequate to the interpretation of the ambiguity that is history as we experience it, and as the modern consciousness has sought to understand and interpret it."[21] The unavoidable implication of Gilkey's affirmations is clear — Christianity can provide a *better* religious substance for cultural existence in history than can any other worldview or cluster of symbols. This is not to say that the only political action that is creative is grounded in Christian symbols, but it *is* to say that the presuppositions of such political praxis "are made explicit, coherent and communicative of power for the future *most adequately* in terms of the symbols of providence, of christology and of eschatology explicated here [in *Reaping the Whirlwind*]."[22]

The problem is that this is not a position that Gilkey has consistently maintained. In *Creationism on Trial* he addresses the relation of the religion of an explicit religious community to the religious centre of culture again. He begins by saying that there are two alternatives that are immediately suspect. The first is theocratic. In this alternative, "the explicit religious center, controlled by a religious institution and by a religious hierarchy with political power..., in turn controls or rules all aspects of cultural life...."[23] In other words, the cultural foreground is strictly controlled by the religious substance which is, in turn, determined by one particular religious community. Gilkey sees this to be the position of the fundamentalist right and its offshoot, creation science. The other alternative is the model of a 'secular' society "with no ultimate vision, no unifying symbols of reality, truth and value at all." The problem with this alternative is that it "is not a human or historical possibility."[24] The religious is constitutive to culture and will always reappear, often in demonic forms.

Gilkey's alternative to these two options is to call for "some form of 'mixed economy.'"

Here the explicitly religious communities of a culture both support and criticize the "civil religion" of the wider cultural life. They do not seek to dominate the various facets of culture by their own laws; they witness on the one hand to the genuine values in the culture's tradition (e.g., equality and justice) and on the other to cultural and social error and evil (in political, economic, and social matters) wherever they find the civil society clearly in the wrong.[25]

This theory of a 'mixed economy' does have some merit. Especially in the face of possible heteronomy it is important to insist that no particular institutional religion should be allowed to dominate society.

But has Gilkey's reaction to the fundamentalist right forced him to abandon the apologetic force of his earlier arguments for the coherence and adequacy of a Christian interpretation of history, culture and personal meaning and the creativity of such an interpretation for cultural formation? In this passage from *Creationism on Trial* he seems to present as an *a priori* principle that the religious vision of a particular community should *never* be the religious substance of a culture. Further, he proposes that the 'civil religion' should continue to take the role of the religious substance and that the 'particular' visions of 'explicit' religious communities should both support and, where necessary, criticize that 'general' civil religion. I would submit that this position is both inconsistent with Gilkey's general understanding of the nature of religious substances, and internally incoherent.

Gilkey would be the first to argue (at least in the writings prior to *Creationism on Trial*) that all religious visions, regardless of how 'implicit' they may be, are 'particular' religious visions. There is no such thing as a 'general' religion. When a particular religious vision comes to cultural dominance and becomes the religious substance of a culture it does not, thereby, lose its particularity. Even the 'civil religion' of modernity in America is a particular vision of life reflective of a combination of post-Enlightenment consciousness and the 'frontier' mentality. The only differences between a civil religion and the religion of an explicitly religious community are, a) the latter is explicit about its religiousness whereas the former is not, and b) the former has come to cultural dominance whereas the latter has not.

If the issue is not really a distinction between 'general' and 'particular' religion, and if the distinction between implicit and explicit is not overly significant, then the real question becomes, *which* particular religious vision will have cultural dominance? Gilkey is worried that if a particular religious vision becomes the religious substance of a culture then heteronomy will follow. In the instances of American fundamentalism, Islam in Iran, and Japanese Shintoism during the second world war, this fear is well justified. But surely the answer cannot be to propose an impossible 'general' civil religion that all members of society supposedly will give assent to. We have seen in both Nazi Germany and Soviet Russia that such civil religions can be equally heteronomous.

Would it not be more helpful to argue (as Gilkey has argued in the past) that one particular religious vision offers a more creative interpretation of history, culture and their ambiguity, and therefore is a viable candidate for providing cultural leadership in our present civilizational malaise? Such an option need not entail heteronomy if that religious perspective is itself not heteronomous and if the pluralist character of society is honoured and constitutionally protected. In such a context all particular religious visions can contribute to cultural formation and even vie for cultural leadership and influence. This option avoids both heteronomy and secular autonomy, while also going beyond the incoherence of a 'mixed economy' approach.[26]

Gilkey's lack of specificity with regard to the relation between particular religious communities and the religious substance of a culture results in a further lack of clarity about the content of a supposed 'civil religion.' I am not saying that he is unclear on the actual content of the present civil religion. On this, I have suggested, he is most helpful. Rather, my question concerns Gilkey's proposed norms rather than his descriptions. What does Gilkey think *ought* to be the religious substance of our culture? It is on this question that his position lacks specificity, and without that specificity his cultural proposals lack clarity and power.[27]

The problem of specificity leads us to another problematic dimension of Gilkey's theology of culture, viz., his proposals concerning relativism, absolutism and the parity of religions.

c) Relativism, Absolutism and the Parity of Religions Revisited
One of the central problems with which Gilkey's theology of culture is concerned is summed up well in the following statement:

> We are in the difficult, though intriguing, position of having at one and the same time to speak an illuminating, healing and transcendent Word to our culture's increasing agony and yet, as a kind of continuation of the Enlightenment even after its own termination..., to recog-

nize with quite new seriousness the relativity of our faith which these encounters with other religions force upon us all.[28]

A relativistic culture in crisis requires an illuminating and transcendent Word, yet that Word must be spoken in full recognition of the relativity of the faith which gives expression to it. This is, says Gilkey, a "continuation of the Enlightenment even after its own termination." My question in this section is whether this dimension of the Enlightenment should be continued or whether it should be allowed to terminate with the rest of the Enlightenment worldview.

I have already argued in chapter four that Gilkey's universalistic response to the problem of relativism and the parity of religions cannot meet his own criterion of eidetic fidelity to the symbolic content of the biblical testimony. I will now argue that Gilkey's emphasis on the relativity and parity of all faiths, including the Christian faith, is also inconsistent with the 'eidetic meaning' of much of his own writings.

In the section above we had occasion to refer to some of Gilkey's proclamations of the adequacy and coherence of a Christian interpretation of history and culture with specific reference to the viability of a Christian religious substance of culture. Those kinds of proclamations can be found throughout his corpus. For example, in *Maker of Heaven and Earth* he says that the Christian faith is "the only sufficient answer" to the anxieties of finitude. One of the reasons for this is that "Christian faith takes evil more seriously than any other viewpoint." Moreover, he concludes that "the idea of creation, and the faith of which it is a part, makes more sense of our experience of being contingent, temporal creatures than does any other alternative viewpoint."[29]

Lest one suggest that this is simply an expression of the 'neo-orthodox' phase of Gilkey's thought, consider the fact that in *Society and the Sacred* he says that Christianity, as a total system of symbols, " can satisfy the mind as a valid symbolic thematization of the totality of concrete experience as no other global viewpoint can."[30] In *Catholicism Confronts Modernity* he says that this system "provides the most adequate and most coherent account of human being in the world." And this adequacy is rooted in the special revelation of the Christ: "Only in the event of Jesus as the Christ is clarity with regard to ultimacy manifest."[31]

In the light of these assertions from the earliest to some of the most recent of Gilkey's publications it is difficult to see how he can really say that all faiths are relative and that they manifest a parity of wisdom, truth and grace. These are all statements of the supremacy of Christianity. If Christian faith is relative for Gilkey, it is, according to these statements, at least the best, most adequate and most coherent of all relative options. This is not much of a relativity, and a very odd notion of parity! Since Gilkey has never published a retraction of these views we must attempt to interpret him in a way that accounts for both these strong statements of the superior adequacy of the Christian symbol system and his equally strong statements of parity and relativity.

In *Message and Existence* Gilkey speaks of the union of the natural, historical and personal dimensions of life in a way that may help us interpret him.

> There thus is latent in this tradition [Christianity], *as in no other I believe,* the possibility of a union of nature, history, and personal existence that is *genuinely inclusive* of the best (and often the greater) wisdom in many other traditions and also that is essential to our present dilemmas.[32]

In this statement Gilkey combines an admission of the 'greater' wisdom of other traditions with an affirmation of the superiority of Christianity as a religion that can integrate this diverse wisdom better than any other viewpoint. While this comes close to unifying the two conflicting tendencies in his thought, it is clear that unity is still not achieved.

Another way in which Gilkey strives for such unity is in his proposal of a 'covenant' with other traditions. Again, we saw in chapter four that such a proposal has great difficulty in being reconciled with eidetic fidelity to a rather clear and central biblical motif. Beyond that, however, there are other difficulties with the covenant model. The only examples that Gilkey gives of past 'covenants' that were creative are the covenants 'with the Greeks' and with modernity. The problem is that neither of these covenants is without profound ambiguity. Gilkey would be the first to point out that the liberal covenant with modernity, complete with its buoyant confidence in the progressive realization of the Kingdom of God in history, was a perversion of the Christian faith and perpetrated the "lie" that modernity told us about ourselves. And do we really want to affirm the synthesis of Christianity with the anti-creational dualism and substantialism that characterized the covenant with the Greeks?

This is not to deny the necessity and even potential creativity of expressing the gospel in the cultural forms of the day. It is to say that such expression must be careful to maintain the integrity of Christian faith. This means that the cultural forms must undergo transformation if they are to be Christianly useful. Of course, Gilkey also realizes this.

> The Christian symbol must rule the use we make of any modern ontology as a superior norm of expression, lest we proclaim a secular ontology as unequivocally Christian, and our gods be different than God. Thus no philosophical system per se, modern or Greek, can be adopted without transformation to fit the symbols of our tradition.[33]

If this is true, then it is also a necessary corrective to Gilkey's notion of a covenant with other traditions. For how could such a covenant really be between equals, on the model of parity, if one partner insists on maintaining a "superior norm of expression" and transforming the symbols and philosophical categories of the other tradition in terms of that norm?

The problem with the model of covenant, then, is twofold: it is in tension with some of Gilkey's own formulations of the "superior norm of expression" of Christian faith, and the only historical covenants presented as models are, themselves, less than totally desirable. Gilkey's case is not made any stronger in the one example of a covenant that he proposes that Christianity and the West should now embark upon. He proposes that we enter into a covenant with the Chinese. Gilkey says that the Chinese revolution can learn from Christianity that one must go beyond social transformation to the redemption of human freedom because all creative revolutions are inherently ambiguous and, therefore, are tempted to fall into fate. What we can learn from China, however, is that the individual is embedded in his or her responsibility to the community and that the common good and community obligations must have priority over the individual good and obligations to the self. Such a reintegration of the false polarity of individual and community is desperately needed in the West.

> If, as I believe, the central social and political crisis facing us at present requires a new synthesis of the tradition of personal freedom with the communal character of human existence, then it is surely modern

China that will provide the inspiration and guidance for the creation of that synthesis.[34]

Indeed this synthesis in China is itself the result of the mutual transformation of the Confucian and Marxist traditions that represents "a genuine covenant, a monument to Mao's genius."[35]

The problem with this proposed covenant with the Chinese is that the Maoist inspired "cultural revolution" of the 1970's has proven that this revolution succumbed to the temptation of heteronomy that Gilkey warned of. But does not this fall into heteronomy itself raise questions concerning both Gilkey's evaluation of Maoism and the propriety of his proposed covenant with that cultural movement? Elshtain points out, against Gilkey, that what happened in Maoist China was not simply the reintegration of the individual into the communal. Rather, in Mao's China we see "the playing out of a repressively enforced consensus that has run roughshod in often tragic and despicable ways over individual 'goods,' beings and identity."[36] Gilkey's unwise evaluation of the Maoist revolution does not commend his covenant model to us.

The difficulty with speaking of a parity of religions and advocating a covenant between diverse religions is that it does not take seriously enough (as we have seen in the case of the covenant with the Chinese) the ambiguous and even demonic potential of religion. This is curious in the light of Gilkey's own emphasis on such a demonic potential. Indeed, this is precisely what Gilkey finds lacking in Wilfred Cantwell Smith's understanding of the universality of faith. Against Smith, Gilkey says that "there cannot be ... very much that is demonic, dangerous or 'invalid' about faith as it appears thus universally, constantly, and uniformly in 'religion.'" Moreover, Smith's hermeneutic of "appropriableness" whereby members of all religions should be able to appropriate to themselves the formulations of a "world theology" implies, says Gilkey, "that in the end there can be no basic disagreement between stances (a true statement about another faith must be appropriable by its participants); nor can there be any possibility of valid criticism or negative assessment of one faith by another — such would of course not be 'appropriable.'"[37]

Further, in Smith's world theology all history becomes *Heilsgeschichte* and therefore, "there is no category of 'special revelation,' a special point in history or consciousness where a special and decisive (if not exclusive) manifestation of 'God' is affirmed to have taken place...."[38] In effect, then, Smith is forced either to deny or to ignore the authority of special revelation or its equivalent (e.g., higher consciousness) in Christian, Jewish, Islamic, Hindu and Buddhist traditions. But one cannot deny that an essential ingredient of every religious tradition is an authority structure that will often resist 'fusion' or synthesis with the horizons of other traditions.

Whether Gilkey's critique of Smith is fair is not my concern here. What is my concern is the possibility that Gilkey's arguments against Smith concerning the demonic potential of religion, the possibility of negatively assessing a religion, and the significance and authority of special revelation in religion, may also be directed at his own covenant model. His negative assessment of faiths such as Iranian Islam, Shintoism in World War II Japan, and North American fundamentalism as demonic is certainly not granting them parity.[39] And the conflicting authority structures and special revelations of Christianity, Islam, Hinduism, Mormonism and the Unification Church do not create a fertile environment for mutually transforming covenants.

At this point it is necessary to return to the question of the relevant criteria for evaluating contrasting religious symbol systems with their conflicting authority structures and claims to truth. As we have seen, however, the finding of such criteria is not easy in a relativistic age. Gilkey suggests a dialectic of one part absolute and two parts relativity. In the light of this dialectic it is not surprising that ultimately Gilkey appeals to Tillich's criterion of the self-negating symbol. Tillich's solution to the problems of relativity/absolutism and particularity/universality was Christomorphic. Christ, as the bearer of the New Being, is one with the divine ground, yet points beyond himself by negating himself. He is a particular manifestation of the universal who, on the cross, sacrifices even that particularity. Therefore he is the final revelation of God and the criterion of all other revelation.[40] Gilkey says that "a self-negating and continually self-negating particularism, if religious, if related to ultimacy ... is, therefore, the only human path or way to universality," and the final criterion of all claims to universality.[41] Here we have in one symbol an absolute that radically relativizes itself.

One of the problems with Gilkey's dialectic of one part absolute and two parts relativity is that it is not always clear what the actual content of that one part absolute is. It sometimes seems that Gilkey is simply saying that one needs *some* absolute in order to have a centre from which to evaluate and respond to the dangerous heteronomies that threaten modern culture. With Tillich's Christomorphism it seems that we have uncovered the content of Gilkey's absolute — the self-relativizing absolute of the Christ. Whether this is an adequate Christology is not the issue here. The issue is whether even this symbol can function as a final criterion for evaluating other religions. Can Gilkey really affirm the symbol of a self-negating Christ as an ultimate criterion of religion and still claim to be affirming the parity of all religions? And is he really replacing the imperialism of the more traditional missionary mentality with a covenant model when he says that the ultimate religious criterion of religion is captured in the symbol of a particular manifestation of the universal engaging in self-negation — a relative absolute? Would not the Muslim, or any other person from a religion that takes its authority structure very seriously, regard such a criterion as yet more Western imperialism? Isn't this simply the imposition of a Western notion of relativity and a Christian notion of self-negation on other religious traditions? Is that why Gilkey never really applies his covenant model to the more authoritarian religious traditions?

Tillich's interpretation of the symbol of the Christ does not get Gilkey off the horns of the relativism/absolutism dilemma. Nor does it provide any better foundation for his model of covenant. I conclude, then, that Gilkey's proposals concerning the relation of Christianity to other religions are, in the end, inadequate.

d) Further Questions

Gilkey's theology of culture is only one dimension of his theological project as a whole. While the focus of our study is this theology of culture, we can only adequately evaluate his contribution by seeing how that theology of culture is rooted in, or in conflict with, his prolegomenon to theology and his constructive theology. This leads to a series of new questions. For example, in what way is Gilkey's insistence on freedom in history founded on his understanding of providence, promise and eschatology? Further, what notion of God is necessary if one wants to affirm this kind of historical freedom? What kind of Christology is necessary to support Gilkey's universalism? How has his doctrine of creation provided a basis for his critique of creation science? These are some of the questions we will address in part four. Even more foundational for a theology of culture, however, is the assumption that a dimension of ultimacy is constitutive to human life. How Gilkey's prolegomenon provides that foundation for his theology

167

of culture will be evaluated in Part III of this book.

NOTES

1 For a similarly positive evaluation see Thomas F. Hosinski, "Experience and the Sacred: A Retrospective Review of Langdon Gilkey's Theology."

2 Tillich, *Theology of Culture*, p. 27.

3 Karl Marx, *Early Writings*, trans. and ed. by T. B. Bottomore (New York: McGraw-Hill, 1964), p. 43.

4 Cf. Harvey Cox, *The Seduction of the Spirit: The Use and Misuse of People's Religion* (New York: Simon and Schuster, 1973), pp. 130-131.

5 Cf. Richard Quinney, "The Theology of Culture: Marx, Tillich and the Prophetic Tradition in the Reconstruction of Social and Moral Order," *Union Seminary Quarterly Review* 34, 4 (Summer, 1979), pp. 203-214; and Frederick Sontag and John K. Roth, "Premise of all Criticism," *Andover Newton Quarterly* 17 (January, 1977), pp. 195-200.

6 Cf. David Tracy, "Response to Gilkey," *The University of Chicago Magazine* 76, 1 (Fall, 1983), p. 14.

7 It is especially on this point that Bob Goudzwaard's cultural analysis can best serve to supplement Gilkey's. Cf. *Aid for the Overdeveloped West* and *Capitalism and Progress.*

8 Walter Wink, "Unmasking the Powers: A Biblical View of Roman and American Economics," *Sojourners* 7, 10 (October, 1978), p. 14.

9 I raise the issue of economism in this section extolling the strengths of Gilkey's theology of culture, rather than in the next section which specifically addresses the weaknesses of his contribution, because this understanding of economism is congruent with the overall thrust and tone of Gilkey's analysis, though not sufficiently developed.

10 Jean Bethke Elshtain, untitled review of *Society and the Sacred, Theology Today* 34, 4 (January, 1983), p. 429.

11 *Society and the Sacred,* p. 3.

12 Consequently, Gilkey would insist that theology of culture is a 'historical science' or 'humanity' and not a social science. In *Reaping* he explains: "Since ontologically the only finite 'substances' or 'entities' in historical being are human persons, we can understand the life of groups only if we apply to them in some analogical form the modes of understanding appropriate to personal existence. Hence the methods of history provide a more helpful empirical base for a philosophical understanding of the nature of historical change and the categories appropriate to it than do those of the social sciences" (p. 39).

13 Elshtain, untitled review, p. 432.

PART 2: THEOLOGY OF CULTURE

14 Though we will see in the next section that Gilkey's unwise affirmation of the Maoist revolution in China does give Elshtain some legitimate cause for alarm.

15 *Reaping*, p. 39. Cf. "Addressing God in Faith," in *Liturgical Experience of Faith*, ed. by H. Schmidt and D. Power, *Concilium*, vol. 82 (New York: Herder and Herder, 1973), p. 75.

16 Cf. *Message and Existence*, pp. 36, 170.

17 Rosemary Radford Ruether, *To Change the World: Christology and Cultural Criticism* (New York: Crossroad, 1983), p. 60. See also her *Liberation Theology: Human Hope Confronts Christian History and American Power* (New York and Toronto: Paulus Press, 1972), ch. 8; and *Sexism and God-talk: Toward a Feminist Theology* (Boston: Beacon Press, 1983), ch. 3.

18 Albert C. Outler, untitled review of *Society and the Sacred*, *The Christian Century* 99, 14 (April 21, 1982), p. 490. He goes on to say, "Gilkey's theological rhetoric is notoriously reticent."

19 Relationship B in our diagram.

20 *Reaping*, p. 153, italics added. Similarly, in *Society and the Sacred* he says: "... I believe it can be shown that a Christian interpretation provides a clearer, more illuminative, and more complete access to the full character of personal and historical experience than any other viewpoint" (p. 39-40). And in *Catholicism* he says that Christianity provides "the *only* cluster of symbols of ultimacy capable of understanding the mystery of our historical being as our age views that mystery" (p. 136), again, italics added. Further, in "Modern Myth-Making," he says that Christian theology "provides the best basis for the self-understanding of secular culture...." (p. 284) Cf. p. 312.

21 Ibid, p. 294.

22 Ibid, p. 295, italics added.

23 *Creationism*, p. 220.

24 Ibid, p. 221.

25 Ibid.

26 This option also assumes a distinction between a religious vision and its institutional embodiment. The proposal is not that any particular religious institution should be granted undue cultural power, but that religious visions, culturally enacted, have such influence. For example, the religious vision of Christianity is embodied in cultic life in the form of the institutional church. For Christianity to have cultural influence beyond the institutional church does not require that the institutional church should have such influence but that the Christian worldview itself should influence areas of cultural life other than the institutional church. If one takes the example of politics, this option would rather see Christians forming political perspectives and alternatives than see the institu-

tional Church more involved in politics.

27 For a more helpful discussion of cultural normativity see Bob Goudzwaard, *Capitalism and Progress*, ch. 19.

28 *Society and the Sacred*, p. 14.

29 *Maker*, pp. 17, 181, 287.

30 *Society and the Sacred*, p. 39.
31 *Catholicism*, pp. 11, 93. Cf. p. 163. For similar Christological sentiments see *Message and Existence*, pp. 247, 250.

32 *Message and Existence*, p. 47, italics added.

33 *Catholicism*, p. 126.

34 *Society and the Sacred*, p. 146.

35 Ibid, p. 148.

36 Elshtain, untitled review, p. 433. The tragic events in the Spring of 1989 in Beijing's Tianamen Square, though unrelated to Mao, underscore the repressive heteronomy of the present regime.

37 "A Theological Voyage With Wilfred Cantwell Smith," pp. 300, 301.

38 Ibid, p. 303.

39 It is also instructive to note that Gilkey never advocates covenants with any of these religious traditions.

40 Cf. Tillich, *Systematic Theology*, I, p. 137.

41 "Tillich: Master of Mediation," pp. 55-56. Cf. "The Role of the Theologian in Contemporary Society," pp. 349-350; and "The New Being and Christology," pp. 308, 311.

PART 3:
Prolegomenon

CHAPTER SIX:
The Dimension of Ultimacy: Evidence

In our discussion of Gilkey's critique of modernity we have had repeated opportunity to refer to Niebuhr's notion of irony. The religious substance of modernity is caught up in irreconcilable contradictions or tensions that result in self-destructive tendencies. The irony is that it is precisely the creativity of modernity that turns out to be also the source of its most demonic and destructive potential. This perception of the ironic dimensions of modernity has its parallel in Gilkey's insistence, in his prolegomenon, that the secular self-understanding also manifests self-contradictory tensions.

In Part II of this study we saw that the purpose of Gilkey's prolegomenon is to establish the meaningfulness of religious discourse by means of a phenomenological and hermeneutical disclosure of a dimension of ultimacy in the most secular dimensions of human life. Such a prolegomenon begins with the assumption that the self-understanding of secular people is in visible tension, if not contradiction, with the way in which they actually live. There is a tension between the secular *Weltanschauung* and *Lebenswelt*. Therefore, Gilkey's prolegomenal thesis is "that the developments of modern life have not made the radical difference on the level of man's existence that the self-understanding of modern man presupposes, and that secular man on the level of his existence is not as 'unreligious' and so as free of the need of mythical language as he thinks." If this is true "then religious discourse can be defended as meaningful by showing that it provides the only means through which we can thematize and symbolize the felt and lived character of existence."[1]

There is a sense in which the adequacy of Gilkey's theology of culture is itself an illustration of the viability of his prolegomenal thesis. If an understanding of modern secular culture in terms of its religious substance does in fact disclose the fundamental dynamics of that culture, then it has been established, at least practically, that there is a religious dimension of culture and that this dimension can only be thematized appropriately by some form of religious discourse. Gilkey's theology of culture has disclosed the mythic foundation of secular culture. The myths that guide this culture must remain "incognito," however, "that is to say, they cannot admit their status as myths, and thus they are forced to appear in another guise, as science."[2] This is simply another dimension of modernity's self-contradiction.

While Gilkey's theology of culture gives further credence to his prolegomenon, it is fair to say that the prolegomenon is, in fact, foundational, both logically and chronologically, for the theology of culture. It is in the prolegomenon that Gilkey first establishes that the dimension of ultimacy is a constitutive dimension of human life, and on that prolegomenal foundation he has erected his theology of culture. In this part of the book I will present a brief exposition and evaluation of that prolegomenon. The discussion will be brief for two reasons. First, the focus of this study is Gilkey's theology of culture and I am interested in the prolegomenon only insofar as it is relevant to that focus. Second, Gilkey's prolegomenon is the dimension of his thought that has received most critical attention. There is no need to rehearse here in great detail what has already been addressed by others. I refer the reader to these other studies.[3]

Gilkey's argument for a dimension of ultimacy can usefully be presented in terms of three bodies of evidence. The first is the evidence for a dimension of ultimacy within the secular self-understanding itself. Gilkey's argument is that a phenomenological analysis of the hallmarks of modernity, viz., contingency, relativity, temporality and autonomy, discloses a dimension of ultimacy in each of these four characteristics.[4] Modernity is also a scientific (if not 'scientistic') culture, however. Consequently, Gilkey's second major argument is a disclosure of the dimension of ultimacy inherent in all human cognition, especially scientific cognition. And, thirdly, because modernity is also suffused with a post-Enlightenment 'historical consciousness,' Gilkey argues that ultimacy is also inherent in historical experience. In this chapter I will briefly expound these three bodies of evidence in this order.

1. The Secular Self-Understanding Revisited
a) Contingency
Each of the four characteristics of the modern spirit can be experi-

enced in both a positive and a negative way. The 'givenness' of life expressed in the concept of contingency is experienced positively when "the reality and power of our *existence* are felt from the inside as joyful vitality."[5] In such experience we feel the power and wonder of life pulsating through us — we are 'energized.' Such an experience of being is the ground of all values, "not *one* among the values of our life, but their basis...." The radical givenness of our existence demonstrates that it is "quite beyond our creation, our control or our determination...."[6] The ultimacy of such experiences accounts for the enduring role that birth and fertility have in religio-mythic consciousness.

Contingency also has a negative side, however.

> As the positive joy of our contingent existence appears when that existence is experienced against the dimension or framework of ultimate being working in and through it, so whenever we feel our contingency threatened, the negative anxiety of contingency reveals itself against a similar infinite horizon, the infinite Void of insecurity.[7]

The contingency of life gives rise to anxiety because ultimately we cannot control contingency. Here the traditional symbol of fate is relevant. Life is experienced in its contingency as fated, as subject to forces beyond our control. Fate is the experience of ultimate incapacity and as such opens up the spectre of the Void to us. Such an infinite Void contains an infinite threat to our being and its meaning. This is the negative face of contingency. It is that which "calls forth in man the need infinitely to buttress the security that guarantees his survival...."[8]

Such attempts are never adequate, however. An infinite threat cannot successfully be faced with finite securities. Rather, infinite threat raises the question of an unconditional security. When contingency is experienced as ultimate threat it "reaches beyond itself to formulate an ultimate question, and thus in the most dramatic way opens up for us the infinite dimension, the unconditional horizon, in which we exist."[9] The anthropological universality of this question "is proof that [humankind] is aware of an unconditional threat of Fate and does look for an unconditioned answer...."[10] Some answer that comes to us from beyond the finite and beyond the conditioned is necessary if we are to experience ultimate security in our contingent being.[11]

b) Relativity

The positive contribution of modernity's experience of relativity is evident in the way in which such a conception 'sets free' human culture in history. Once we acknowledge that cultural creations are relative and not tied to static and changeless structures, there arises an optimism that is creative of new cultural forms. This optimism came to its clearest expression in the myth of progress. But it is precisely the demise of this myth that brings to our attention the negative side of relativity. The progress motif has functioned as a constant and absolute in a world of flux and relativity. As long as we believed in progress all of our relative cultural formations could be set "into an ultimate context which was built into the very grain of things and so which could not pass away."[12] The very belief in progress was ultimate in character. The demise of that belief raises ultimate questions anew.

The question that the progress motif answered was the question of the meaning of human life in all of its relativity. Progress was the ultimate context of meaning within which relative meanings could be grasped. However, "when the ultimate context of meaning within which the culture had existed has begun to disintegrate, then within this now dissolving cultural whole even the small, proximate, and relative meanings that make up its concrete life themselves disintegrate and vanish." Moreover, it seems that "relative meanings cannot exist *as meaningful* unless they subsist within a historical horizon of ultimacy."[13] When there is no permanency, no constancy, and no ultimate context of meaning, then relativity highlights the precariousness of human culture, and the spectre of ultimate meaninglessness is raised. The threat of the Void returns. Total relativity results in total meaninglessness and a directionless culture. No culture can survive under such circumstances.

When people stare into the Void of total relativity and meaninglessness, "then only the awareness of an unconditional context of meaning, of a purpose or *telos* in events that is not fragile and that transcends even what they love [i.e., their own cherished and 'relative' meanings], can put meaning back into life."[14] Proximate meaning must participate in a context of ultimate meaning in which our fragmentary lives find themselves completed and fulfilled. Such a sense of ultimate meaning "is the basis, not the effect, of our willing and doing."[15] And because the threat to such meaning is ultimate, so the answer must be unconditioned. Like the issue of ultimate security raised by contingency, the ultimate context of meaning entailed in relativity cannot be created by finite humanity. Rather, as an unconditioned and ultimate context of meaning it comes as a gift. In part four we will see that this sense of ultimate meaning is theologically explicated in the doctrines of creation, providence and eschatology.

c) Temporality

Modernity has both realized and affirmed the fundamental transience of reality. "Temporality defines all of creaturely existence, and thus all of its actuality; things, persons and communities come to be and *are* in time, in passage into the future."[16] Similar to relativity, the positive side of temporality is that life is open to change, development and growth. But temporality also poses a threat — it is ambiguous.

> This ambiguity is experienced as anxiety about temporal passage, an anxiety both for ourselves as individuals and for the wider history in which we participate. It raises in all of us what we can only call the "religious" questions, first, of our mortality as individuals, and secondly of the direction of temporal passage in social history—questions which we must all deal with in one way or another.[17]

Again we face the Void — only this time it is the Void of mortality which nothing finite can overcome. A profound understanding of our temporality sets us on a search "for what will last, a temporal embodiment, so to speak, for some eternity transcendent to mere passage that has been lost, and an assurance about a directed structure of time in which both we and what we value will not vanish away into nothingness."[18] Therefore, temporality, like contingency and relativity, gives rise to ultimate questions that disclose a dimension of ultimacy inherent (though often ignored) in secular life.

d) Autonomy

In the above three characteristics of modernity we have seen that Gilkey's phenomenology of secular experience usually discloses a dimension of ultimacy in the negative experiences entailed in contingency, relativity and temporality. The ultimate appears to us primarily in its absence, as a Void. In his phenomenological analysis of autonomy, however, it is as much the positive as the negative side of autonomy that discloses a dimension of ultimacy.

The positive experience of freedom means that there are no heteronomous norms established by either the church or state that have an absolute authority to which we are subject. Rather, humans must engage in a process of self-determination through the choice of norms relevant to their cultural and historical context. But this choice already uncovers a dimension of ultimacy in human freedom. While we are free from the imposition of heteronomous norms over us, we are not free to escape the problem of norms entirely. Indeed, one of the central causes for modernity's demise is the loss of any foundation for socio-cultural normativity. Daniel Bell says, "Western society lacks both the *civitas*, the spontaneous willingness to make sacrifices for some public good, and a political philosophy that justifies the normative rules of priorities and allocations in society."[19]

While Gilkey is critical of Robert Heilbroner's scenario of a future with no such autonomy, the autonomy that he envisages is one in intimate relation to norms. Indeed, Gilkey argues that a phenomenology of choice discloses that in every enactment of freedom by choice "is the concurrent affirmation of a standard in terms of which deliberation evaluates alternatives and so in terms of which the choice is made."[20] Such normative standards are the inevitable guides of freedom's actuality.

> If he [i.e., Western man] is himself to guide his own life in freedom, he can do so only in relation to some view of human excellence which grasps him as an embodiment of authentic existence and in relation to some form of community which he finds creative of this style of life. Norms which structure communal life and so which participate in some mode of ultimacy are, we suggest, inescapable, even in modern autonomous culture.[21]

Such norms are not an alien limitation of freedom, but are intrinsic to its very enactment.

> To be itself, freedom points beyond itself to a standard or image by which it is directed and shaped and inescapably that norm has for the freedom which it shapes the character of ultimacy and sacrality — for it is the source and foundation of our own existence as we create it, and of all value and good to that existence.[22]

This constitutive role of norms in our exercise of freedom points to ultimate, though usually preconscious, questions such as, "Who am I?", "What kind of person do I want to be?", "What is right and wrong?", and "What is the most desirable good, or end of life?" We mold our lives in terms of the norms that are entailed in the answers we give to those questions. Combined, these norms set an ultimate standard "to which we give our lives, in expectation that through it our lives will be fulfilled." This is, of course, an essentially religious stance: "for our god is whatever it is to which we give our lives, and from which we expect in turn to receive all our blessings."[23]

Ultimacy can also be disclosed in the negative experience of freedom, however. As soon as one acknowledges that there is a standard or model of normative existence, one then knows oneself to be "obligated." That obligation immediately opens up the possibility of failure and guilt. The model of normative life to which we commit ourselves seems to refuse incarnation. The ambiguity of human freedom means that our freedom "is not simply a freedom capable of choosing and then following its own ideals," because, inevitably, "an evil that was not a part of our purpose ... appears from nowhere as an aspect of what we have done."[24] Using language similar to St. Paul in Romans 7, Gilkey says, "Something in ourselves, that we perhaps did not know was there, prevents our enactment of this image; we seem unable, perhaps even strangely unwilling, to become what we thought we really wanted to be."[25] The anxiety, guilt and loss of self-respect that results from this failure generates a search for an ultimate healing. The depth and inevitability of our failure disclose the ultimate nature of the problem. A finite answer will never be totally sufficient. We search, says Gilkey, for an ultimate redemption, an infinite source of forgiveness, and an unconditional acceptance of us in all of our waywardness. Therefore, both the norms that are required for the positive enactment of freedom, and the forgiveness that is necessary when freedom falls, disclose a dimension of ultimacy in the very experience of secular autonomy.

2. Scientific Cognition Revisited
In chapter two we saw that the primary arena within which autonomy is exercised in modernity is in the free investigation of science. In Gilkey's critique of modernity's conception of science he argues that, rather than making religion irrelevant, a scientific culture gives rise to dilemmas that can best be described as religious in nature. This perspective within his theology of culture raises the question of whether there is a religious dimension not only of contingency, relativity, temporality and autonomy, but also of scientific cognition itself. Gilkey's answer, that an analysis of such cognition does disclose a dimension of ultimacy in science, forms a second body of evidence

for his prolegomenon. Traces of ultimacy can be disclosed by a phenomenological (and transcendental) analysis of the passion to know, the role of global visions and theories in science, and the act of scientific judgment.[26]

a) The Passion to Know

The most fundamental basis of science as a human enterprise is the urge, passion or drive to know. Humans have an unceasing dissatisfaction with not knowing. Bernard Lonergan describes this passion in terms of "self-transcendence"—the constant urge to go beyond one's present state of knowledge.[27] Gilkey notes that "all scientific repugnance at prejudice, the closed mind, unexamined answers, and lack of rigor in facing uncomfortable truths, depends on this underlying *eros* to know."[28] Ironically one can only achieve 'disinterested' objectivity if one has a passion to find and adhere to the truth. Such a passion entails a commitment to the truth, an affirmation of the good of knowing for its own sake. This affirmation is not the result but the foundation of cognition. It is, therefore, unconditioned.

> It involves ... an affirmation of the reality and value of the Logos in concrete existence: the reality of a rationality characterizing that which is to be known, and so which is there to be found even if I have not and cannot demonstrate its existence; and a commitment to the ultimate value of that search and achievement.[29]

Such commitments and affirmations disclose an ultimate dimension at the foundation of scientific cognition.

b) Theories and Science

Since the publication of Thomas Kuhn's *The Structure of Scientific Revolutions*, it has become increasingly common to recognize the role of paradigms or theoretical frameworks in all scientific inquiry. No one simply 'attends to the facts.' Science uses methods and those methods presuppose certain theories about the data.[30] Gilkey reflects the shift in philosophy of science away from a narrow empiricism (or even a falsificationism) when he says that "objective inquiry takes place only within a presupposed framework — else it cannot take place at all." And further: "Scientific procedures and theoretical structures subsist within total world views or cosmologies which must be overthrown if a new *fundamental* scientific theory is to be accepted, explored, and enlarged."[31] In order for humans even to begin to think scientifically they must "believe *something* of ontological generality about the character of reality as such and the relation of their minds to it...."[32]

Such a commitment to a view of reality as a whole functions in science as a conditional absolute. Gilkey quotes Stephen Toulmin: "These ideals of natural order have something absolute about them."[33] These fundamental assumptions are the "transcendental preconditions of methodical thinking, not explicit objects of such thinking; we think *with* them and not *of* them."[34] The absolute character of such assumptions points to their religious or ultimate character. Like religious beliefs they are not, in the end, provable. Rather, they are the foundation of all subsequent proof (or falsification). They are 'self-validating' and 'self-accrediting.' Kuhn also notes that there is something religious about such paradigmatic frameworks when he says that "the transfer of allegiance from paradigm to paradigm is a conversion experience that cannot be forced." Indeed, such a conversion, says Kuhn, requires "faith."[35] Consequently, even modern autonomous science is a "faith seeking understanding" and therefore is rooted in a dimension of ultimacy.

c) Scientific Judgments

Scientific inquiry has a *telos*, a goal. That *telos* is to understand the real and therefore to make judgments on the real: "we conceive in order to judge."[36] Judgments, however, have conditions that must be met. Those conditions are rooted in the paradigms or theoretical frameworks that we discussed above. When we judge a theory to be true, we conclude that the conditions have been fulfilled and that no important questions have been left unanswered. The judgment is, then, virtually unconditioned. We hold such and such to be the case without conditions. Such judgment, common as it is in scientific cognition, "bespeaks an experience of the overcoming of this infinity of conditioning qualifications — that now the proximate judgment is unconditioned and this finite truth can be affirmed."[37] To know is to step beyond relativity. Therefore, in all such knowing we have "a prethematic sense or prehension of something nonrelative within our cognitive grasp." Indeed, this prehension of the nonrelative is no less than "a necessary 'transcendental condition' for our being able to know at all."[38]

Not only can we discern traces of ultimacy in the making of

cognitive judgments, says Gilkey, but further, the very making of such judgments is itself grounded in our undeniable awareness of ourselves as knowers.

> Fundamental to the proximate judgments that make up science, therefore, is a still deeper unconditioned certainty and awareness than that which relates to the content of the judgment, namely that in this situation I know myself with certainty as a knower.[39]

Here again we reach bedrock — a dimension of ultimacy constitutive to and foundational for scientific cognition.

Gilkey says that ultimacy "is not the result of knowing, but a condition of knowing."[40] The grounds, foundation or condition for the possibility of knowing necessarily transcends knowing itself. When we speak at this level "our language penetrates into a deeper region of mystery, where affirmation and assertions are based more on deep intuitions and faith than on argument — since we are dealing with the foundations of all argument."[41] Therefore, we uncover traces of ultimacy in the midst of even the most secular scientific cognition.

3. Ultimacy in Historical and Political Experience

Concomitant with an emphasis on contingency, relativity, temporality, autonomy and scientific progress, modernity is also, as we have seen, a culture characterized by 'historical consciousness.' Recognizing the inherent historicity of all cultural formations gives political action greater room for directing and changing history than was possible in the pre-modern medieval West. Gilkey argues that such historico-political experience also discloses a dimension of ultimacy if one looks at the nature of politics in relation to being, meaning, and the moral dimension. The argument presupposes, however, at least two ontological features of historical process itself, namely, the relations of individual to society and destiny to freedom. Some brief comment on each of these is a necessary introduction to Gilkey's prolegomenal claim that historico-political experience is rooted in a dimension of ultimacy.

Gilkey says that history has to do with the career, in time, of communities or groups. "They, not individual men and women, are the subjects of historical life, and it is *their* history that is here our primary concern." Indeed, "the actions of individuals become *historical*, achieve effectiveness and significance on the plain of historical life, only insofar as they are received by, affect and so mold the life of communities."[42] While there is clearly an important distinction to be made between the individual and the group to which he or she belongs, there is no basis for the sharp individualistic dichotomy between inner experience and objective social reality. "The *ways* we experience our world even on the most individual level are determined for us socially, i.e., by forms of experience and interpreting that experience that are characteristic of our society." Moreover, whatever we experience of the objective social world, "is a 'world' formed by human consciousness and intentionality." That social world is formed by a communally shared system of meanings, values and norms that is also affirmed by the individual consciousnesses of the members of that society.

> Thus the internal relations of individual to society run both ways: the content and tone of the individual's experience is continually qualified and shaped by the structure and by the shared experiences of the group, and the social reality in which he or she lives is constituted by the shared consciousnesses of that society's individuals.[43]

This ontological interaction of individual and society also leads Gilkey to suggest that groups can be best understood in terms of an analogy with personal existence. Groups, as well as individuals 'act' in history. Groups, like individuals, manifest a self-awareness, a shared consciousness enshrined in myths. And in terms of that self-awareness groups manifest intentionality in history. Indeed, Gilkey agrees with R. G. Collingwood that such intentionality is the *sole* object of historical inquiry, the only form of causality that is legitimately described as historical.[44] Therefore, the so-called 'determining factors' in history (e.g., the patterns of trade, injustices, colonial or economic expansionism, changes in the balances of power, availability of raw materials, etc.) only provide the external conditions and limits within which human intentionality functions. This leads to the second ontological element of history that Gilkey discusses.

Gilkey argues that "the fundamental ontological structure for groups and so for historical passage is the polarity of destiny and freedom, the inherited 'given' from the past on the one hand, and the present human response in the light of possibilities for the future on the other."[45] Destiny is the 'given' of historical existence. It includes the material environment, habitual modes of relationship established by past generations, slow, unintentional changes such as the growth of the free market system, and the unplanned coming together of these various factors into a new constellation of conditions. This given is contingent in itself, but necessary for us because it sets the stage for our response. That response is the other pole of historical existence, namely, freedom. While destiny refers to the actuality of our present historical condition, freedom uncovers new possibilities inherent in that actuality. Freedom captures the essence of human intentionality. In freedom we respond to the actuality of our present historical situation. Indeed, "the new in historical action arises out of the union of destiny with freedom, of given actuality with relevant possibility." It is freedom which makes history *history* and not merely determined occurrence. And this freedom "is incarnated in the corporate action of each community, i.e., in its political life."[46] Politics, as the search for the public good, is the arena within which each group affirms its freedom, deals with destiny and enacts its will. If there is a dimension of ultimacy foundational to historical experience, then it will best be disclosed in an analysis of political life.[47] To this we now turn.

a) Politics and Being

Like the awareness of contingency, the awareness of our own being is the ground of all creative self-determination. The joy of being is the most fundamental of all joys. But that also means that the anxiety about non-being is the most fundamental of our anxieties. The ontological interrelation of individual and society gives this anxiety a political significance. We *are* only in community, our being and its continuance are indissolubly linked to the strength and being of the community to which we belong. Gilkey comments: "on the power of the group, its power to be, to continue to be and to direct its own future, its power to escape subjection to fate, depends the power to be of each member."[48]

Groups are, however, contingent, temporal and relative. They come into being and go out of being. A threat to the being of a group, therefore, is a threat to the being of each member. As we have seen in our discussion of contingency above, such a threat is ultimate in character. This threat is most poignantly experienced in historical experience is when destiny becomes fate; "... when we experience the given and the ongoing changes it represents as overwhelming and oppressive, as destructive of our powers and so of our freedom." Gilkey explains: "As a given which our freedom and intentions cannot in any way direct or determine, and so as a given alien to our potentialities and aims, fate is that in our experience of history which is the ultimate threat to our personal and communal being in the future."[49]

To be human is to be a free and intentional being. To be fated, then, is to be stripped of one's humanity. Politics is the communal attempt to wrest destiny from fate. "Political action seeks basically to evade fate, to transform the given in all historical life into a destiny which our freedom can in some measure control and direct."[50] And it is because government has this fundamentally ontological role of maintaining freedom in the face of fate that it takes on an air of majesty and sacrality. While such a sacrality can *often* give government and politics a fanatical character ("we *must* maintain our historical destiny as a nation or race even if that means reducing the destiny of other nations or races to fat?"), it *always* means that government and politics are inescapably related to myth. The 'care' that we have for our being in time and the shape of our temporal process unavoidably raises the question of an ultimate sovereignty in history. Therefore, historico-political experience is only adequately thematized by myths which "function as essential answers to the deepest, desperate questions of historical being, to human being in passage, and so ... provide the grounds for the possibility of human freedom in that passage...." Indeed, it is only in relation to such myths that any government can claim ultimate legitimacy because "legitimacy is established by relating governmental power to what is conceived to be the ultimate sovereignty of history, to the grain and texture of the movement of historical time."[51] Moreover, the hope that is a requisite of any creative political action is also grounded in the faith that the ultimate sovereignty of history, expressed in the communally affirmed mythos, is such "that it will not crush our political actions but may be participated in by them."[52]

This leads us to Gilkey's second argument for a dimension of ultimacy as a constitutive dimension of political experience.

b) Politics and Meaning

Political activity is not limited to securing destiny and freedom in the face of fate. It is also unavoidably teleological, directed at what is conceived to be of the highest value and meaning. In fact, one of the most debilitating results of the experience of fatedness is that it robs historical life of all value and meaning. A sense of the meaningfulness

185

of our historico-political life is also lost when people lose a sense of *eros* or participation in the dominant mythos.

The relation of politics to meaning raises the question of the religious substance of culture that we discussed at some length in chapter two. Human immersion in passage, and the ability to direct that passage, "create together the necessity of giving to the sequences of time a *logos*, a structure of order and meaning in terms of which both understanding and purposive action become possible." It is because creative political action presupposes a vision of the structure and meaning of the total sequence of historical events that myths, or symbolic visions of reality as a whole, "appear as basic to all important political speech, and that a general vision of history is presupposed in all historical understanding...."[53] Each culture, then, has a way of life which "gives meaning and value, as well as form and structure, to all its activities."[54]

While Gilkey's argument concerning the relation of politics and being parallels his phenomenological analysis of contingency and temporality, and the threat of non-being, his argument here is most closely parallel to his analysis of relativity. All relative or proximate meanings or values in personal or political experience participate in a context or horizon of ultimate meaning, or an ultimate order for history.

The third argument for ultimacy in historical and political experience is based on the relation of politics to the moral dimension of life and is parallel to Gilkey's discussion of autonomy.

c) Politics and the Moral Dimension

We have seen that Gilkey takes it to be an ontological given that human beings are free in history. The manner in which that freedom is historically enacted is always related to a moral dimension. This is another side of the teleological character of political acts. Human autonomy is directed by what is conceived to be the good. Just as government has an air of majesty because it is the source of power to protect being against non-being, and is legitimated by its perceived contact with the ultimate sovereignties of history, so also government is seen to be majestic, legitimate and sacred when it is perceived to be moral. When that perception (and reality) is not present, the government will eventually falter. "Moral corruption is as virulent a disease threatening the existence of a community as can be the loss of its access to the raw materials necessary for survival."[55]

Historical and political morality, however, presuppose some model of authentic self and an authentic society.

> As politics cannot function without an ultimate vision of the *structure* of historical communal life, so politics cannot and does not function without a corresponding vision of an ultimate *norm* for history's life.

Moreover, the visions of the *structure* and the *norm* for historical life form a fundamental unity because "no political action is possible unless what is regarded as ultimately authentic and good is also regarded as the most real."[56] Ontology and ethics, the 'is' and the 'ought,' and 'facts' and values' can never be totally separate. They form an indissoluble unity in the religious substance of any culture.

Gilkey concludes on the basis of these three arguments that political experience is "unavoidably religious" because it "exists within a horizon of ultimacy." "Its actions are engendered by the ultimate concerns of being and meaning; its judgments are grounded in ultimate norms; and its *élan* is enlivened with an ultimate hope for the future."[57] It is this dimension of ultimacy in politics, however, which can inject both the demonic and the creative (or transformative) into history. History is ambiguous. But it is precisely "the demonic character of even the most moral political action [which] leads to the transcendent as the only creative form of ultimacy in political and historical life."[58]

To summarize, Gilkey's prolegomenon argues that phenomenological analyses of the central features of the secular self-understanding (contingency, relativity, temporality, autonomy), the very processes of scientific cognition, and the dynamics of historico-political experience, disclose a dimension of ultimacy in the most apparently 'secular' areas of our individual and communal lives. The reality of such a dimension is clearly foundational to any theology of culture. In the next chapter I will discuss some of the constitutive characteristics of this dimension of ultimacy. Because of the complexity of some of the issues before us, 'exposition' and 'evaluation' will be intertwined in this chapter.

NOTES

1 *Naming,* pp. 248-249. Cf. "New Modes of Empirical Theology," pp. 356, 360.

2 "Modern Myth-Making," p. 290.

3 Cf. R. L. Littlejohn, *Gilkey's Phenomenology of Ultimacy,* ch. 4; D. R. Stiver *Converging Approaches,* ch. 3; John Shea, *Religious Language,* ch. 5; Michael Bruce Beaugh, *The Development of the Concept of Meaningful Existence,* ch. 7; and J. S. Marai, *The Problem of God-Language,* ch. 3B. The most extensive expositions are found in Littlejohn and Shea.

4 Cf. ch. 2, section 5 above. A concise summary of Gilkey's argument can be found in "The Problem of God," pp. 12-15.

5 *Naming,* p. 315.

6 Ibid, p. 317. In the light of Gilkey's more recent discussion of the Buddhist emphasis on non-being, or Nothingness, he would probably modify these typically 'Western' affirmations of being. Cf. *Society and the Sacred,* ch. 9: "The Mystery of Being and Non-Being;" and "The Political Meaning of Silence," *Philosophy Today* 27, 2/4 (Spring 1983), pp. 179-180.

7 Ibid, p. 320.

8 Ibid, p. 321.

9 Ibid, p. 320.

10 Ibid, p. 330. Recognizing the limits of any prolegomenal argument, Gilkey is careful to distance his claim to have disclosed the ultimate dimension of contingency from the cosmological argument for the existence of God. Cf. pp. 328-329, n.8, and 331.

11 A similar argument is advanced by Wolfhart Pannenberg in *What is Man?,* trans. by D. A. Priebe (Philadelphia: Fortress Press, 1970), ch. 3.

12 *Naming,* p. 343.

13 Ibid, p. 345. Again, a similar argument has been advanced by Pannenberg. In *Theology and the Philosophy of Science* he says that "every specialized meaning depends on a final all-embracing totality of meaning in which all meanings are linked to form a semantic whole" (p. 216). Critically appropriating both Gadamer's "unexpressed horizon of meaning" and Polanyi's "tacit coefficient of speech," Pannenberg argues that such an ultimate context of meaning is implicitly invoked in every experience of particular meaning:

> The immanent analysis of the perception of meaning ... can easily show that all perception of individual meanings has as an implicit component the assumption of a totality of meaning, by reference to which the individual perception first receives its determinate meaning (pp. 200-201).

Further, a totality of meaning is similar to Gilkey's notion of the religious substance of culture because it functions as the 'worldview' or 'spirit' of a culture. Cf. pp. 84-103 [esp. 101-102], and 433ff.

Cf. Hans-Georg Gadamer, *Truth and Method* (2nd. ed.; New York: Crossroad, 1985), pp. 269ff, 337ff; and Michael Polanyi, *Personal Knowledge: Toward a Post-Critical Philosophy* (Chicago: University of Chicago Press, 1958), part 2 (esp. pp. 86ff); and *The Tacit Dimension* (Garden City, N.Y.: Doubleday, 1966), ch. 1.

For a more complete discussion of Pannenberg's notion of totality see the present author's *Futurity and Creation: Explorations in the Eschatological Theology of Wolfhart Pannenberg* (published thesis; Toronto: Institute for Christian Studies, 1979), ch. 3.

14 Ibid, pp. 354-355. Cf. "Addressing God in Faith," p. 72.

15 Ibid, p. 352.

16 *Reaping*, p. 245. Cf. p. 301: "Being is temporality, process; and our every experience of our being, and our reflections on our being drive toward an ontology of temporal process."

17 *Naming*, pp. 358-359.

18 Ibid, p. 361.

19 Bell, *Cultural Contradictions of Capitalism*, p. 25. Commenting on Bell's social analysis, Bernard Zylstra said, "Normative questions may indeed be raised but normative answers cannot be given" ("A Neo-Conservative Critique of Modernity: Daniel Bell's Appraisal," *Christian Scholar's Review* 7, 4 (1978), p. 354).

20 *Naming*, p. 374. Vincent Brummer makes a similar point in his *Theology and Philosophical Inquiry: An Introduction* (Philadelphia: Westminster Press, 1982): "... all value judgments and ascriptions of meaning are founded on assumed norms. Such norms are founded on higher norms or ideals; so that we justify our value judgments by appealing to norms, and such norms are, in turn, justified by pointing out that they are consistent with higher norms and ideas to which we ascribe." Further, "... everyone determines and guides his whole *way of life* in the light of the total set of norms and ideals that he accepts and allows to direct his life" (p. 132).

21 Ibid, p. 372. Similarly, Bob Goudzwaard says that every genuine process of disclosure whereby human freedom creatively forms culture "requires the recognition and fulfillment of norms." Without such norms a cultural movement "immediately loses impetus and effectiveness; without norms our values and standards, too, lose all material content...." And Goudzwaard recognizes, with Gilkey, the ultimate character of these norms when he says that "norms can never be formulated outside of a committed life perspective...." (*Capitalism and Progress*, p. 210).

22 Ibid, pp. 374-375. Again, cf. Goudzwaard: "Norms are not intended to rob us of our freedom; rather, they enable us to retain life and liberty, to prevent us from threatening the lives of ourselves and others" (*Capitalism and Progress*, p. 211). Richard Middleton and I present a similar perspective in, *The Transforming Vision*, pp. 155-159.

23 Ibid, p. 377. Cf. "Addressing God in Faith," p. 72.

24 Ibid, p. 388.

25 Ibid, p. 385.

26 For similar analyses, cf. David Tracy, *Blessed Rage for Order*, pp. 94-100; Ian Barbour, *Issues in Science and Religion* (New York: Harper Torchbooks, 1971), ch. 6 and 9; Karl Rahner, *Spirit in the World*, trans. by William Dych (New York: Herder and Herder, 1968), pt. II, ch. 3; Herman Dooyeweerd, *A New Critique of Theoretical Thought*, I, Pt. I (Prolegomenon); and the present author's more modest contribution in *The Transforming Vision*, ch. 11 and 12.
  Gilkey's phenomenology of scientific cognition is itself dependent upon Bernard Lonergan, *Insight: A Study of Human Understanding* (London: Longmans, 1964); Thomas Kuhn, *The Structure of Scientific Revolutions* (rev. ed.; Chicago: University of Chicago Press, 1962); Stephen Toulmin, *Foresight and Understanding* (New York: Harper Torchbooks, 1961); and Michael Polanyi, *Personal Knowledge*, and *Science, Faith and Reality* (Chicago: University of Chicago Press, 1964).
  For further discussion of Gilkey's understanding of the relation between religion and science see Anne Marie Clifford, *The Relation of Science and Religion/Theology in the Thought of Langdon Gilkey* (unpub. Ph.D. dissertation; The Catholic University of America, 1988).

27 Bernard Lonergan, *Method in Theology* (New York: Herder and Herder, 1972), pp. 104-105. Pannenberg's anthropological concepts of exocentricity and *Weltoffenheit* carry a similar meaning. Cf. *What is Man?*, ch. 1; and *Anthropology in Theological Perspective*, esp. ch. 2.

28 *Religion*, p. 49. Albert Einstein was referring to this very passion when he said, "Science can only be created by those who are thoroughly imbued with the aspiration towards truth and understanding. This source of feeling, however, springs from the sphere of religion." Quoted by David Price et. al., *Teaching Science in a Climate of Controversy* (Ipswich, MA: American Scientific Affiliation, 1986), p. 9.

29 Ibid, pp. 50-51.

30 N. R. Hanson notes that all facts are "theory-laden" in *Patterns of Discovery* (Cambridge: Cambridge University Press, 1965), ch. 1; and Paul Feyerabend notes that "every methodological rule is associated with cosmological assumptions, so that using the rule we take it for granted that the assumptions are correct." Quoted by Alan Storkey, *A Christian Social Perspective* (Leicester, England: InterVarsity Press, 1979), p. 100.

31 *Religion*, pp. 44, 45. For an excellent discussion and integrated response to some recent developments in philosophy of science see Clarence Joldersma, *Beliefs and Scientific Enterprise: A Framework Model Based Upon Kuhn's Paradigms, Polanyi's Commitment Framework, and Radnitzky's Internal Steering Fields* (published thesis; Toronto: Institute for Christian Studies, 1982.)

32 Ibid, p. 53. See also Gilkey's article, "Nature, Reality and the Sacred: A Meditation in Science and Religion," *Zygon* 24, 3 (September 1989), pp. 283-298.

33 Cited in *Religion*, p. 52.

34 Ibid, p. 53.

35 Kuhn, *The Structure of Scientific Revolutions*, pp. 150, 158. Kuhn also compares a paradigm shift to a "gestalt" shift and argues that even perception is dependent on a pre-perceptual paradigm (pp. 112, 120). In this way paradigms are similar to 'visions of' and 'visions for' life. For further discussion of the relation between a "gestalt" formed by fundamental assumptions or beliefs and perception, see Nicholas Wolterstorff, *Reason Within the Bounds of Religion* (Grand Rapids, Mich.: Eerdmans, 1976), p. 49; and Michael Polanyi, "The Scientific Revolution," in *Christians in a Technological Age*, ed. by H. White (New York: Seabury Press, 1967), pp. 34-36.

36 *Religion*, p. 56.

37 Ibid, p. 57.

38 Ibid, p. 58.

39 Ibid, pp. 59-60.

40 "Empirical Science and Theological Knowing," p. 96. Cf. Gilkey's untitled review of Karl Rahner's *Spirit in the World*, *Journal of Ecumenical Studies* 7, 1 (1970), p. 142.

41 *Religion*, p. 63. Cf. *Catholicism*, pp. 164-165; and *Message and Existence*, pp. 27-28.

42 *Reaping*, p. 37.

43 Ibid, pp. 38-39.

44 R. G. Collingwood describes this intentionality primarily in terms of 'thought': "The processes of nature can therefore be properly described as sequences of mere events, but those of history cannot. They are not processes of mere events, but processes of actions, which have an inner side, consisting of processes of thought; and what the historian is looking for is these processes of thought. All history is the history of thought" (*The Idea of History*, ed. by T. M. Knox (New York: Oxford University Press, 1956), p. 215).

45 *Reaping*, p. 43.

46 Ibid, pp. 44-45. Cf. *Catholicism*, p. 144: "Politics is the art of grasping and utilizing the possible latent within the present."

47 It should be noted that Gilkey seems to be using the term 'politics' in a very general way. It would be to misread Gilkey to interpret him to be advocating an absolutistic view of politics whereby the way in which *that* sphere of cultural life responds in freedom to historical destiny is finally determinative for all other spheres. He leaves himself open for such a misreading, however, by failing to note that political action is only *one* way in which humans form history. All other cultural institutions engage in the same process of utilizing the possible latent within the

given — whether they be families, business enterprises, churches, schools, or voluntary associations. Therefore a phenomenological analysis of any of these institutions should, in principle, be able to disclose a dimension of ultimacy in historical experience as effectively as such an analysis of politics.

For an ontological analysis of the structure and relation of these various societal institutions, cf. Dooyeweerd, *A New Critique of Theoretical Thought*, III, pt. II.

48 Ibid, p. 48.

49 Ibid, pp. 49-50.

50 Ibid, p. 51.

51 Ibid, p. 54. Cf. "Theology and the Future," p. 257.

52 Ibid, p. 56.

53 *Society and the Sacred*, p. 60.

54 *Reaping*, p. 60.

55 Ibid, p. 64. This observation is verified by recent historical events. One need only think of the demise of the Shah of Iran, Duvalier in Haiti, Somosa in Nicaragua, Marcos in the Philippines, or Amin in Uganda, to see that when a government loses the confidence of the population because it can no longer be seen to be moral, it can only maintain power by means of military suppression of unrest—though even this can only be a short-term solution.

56 Ibid, p. 67. Gilkey goes on to say: "For every moral norm by which we judge the present, and every moral hope by which we bear in anticipation the unknown future, is taken by us to be an aspect of the ultimate grain of history itself, to be ultimately real as well as ultimately good." Cf. "Religion and the American Future," p. 13.

57 Ibid, p. 68.

58 Ibid, pp. 68-69.

CHAPTER SEVEN:
The Dimension of Ultimacy: Characteristics[1]

It is clear that the overriding cultural context in which Gilkey's theology has been formed and the religious situation that he addresses himself to is the secularism of the modern West. In such a secularism, says Gilkey, the ultimate has been "eclipsed," resulting in "the absence of the religious, transcendent or ultimate dimension or reference in all the facets of life, and the consequent derivation of all standards and goals solely from the natural and social environments in which men live."[2]

His response to this situation has been singular. Such an eclipse of ultimacy is not possible. The religious can never be totally absent from human life. As early as his first book Gilkey insisted that human life is best understood as *homo religiosus*.

> Whether he wishes it or not, man as a free creature must pattern his life according to some chosen ultimate end, must center his life on some chosen ultimate loyalty, and must commit his security to some trusted power. Man is thus essentially, not accidentally, religious, because his basic structure, as dependent and yet free, inevitably roots his life in something ultimate.[3]

And we have seen that his whole prolegomenal argument has attempted to disclose such a dimension of ultimacy in ordinary experience.

In this chapter I will address three questions. First, what are the characteristics of this dimension of ultimacy? Specifically, in what way is it a *dimension* of human life at all? Second, what is the nature of the language that is most appropriate to thematize this dimension and how is that language related to other modes of discourse? And third, what is the relation of a dimension of ultimacy to the Ultimate itself? It is only by addressing these questions that certain elements of Gilkey's theology of culture can be fully understood and evaluated.

1. *Homo Religiosus* and the Dimension of Ultimacy
a) Limit Questions

It has become common in much contemporary theology to speak of the "questionableness" of human existence.[4] Our existence drives us to ultimate questions. These questions are ultimate "because answers to them are foundational for all else we are and do." Or, more specifically, they are "limit" questions "because each one seems to appear at the outer limits of our capacities and powers, at the edge, so to speak, of our finitude."[5] Here Gilkey is, like many others,[6] dependent on the philosophy of Stephen Toulmin. In his book, *An Examination of the Place of Reason in Ethics*, Toulmin says that any form of reasoning can be pushed to a level of questioning that can only be described as being at the "limits" of rationality. Such questions are religious in nature because they confront us with the very foundations of our finite being and the very foundations of our rationality.[7] Similarly, the phenomenological existentialist philosopher, John Wild, speaks of these questions as being at the "boundary" of our existence.[8]

Such questions address issues "of ultimate origins (where did it *all* come from), of ultimate worth (what is the point or meaning, the *why* of life), of ultimate destiny (where are we all going)."[9] Beyond the scientific questions of proximate origins (*how* questions) and beyond the philosophical questions of ontological structure (*what* questions), we are driven to ask existential questions about the mystery and meaning of our lives (*why* questions). These questions are "peculiarly 'religious' in character." "That is, they ask about the ultimate ground and meaning of our existence, they search for a faithful and healing answer to our deepest problems, and they are answered in terms of affirmation and trust, rather than in terms of proof and demonstration."[10]

b) A 'Dimension' of Ultimacy

The inevitability and universality of such questions in human life discloses a dimension of life which has assorted characteristics.

> What is shown is that man is a religious being whose experience of the sacred, both positively as the ground, limit, norm, and resource of his life, and negatively as the infinite and uncontrollable threat to his life, characterizes his humanity and provides the only way of understanding rationally the positive characteristics of man's autonomy and of his creative powers, and the negative uses he makes of those powers.[11]

While Gilkey describes this dimension in various ways, we could summarize his description in the following terms: the dimension of ultimacy discloses the ultimate ground (basis, source), limit (horizon), norms (values) and meaning (hope) of human life, both in terms of its creative possibility and demonic potential (ambiguity).[12] Such a dimension of ultimacy is not an optional matter of preference simply for those who are religiously inclined. Gilkey's claim is much more comprehensive.

> It is, in fact, in relation to this dimension of his experience that man becomes man, that the uniquely human characteristics of our life appear. Built into his experience of himself and his world is a dimension that transcends both his selfhood and his environment, and that makes him human.[13]

If we grant that Gilkey has in fact disclosed a dimension of ultimacy with something like these kinds of characteristics, then the question that remains to be answered is the relation of this dimension to other dimensions of life. Gilkey's answer to this question is, however, not totally clear. On the one hand he says that the dimension of ultimacy appears "in relation to every significant aspect of man's being."[14] Yet, on the other hand, ultimacy is also one dimension of our multi-dimensional lives.[15] How is it that one dimension can be manifest in every significant aspect (dimension) of human life?

The issue is clouded further by the way in which Gilkey mixes the metaphors of *transcendence* and *centre*. In the quotation in the paragraph above we saw that the dimension of ultimacy "transcends" both human selfhood and the environment. In other places he says that "ultimacy appears as *transcendent* to our finite powers," even as "transnatural."[16] Insofar as this is a dimension that appears only at the limits of secular experience, "its phenomenological character is *qualitatively* different from all we call the natural world."[17] Yet this is a dimension that has been disclosed *within* ordinary experience. Therefore Gilkey endeavors to speak of it in terms which neither separate ultimacy from secular life (as the metaphor of transcendence seems to do) nor identify ultimacy too strongly with secular life.[18] It is in this context that he uses the metaphor of centre.

> My thesis is that a dimension of ultimacy does in fact appear at the center of each significant facet of man's being in the world, and that it is this dimension which grounds man's powers, possibilities, and joys, and also

195

which man experiences as a threat to his being and his value.[19]

It is from this spiritual centre that the total self can exist as a unity.[20] More questions arise. How can a transcendent dimension that transcends our selfhood, our environment and our finite powers also be the unifying centre of that selfhood and those finite powers? How can Gilkey speak of a 'dimension' of life which is both within and beyond ordinary life — especially when he has disclosed this dimension precisely by means of an analysis of ordinary life?

c) Dimension, Centre, Transcendence

Perhaps we can bring some clarity to this somewhat confused state of affairs if we make clearer distinctions among Gilkey's three terms, viz., dimension, centre, and transcendence. The place to begin is by asking whether the dimension of ultimacy, in Gilkey's thought, is a *dimension* at all. For example, when Gilkey says that history is multi-dimensional and that one of those dimensions can be described as a dimension of ultimacy, it is fairly clear what he means.[21] We can easily think of other dimensions that are manifest in history. History has to do with human cultural formation, political power, economic systems, legal structures, abundance and scarcity of resources, moral decisions, philosophical ideas and artistic expression. Therefore it manifests, among others, formative, political, economic, juridical, physical, ethical, theoretical and aesthetic dimensions. All of these are constitutive of historical reality. To say that there is also a religious dimension of history is to disclose, as Gilkey has done admirably, the role of ultimate visions, norms and eschatological expectations in historical formation. Further, understanding how this dimension functions in history provides insight into some of the foundational reasons for why cultures are formed the way they are, why political and legal structures take on an air of sacrality, why resources are used in certain ways in different economic systems, why the moral fibre of a culture is what it is, and why one culture develops philosophical thought and artistic styles so different from another culture. What this description of historical experience suggests is that not only are there various constitutive dimensions of historical experience, including a religious dimension, they are also all integrally interrelated. In this instance we have suggested how the religious dimension is manifest as a *moment* in all of the other dimensions.[22]

The term dimension is a spatial metaphor. This is both its strength and its weakness. The strength of the metaphor is that it delineates a space or sphere of life which is characterized in one way and not in another. The religious dimension is related to but not the same as the political, emotional or economic dimensions. Nor can one dimension be reduced to another without sacrificing the integrity of that dimension. For example, the religious dimension is misunderstood when it is reduced to the emotional dimension (whether the reduction be pietistic or psychoanalytic). Yet such a reduction is possible precisely because there is a legitimate and constitutive emotional side to the religious dimension.

Herein is, also, the limitation of the metaphor. It is difficult to conceive of dimensions, or irreducible spheres, interrelating and interpenetrating one another. Yet to speak in such a way seems to be necessitated by the phenomenological evidence. Perhaps a more biotic metaphor would help. We could say that reality manifests a diversity of *functions* and that a multi-dimensional, or multi-functional analysis will attempt to account for these various irreducible ways or modes of being-in-the-world. Such functions, however, are always functions of something. In this regard, I find it helpful to follow Hendrik Hart's description of anything that functions (a rock, a bird, a tree, a person, etc.) as a *functor.* For example, a person thinking is a functor (person) functioning in a certain kind of way (thinking). Just as 'thinking' does not think, only people do, so it is that only functors function. That functioning is related to, but ought not be reduced to, other forms of functioning.[23] Thinking can not be legitimately reduced to the physical-chemical interactions of brain cells, though it is foundationally related to such interactions.

Whether we use a term like dimension or function (or, for that matter, 'aspect,' 'modality,' or 'way-of-being') the state of affairs that we are attempting to elucidate includes various dimensions or functions in interrelation. One of those dimensions or functions is appropriately described as a religious dimension, or a dimension of ultimacy. My question has been whether Gilkey's dimension of ultimacy is a dimension in this sense. I think that it is not. The metaphor of dimension refers to some sphere or space that is filled. Multi-dimensionality, then, refers to a whole that is made up of various unique and separate (though related) spheres. Similarly, a function is one way or mode of being among others. However, we have seen that Gilkey describes the dimension of ultimacy either in terms of transcendence, and therefore qualitatively different from our natural lives, or at the centre of each significant facet of human life in the world. In neither case is the metaphor of dimension (or function) appropriate. That which is transnatural and qualitatively different from our natural life cannot be a dimension of that life. Nor is it easy to imagine how the centre of one's life, the unity of the self, can be one dimension of that self, among others. It would appear necessary to distinguish between the religious dimension of life, the unified centre of the self, and the transcendent referent of that dimension which is the ground of that unity. This is not the place for a full elaboration of an alternative anthropology, but a few comments are in order.

In chapter two we saw that Gilkey's definition of religion is closer to the broad approach of Clifford Geertz than it is to the narrow constrictions of Melford Spiro. Religion is more a matter of a total, committed way of life than a set of particular kinds of beliefs related to cultic institutions. A theology of culture is only possible within such a broad definition of religion. Yet we now see that it is impossible to speak of a religious dimension of culture without giving that definition some functional specificity. If it is a dimension among other dimensions, then what are its irreducible characteristics? By not addressing this question of the focus of the religious dimension of life, Gilkey, in effect, collapses the religious dimension into the unifying centre of the self. In cultural terms he speaks not so much of a specific religious dimension of cultural life, but of a more general religious substance. While such an approach has clear strengths (as I noted in chapter five, section one) it also results in some of the problems I am here addressing.

James H. Olthuis has used the terms 'heart' and 'belief' to refer to what I am here calling 'centre' and 'dimension of ultimacy.' The two must be kept distinct. He says, "If the distinction between the heart (as the root unity of man's total functioning) and belief (as one way of functioning) is not made, the belief dimension is wrongly identified with or considered exhaustive of man's spirituality."[24] One is then forced into either a dualism whereby the religious is separated from the non-religious dimensions of life, or a monism which spiritualizes all of life in such a way that both sacrifices the independence and integrity of the non-religious dimensions of life and compromises the role of will or decision in the making of faith choices. We will see below that Gilkey's theology of culture manifests both of these tendencies. His discussion of the relation of religion and science in the context of the creationist controversy tends to be dualistic (against his best intentions), and his understanding of the parity of religions tends toward monism.

Maintaining a distinction between the religious dimension (belief) and the spiritual centre of the self (heart) allows one both to affirm the profound spirituality of all of life (which is the strength of the broad definition of religion) and to recognize that the explicit focussing on ultimates (or limit questions) is characteristic of one kind of human experience, or one dimension of human life (which is the strength of the narrow definition of religion). Again, I find Olthuis to be helpful. Using "faith" to refer to what he earlier called "belief," he says,

> ... faith is one of the ordinary modes of human existence, of which all are equally human, equally personal and equally spiritual. However, although the faith mode is no more spiritual than any of the other modes, it is by means of the function of faith that the intrinsic spirituality of the whole person comes to explicit consciousness and awareness. By way of the function of faith we surrender ourselves to the ultimate; we give over and let go to the god in whom and from whom we receive certitude and the ground of our existence.[25]

The reason that it is so easy to succumb to the temptation to conflate the religious dimension and the spiritual centre of human life is precisely because it is the unique role of this dimension to bring that spiritual centre to explicit consciousness and awareness.

The religious dimension is appropriately called a depth or limit dimension because it opens life up to the question of its ultimate foundations.[26] It brings to expression that heart-directedness or spiritual centre of life that integrates, unifies and directs all of life in its multi-dimensionality. In biblical terms, this dimension "confesses with the mouth" that which is "believed in the heart."[27] It is the spiritual centre of human life which characterizes all of life as spiritual, as religious in the broadest sense of the term. It is also this centredness and spirituality that discloses the fundamental character of human life as relational. To be a unified human being is to be in relation to that which is taken to be ultimate.

At this point, perhaps we can speak of transcendence with more clarity. I have already argued that the dimension of ultimacy, as a dimension, among others, of ordinary life, is uniquely related to, yet distinct from the spiritual centre or heart unity of life. This, I suggest, clarifies Gilkey's ambiguous use of the terms 'dimension' and 'centre.' Yet we have also seen that Gilkey refers to the dimension of ultimacy as transnatural, transcending our selfhood and our world. This, I submit, is confusing. How can a dimension of the world transcend the world?

There may be a way out of this confusion, however. That heart-unity which is brought to explicit confessional expression in the religious dimension discloses, I have argued, the relational character of the human person. We are who we are in relation, not only to each other, the environment and our past, but also, most foundationally, in relation to that which is taken to be the ultimate origin, meaning and goal of life. That ultimacy is, by definition, transcendent to our personhood in both its spiritual centredness and multi-dimensionality. Neither the religious dimension nor our spiritual centre is transcendent or transnatural. Both are thoroughly natural and ordinary. Through them, however, we are related to that which is ultimate and, therefore, that which transcends our life. We are related, in our centredness and multi-dimensionality, to ultimate foundations. But neither our centredness nor any of our dimensions is that foundation. Rather, that which is the ultimate foundation (source, ground, limit) is the foundation of our life in its centredness and in all of its rich multi-dimensionality.

Gilkey's prolegomenal analysis of the dimension of ultimacy suffers from an underdeveloped understanding of human multi-dimensionality. He has failed to distinguish clearly the dimension of ultimacy as a constitutive ontic dimension of ordinary life from the heart-unity or centre of the self which functions in diverse ways (including religiously). He has also lacked clarity in distinguishing these anthropological structures from the transcendent or ultimate foundations to which they necessarily relate. In the next section we will see how these problems manifest themselves in Gilkey's under-standing of religious language. Following this I will return to the question of the relation of the dimension of ultimacy to the transcend-ent which is its referent and ask whether Gilkey further conflates the dimension of ultimacy and the Ultimate itself. The discussion of religious language has direct bearings on our evaluation of Gilkey's response to the creationist controversy, and the question of the relation of the dimension of ultimacy to the Ultimate is relevant to his approach to the parity of religions. In the former instance, Gilkey manifests what I have called dualistic tendencies, in the latter he manifests monistic tendencies.

2. Ultimacy and Religious Language
a) The Meaningfulness of Religious Language
It is important to recall that the initial impetus of Gilkey's prolegomenon was to answer the charge of both radical theology and analytic philosophy that religious language was not only untrue or misdirected, but it was also void of all possible meaning. Religious language, it was argued, was meaningless because it could demonstrate no relation to experienced reality. Religious concepts had no experiential home. It was this challenge that made a prolegomenal inquiry necessary.

> These questions of compossibility, of potential actuality, are questions of the relation of concepts to experience; and consequently the radical question of meaning drives theological reflection beneath its own accustomed materials and authorities to the examination of ordinary experience. The purpose of such an inquiry is to find those dimensions or regions of ordinary experience to which the language of religious symbol has reference, and so in terms of which such symbols can be said to have legitimate meaning and real possibility.[28]

In chapter one (section three (b)) we saw that Gilkey assumes a phenomenological understanding of the relation between meaning and experience. It is in this sense that he uses the term reference. Language is only meaningful (and therefore potentially true) if it has reference to a particular dimension or aspect of concrete experience. The issue is not so much one of the univocal reference of declarative propositions (as in the referential theory of meaning), but, more modestly, the relation between a particular language game and a real dimension of human life that is appropriately brought to thematic expression in that language game. Gilkey's prolegomenon has, I conclude, disclosed such a religious dimension, though I have been critical of Gilkey's unclear description of that dimension. The question that must now be addressed is the nature of the language that brings that dimension to thematic expression. Borrowing a phrase from Wittgenstein, what are the "family resemblances" of the religious language game?[29]

b) Religious and 'Ordinary' Language
In the light of the ambiguities we discovered in Gilkey's description of the dimension of ultimacy it is not surprising that some similar ambiguities appear in his discussion of religious language. We have

seen that Gilkey argues that religious language has meaning only if it has reference to ordinary experience. Religious symbols can be true for us only if they make sense of our experience of the world and uncover "the hidden, complex, and mysterious actuality of our human existence generally and of the actual situation of each one of us individually."[30] Indeed, not only does such language have reference to ordinary experience, it also *shapes* that experience. We do not so much make symbols as they make us — they tell us what reality is really like and what authentic humanity really is.[31] While such language is inextricably connected to ordinary reality, however, Gilkey also acknowledges that this language is opaque. Herein is the beginning of the ambiguity. Religious language is also a strange and unusual use of language, manifestly different from "ordinary discourse." It may have reference, but unlike the reference of any kind of empirical propositions.[32] This mode of address is both "special" and somewhat "queer."

The fact that this language is odd does not mean that it can be dismissed as the idiosyncratic way in which certain kinds of religious people choose to speak, however. Rather, such language is inescapable precisely because the dimension of life that it thematizes is also inescapable and inherent in our humanness. Moreover, this mode of discourse is irreducible. It cannot be reduced to any other form of discourse. It is not merely 'emotive' or 'metaphysical' or 'moral.' It is a mode of discourse with its own necessary and irreducible characteristics.[33] The problem is that two of these characteristics (viz., that this language is both disclosive of ordinary experience and at the same time an opaque mode of discourse which is manifestly different from ordinary discourse) are in tension with each other. This tension is parallel to the problem, discussed above, of how the religious dimension could be an ordinary dimension of life and also be described both in terms of the centre of life and also transcendent to life.

c) Symbols and Myths
The difficulty we encounter at this point comes to sharper focus in Gilkey's description of symbols and myths. Religious language is necessary, we have seen, as a mode of discourse that addresses ultimate questions and answers. Such discourse is not, however, the same as univocal or literal language. Rather, ultimate issues can only be addressed symbolically.

A fundamental point of view, a particular apprehension of the ultimate context in which we exist, cannot ... become creative or be transmitted unless it has appropriate, consistent, and relevant symbolic expression. Symbols illumine, structure, bring to light, and reveal to us the tonal characteristics of our felt being in the world.[34]

It is the nature of such symbols to be polysemic and to manifest a double intentionality. They have a double reference because they refer both to finite reality and to the transcendent which is revealed by reference to that finite reality. Just as the symbol can have power only if it participates in the reality to which it points, so also can we truly affirm a symbol and receive what the symbol gives only if we participate in the transcendent through its mediation.[35] Moreover, we are drawn to such participation only if these symbols make sense of our experienced world.[36]

Our experienced world is, however, temporal and historical. When symbols are related to historical passage they take on a story form, they become myths.[37] Gilkey defines myth as follows:

Myth, as a form of language, uses a story form, phenomenal or ontic language descriptive of events in space and time and of actors in those events, to describe or illumine structures and relations that transcend that phenomenal and that ontic manifold.[38]

Similarly, in an earlier article, he described myth as,

... a certain mode of language, whose elements are multivalent symbols, whose referent in some strange way is the transcendent or sacred, and whose meanings concern the ultimate or existential issues of actual life and the questions of human and historical destiny.[39]

Homo religiosus is necessarily *homo mythicus* because ultimate questions of origins and destiny can only be answered in the form of myth. Myth portrays both the horizon (destiny) and ground (origin) of the world by telling a story, the form of which entails actors and events in time, but the content of which is the ultimate and transtemporal.[40] The question to pursue further is precisely this relation between religious language characterized as symbolic-mythic discourse on the one hand, and empirical, natural and historical reality on the other.

d) Religious and Scientific Language
Gilkey has said that "it is of the essence of modernity to believe that

myth is part of the infancy of man, to be outgrown in the scientific and autonomous age of modernity."[41] While his own disclosure of the mythos that forms the religious substance of modernity sufficiently disproves the modernistic devaluation of myth, Gilkey must still find a way to relate mythic and scientific language if he is to develop a theology of culture in the context of modernity. The way in which he has addressed this problem has not been totally consistent, however.

In *Maker of Heaven and Earth* Gilkey makes a sharp distinction between scientific questions of proximate origins and religious questions of ultimate origins and concludes that "the inquiries of the physical sciences and those of theology are now seen to be asking *fundamentally different* kinds of questions, in *totally different* areas of thought and experience."[42] While science asks "how" questions, religion addresses "why" questions. The former questions are answered in the "explanations" of the natural sciences and the latter strive toward human "understanding." Indeed, we often find "that we must transcend and even *relinquish* an explanation of 'how' it [i.e., creation] happened if we are to understand 'why' it happened."[43] It is not that religion and science contradict each other, they simply are addressing different issues. At best, religion "supplements" science.[44]

This way of distinguishing religious and scientific thought and language could appropriately be described as dualistic. Any potential conflict between science and religion is avoided by insisting that the two are simply addressing different levels of life. This dualism comes to its sharpest expression in the way in which Gilkey will, on occasion, describe the relation of symbolic-mythic language to facts. Gilkey says that while religious language is clearly assertive, that is, it is saying something about a real state of affairs, its assertions are "non-empirical" — they inform us of no "matters of fact."[45] Myths have no literal reference. A myth like the story of the creation and fall of humanity "has no inherent and original factual content; its meaning is not intrinsically tied to any particular, individual event in history."[46] Indeed, Gilkey goes so far as to say that "a myth can only be true as a *religious* affirmation, if it is untrue as a literal description of fact."[47] Therefore he concludes that "religious truth ... does not tell us any new 'facts' about other finite things in the created world, nor add at all to our descriptions of its observable character, structure, or development."[48]

Almost all of the references in the above two paragraphs are taken from *Maker of Heaven and Earth*. In 1961, however, Gilkey published an

204

article that would appear to have cut the ground out from under such dualistic formulations. In "Cosmology, Ontology and the Travail of Biblical Language," Gilkey asks whether the neo-orthodox rejection of the univocity of religious language has not resulted in equivocation.[49] Specifically addressing the "Biblical Theology" movement he argues that speaking in theological and mythical terms of "God's mighty acts in history," of events that are also explained (by the same people) in purely scientific and naturalistic terms, leaves one in a hopeless dualism. The result is that such mighty acts are reduced from God's objective activity in history to the mere inward beliefs of the biblical (and contemporary) writers. In response to this dualism of belief and historical event, Gilkey insists that there must, in fact, be special events in history, not just our belief in them. He goes on to say that "only an ontology of events specifying what God's relation to ordinary events is like, and thus what his relation to certain special events might be, could fill the now empty analogy of mighty acts, void since the denial of the miraculous."[50]

This article is tacitly a critique of the dualistic and neo-orthodox tone of *Maker of Heaven and Earth*.[51] There are, however, two problems with the role that this article plays in the Gilkey corpus. The first problem is that Gilkey only *proposes* an "ontology of special events" as a prerequisite for meaningfully speaking of mythic events having historical factuality, he never develops such an ontology.[52] The second problem is that while Gilkey has developed a more integral way to speak of the myth/fact relation (which I will discuss further below), he has also reverted to the same terms found in *Maker of Heaven and Earth* in his more recent work, *Creationism on Trial*.

Gilkey's testimony for the American Civil Liberties Union at the 1982 'creationist' trial in Arkansas maintained that creationism or creation science should not be taught as science in public school biology classes because it is a religious, not a scientific, theory. While he does not retreat from his arguments concerning the religious dimension of science (arguments used by the creationists in their own defense), or his claim that science has played an idolatrous role in western culture, he nevertheless finds himself supporting the mainline scientific establishment (a paradoxical position for Gilkey to find himself in) and advocating a fairly traditional religion/science distinction. As in *Maker of Heaven and Earth* he insists that science is only concerned with proximate origins (how questions), not the religious issue of ultimate origins (why questions).[53] While science is concerned with objective data and observable, repeatable facts, religion is concerned with the world as a whole. Science, therefore, asks objective questions and religion asks questions of ultimate meaning. Whereas the final authority in science is logical coherence and experimental adequacy, the final authority for religion is God and revelation, neither of which are, in principle, falsifiable. The language of science is quantitative and univocal while religious language is personal and symbolic.[54]

In a rather facile way Gilkey sums up the distinction between religious and scientific language by saying that "whenever finite things or persons are related to God, there is religious discourse or theories about them; whenever they are related merely to each other, one has 'secular' discourse, not religious discourse."[55] I say that this position is facile because it loses touch with the depth of analysis we have seen elsewhere in Gilkey's theology of culture. There we have seen that the genius of his approach has been to discern the religious dimension of the most apparently secular aspects of our culture, including science. Once one understands the role that a religious vision of life (or religious substance) plays in culture, then a simplistic religion/secular dichotomy is no longer helpful. Yet it is precisely this kind of a dualistic tendency that can be discerned in Gilkey's argument against creationism.

One of the arguments advanced by the creationists was, in fact, borrowed directly from Gilkey's phenomenological description of the religious dimension of science.[56] If all science proceeds on the basis of presuppositions that are ultimately religious in character, they argued, then why should only 'secular' presuppositions be allowed in the classroom and not 'theistic' ones?[57] Gilkey's response to this question was to introduce a distinction between the metaphysical and epistemological presuppositions that make science possible and the methodological presuppositions that are merely rules of procedure. This is a distinction that had not been made in his writings prior to the book on creationism. The metaphysical and epistemological pre-suppositions parallel what we have seen to be the religious dimension of science. Science is only possible if certain things of ontological generality are believed about the world. These include the reality, uniformity, intelligibility and ordered contingency of the material world, and the possibility of human minds to grasp that order in a context of inter-subjective research and testing. These presuppositions are both religious and cultural in character. They are also distinct from the methodological assumptions of science. These rules of procedure function as the 'canons' of science. They amount to the scientific method that is absorbed by scientists in their training.[58] One such canon that is most relevant to the discussion with creation-science is that "no supernatural force or cause from outside the system can be a part of scientific explanation."[59] This methodological assumption is not a matter of atheism, says Gilkey, but a recognition of the limitation of science. It is a matter of the "secularity" and "methodological non-theism" of science.[60]

The significance of the distinction between metaphysical and epistemological assumptions in contrast with methodological assumptions is that it allows Gilkey to counter the creationist presuppositional argument. He can now claim that the distinction between a theistic and naturalistic interpretation of science is religious or theological in character, not scientific, because "... one is here dealing with the metaphysical or theological presuppositions of science, not with science itself, and that is a very different level of thought, of discourse, and of truth."[61]

The implication of this argument, however, is that while there may be legitimate religious disagreement at the level of the metaphysical and epistemological presuppositions of science, there can be no such disagreement with regard to methodological presuppositions. If the creationist wants to be scientific then he or she will have to abide by the rules and canons (an interesting word!) of *the* scientific method. It is almost as if the scientific method is an eternal, timeless and religiously neutral truth. The problem, however, is that methodological assumptions are themselves derivative. They are formulated in terms of the prior assumptions that Gilkey describes as metaphysical and epistemological. All methodological rules are associated with, and expressive of, such cosmological assumptions. Indeed, this was precisely what Gilkey persuasively argued in *Religion and the Scientific Future*:

> Ultimately, then, since objective rules or criteria do not explain the bases of our most cognitive judgments, we must acknowledge that the most significant factors determinative of what we assert to be true or false are those ideals of natural order, and back of them that general view of the nature of things, which determines what for us are valid data and what for us is a useful method of inquiry.[62]

If this is true (and I think that it is) then Gilkey's more recent distinction between metaphysical and methodological presuppositions is a forced and invalid attempt to counter what appears to be a valid argument from the creationist side.

On Gilkey's own terms it would be more appropriate to argue that the theistic assumptions of the creationists, together with the methodological implications of those assumptions, are, in themselves, insufficient, and that they cannot, therefore, provide an adequate foundation for fruitful scientific research. To construct an artificial distinction between metaphysical and methodological presuppositions is both as facile and as dualistic as the distinctions we saw above between religious and scientific language.

e) From a Dualistic to an Integral View of Religious Language

I have suggested that Gilkey's separation of religious language from ordinary, factual, univocal and scientific language is understandable if one sees this separation as parallel to his separation of the religious dimension of life from all other 'ordinary' dimensions of life. At the same time, however, this dualistic tendency in his approach to religious language is odd in the light of both his repeated critique of theological dualism and his own more integral formulations concerning religious language.

An overemphasis on the uniqueness and opaqueness of religious language tends to a dualism in which religious symbols and myths lose any effective contact with ordinary life. Whether one thinks of the traditional nature/grace dualism or the more recent *Geschichte/Historie* distinction with its parallel Christ of faith/Jesus of history dichotomy, the result is the same—religious language is divorced from our actual *Lebenswelt* and relegated to an existential religious realm of 'encounters' or 'I-Thou' relationships. The problem with such a dualism, according to Gilkey, is that "our most fundamental Christian symbols refer to precisely that life-world and not to some other zone; they are here to shape, thematize, empower and direct ordinary life to its natural good, not to shape some other level of existence somewhere else."[63] In order to grasp how such symbols thematize, empower and direct ordinary life one needs a more integral understanding of religious language. Such an understanding, in manifest tension with the dualistic tendencies we have been discussing, can also be discerned in Gilkey's thought.

Like the religious dimension that it brings to linguistic expression, religious language is both irreducible and interrelated with all other modes of discourse. "While it is in its own way different from each of these types of ordinary discourse, religious language necessarily has relations to each of them."[64] It is this irreducibility, yet profound relatedness of religious language that is absent in Gilkey's more dualistic formulations.[65]

Religious language cannot be totally separated from ordinary life precisely because its very meaningfulness depends upon its ability to thematize that dimension of life. Therefore religious language must have, in its own unique way, concrete reference to the factuality of reality. That factuality encompasses both the historical events to which religious language refers and the present factuality of our lives. The question is, in what irreducible way does religious language disclose dimensions of our historical and present factuality? The answer, of course, is that this mode of discourse is religious in character, disclosing the religious dimension of reality. But what does that mean? To explicate this I will first take the example of historical events.

Biblical narratives often have reference to historical events. Therefore, Gilkey agrees with Wolfhart Pannenberg's critique of the a-historical theology of Bultmann. In a faith which is as historical as Christianity, the historical investigation into the events and facts related to its fundamental symbols is inescapable.[66] Gilkey explains:

> Significant religious symbols—and the myths that group them together into "stories"—arise in special experiences where an unusual encounter has taken place, where the transcendent and the sacred has manifested itself in a special manner....

Further, "a factual element accrues to any set of religious symbols because these arise out of a series of past events into the present by a tradition."[67] Therefore the fact/myth dichotomy discussed above is totally inappropriate. Yet, religious language refers to historical events in a unique way, from its own perspective. Mythical language describes historical events from the perspective of ultimacy. Such language discloses the depth dimension of historical events. For example, the gospel narratives tell the story of the man Jesus of Nazareth in terms of the incarnation — the depth meaning of this man's life is that he is the Son of God, the promised Christ.[68] Similarly, the narrative of the Hebrew scriptures tell the story of Israel's history in terms of the covenant. The focus of such language, then, is to describe real events in terms of ultimacy.[69]

Another way in which Gilkey describes the relation of symbols and myths to historical factuality is to say that the cluster of symbols that characterize Christianity provide us with "an ultimate horizon" and a "general framework within which we interpret all facts."[70] These symbols and myths encompass the totality of experience: "they tell us the ultimate character and the pattern of the whole of reality...."[71] And in this context we can interpret the meaning of particular facts and events within that whole. While we should be cautious that such language does not reintroduce an unwarranted fact/value dualism into our approach to the relation of myth and factuality,[72] the predilection of symbolic-mythical language for a comprehensive understanding of the totality of reality that serves as the ultimate horizon or context in which historical events occur, does clarify the way in which myths and historical factuality relate.

If religious language provides the interpretative context for disclosing the depth dimension of historical factuality, then does it function in the same way for the factuality of present experience? Gilkey argues that it does. Religious language is related to other modes of discourse such as empirical discourse, philosophical or abstractive language, existentially self-involving discourse and moral language,[73] and it has reference to the same referents (or states of affairs) as these other modes of discourse. The fact that reality is multi-dimensional requires that we engage in various modes of discourse or language games in order to grasp any referent in all of its richness.

For example, Gilkey's theology of culture speaks of cultural formation and history in terms of the religious substance of culture. That is, religious language is necessary to disclose the dimension of ultimacy inherent in any culture. One could just as legitimately speak in sociological or political terms of the same state of affairs because cultures also manifest social and political dimensions. Similarly, one could speak of the natural environment in scientific terms or (as is more often the case today) in economic terms because these too are legitimate dimensions of nature. To disclose the depth meaning of nature in terms of the symbol of 'creation' would be to engage in another mode of discourse — the religious. There is, therefore, both unity and diversity in our language. We refer to unified referents with a diversity of modes of discourse in order to grasp those referents in their multi-dimensionality.

In this light it is possible to be even more specific about the unique focus of religious language.

> The direct purpose of religious speech is to express what creates, founds, or establishes life (its ground and ultimate horizon), what is experienced as most deeply disturbing or threatening to it (its most fundamental principle of evil or alienation), and what is experienced then as rescuing or restoring it (its redemptive or saving powers).[74]

In this focus, religious language can address itself to any area of life and any present factuality. Herein we see the fundamental relatedness of this mode of discourse to all of life in its multi-dimensionality. Without such a relatedness a *theology* of culture would be impossible. With it, the dualistic tendencies discussed above are inappropriate.

We have seen that Gilkey's prolegomenon establishes that there is a religious dimension which is a constitutive dimension of our life and that this dimension is thematized by means of religious discourse. Such discourse is, therefore, in principle, meaningful. This dimension and this language refer us to that which is Ultimate. The question that remains to be explored, then, is the relation between the dimension of ultimacy and the Ultimate.

3. A Dimension of Ultimacy and the Ultimate
a) Naming a Dimension
In section one of this chapter I argued that Gilkey has not clearly explicated the relation of the dimension of ultimacy to what I called the heart-centredness or spiritual unity of human life. Further, his language becomes even more confusing when he relates the religious dimension and the spiritual unity of life to the transcendent. One cannot coherently speak of a dimension of life as being transcendent to that life. We have also seen that this confusion has unfortunate consequences for Gilkey's discussion of religious language because the connection of such language to the transcendent could mean that it loses touch with concrete life. We need, then, to explore more fully the relation of this dimension of ultimacy to the Ultimate in Gilkey's thought. We will see both that the ambiguities addressed above continue to be manifest in his discussion of this relation and that his views on the ultimate/Ultimate relation are foundational to the way in which he addresses the problem of the parity of religions.

My question is: what is the relation between the dimension of ultimacy, which has been disclosed in Gilkey's prolegomenon, and the Ultimate to which such a dimension necessarily has reference? At first sight this does not appear to be an overly problematic question. Gilkey clearly insists that his prolegomenon is not a natural theology.[75] Phenomenologically disclosing a dimension of ultimacy is neither proof for the existence of God nor evidence that any particular religious symbol system has more adequately thematized that dimension than any other. Such a disclosure simply establishes that religious language is meaningful — it makes no claims regarding the truth of such language.[76]

It is also the case that Gilkey unequivocally says that "this dimension [of ultimacy] in our world is not by any means simply or directly 'God,'" though it provides the possibility of a relation to God if there is a God.[77] This is why R. L. Littlejohn can confidently say that "Gilkey does not hold that the dimension of ultimacy can be phenomenologically identified with God." Indeed, Littlejohn says that Gilkey "makes a sharp distinction between the ultimate dimension in human experience as an experiential range of reference and God as the actual referent which can appear in this range."[78] While we have seen in chapter one that this distinction between an experiential range of reference and the actual referent which can appear within that range is a helpful way to characterize Gilkey's position in contrast with a referential theory of truth,[79] I are not sure that the relation of the dimension of ultimacy to the Ultimate, or God, is quite as clear as either Littlejohn or Gilkey himself suggest.

In the very next sentence, following the apparently unequivocal statement that the dimension of ultimacy is not God, that I cited above, Gilkey goes on to say that "for many and varied important reasons, Christians *name* this dimension or region of ultimacy by the symbol of God and define it further in terms of that symbol."[80] There is obviously some ambiguity here. Why would Christians *name* a dimension of human life which Gilkey has just said is not by any means 'God,' by that very name? How could a *dimension* of life which refers us beyond that life to our ultimate ground and horizon also be that to which it refers us? Is Gilkey really saying that this dimension is appropriately named God? Has he conflated the dimension *of* ultimacy and the Ultimate? Does he merge the human *experience* of ultimacy with the Ultimate? I suggest that, against his best intentions, this is precisely what he does.[81]

Moreover, this conflation of the dimension of ultimacy and the Ultimate is a natural consequence of the confusion I noted in section one of this chapter concerning the supposed transcendence of this dimension of life. There we saw that Gilkey has failed to distinguish clearly between the transcendent to which this dimension refers and the dimension itself. Somehow the dimension of ultimacy transcends our selfhood and environment. While I have already argued that this is an unhelpful way to speak of a dimension of life it now becomes clear that this undifferentiated identification of the dimension of ultimacy with transcendence can easily result in the conflation of the two.

If the ambiguity in Gilkey's description of the dimension of ultimacy/Ultimate relation was simply a minor matter of unclarity on one point, then it would not be necessary to dwell on it at any length. The problem is that this conflation decisively informs Gilkey's theology of culture, especially with reference to his discussion of the parity of religions, universalism and his proposed model of a covenant between Christianity and other religious traditions. While I have already voiced my criticisms of this side of his theology of culture at some length above, I can now take that critique a step further.[82]

b) Ultimacy, the Ultimate and Universalism

If one discloses a dimension of ultimacy in the life of a person or a culture has one, thereby, disclosed a relatedness to God in the life of that person or culture? This is a difficult question. In the context of a prolegomenon Gilkey would have to answer in the negative. Disclosing a dimension of ultimacy is no more than uncovering a legitimate dimension of human life that has been, for assorted reasons, hidden or forgotten. By establishing that there is such a constitutive dimension of human life one is simply proving that human beings face ultimate or limit questions and that, in answering these questions, they are related to something that functions as ultimate in their lives. That something need not be God — indeed, it could just as easily be an idol. We could say, then, that a phenomenological analysis of the dimension of ultimacy discloses a dimension with certain *structural* qualifications (e.g., a concern with limit, ground, horizon, etc.). That analysis also discloses, however, that this dimension manifests what might be called a *directional* characteristic.[83] That is, it is a constitutive characteristic of such a dimension to answer the limit questions in a certain way, to go in one direction and not another, or, to use Ricoeur's phrase, "to take a stand somewhere."[84] It is structurally impossible to be a-religious — the human creature is *homo religiosus*. This is a universal, structural characteristic of human life. And that structural dimension of life receives existential concreteness and clarity in terms of directional choices and particular commitments.

What I am here describing as the relation of structure and direction is evident in Gilkey's own theology — though he never uses these terms. In part IV of this study we will see that Gilkey's view of creation and fall affirms a creation that is (in my terms) structurally good though profoundly misdirected because of the taint of sin.[85] We will also see in his theology of providence that history manifests an ontological structure which he describes as the relation of destiny and freedom. When freedom falls into sin, however, destiny becomes misdirected and results in fate.[86]

The distinction between structure and direction was also evident in my discussion of Gilkey's theology of culture. Science and technology are not, in themselves, evil. Rather, they are good dimensions of human creativity. When, however, they are misused in service of human concupiscence, then they are misdirected and take on a demonic potential.[87] Such cultural misdirection is rooted in the religious substance of a culture which also displays a structure/direction relationship.

> Community inescapably has a religious substance, but that substance can be at once creative and infinitely destructive, the source of the danger of each community to the peace, security, and well-being of other communities.[88]

While the "inescapability" of communities having a religious substance is a structural given, the ability of such a substance to be both creative and destructive is evidence of the equally inescapable directionality of each religious substance. It is on the basis of this potential (and actual) misdirection of the religious substance of modernity that Gilkey can engage in a theological critique of modernity.

The question that we need to address further, however, is whether Gilkey also discerns misdirection in the religious substance of other traditions. If he does have such discernment then what are the implications of this for his approach to the problem of pluralism and the parity of religions? Again, Gilkey's position is not totally clear. On the one hand he seems to affirm the distinction between a universal structure and particular direction, and on the other hand this very distinction is "puzzling" for him. Specifically discussing Christian religiousness he says:

> The ultimate puzzle for theological language is the uniting of these two elements of our deepest experience, the one universally human, and the other uniquely Christian: the mysterious depths of our human existence with its joys and terrors on the one hand and the claiming and saving power of the figure of Jesus on the other.[89]

This puzzle concerning the relation of the universal and the particular is directly related to the question of the relation of the dimension of ultimacy to the Ultimate. At the mysterious depths of all human existence is a dimension of ultimacy. This is universal and structural. How people relate to the Ultimate varies from one tradition to another. For some, the Ultimate is taken to be a monotheistically conceived God, for others a mystical Oneness, and for even others economic growth and technological power function as the Ultimate. How one *relates* to the Ultimate, then, is particular and directional.

In his discussion of *religion* as a universal dimension of life and its relation to *religions* as particular manifestations of the Ultimate, Gilkey attempts to maintain the distinctions we are here addressing.[90] That attempt, however, is not successful. The ambiguity arises in Gilkey's tendency to move too easily and too quickly from the religious substance of a culture to a manifestation of the 'sacred' in that culture. For example, in *Society and the Sacred*, he combines two questions: "where in ordinary experience does (a) religious language find common usage, and (b) where does an experience of the sacred and ultimate make its appearance?" His answers read: "religious or mythical speech appears in all contemporary political speech, and when any culture is expressing its most ultimate convictions, norms, and expectations; and the sacred is manifest most commonly to us — as to all cultures — in and through the forms, usages and requirements of our common life."[91]

My problem with this formulation is that while the answer to the first question concerning religious speech is both clear and well substantiated by Gilkey's theology of culture, the second answer is neither clear nor substantiated. When Gilkey refers to an "appearance" of the "sacred" and "ultimate" in and through the forms and usages of our common life (which are themselves rooted in a religious substance of ultimate convictions, norms and expectations), is he saying that the "Sacred" and "Ultimate" appear here, or only that that which this particular culture takes to be sacred and ultimate are manifest in this way? It would seem that he is, in fact, saying the former, not the latter. The problem is that Gilkey's own theology of culture has shown that that which is taken to be ultimate in a tradition such as western modernity is not the Ultimate at all, but idolized dimensions of the creaturely. If a culture's ultimate convictions, norms and expectations revolve around an unquestioning faith in science and technology (as has been the case in modernity) then these dimensions of life will take on sacral characteristics. They will function as that which is ultimate in that culture.

That Gilkey does identify the religious substance of a culture with the presence of the divine or Ultimate in that culture is especially clear later in his discussion of the parity of religions and universalism. Attempting to present a biblical case for universalism, he argues that "each creative culture, insofar as it lives on a religious substance, is established in and through the divine, apprehended and received, to be sure, in different ways than this, but nonetheless grounded here."[92] While I have already offered a critique of this argument earlier in this study,[93] what is important to note here is that Gilkey is making the unqualified claim that insofar as a culture lives on a religious substance (and all cultures do!) it is, thereby, established in and through the divine presence.

In another passage, also discussed previously, Gilkey explicitly identifies the structural phenomenon of cultural religious substances with both general revelation and universal redemption. Not only does each culture have a religious substance "which represents its appropriation of and response to the divine," and which is evidence of "the creative and providential activity of God present and manifest throughout nature and history," but also, this divine presence manifest in every religious substance is universally redemptive.[94] While the move from providential presence to universal redemption is, I have argued, unfounded, what is of greater significance in this context is Gilkey's move from religious substance, which represents a "response to" the divine, to an affirmation of the universal providential presence of God in all historical cultures. It may well be true that the doctrine of providence only has meaning if that divine historical presence is universal. But this does not mean that one can assert without qualification, as Gilkey seems to be doing, that all religious substances manifest this providential presence. A culture's religious substance is a response to the divine and that response can be (and often is) profoundly distorted, misdirected and idolatrous, as Gilkey himself would also say.

If Gilkey acknowledges the response character or directionality of the religious dimension of life (and the religious substance of culture) then how can he so easily move from an affirmation of a dimension of ultimacy to what appears to be a rather unambiguous and undifferentiated affirmation of the creative presence of the Ultimate in all cultures? On one level the answer to this question is that Gilkey wants to have a theoretical foundation for his belief in universalism. If the Ultimate is always that which is manifest in all religious substances, then the groundwork has been laid for such a universalism. But, perhaps there is a deeper reason within his theoretical understanding of ultimacy which explains this affirmation of the universal and redemptive presence of the Ultimate. If the dimension of ultimacy is appropriately named God and if the dimension of ultimacy and the Ultimate to which it has reference are in fact conflated, as I have shown to be Gilkey's view, then any disclosure of a religious substance or dimension of ultimacy in a culture will serve as conclusive evidence of the divine presence in that culture. It is this conflation that provides the theoretical foundation for Gilkey's approach to the parity of religions.

c) Universalism and Monism
I also suggested above that while Gilkey's lack of clarity concerning the religious dimension as an ordinary dimension of life led to dualistic tendencies in his understanding of both this dimension and the religion/science relation, his lack of clarity concerning the relation of this dimension to the transcendent or Ultimate results in monistic tendencies. I can now explain how this is the case.

Gilkey's approach to the parity of religions is monistic in the sense that it affirms a fundamental unity or oneness of world religions. This unity is affirmed because all world religions, and all historical cultures, manifest a dimension of ultimacy. Since that dimension is conflated with the Ultimate itself, all such traditions and cultures are related to the Ultimate. Since the Ultimate is one, the different ways of relating to it are, at best, relative.

Our experience tells us that God is related as creative ultimacy to all humans—and to all creatures alike—and that the differences between

217

our responses to this relation — in our being, our loving and our creativity — are at best relative differences.[95]

My problem with Gilkey's position is that it fails to take seriously enough the response character or directionality of the religious dimension. This has two consequences. First, if the dimension of ultimacy is effectively conflated with the Ultimate, then how can it still entail a response to the Ultimate? The response character of this dimension can only be maintained if it is clearly distinct from the Ultimate to which it responds.

The second consequence of this monistic tendency is that it compromises the role of will or decision in making faith choices. Such a compromise undermines the directionality of the religious dimension, fails to account for the possibility of radical misdirection, and relegates choices of ultimate concerns to relative differences.

4. Evaluative Conclusions
In this part of the book we have seen that Gilkey's theology of culture is founded upon his prolegomenal analysis of the dimension of ultimacy. The disclosure of such a dimension makes a 'theology' of culture a meaningful venture. In chapter six we reviewed Gilkey's evidence for such a dimension and found his argument compelling.

In chapter seven we have discussed Gilkey's understanding of the characteristics of that dimension, the nature of the language that brings the religious dimension to thematic expression, and the relation of the dimension of ultimacy to the Ultimate itself. Insofar as this whole chapter has been an evaluation of Gilkey's position, there is no need to rehearse again my difficulties. I have found problems throughout his analysis of ultimacy. I have also argued that these problems have a direct bearing on the aspects of his theology of culture that I have found less than compelling.

The question that remains to be addressed is how Gilkey's constructive theology relates to his theology of culture. This will be my concern in the final part of this book.

NOTES

1   An edited version of this chapter has been published elsewhere as "The Dimension of Ultimacy and Theology of Culture: A Critical Discussion of Langdon Gilkey," *Calvin Theological Journal* 24, 1 (April 1989), pp. 66-92.

2   *How the Church*, pp. 20-21. Cf. "Secularism's Impact on Contemporary Theology," p. 64.

3   *Maker*, p. 193.

4   For a survey of this theme in the thought of Barth, Bultmann, Tillich and Ebeling, see Pannenberg's article, "The Question of God," in *Basic Questions in Theology*, II, trans. by G. H. Kehm (Philadelphia: Fortress Press, 1971), pp. 210-233.

5   *Society and the Sacred*, p. 110. Cf. *Creationism*, pp. 214-215, 257-258, n.1.

6   Cf. especially, Tracy, *Blessed Rage for Order*, ch. 5.

7   Cf. Stephen E. Toulmin, *An Examination of the Place of Reason in Ethics*, ch. 14. Gilkey is critical of Schubert Ogden's use of Toulmin's notion of limit questions as the basis for his own rational and logical form of metaphysical philosophy because such questions are at the limits of rationality and therefore beyond the scope of the rational categorizations of argumentative reasoning. "Theology in Process: Schubert Ogden's Developing Theology," *Interpretation* 21 (October 1967), pp. 455-456.

8   Gilkey quotes Wild: "To reflect upon these boundaries seriously is to raise the ultimate questions of our existence. The way we face them reveals the kind of being we are, for the way a finite being holds itself with respect to its ultimate limits is the very core of that being...." In *Naming*, p. 308, n. 2.

9   *Creationism*, p. 114.

10   *Maker*, p. 28. Cf. pp. 24-29, 66-69.

11   "New Modes of Empirical Theology," p. 357.

12   Cf. *Naming*, pp. 296, 313-314; "Dissolution and Reconstruction," p. 34; and *Catholicism*, pp. 187-188.

13   *Naming*, p. 254. Cf. "Dissolution and Reconstruction," p. 35: "*Nothing* about man's behavior and experience can be finally understood except through this 'religious' dimension, where he seeks the ultimate or sacred and he finds it either in God or himself."

14   "New Modes," p. 359. Cf. *Naming*, p. 307.

15   Cf. *Reaping*, p. 121: "History is multi-dimensional; human societies live, move and act in this multi-dimensional history.... Further, *one* dimension of this multi-dimensional reality of history and of social change was found to be a dimension of ultimacy, a horizon of transcendence and of sacrality (emphasis added)."

6 *Naming*, p. 313. Cf. "Response to Berger," p. 492.

17 "Response to Berger," p. 494.

18 Cf. *How the Church*, p. 55: "The religious or holy, then, is properly not a category either totally separated from the secular or completely identified with it. Rather it is that which relates us to the source of our life and the goal of its meaning, and thus that which conditions and ultimately directs all our secular existence."

19 "New Modes," p. 358.

20 Cf. *Naming*, p. 392.

21 Cf. footnote 14 above.

22 I am depending here on Herman Dooyeweerd's analysis of the irreducible modalities, dimensions or aspects of creaturely life, and the interrelation of those modalities. Cf. his *A New Critique of Theoretical Thought*, II, pt. I. For introductory discussions of this theory see, L. Kalsbeek, *Contours of a Christian Philosophy*, ed. by Bernard and Josina Zylstra (Toronto: Wedge Publishing, 1975), esp. ch. 7-13; Jacob Klapwijk, "The Struggle for a Christian Philosophy: Another Look at Dooyeweerd," *Reformed Journal* 30, 2 (February 1980), pp. 12-15; "Dooyeweerd's Christian Philosophy: Antithesis and Critique," *Reformed Journal* 30, 3 (March 1980), pp. 20-24; and Brian J. Walsh and Jonathan Chaplin, "Dooyeweerd's Contribution to a Christian Philosophical Paradigm," *Crux* XIX, 1 (March 1983), pp. 8-22.

23 Cf. Hendrik Hart, *Understanding Our World: Toward an Integral Ontology*, Christian Studies Today Series (Lanham, MD: University Press of America, 1984), ch. 3 and 4.

24 James H. Olthuis, "Towards a Certitudinal Hermeneutic," in *Hearing and Doing: Philosophical Essays Dedicated to H. Evan Runner*, ed. by John Kraay and Anthony Tol (Toronto: Wedge Publishing, 1979), p. 76. For a similar perspective see Arnold H. DeGraaff, "Towards a New Anthropological Model," in the same volume, pp. 97-118. Olthuis places his view of the faith dimension in the context of a developmental model in his article, "Faith Development in the Adult Life Span," *Studies in Religion/ Sciences Religieuses* 14, 4 (1985), pp. 497-509.

25 James H. Olthuis, "Straddling the Boundaries Between Theology and Psychology: the Faith-Feeling Interface," *Journal of Psychology and Christianity* 4, 1 (Spring 1985), p. 10. For a discussion of the importance of such distinctions in "religious and moral education" see J. Harry Fernhout, *The Relation of Religion or Faith to Morality According to Lawrence Kohlberg and James Fowler* (unpub. M.A. thesis; University of Toronto, 1982), esp. pp. 182-195; and J. Harry Fernhout and Dwight Boyd, "Faith in Autonomy: Development in Kohlberg's Perspectives on Religion and Morality," *Religious Education* 80, 2 (Spring 1985), pp. 287-307.

26 Cf. Hart, *Understanding Our World*, p. 183. For Dooyeweerd's analysis of this dimension, cf. *A New Critique of Theoretical Thought*, II, pp. 291-330.

27 Cf. Romans 10:9.

28 *Naming*, p. 20.

29 Cf. Wittgenstein, *Philosophical Investigations*, ¶ 67.

30 *Message and Existence*, pp. 135-136. Cf. *Catholicism*, pp. 12, 145; *Reaping*, pp. 147-148; and "The Universal and Immediate Presence of God," p. 40.

31 Cf. "Symbols, Meaning and the Divine Presence," p. 251; and *Catholicism*, p. 113.

32 Cf. *Naming*, pp. 286, 298-299.

33 Cf. *Naming*, pp. 287, 295; also "Responses to Berger," p. 493.

34 *Naming*, pp. 419-420.

35 Cf. *Catholicism*, pp. 165-167; "Tillich: Master of Mediation," p. 46; Tillich, *Systematic Theology*, I, pp. 239-241; and Ricoeur, *The Symbolism of Evil*, p. 15.

36 Cf. *Reaping*, pp. 148-149.

37 Ricoeur views myths as second degree interpretations of symbols. Cf. *The Symbolism of Evil*, p. 18: "In this sense symbols are more radical than myths. I shall regard myths as a species of symbols, as symbols developed in the form of narrations and articulated in a time and space that cannot be co-ordinated with the time and space of history and geography according to the critical method." Gilkey's views closely follow Ricoeur's.

38 *Reaping*, p. 150.

39 "Modern Myth-Making," p. 283. Cf. *Religion*, p. 66.

40 Cf. *Religion*, p. 103; *Catholicism*, pp. 85-87; and *Maker*, pp. 281, 288.

41 "Modern Myth-Making," pp. 290-291.

42 *Maker*, p. 34, emphasis added. Cf. *Naming*, p. 422.

43 Ibid, p. 69, emphasis added. For a critique of the distinction between explanation and understanding and its implication for the dichotomy in the western academy between the *Naturwissenschaften* and *Geisteswissenschaften*, see Pannenberg, *Theology and the Philosophy of Science*, ch. 2 (esp. section 5); and Ian Barbour, *Issues in Science and Religion*, ch. 7.

44 Ibid, p. 133.

45 *Naming*, p. 286.

46 *Maker*, p. 283.

47 Ibid, p. 285.

48 Ibid, p. 132.

49 I have also discussed this article in chapter one, section two of this book.

50 "Cosmology, Ontology, and Biblical Language in Travail," p. 200.

51 Gilkey acknowledged this in a discussion with the present author. "Interview," November 28, 1984. Cf. above, **Introduction**, section two.

52 Again, Gilkey verbally acknowledged this in the interview referred to in note 51. Neither *Reaping* nor "Events" explicitly address this problem.

53 Cf. *Creationism*, pp. 33-34, 49-51, 120-122.

54 Cf. *Creationism*, pp. 108-112.

55 *Creationism*, p. 113.

56 Cf. our discussion above in chapter six, section two (a).

57 Gilkey summarizes the creationist argument as follows: "But if all scientific thought has undemonstrable presuppositions, and if every form of thinking, therefore, bears with it a 'religious aura,' does this not give point to the creation-scientist critique that evolutionary science represents in fact a secularistic 'faith,' not an 'objective theory,' even that it is an instrument of atheistic and humanistic religion?" (*Creationism*, p. 134).

58 Cf. *Creationism*, pp. 65-69.

59 *Creationism*, p. 112.

60 Cf. *Creationism*, p. 115.

61 *Creationism*, p. 135.

62 *Religion*, p. 55.

63 "Symbols, Meaning and the Divine Presence," p. 253.

64 *Naming*, p. 288.

65 It is, therefore, intriguing that in the very same book in which he advances such dualistic formulations to counter creationism he also says that explicating the unified relatedness of religious and scientific thought is an essential task of philosophical theology: "Perhaps, then, the major philosophical and theological task of our time is represented by this question, as old as the tradition of reflection itself: How are the many diverse ways of thought in a culture — its technical and scientific thought, its social and political thinking, its artistic and moral experience and reflection, and its deepest and so religious convictions — to find coherence and unity, that is, together to achieve coherence, mutual credibility and effectiveness?" (*Creationism*, pp. 207-208).

66 Cf. *Catholicism*, p. 120. For Pannenberg's critique of kerygmatic theology and insistence on the historicity of Christian faith, see his *Revelation as History*, trans. by

D. Granskou (London: Macmillan, 1968), ch. 1, 4; *Basic Questions in Theology*, I, ch. 1, 2; *Faith and Reality*, trans. by J. Maxwell (Philadelphia: Westminster Press, 1977), ch. 2, 5, 6; and "The Revelation of God in Jesus of Nazareth," in *Theology as History*, ed. by J. M. Robinson and J. B. Cobb Jr. (New York: Harper and Row, 1967). For helpful critique of Pannenberg's position see F. II. Klooster, "Historical Method and the Resurrection of Jesus in Pannenberg's Theology," *Calvin Theological Journal* 11, 1 (April 1976), pp. 5-33; I. G. Nicol, "Facts and Meanings: Wolfhart Pannenberg's Theology as History and the Role of the Historico-Critical Method," *Religious Studies* 12, 2 (June 1976), pp. 123-139; and D. Holwerda, "Faith, Reason, and the Resurrection in the Theology of Wolfhart Pannenberg," in *Faith and Rationality: Reason and Belief in God*, ed. by Alvin Plantinga and Nicholas Wolterstorff (Notre Dame: University of Notre Dame Press, 1983), pp. 256-316.

67 *Religion*, p. 128-129. Gilkey goes on to say that any living symbol in the Jewish or Christian traditions "has, as part of its meaning and crucial to its validity, reference to the factuality of the past, and especially to those events creative of that tradition."

68 Cf. *Maker*, pp. 260, 282.

69 James H. Olthuis calls this the "certitudinal" focus of scripture. Cf. his "Towards a Certitudinal Hermeneutic," and his *A Hermeneutics of Ultimacy: Peril or Promise?* (with Clark H. Pinnock, Donald G. Bloesch and Gerald T. Sheppard), Christian Studies Today Series (Lanham, MD: University Press of America, 1986).
It is important to underline the fact that if religious language is to disclose a dimension of ultimacy of any event it must have reference to a particular state of affairs. In response to Bultmann, John Macquarrie asks: "Does it ... make sense to talk of 'dying and rising with Christ' without an assurance that, in some sense, Christ actually died and rose?" (quoted by Thiselton, *The Two Horizons*, p. 273).

70 *Catholicism*, p. 100.

71 *Creationism*, p. 212.

72 Again, Pannenberg has offered a helpful corrective. He strives to reinstate "the original unity of facts and their meanings" because the meaning of an event is "inherent" in that event in its historical context, not added to it from the outside. Cf. *Theology as History*, pp. 126-127; *Faith and Reality*, p. 62; and *Basic Questions in Theology*, I, p. 86. Cf. also, Thiselton, *The Two Horizons* pp. 74-76 (on Pannenberg), 213-223, 245-251 (on Bultmann), 359-361 (on Wittgenstein).

73 Cf. *Naming*, pp. 288-293.

74 *Creationism*, p. 215. It is interesting to note that in this description of the purpose of religious language Gilkey essentially follows the overall thrust of the biblical worldview, viz., creation, fall and redemption. I will address this further in part IV.

75 Cf. chapter one, section three (f).

76 Cf. chapter one, section three (d).

77 *Naming*, p. 254.

78 *Gilkey's Phenomenology of Ultimacy*, pp. 122, 162. It should be noted that Littlejohn offers no textual evidence for this interpretation — not even the reference that I have provided in the previous note.

79 Cf. chapter one, note 58.

80 *Naming*, p. 254. Cf. "The Universal and Immediate Presence of God," pp. 100, 103; and "New Modes," p. 366.

81 Therefore, in contrast with Littlejohn, we agree with D. R. Stiver's interpretation. Summing up the "natural theologies" of Rahner, Gilkey, Küng, Tracy, Ogden and (even!) Mascall, he says that the "new style" natural theology proposed by these thinkers "does not shrink back from declaring that awareness of ultimacy or a horizon of mystery is actually an awareness of God." *Converging Approaches*, p. 267 (cf. p. 260). Whether this is an adequate interpretation of all of these thinkers is a matter on which we will reserve judgment. That such an interpretation seems to be valid with reference to Gilkey we are convinced.

82 Cf. chapter five, section two (c).

83 I have discussed the structure/direction distinction further in *The Transforming Vision*, pp. 88-90; and "Dooyeweerd's Contribution," pp. 17-18.

84 Cf. *The Symbolism of Evil*, pp. 308, 355.

85 Cf. *Maker*, pp. 159-160; *Message and Existence*, pp. 128-129; and "Heilbroner's Vision of History," p. 231.

86 Cf. *Reaping*, pp. 49-51, 126-127.

87 Cf. *Reaping*, pp. 260-261; *Society and the Sacred*, p. 84; and "Culture and Religious Belief," p. 11.

88 *Message and Existence*, p. 214.

89 "Dissolution and Reconstruction," p. 38.

90 Cf. *Society and the Sacred*, pp. 158ff.

91 *Society and the Sacred*, p. 22.

92 Ibid, p. 68.

93 Cf. chapter four, section two.

94 *Society and the Sacred*, p. 163.

95 *Reaping*, p. 298.

PART 4:
Constructive Theology

CHAPTER EIGHT:
Gilkey's Constructive Theological Reflections

Langdon Gilkey is a systematic theologian who has not produced a systematic theology. The closest he has come to a systematic articulation of the Christian faith has been his introduction to Christian theology, *Message and Existence* — a book he refers to as a "baby systematic" which "dodges" the "stupendous and intimidating scholarly and intellectual requirements of a full systematic theology."[1] Indeed, since the "death of the giants" (most notably, Barth and Tillich), little explicitly systematic theology has been produced (with the possible exception of Rahner). For example, if one surveys the topics addressed at meetings of the American Academy of Religion over the last two decades, one will note a steady decrease in discussion of traditionally theological topics. And while there may be some discussion of specific doctrines (most notably, Christology and God/Goddess) there is almost no discussion of the broad topic of systematic theology as a whole. In terms of Gilkey's threefold categorization of theology it is fair to say that questions of prolegomenon (including methodology, anthropology, phenomenology and philosophy of religion) and theology of culture (including ecology, religious pluralism, feminism, ethics, and the crises of modernity) have dominated the scene, leaving little room for systematic theology.

An analysis of Gilkey's thought, however, is not complete without at least some discussion of his constructive theology. Recall that in his methodological proposal (as outlined in chapter one) the prolegomenon is a prolegomenon for constructive theology, and the theology of culture is an outworking in praxis of the eidetic, experiential and reflective meaning that has been disclosed in a constructive theology. A discussion of this constructive theology is, therefore, essential. As with my interpretation and evaluation of his prolegomenon, this discussion will be limited and focussed in terms of the overall aim of this study, namely, an explication and evaluation of Gilkey's thought primarily in terms of his theology of culture. In this part of the study, then, I will not attempt a thorough evaluation of every aspect of Gilkey's constructive theology. Rather, I will address his constructive theology in terms of its foundational continuity (or discontinuity) with his theology of culture.

Focussing the analysis in this way does not eliminate all of the interpretative problems, however. I have already noted that Gilkey has not written a "systematic" theology. At best he has engaged in various constructive theological reflections. This lack of a clearly explicated system does not mean that Gilkey's reflections on assorted theological symbols, doctrines and themes (e.g., creation, providence, sin, Christology, eschatology, etc.) are unrelated or disjointed. The problem for the interpreter of Gilkey's thought is to discern how these reflections are, in fact, interrelated. I suggest that the best way to see this interrelation is by paying attention to what Gilkey describes as the dialectical structure of Christian faith. After briefly describing this dialectic I will interpret Gilkey's constructive theological reflections in terms of the three stages of the dialectic.

1. The Dialectical Structure of Christian Faith
In response to Gilkey's critique of Jonathan Schell's book, *The Fate of the Earth*, David Tracy noted the dialectical character of Gilkey's comments:

> For if you notice, every one of his [Gilkey's] statements was dialectical from the beginning of the critique to the end of it. That is to say, when freedom is discussed, it is discussed in relation to fate and destiny, for example. Or when history as invention is discussed, it also is discussed in relation to history as in some way given.[2]

What Tracy has noted in this one instance is also an important comment on the whole of Gilkey's work. His thought is suffused with dialectical interrelations. The *modus operandum* of his theological project as a whole is the dialectical interaction of the Christian tradition and modernity, the symbols that constitute a Christian *Weltanschauung* and the present *Lebenswelt*, message and existence. "In this interaction the symbols give that world of experience ultimate coherence, order, illumination, and healing—in turn, experience in its contemporary form provides the symbols with relevance, reality, and validity."[3] Further, the role of religion as both the legitimation of culture and its potential revolutionary undermining is also dialectical.[4] Entailed in this dialectic is a simultaneous 'yes' and 'no' in the religion/culture relation. In order for the religious symbols of a particular religious tradition to be meaningful there must be some positive relation between those symbols and the religious substance of the culture. Yet, these symbols must also give rise to a prophetic protest against the demonic pretensions of that culture.[5]

Such dialectical themes are apparent in other dimensions of Gilkey's theology of culture as well. For example, the problems of relativism and absolutism can only be overcome by means of a dialectic of one part absolute and two parts relativity. We have also seen that the cultural career of modernity itself displays certain dialectical tensions. That which is clearly most creative in modernity (its science and technology) becomes, in time, that which is the greatest threat to its future. The creative dialectically becomes its opposite — the demonic.

This dialectic within modernity is, says Gilkey, common to all cultural history. Indeed, there is a cycle to cultural history discernible in the Hebrew Scriptures' narratives concerning Israel that is analogically applicable to all cultures. Every creative culture believes, in some way, in its own divine or ultimate constitution — that somehow this culture represents, at least in its inception, an authentic expression of human life together in history. That belief is usually expressed in the culture's most primordial myths. Yet every culture also has the experience of estrangement, guilt and judgment — the sense that somehow the culture has failed and has not lived up to its hopeful expectations. This pattern of ultimate constitution and eventual judgment is, says Gilkey, common to all cultural history. If cultural historians and analysts do not account for this dialectic, then "they either emphasize the positive structure and harmony of passage and the possibilities of historical life ... in an unwarranted and soon-to-be falsified optimism, or, concentrating so heavily on the actuality of evil, they speak only of fatedness, failing to discern the new possibilities and the forces of reconciliation latent in historical experience."[6] The way beyond the starkness of this either/or is to affirm both by recognizing that there is a third stage or moment in cultural history, namely the experience of a promised renewal. Such an experience of promise is implicit in all movements of revolution and reform. The belief in the possibility of the new and of healing in history is universal. For a culture to continue it must always be in a dialectical tension of divine or ultimate constitution, prophetic judgment and prophetic hope.[7]

This dialectic, common in all cultural history and discernible in the Hebrew worldview, is also the underlying structure of Christian faith. The structure of the gospel, says Gilkey, manifests "a dialectic of affirmation, of negation, and then a higher reaffirmation that, in overcoming the negative, also transmutes the originating positive."[8] For example, the Christ is the manifestation of God, but this is a manifestation in weakness, a manifestation that must be negated in his passion. Only by moving from affirmation and through negation does the Christ receive reaffirmation in the resurrection. "The originating affirmation is true, but, taken undialectically, it is false; the negative represented by estrangement is also true, but, taken undialectically it too is false."[9] Therefore Gilkey argues that "this dialectic persists ... as the fundamental formal structure of Christian symbolism, what it is that is unique to the Christian understanding of reality and of existence."[10] Consequently, Gilkey makes the following claim:

> To reinterpret this fundamental dialectic in and for each age is the major task of theology. I suspect that it is more crucial for a theology, or for preaching, that it is faithful to this dialectic than that it adopt any particular philosophical scheme.[11]

We must be faithful to this dialectic not only because it is the structure of the gospel story but also because this gospel story is itself embedded in a cluster of symbols which is inherently dialectical. The overall pattern of creation, fall and redemption encapsulates the flow of the biblical worldview.[12] It also corresponds to what Gilkey describes as the dialectical interrelation of affirmation, negation and reaffirmation.[13] Our most primordial reality and our most foundational myth is that of creation. And creation is unambiguously affirmed as good. This affirmation, however, is compromised by the negation of the fall. If the thesis is our essentially good nature as creatures, then the antithesis is the estrangement of human creatures. Therefore, a new moment is necessary if the goodness of creation is to be reaffirmed and estrangement overcome — this is the moment of redemption.[14]

The dialectic of creation, fall and redemption is parallel to the dialectic of rational, incredible and credible discussed in chapter one.[15] By means of a synchronic analysis of the structure of creaturely being (especially in its historicity), natural theological arguments can be advanced which will establish the rationality of positing a divine ground and context for that being. This is the ontological task of constructive theology. In this context Gilkey has reinterpreted the ontological meaning of the doctrine of providence, together with the implications of that reinterpretation for our understanding of God. Ontological and synchronic analysis, however, is never sufficient in itself to comprehend the complexity of being in history. The diachronic character of historical being includes alienation, estrangement and fatedness. Therefore, "the concrete reality of historical being as both temporal and estranged now challenges the rationality and meaningfulness of finite existence, the sense of the reality of God, and as a consequence the rationality of religious or Christian belief."[16] That which appeared as rational in synchronic analysis is negated and becomes incredible in diachronic analysis. The goodness of creation and the rationality of providence are incredible in the light of the fall. The fall is incredible because, as a warping of ontological structures, it cannot be rationally explicated in terms of those structures. But while the divine as ground of our being is obscured in estrangement, it can now manifest itself as redemptive precisely in relation to that estrangement. Redemption, then, is the third stage of the dialectic.

Redemption is not rational, however, because "it is not present in the analyzable essential structure of historical being." Rather, redemption is "given" to that historical being as a credible "answer to the warping and self-destruction of that structure."[17] Further, it is important to note that rationality and credibility "are dialectically interdependent such that the rationality of the one and the credibility of the other disappears if either element is separated or isolated from the other."[18] Without a rational foundation the credibility of redemption is dissolved, and without that credibility the rational foundation is subverted. Gilkey sums up the dialectic as follows:

> On the one hand, no redemptive possibilities are fully rational or even credible unless their grounds are rationally coherent with the essential structure of our being; on the other hand, concrete existence makes the very rationality of theism incredible unless the reality of redemptive grace is found in some way credible.... There is a dialectic of rationality, incredibility, and credibility that constitutes the formal structure of Christian belief, with the negative estrangement initiating the movement from one moment to the other.[19]

This dialectic, I suggest, is the best entry into understanding the interrelation of Gilkey's constructive theological reflections. I will proceed to explicate and evaluate those reflections in these terms.

2. The Rationality of an Ontological Reinterpretation of Providence
a) Theology and Ontology

Langdon Gilkey has been concerned with the interface of theology and ontology throughout his career. The central question he addressed in his doctoral dissertation was: "can there be metaphysics that is both genuinely Christian and truly philosophical?"[20] The purpose of that thesis was "to state the doctrine of Creation in such a way that the primacy of revelation is maintained while at the same time the possibility of an empirical and rational metaphysical analysis of finitude is upheld."[21] A revelational theology and a rational metaphysics need not be antithetical, Gilkey argued. This concern was also manifest in the book which indirectly was based on the dissertation. While Gilkey is fully cognizant of the limits of ontology in *Maker of Heaven and Earth*,[22] he also speaks of the possibility of a "Christian philosophy"[23] and the necessity of "a sound Christian ontology" as "the basis of a coherent biblical theology."[24]

Gilkey's shift away from such a revelational and 'biblical' theology did not entail a shift away from ontological concerns. Indeed, it was precisely the apparent vacuousness of biblical theology's language of God's 'mighty acts' in history that led Gilkey to argue that it was necessary to formulate an "ontology of events." "What we desperately need is a theological ontology that will put intelligible and credible meanings into our analogical categories of divine deeds and of divine self-manifestation through events."[25]

It was not by means of ontological analysis, however, that Gilkey attempted to establish the meaningfulness of religious language. As we have seen, his prolegomenal work, *Naming the Whirlwind*, is decidedly non-ontological.[26] Gilkey's prolegomenon engages in an ontological *epoché* in which ontological questions are "bracketed out."[27] The prolegomenon "is an 'ontic' rather than an 'ontological' analysis since the meaning for which it searches is of ... the relation of words to lived experience, rather than the relation of symbols to the universal structures of being."[28] In *Naming the Whirlwind* ontology is seen as a post-prolegomenal enterprise.

The ontological *epoché* of *Naming the Whirlwind* was not a departure from Gilkey's concern with the ontological meaning of theological symbols, however.[29] Rather, it is best understood as laying the prolegomenal foundation for the theological and ontological reflection found in *Reaping the Whirlwind*. But even the insistence that prolegomenal reflection is pre-ontological was short-lived. Part I of *Reaping the Whirlwind* is presented as a prolegomenon that is foundational to the reinterpretation of providence found in Part II. That prolegomenon (especially chapters one and two) is essentially an ontology of historical passage. In summary, Gilkey's argument in these pages is that the very ontological structure of historical passage calls forth both mythical categories and theological reflection on the notion of providence. I will explicate his argument further in the next two subsections.

Ontological reflection is inescapable if it is to be established that religious language is not only meaningful, but also true.[30] One criterion by which religious language is to be judged is its universal applicability. Such a criterion requires the elaboration of a "Christian philosophy," together with ontological elucidation, if the criterion is to be met.[31] Gilkey follows Tillich's understanding of ontology as a discipline concerned with uncovering the fundamental unifying structures of reality. "It is the precise task and aim of ontology ... to provide categories in terms of which every aspect of our experience may be interpreted."[32] Theology and ontology are not special disciplines concerned with specific and limited dimensions of human life. Rather, they are both concerned with reality as a whole. Similar to ontology, "the scope of theology is inclusive of all else that we experience and think...."[33] Therefore, if a theological symbol is to be meaningful reflectively for us and articulate what is true for us it "must be systematized and related to all else that we hold to be true and so to shape reality as a whole for us."[34] This is a necessary (though not sufficient) condition for validating Christian symbols.

Asserting that theology needs philosophical and ontological elaboration is not without its problems, however. For theological symbols to be meaningful reflectively for us their reinterpretation must be in terms that relate to our present understanding of the world. What, then, is the relation of traditional and ancient symbols to modern ontological conceptions? Gilkey's answer to this question is somewhat ambiguous. In one passage he says that "constructive theology requires for its completion the conceptuality of a modern ontology, given to it *on loan* from some example of contemporary philosophy."[35] The metaphor of 'borrowing' an ontology is unfortunate and does not do justice to Gilkey's position. How does one know *which* modern ontology is most appropriate for a faithful elucidation of Christian symbols? Are there any criteria by which we could decide whether Tillich's borrowing from Heidegger or Cobb's borrowing from Whitehead is more appropriate? Gilkey seems to be aware of these problems when he says,

> The Christian symbol must rule the use we make of any modern ontology as a superior norm of expression, lest we proclaim a modern secular ontology as unequivocally Christian, and our gods be different than God. Thus no philosophical system per se, modern or Greek, can be adopted without transformation to fit the symbols of our tradition.[36]

The relation of theology and ontology is, therefore, dialectical. While theology depends upon ontology in order to explicate the reflective meaning of its symbols, ontology is itself dependent on those very symbols for its presuppositional foundations. As early as his dissertation Gilkey has insisted that metaphysics is not logically prior to theology precisely because theology is at the centre of metaphysics.[37] Similar to Ricoeur's dictum that "the symbol gives rise to thought,"[38] Gilkey argues, in *Naming the Whirlwind,* that "the basis ... for any speculative ontology is the reception in experience of a 'revelation' of the ultimate order of things, a revelation which is not so much the result of speculative thought as its ground."[39] Revelation, understood as myths and symbols, both shapes our being in the world and provides the ultimate and foundational framework for all ontological reflection. That ontological reflection analyzes the structures of being in the world and, thereby, provides an ontological foundation for the reflective reinterpretation of those symbols.[40]

From this discussion we see that theology and ontology need and complement each other because, a) both are modes of reflection directed to reality as a whole, and b) revelation and ontology are dialectically interrelated. There is, however, a third reason why theology (especially theology of culture) finds it necessary to engage in ontological reflection. We have seen in Part II that a creative theology of culture must be founded in historical discernment, affirm the ambiguous (yet real) role of human freedom in the shaping of history, and have a basis for future hope. All of these require an ontology of historical passage. The discernment of the historian is grounded in an *ontological* perspective which determines "his use of his data and the shape and meaning of all of his explanations."[41] And the affirmation of both the role of human freedom in history (against any form of determinism) and the openness of the future is only possible if "the ontological structure of historical being is discriminated."[42] To Gilkey's elaboration of that ontological structure we now turn.

b) An Ontology of History

We have seen in chapter two that relativity, contingency and temporality are essential characteristics of the modern view of the world. Perhaps the greatest distinction between modern Western thought and medieval/ancient thought (using these categories as broad ideal types) is that modernity views change to be of the essence of being, not merely an appearance. Gilkey comments that "for the modern consciousness change engulfs all reality ... rather than only a lower, less real level of reality," because "change is for us not the appearance, disappearance and appearance again of a limited number of permanent and changeless forms but the disappearance of old forms and the appearance of quite new ones."[43] That which is real is in process, "every present is pregnant with change and thus with new possibilities for the future."[44] Any reflection on being is driven, therefore, to "an ontology of temporal process," an ontology of historicity.[45]

Such an analysis uncovers, says Gilkey, the ontological structure of historical passage in terms of the polarity of destiny and freedom: "the inherited 'given' from the past on the one hand, and the present human response in the light of possibilities for the future on the other."[46] The destiny which is historically given to each present includes the material environment in its present state of depletion or fruition; modes of social relationships governed by the religious substance of culture up to the present time; the slow, unintended changes that have occurred in both the material and socio-political environments; the radical and drastic changes that have been effected by the past exercise of human freedom; and the contingent coming together of a multiplicity of factors into a new constellation of historical conditions. Destiny refers to the given actuality of historical experience. Before it we realize that "we are in every regard dependent on other beings, and thus is the fact that we are here at all radically contingent, contingent on an infinity of other events and entities over which we have little or no control."[47] Consequently, all historical explanation begins with a reconstruction of the initial conditions out of which an event arose. The given conditions are *necessary* conditions for any event to occur. They are not, however, *sufficient* conditions.[48] For this we need to consider the other side of the polarity—freedom.

Historical events occur in relation to previous events and conditions. This is destiny. Yet no event in history is totally determined by such conditions. The radical contingency of historical events means that no event *had* to occur in the way in which it did. There is always some form of volition involved — this is what Gilkey calls freedom. Destiny "sets the stage for our response, and is thus the ground and limit of our freedom."[49] While we are limited by the given actuality of our present historical situation, our response to that situation is, nevertheless, free. The given calls forth response, actuality is changed by possibility, and destiny is transformed (either creatively or demonically) by freedom. If the experience of destiny is the experience of being immersed *in* history, then the experience of our historical freedom gives us a sense of being *out* of history. "We are in history as dependent on the conditions given from beyond ourselves; we are 'out' of it as capable of responding in novel ways to those conditions."[50] We are both embedded in time and transcendent over it. The human being is "a self-transcending finitude that continually synthesizes past and future into a new present, that relates our given destiny to our present freedom, and that unites in thought and deed our present actuality and our future possibilities."[51] This is the basic structure of human temporality.

Gilkey's understanding of the ontological polarity of destiny and freedom is, perhaps, his most significant deviation from the thought of Paul Tillich. For Tillich, the basic ontological structure is the polarity of self and world. The polarity of destiny and freedom is then seen as one of the elements of the self/world structure.[52] Gilkey reverses this pattern, giving ontological priority to destiny/freedom.

> Destiny refers to the entire inheritance of this moment from its immediate past; it is therefore referent *both* to the "world" with which we have to deal *and* to the "self" formed by the past which deals with that world. In a temporalistic account of being, destiny temporalizes the polarity of self and world into an inheritance to be balanced by present freedom; union of the two creates the "event" in the present which then becomes "world" and "self" or destiny, for the next present, for the future. Because process and freedom are basic ontologically, the primary ontological structure is for us constituted by destiny and freedom, actuality and possibility, not by world and self.[53]

It is this polarity of destiny and freedom that provides an ontological foundation to Gilkey's theology of culture. He can reject any historical and cultural analysis which is fatalistic precisely because the ontological structure of historical passage includes freedom as a constitutive element. All political action is dependent upon this polarity of destiny and freedom because politics is the art of creatively responding, in freedom, to an inherited destiny.[54] If our destiny has been to inherit a 'time of troubles' and to find ourselves at the end of an historical epoch, then it is to that destiny that we must respond.[55]

A 'time of troubles' also requires confidence in an open future. Gilkey can assert, against Heilbroner, that "no determined future is the truth" precisely because of the destiny/freedom polarity. But even this ontological structure cannot, ultimately, guarantee an open future. In a nuclear age it is quite possible that human freedom could close the future. Therefore it becomes necessary to add to this ontological structure an ontological horizon of ultimacy.[56] Beyond the ambiguity of human freedom an open future requires the possibility of promise. "Such faith in a nonfated future, in the continuity of open possibility, and in the divine completion of our every abortive creation is now more necessary than ever."[57] If the polarity of destiny and freedom provides the ontological foundation for Gilkey's reinterpretation of providence, then the crisis of modernity is its most immediate cultural context. It is this reinterpretation that we must now examine.

c) Providence Reinterpreted

Gilkey says that the primary task of his reinterpretation of providence "is to seek to understand the relations of God to the unity of destiny and freedom, to the unity of the past which he upholds, to the freedom which he calls into being and the new possibilities which he offers history."[58] Such a reinterpretation is imperative, he has suggested, if we are to respond to our 'time of troubles' with courage, serenity and creativity. If the faith in progress which replaced a traditional understanding of providence is in crisis, then perhaps a reinterpretation and reappraisal of providence is in order. But that reinterpretation must be appropriate to the modern context. For Gilkey this means that such a reinterpretation can be neither supernaturalistic nor dualistic. Nor can providence be affirmed in any way which compromises human freedom.

Providence must not be understood in terms of supernatural

237

interventions in history because that would abrogate the naturalistic principle of understanding that is foundational to all modern science. Therefore, Gilkey's reinterpretation focuses on God as the ultimate ground of historical institutions, the source of their meaning, the criteria for their evaluation and the resource for their future possibility. God is not one cause among many in historical events. Rather, Gilkey argues that "God can be intelligibly said to 'act' in and through the secondary 'causes' of destiny and freedom ... and yet to have a constitutive, critical and renewing role in that process...."[59]

A non-supernaturalistic understanding of providence must also avoid the dualism that became common in neo-orthodoxy, says Gilkey. To speak of God's 'mighty acts' in history and still understand those acts in purely naturalistic terms is equivocation. To say that such language has no direct reference to actual events in the space-time continuum but, rather, refers to the inward and personal faith of an existential 'encounter' is dualism. Gilkey suggests that it is precisely such a dualism that is the cause of the eclipse of providence in neo-orthodox theology. If God's providential relation to the world is irrelevant to faith because God is only related to humans in their inward, spiritual dimension then "clearly a metaphysical dualism of some sort is implied."[60] The ultimate implication of this dualism is that "a God who is neither the Creator nor the Ruler of nature becomes also an alien intruder into temporal history."[61] Such a God is neither the God of the biblical witness and Christian tradition nor relevant to a culture suffused with a profound awareness of temporality. Therefore, Gilkey concludes that neo-orthodox dualism will not be helpful in reinterpreting the doctrine of providence in the context of the crisis of modernity.

A theology of providence that is neither supernaturalist nor dualistic and which wants to affirm God's meaningful and real presence in history must also be able to affirm the constitutive role of human freedom in that history. Any deterministic understanding of providence would be in conflict with the very ontological structure of historical passage as destiny and freedom. Such an understanding would be neither reflectively coherent, existentially adequate, nor appropriate to the eidetic meaning of providence. Providence is not in opposition to human freedom in history. Rather, Gilkey argues (following Augustine) that in the eidetic meaning of providence "the divine sovereignty is maintained in history ... *through* the action of creatures and *through* their willing, by an inward, hidden and yet purposeful power working within the natural unfolding of events out of their causative factors."[62] Providence has to do with a faith in and discernment of that inward, hidden and yet purposeful power.

Human life in history, freely responding to and reshaping destiny, gives rise, says Gilkey, to the most fundamental of all theological questions.

> As human beings in passage "make" history by uniting a given actuality and future possibility, destiny and freedom, into *event*, is there such a principle or factor uniting past actuality and not-yet possibility, destiny and freedom in their widest scope, an ultimate creativity and sovereignty in history that makes intelligible the ultimate dimension or horizon of history and the quest for an ultimate order and a sacred norm?[63]

According to Gilkey this question receives its most intelligible and rational answer in the notion of providence. His argument surprisingly takes on the form of a natural theology.[64] He acknowledges, however, that any natural theological argument is dependent upon pre-ontological intuitions. "Argument articulates, it does not create, the most fundamental intuitions or presuppositions within which we live—though arguments can open us to these intuitions and can hold our minds fast to their reality."[65] Aware of this disclaimer I will briefly summarize the argument.[66]

The argument is formulated in three stages, each addressing a significant relation in the process of historical passage, viz., the relation of past to present, the present to freedom and self-actualization, and the present to the future. The relation of past to present raises the following question: "how is it that achieved actuality, if it is constituted by events and not by enduring and so determining substances or essences, presents itself in each moment as a given, a destiny over time from the now receding past?" "If all is temporal and contingent, if all passes into a vanished and so ineffective past in coming to be, then how is the continuity of existence possible?" Such ontological continuity is only possible, argues Gilkey, if there is some "élan or power of process by which each achieved moment is projected beyond its passing self to become the ground or the origin ... of the next moment. For finite being to be and to be contingent in passage, there must be a power of being transcendent to that contingency and to that continual passing away,"— "that which essentially conquers or overcomes temporality and contingency."[67] That power of being is what Gilkey describes as the preserving or sustaining providence of

God.

God's preserving providence is the continuing power of being which overcomes the non-being of temporality. It is, therefore, "the ground or condition of the *possibility* of secondary causality, i.e., of the continuation and effectiveness of the destined past in the living present."[68] In terms of the ontological structure of historical passage, it is the preserving or sustaining providence of God that "brings destiny forward, so to speak, to come to union with freedom into event, and that is the ever-creative ground for the self-actualization and so the 'reality' of the creature."[69] This leads to the second stage of the argument.

According to Gilkey, historical self-actualization is dependent upon the effective presence, or endurance of the past into the present. Destiny is grounded in the preserving, or sustaining, providence of God. Self-actualization can not be merely an *effect* of the past, however, if it is to be a *self*-actualization. "All finite being is a becoming-to-be in itself and through itself, a projection of itself as a retrieval of its past destiny into new possibilities, and thus a constitution of itself through itself."[70] Such self-actualization is, of course, the freedom side of the destiny/freedom polarity. But freedom is not self-grounding. Gilkey notes that "we do not ... cause our freedom, our capacity to decide and to shape. It too is *given* to us as a basic power in ourselves, that is itself the basis for all we do and create."[71] There must be, then, a power of being that is "the ground of each self-actualizing occasion, a ground for the present as a duration of free and intentional unification of its given past with its possible future."[72]

The providence of God does not conflict with the processes of free self-actualization in history—it is the ground from which all such self-formation arises. Gilkey calls this ground of present self-actuality the creative "accompanying" or "concurring" providence of God. Just as God is the ground of our destiny (preserving providence) so also is God the ground of our freedom (concurring providence). In the third stage of Gilkey's argument the claim is made that God is also the ground of our future possibilities.

Free self-actualization in the present depends upon a future that is open, that is characterized by real possibility. Like past actuality, future possibility both has no actuality (it is still possibility) yet is somehow effective in the present. A possibility that effects actuality but which has no actuality in itself raises again the question of God. Gilkey claims that "possibility, which can be effective only in relation to actuality, must be in relation to an actuality of transcendent scope, an actuality that is capable of holding within its power of envisionment the entire and so open realm of possibility."[73] That transcendent actuality is the ontological ground for novelty, openness and future possibility. It is a primordial actuality that can envision all possibility as possible.[74] Gilkey refers to this transcendent and primordial actuality as the envisioning providence of God.

The relation of this divine and providential actuality to historical self-actualization does not negate the latter. Self-actualization is free. We have seen in chapter six, however, that human freedom is necessarily related to ultimacy as the source of the norms that guide its actualization.[75] This dynamic reappears in the relation of present actuality and future possibility. Novel possibilities must be ordered in terms of graded options that are more or less relevant to present actualities and desired future actualities. Gilkey argues that such an ordering is grounded in God's ordaining, ordering or envisioning providence. "One of the creative roles of God … is that he gives to each occasion, and so to each person and community, an ordered vision of possibility, a leap beyond the present actuality yet one in relation to it. Thus is our creativity possible."[76] Through participation in this envisionment we apprehend the possibilities that are relevant to our situation and freely actualize (or fail to actualize) these possibilities according to our own will. Thus, envisioning providence is both the ground of possibility and that which guides self-actualization.

If providence as 'preservation' provides an ontological basis for understanding the continuing causality of being in history and 'concurring' providence provides an ontological basis for understanding the freedom of the self-actualizing present, then providence as 'envisionment' "provides an ontological basis or explanation for the normative, the 'ought' characteristic of relevant and new possibility as it impinges on our present."[77] Providence not only grounds our experience of historical passage, it also directs that passage and makes a claim upon our self-actualization to act wisely and responsibly.

Reinterpreting providence in non-dualistic and non-supernaturalistic terms as referring to the ground of historical passage (preserving providence), present self-actualization (concurring providence), and future possibility (envisioning providence) has significant implications for our understanding of God. While a complete elucidation of Gilkey's reinterpretation of God would not be appropriate in this context, a brief discussion is in order.[78]

d) "God" Reinterpreted

Gilkey's reinterpretation of God focuses on three dimensions of the divine being, viz., God's self-limitation, temporality and changeability. While all three notions mark a departure from the classical understanding of God as omnipotently sovereign, eternal and immutable, Gilkey attempts to maintain the classical categories in polar tension with the categories of his reinterpretation. The various polarities of immanence and transcendence, relatedness and absoluteness, conditionedness and unconditionedness, and temporality and eternity are all expressive of God's being and must be kept in dialectical tension with each other.[79] If classical theology tended to focus on the second term of this list of polarities, then it is fair to say that much post-neo-orthodox theology attempts to redress the balance by focussing on the first terms. At least this is true of Gilkey's constructive theological reflections.

The first change in the conception of God that Gilkey proposes is the notion of God's self-limitation. If there is one thing that providence cannot mean, if it is to be intelligible to the modern consciousness, it is that God is the ordainer of each present and the sole shaper of all historical process. If this were the case then it would not be possible to account for freedom in history in any meaningful way. In fact, this has been one of the most important atheist complaints about Christianity. The eschatological theologians (most notably Pannenberg and the early Moltmann) attempted to address this problem of an omnipotent God who erases all human freedom in history by rejecting the theistic view of an almighty Lord over the present and replacing it with a God whose being is futural, characterized by promise.[80] Whitehead, and his followers, responded to this problem by reducing God to finitude, as "one metaphysical factor balanced by other equally permanent and equally real factors."[81] Against the eschatologists, Gilkey argues that the problem of human freedom in the God/creation relationship is not a matter of tense which is resolved by a futural God. Indeed, "these issues can be resolved only by rethinking ontologically the way the God of the present acts in relation to human freedom and to the possibilities of the future...."[82] And against the Whiteheadians he argues that a God that is one metaphysical factor among others is not God at all.

If we are to affirm the genuine human freedom to engage in self-actualization and not relegate God either to the future or to one metaphysical factor among others, then we will need to conceive of the self-limitation of God. While God brings the past into the present (preserving providence), grounds present freedom (concurring providence), and offers new possibilities (envisioning providence) in none of these activities is God all-determining.[83] Rather, God must be understood as self-limited in relation to creaturely freedom. God, as the creative ground of our being is "essentially *self-limiting*, producing a free, contingent being that is not God or a part of God and whose actions are not God's actions, for finite actuality comes to be through its own actualization of its destiny."[84] Consequently, God's action in history is both *through* our freedom and *limited* by our freedom.[85] Indeed, freedom is only possible if God is so self-limited.

This understanding of God's self-limitation also gives Gilkey an entry into understanding God in relation to the being/nonbeing polarity. While he often speaks of God's creativity and preserving providence "overcoming" nonbeing,[86] he also suggests that a relative nonbeing is part of the divine life. Following Kierkegaard, Gilkey argues that while only an omnipotent God could create free beings, so also God "steps back" and "qualifies his own infinite being with nothingness, and thus alone does God give room for that freedom which infinite being creates." Therefore, "nonbeing in the divine ground of all must be there if finite being is to be there at all."[87] As we will see in section four below this dialectic of being and nonbeing is also significant in Gilkey's understanding of the gospel.

The God that is characterized by self-limitation is also a God that is temporal. If the future is really open, then God must be radically redefined in terms of temporality.[88] The modal distinction between actuality and possibility that is fundamental for finite being is also fundamental for God. Gilkey explains:

> Actuality *is* not as actuality until it actualizes itself in creativity.... Thus the future, even for God, is possibility and not actuality. God's relation to the future is thus a relation to possibility and not to actuality.... God thus experiences temporal passage as constitutive and so essential to his own being: the past as achieved actuality, the present as self-achieving actuality and the future as possibility.... As, however, the ground of a process that mediates possibility into actuality, he himself participates in that passage from possibility into actuality and so in that sense is temporal. Thus, since the temporal process or becoming of possibility is an aspect of the divine being *itself*, God is essentially dynamic, living and active.[89]

Therefore, God's relation to flux and becoming is essential, not merely accidental.

Another way in which Gilkey describes the temporality of God is by uniting the notion of God as logos with the envisioning providence of God. According to Gilkey, logos does not refer to a static, timeless order of repeated forms. Rather, "the divine logos is a creative vision of future possibility, arising out of the infinite divine love...."[90] This *logos,* or envisioning providence of God, evokes novel possibilities that lure history forward.[91] Yet this also illustrates God's temporality because, if God 'lures' the world into as-yet-unactualized possibilities, "then the future God faces is also open, undecided; it is characterized for God, as for us, by possibilities, not by actualities already decided in eternity."[92] Therefore, freedom and the openness of history are affirmed and God's temporality must be recognized.

Gilkey's affirmation of divine temporality is always in dialectical interrelation with God's transcendence, however.[93] Recall that Gilkey's argument for the rationality of believing in preserving providence is that there must be a power transcendent to temporal passage which is the ground of that passage. Even futural possibility, he has argued, must be related to some form of an eternal actuality. The way that Gilkey attempts to bring temporality and eternity, and possibility and actuality together is by speaking of God's temporality as a distinct *kind* of temporality.

> Thus, in participating in every duration of temporal passage, God is *not* contingent as are his temporal creatures: he does *not* arise out of a process of which he is not the ground; he is *not* dependent for his being and so vulnerable to a process he does not found; *nor* does he pass away into a process which has given him birth.[94]

Providence is the work of a God "who is in dynamic process but not subject to process."[95] As the ground of being of all process (preserving providence), and as the condition for each moment, God is present in each moment, and yet transcendent to each moment as well.

> God transcends time as the source of the movement of the process of finite being in the dynamic creative divine life; he is in time as illustrating in his own creative life the modal distinction between potentiality and actuality, the becoming of actuality out of possibility.[96]

Therefore, Gilkey can also affirm God's aseity. "He is *a se* as the continuing, creative and so temporal ground of temporality."[97]

In classical theology an affirmation of the aseity of God is always coupled with the doctrine of divine immutability. It would follow, then, that a reinterpretation of the divine which includes temporality as essential to the divine being would also view the divine being as mutable, in a process of becoming. That which is temporal is subject to change. This is the third way in which Gilkey's reinterpretation of God shifts away from the classical conception. We have seen above that the modal distinction between actuality and possibility is as fundamental for divine being as it is for finite being. This being the case, Gilkey argues that God "*himself 'becomes'* or is subject to change."

> As history changes, therefore, so inescapably God changes, for God is in essential relation to a world he does not in its final and determinative form ordain or make — although each aspect of its being comes to be through the power of his creative being and through the possibilities of his providential envisionment.[98]

Gilkey's affirmation of the changeability of God is not undialectical, however. Similar to his view of the temporality of the divine being, he says that God's changeability is a unique kind of changeability. To be subject to change is to be dependent, contingent and conditioned. God, however, is self-sufficient, necessary and unconditioned.[99] The two poles must be kept in dialectical interrelation.

> In being affected and related, in changing over time, God is not dependent on other entities or factors for his/her being, nor is he/she correspondingly threatened in his/her being. As the source of all over time — and thus *in* time — God is not contingent but necessary in being; as the uniting principle of past, present and future — and thus *in* time — God transcends temporality; as the actuality envisioning the infinite realm of possibility — and thus sharing in potentiality — God is infinite.[100]

While Gilkey acknowledges that the notion of a being which is temporal and changing yet transcends time and is infinite and unconditioned is paradoxical, if not contradictory, he nevertheless insists that this paradox must be affirmed if we are to affirm both God's immanent involvement in creaturely life and divine transcendence.[101]

In summary, Gilkey's reinterpretation of the symbol of God proposes a dialectical understanding of God that includes the notions

245

of self-limitation, temporality and changeability. This reinterpretation of God flows naturally from his reinterpretation of providence. A God who is the ground of historical passage (preserving providence), present self-actualization (concurring providence), and future possibilities (envisioning providence) must also be a God who is self-limited, temporal and changeable, though also omnipotent, eternal and unconditioned.

While the reinterpretation of God is made necessary by the reinterpretation of providence, the reinterpretation of providence is presented as made necessary by the very structure of historical being. Gilkey's argument is that the ontological structure of history as the relation of destiny and freedom rationally necessitates a doctrine of providence. This doctrine of providence accounts for both the ground of historical passage and the openness of that passage — the effectiveness of the historical past, the freedom of the present and the possibilities of the future. Therefore, "the ontological structure of historical being ... proclaims the rationality of theism."[102]

We have seen repeatedly, however, that that ontological structure and that rationally grounded understanding of providence necessarily includes freedom in history as a constitutive element. And it is precisely that freedom which makes a fall, sin, and estrangement possible. The actuality of such estrangement leads us to the second stage of the dialectic — the stage of incredibility that seems to negate the first stage of rationality.

3. The Incredibility of Estrangement

Gilkey's ontological reinterpretation of providence in terms of a past destiny that is given to us replete with creative opportunities, a present in which we transform our destiny in freedom, and a future that is open, represents a contemporary interpretation of what the biblical and traditional witness called the goodness of our created state. This reinterpretation of providence constitutes an affirmation of the ontological structure of creaturely historical being. Such affirmation is where Christian theology begins — it is the first stage in the dialectical structure of the Christian worldview.

An affirmation of the goodness of creaturely being which is undialectical, however, has no contact with the actuality of that being. That which is made ontologically possible because of freedom is, in fact, an historical actuality. We have seen in our discussion of the decline of modernity that one of the central shortcomings of modernity was its unfounded faith in the goodness of human freedom and the potential of freedom to be the fuel of progress. This faith, together with its externalization of evil, failed to account for the ambiguity of the self in its freedom, and the bondage of the human will. The propensity of science and technology to be used both for good and evil, creatively and demonically, is evidence enough that freedom is not necessarily a matter of being free *from* evil — it could just as easily be freedom *for* evil.

The ambiguity of freedom in the career of modernity is symptomatic of the human condition as a whole. Regardless of our affirmations of the goodness of temporal being we cannot escape the fact that the human condition is one of estrangement. Indeed, the reality of evil renders the rational arguments for God's providential presence in creation incredible. Such arguments are ontological — they discern the underlying structures of being. Evil and sin, however, are not ontological categories. Essential to any Christian understanding of evil is the conviction that creation and fall are distinct. Evil is a perversion of a good creation.[103] Such evil, however, has its entry into creation through one of the constitutive elements of creation, viz., freedom. "For freedom was just the kind of finite structure which, although good in itself as a creation of God, nevertheless had the capacity to pervert and distort itself, and so to misuse both its powers and its own goods."[104] The Christian understanding of evil does not attempt to attribute evil's cause to anything beyond the human will.[105] Sin is the misuse and corruption of freedom.

> It is, therefore, in freedom and so in spirit that sin arises, when the finite self ceases to depend on its creator and sovereign and depends entirely on itself. In that estrangement from God arising out of freedom, the self becomes estranged from its own ultimate security and meaning and is therefore driven into estrangement from itself, its community, and its world.[106]

While the possibility of sin is explicable in ontological terms, its actuality is not. Gilkey argues that "because sin is an estrangement of our essential structure, an alienation from our nature, a misuse of freedom in which freedom itself is bound, it is not possible to describe it in ontological terms — for ontology knows only structure and not its misuse."[107] Sin is a "warping" of ontological structures.[108] As the result

247

of freedom it is never ontologically "necessary" though it may appear as existentially "inevitable."[109]

Freedom is not the only ontological structure that is warped, or distorted, by sin — so also is destiny. While sin may begin as an inward act of estrangement it also has outward consequences, the most significant of which Gilkey describes as 'fate.' "As freedom becomes sin in human experience, so destiny becomes fate."[110] Destiny becomes fate when it leaves no room for free and creative response and is, therefore, "that in our experience of history which is the ultimate threat to our personal and communal being in the future."[111] Consequently, Gilkey describes fate alternately as an "ultimate Void"[112] and a "demonic *kairos*"[113] that strips us of our humanity by denying us the freedom of self-actualization and by closing the future to us. This is the experience of the oppressed who are rendered powerless by the sin of the powerful and who, thereby, have literally no control over their destiny.[114] For such people destiny is fated.

Fate, like sin which is its origin, is not an ontological category, however. Fate is not a 'given' of being. If fate was a constitutive element of being itself then all movements for political liberation would be without ground. All political action assumes that fate is a distortion of temporal life and therefore seeks to "maintain history as destiny and to banish history as fate."[115] It is this struggle against the ultimate threat of fate that gives politics its sacred or mythical character as well as its potential fanaticism whereby one culture's destiny will be maintained by imposing fate on another culture.[116]

Insofar as providence is understood as the ground of both destiny and freedom it is clearly antithetical to fate.[117] Consequently, any theology which will affirm providence inescapably will be a political theology dedicated to social liberation. If the ontological structure of history is not fated then those who in existential actuality are the victims of fate must be set free.[118] But Gilkey is also opposed to the apparent identification of political liberation and salvation that he discerns in liberation theology. Clearly indebted to Niebuhr, he insists that "the basic problem of historical existence is not fate — the loss of human beings of the possibility of self-determination; rather, it is sin, the corruption of their freedom — for fate as a category of historical being arises from sin, fate is the character of history enacted by human beings."[119] Therefore, social liberation can only attempt to conquer the consequences of sin, not sin itself. "Only a new relation of mankind to God, to self and to the neighbor can achieve that goal, an achievement far beyond the range of political activity."[120] This leads us to the third stage of Gilkey's dialectic — the credibility of redemption.

4. The Credibility of Redemption

The rationality of belief in theistic providence is grounded in the ontological structure of history as destiny and freedom. When that structure is warped into fate and sin we enter into the negative moment of the dialectic which seems "to overwhelm the positive thesis constituting the rationality of theistic providence and to make the latter incredible."[121] The original affirmation which is ontological in character is negated by the existential reality of estrangement. But the dialectic is not complete until we consider whether a third stage of redemptive reaffirmation is credible.[122]

a) From Rationality to Credibility

The dialectic of Christian faith begins in affirmation. That affirmation, expressed in the reinterpretation of providence, is rational because it is rooted in a synchronic analysis of being. The second stage, however, brings us beyond synchronicity to an awareness of the diachronic character of historical being as estranged. Therefore, a third stage which will both reaffirm the initial affirmation and redress the negation of the second stage will also require categories of understanding that go beyond synchronic structures. Such categories are "not directly derivable from the given structure of ordinary experience, which being in self-contradiction calls for rescue from beyond itself."[123] We must, then, move "beyond ontology" to "credible myth." Gilkey explains that "though ontology has a vital role in the understanding of history, any comprehension of history as a whole, and so any theological understanding, has the form of a global 'myth' and not of a systematic ontology...."[124] The diachronic actuality of estrangement means that "the divine work of providence as possibility, as the principle of creativity and the new in history, is *not enough*," and "must, therefore, be supplemented by incarnation, atonement, and ultimately by eschatology."[125] We must go beyond providence to the deeper need for redemption.

The third, redemptive stage of the dialectic is the stage of credibility, not rationality, because the reality and possibility of redemption is not derivable from the universal, given structure of history. Rather, it is given to history as an answer to the warping and self-destruction of that structure.[126] Redemption is experienced as a gift. "This redemptive moment is different from the other two in that unlike the others it 'comes'; we are not 'thrown into' ... redemption as we are into creaturely being and estranged existence, which are both already there."[127]

To say that the Christian understanding of the gift of redemption is credible is to say that "it can satisfy the mind as a valid symbolic thematization of the totality of concrete experience...." These symbols "'fit' the shape of the experience they claim to adequately thematize."[128] They cohere with a deep affirmation of the goodness of creaturely life, take seriously the estrangement of that life and redemptively reaffirm creation by redressing that estrangement.

The dialectic that Gilkey discerns to be the structure of Christian faith also reappears *within* his discussion of the third, redemptive stage. The Christ-event itself manifests a dialectic of affirmation, negation and reaffirmation as can be seen in the respective categories of incarnation, atonement and eschatology (including resurrection and Kingdom of God). Recognizing that we will not even approach a full explication of any of these categories, I will briefly summarize Gilkey's understanding of redemption in these terms.

b) Incarnation

If the doctrine of providence discloses God as the ultimate *being* from which free beings flow into process and continue in being, and the creative *logos* which lures free beings to new possibilities, then the incarnation discloses God as "a divine *love* through which these creatures are brought back into relation with one another and into the divine life."[129] In a creation characterized by estrangement, redemption is only possible if there is a principle of reconciliation and reunification — that principle is the divine love revealed in the incarnation of Jesus the Christ. The incarnation portrays a God who affirms creation, even in its waywardness. The incarnate Word of John's prologue is both the divine power through which all things are created and preserved, and the divine love that forgives sin and reconciles an estranged creation. In Jesus the Christ the divine power of God which is the ground of all being is revealed as love. And the unity of that power and love gives a credible and confident hope that evil can be conquered and estrangement overcome.[130]

The unity of the power of being and the divine love that is manifest in Jesus has a significant implication for the relation of creation and redemption. Redemption is not necessary because there is something deficient in our created nature. Rather, "redemption fulfills creation; it does not transform it into something else or even something higher, as if to fulfill our created human natures were not a high enough goal for a human existence...."[131] Moreover, "it is above all clear that when God's will and purposes reign, human existence becomes recreated, rescued and fulfilled. God's deepest will is, therefore, for the total well-being, the completion of the fullness of joy in human life."[132]

The incarnation affirms human creatureliness and has as its goal the redemption of that creatureliness. Such a goal is credible because the incarnate one is a model or a paradigm of authentic humanity. In the Christian understanding of the person of Jesus, "the possibilities of human existence are here defined and enacted, and thus the requirements of being fully human for the first time are made plain."[133] In Jesus we see true humanity. He lives under the same conditions of humanity, yet those conditions do not distort or warp his possibility of full humanity. In Tillich's terms, "the paradox of the Christian message is that in *one* personal life essential manhood has appeared under the conditions of existence without being conquered by them."[134] Because essential humanity has appeared in actuality in Jesus the possibility of such authenticity is placed before us. That possibility can only be realized, however, if our estrangement is overcome.

c) Atonement

The story of the passion of Christ dominates the gospel narratives. While incarnation discloses the unity of the power of being and the divine love, the redeeming purposes of that love can only be fulfilled in powerlessness and nonbeing. In this sense the affirmation of the incarnation meets negation in the passion. In Jesus the Christ, "the creative power of being and of life appears in existence as weakness, powerlessness, suffering, and even sin in order precisely to effect on a new level a new creation and a new being beyond negation."[135]

The suffering of Jesus manifests God's alienation from the present powers of history. Such powers, however, are the results of human self-actualization. Therefore, the redemption of those powers must be through God's self-limitation, powerlessness, passion, and even nonbeing.

If God is to redeem history as history, and give it its own meaning, it must

251

be through our wayward freedom and not overagainst it, through participation in the full human condition and not through the eradication of it.[136]

Only the God who is the ground of our freedom can redeem us without destroying that freedom. Such redemption, however, is through suffering the consequences of our freedom.

This interrelation of human freedom (in all of its estrangement) and the divine self-limited powerlessness of the passion is foundational for Gilkey's understanding of atonement. If the redemption of human freedom is to be accomplished in such a way that that freedom is restored and not eradicated, then that redemption will require a human response to a divine example. Thus Gilkey's understanding of atonement tends to be Abelardian. Jesus is an example of suffering love which calls forth a response of love and gratitude.[137] The healing and redeeming presence of God is manifest in his suffering, but not effected. Redemption is effected when human beings respond to that example of suffering love and re-establish a relationship of dependence and trust with God.[138] In this re-establishment human nature is fulfilled, not enchained. The divine participation in estrangement is "the beginning of a reawakening to the divine presence in all of creaturely life, an acceptance of our acceptance by that continuing presence, and so a return in the spirit to what has always been the case: our dependence ontologically and providentially on God."[139] While it is the Christ on the cross who calls us to such a renewed relationship, it is the risen and eschatological Christ who guides us into a new life in the Kingdom of God.

d) Eschatology

Gilkey's theology, like that of his mentor, Reinhold Niebuhr, is better characterized as a *theologia crucis* than a *theologia gloriae*. Indeed, he thinks that a theology which takes seriously the themes of estrangement, atonement and reconciliation provides one with a better foundation for a theology of culture (especially if that culture is in decline), than does a theology which focuses on messianic victory and eschatological hope.[140] Consequently, themes such as the resurrection, eschatology and the Kingdom of God are not fully developed in Gilkey's work.[141] Yet no theology is fully Christian or even approaches completion if such themes are not addressed. Gilkey realizes this. The relation of *theologia crucis* and *theologia gloriae* is dialectical. The life that is the goal of redemption is only achieved because he who is the New Being suffers nonbeing. Life through death, resurrection through the cross — these are the central themes of redemption.

Gilkey does not address at any length questions of the historical actuality of Christ's resurrection. He is content to affirm that the early church certainly believed that this event happened and that that community accounted for its own rebirth by reference to the reality of the risen Christ in its midst. To accept the early church's self-understanding (and Gilkey does) is to accept its interpretation of the resurrection in its kerygma.[142] The resurrection is the foundation of Christian eschatological hope. The culmination of the Christ-event in the resurrection is a proleptic manifestation of humanity's ultimate (and common) destiny.[143]

Any intelligible eschatology, however, must maintain a continuity between *all* of past and present experience (not just *one* past event) and the eschatological future. Specifically arguing with the early Moltmann's theology of hope, Gilkey says that "in the most concrete sense, God will not be in the future as he promises if he has not already been [active in the past], and if he has not been active in the life of secular culture, as well as in the promises given to the churches."[144] Consequently, eschatology must fulfill, not negate, providence. Indeed, eschatology and providence "are dialectical or polar concepts that imply and require each other if historical and temporal passage be real."[145] "As providence is the historical presupposition for eschatology, so is eschatology the defining and controlling symbol for providence."[146]

Without God's providential passage in history, eschatology is pure utopianism and without eschatology, providence has no ultimate direction. Indeed, Gilkey's understanding of eschatology is intimately connected with the envisioning character of providence. Eschatology provides a vision which lures us to the promised future. But eschatology also goes beyond providential envisionment because eschatology goes beyond the ambiguity of human history. Because no historical community could ever actualize the eschatological vision, such a vision has a reference which is transcendent to history. Eschatological images, therefore, represent a lure of possibility beyond possibility.[147]

The central eschatological image in Christian theology is the Kingdom of God. In the ministry of Jesus the Kingdom is revealed as the *logos* of history that functions as both the lure and norm of that history.

> The Kingdom provides the norm for the social context in which love occurs. In providing that norm it both challenges the warped relations of the present and "lures" our social, that is, our political action into a new and more creative future.[148]

This Kingdom is both objectively historical, affecting all of history and all institutions in society, and yet is also manifest inwardly in the lives of men and women "as a radical qualification of their most fundamental personal and inward attitudes, commitments and trust...."[149] Because the Kingdom of God redeems human destiny it restores freedom and participation in community resulting in "a new synthesis of individual self-actualization with the common good, of socialist economic responsibility and universal participation with democratic self-determination and freedom." While communal self-actualization characterizes the image of the Kingdom, so also is God portrayed as its centre. It is, therefore, a theonomous Kingdom.

The lure of this eschatological Kingdom is the foundation of Christian praxis because it "reveals the alienation and so the injustice of the present," and "opens the present to new possibilities in contrast to what is." Moreover, "eschatology provides the only continuing ground for radical criticism" because "the Kingdom transcends those who seek to bring it...." Finally, "by its affirmation that the Kingdom is the divine goal toward which the future points, eschatology grounds the eros of all political action and political hope in what is taken to be the most real in history."[150] In the light of the image of the Kingdom, socio-political action proceeds in hope because that Kingdom reaffirms the goodness and structures of historical being by leading humankind beyond estrangement to redemption.

5. Evaluative Conclusions

This chapter represents neither a complete elucidation of systematic theology nor a complete discussion of all of Langdon Gilkey's constructive theological reflections. Rather, I have attempted to present the broad structural contours of those reflections. Employing Gilkey's understanding of the dialectic of rational, incredible and credible as a hermeneutical key to those structural contours has given us access to some of the most important themes that Gilkey has addressed. Since it has not been Gilkey's intention to present a full systematic theology I will not evaluate these reflections in terms of what would be required for such an enterprise. Rather, I will be concerned primarily with the relation of these reflections to Gilkey's theology of culture and to their own intelligible coherence.

a) Constructive Theology and Theology of Culture

It is not difficult to demonstrate the interrelation of Gilkey's theology of culture and his constructive theological reflections. The two are mutually interdependent and reinforce each other. Indeed, Gilkey's understanding of the dialectical structure of Christian thought in terms of affirmation, negation and reaffirmation has a direct parallel in his understanding of the pattern of constitution, judgment and renewal which is universal in cultural history. Consequently, Gilkey's theology of modernity in decline is a placing of the culture of modernity on this dialectic and an observing of how this dialectic works itself out in our cultural history.

Both Gilkey's theology of culture and prolegomenon establish that a dimension of ultimacy is a constitutive element of historical passage. His theological reflections on the doctrine of providence represent a Christian interpretation of that dimension of history. We have seen that that reinterpretation is rooted in an understanding of the ontological structure of history as destiny and freedom. Such an ontology is also foundational to theology of culture. Affirming both ontologically and theologically (in the category of concurring providence) that freedom is an essential element of history provides the theologian of culture with a basis from which to oppose all forms of oppression and fate.

Further, the appearance of fate in history can only be fully explicated in terms of a theological interpretation of estrangement as the warping and deforming of destiny and freedom into fate and sin. If fated history is to be reopened, such estrangement must be overcome in redemption and eschatology. Moreover, if creaturely life is to be truly reaffirmed then providence and eschatology must represent a unity, and redemption must be understood as the restoration of creation.

In terms of these broad structural contours of his thought, Gilkey's theology of culture and constructive theology are both mutually supportive and, to me, generally convincing. This is not to say that his constructive theological reflections are without problems, however. To some of these problems I now turn.

255

b) Providence Revisited

I have noted that Gilkey's argument for the rationality of theistic providence surprisingly takes on the form of a natural theology. This natural theological argument is surprising because prior to its formulation, Gilkey had argued against the enterprise of natural theology *per se.* I suggest that this natural theology still seems somewhat out of place in Gilkey's corpus. While Gilkey acknowledges that his natural theological argument for providence rests upon certain pre-ontological intuitions he seems, nevertheless, to be forced into the same problems that plague all such arguments. Natural theology tends to ask questions ("if all events have causes then what is the first cause?") or suggest concepts ("that than which no greater can be conceived") that have little, if any, existential contact with real life, and serve only to justify the argument that will then be erected on them. Consequently, such arguments tend to be neither existentially satisfying nor logically convincing to people who do not acknowledge the self-evident importance and legitimacy of such questions or concepts. Gilkey's argument suffers the same weakness.

For example, the argument begins by asking how it is that achieved actuality, which is constituted by events and not by enduring substances, presents itself in each moment as a given, a destiny over time from the now receding past. "If all is temporal and contingent, if all passes into a vanished and so ineffective past in coming to be, then how is the continuity of existence possible?"[151] It would seem to me that while this kind of question might occur to someone who was attempting to argue for the rationality of preserving providence, it is, nevertheless, not self-evidently meaningful. The question is about the effectiveness of the past, given the temporality and contingency of reality. But the question only has meaning if one accepts that such temporality and contingency renders the past "ineffective." That is neither self-evident nor empirically justified. The self-actualization of past cultures has historical effectiveness in a myriad of ways — in the language, customs, traditions, mores and worldviews that are passed on from generation to generation; in the architecture and artifacts that remain; in the abiding (though also changing) religious, political and economic institutions; and in the texts of the past. Since the past is clearly effective, Gilkey's question is counter-intuitive. One does not need to appeal to preserving providence in order to give a rational account of historical continuity.

Consider also the third stage of Gilkey's argument. The future is only open if it is characterized by real possibility. But, since possibility can only be effective if it is in relation to some actuality, then the possibility of the open future must be in relation to an actuality of transcendent scope, viz., God. We need God as a primordial actuality to envision possibility as possibility, Gilkey argues. Again, this is certainly far from being self-evident. It may well be the case that possibility obtains only in relation to some actuality. But why do we need to appeal to a transcendent actuality? Why would not present actuality suffice? The future is open and full of possibility because present actuality is characterized by imaginative freedom that will undoubtedly effect new things in the future. This is an account of future possibility that has no need to refer to an actuality of transcendent scope. Therefore, I conclude that Gilkey's natural theological arguments are less than convincing.

This leads us to question the epistemological status of Gilkey's natural theology. Is his presentation of providence really rational? Gilkey is saying that life in historical passage is only rationally explicable if interpreted with reference to theistic providence. This, I am saying, is not sufficiently established. Therefore, on Gilkey's terms providence is not rational. This does not mean, however, that his interpretation of providence is without ground and totally unconvincing as an interpretation which illuminates our life in historical passage. Rather than presenting his view of providence as a rational natural theology, I would suggest that Gilkey's argument is better seen as a reinterpretation of a doctrine which is grounded in both Scripture and tradition. This reinterpretation articulates a Christian understanding of the depth meaning or ultimate dimension of history and can be evaluated in terms of its eidetic fidelity to that tradition, existential appropriateness for the present cultural context and reflective coherence in terms of the ontological structure of history. Whether this reinterpretation meets such criteria will be discussed more fully in the next two subsections.

If Gilkey's argument is not 'rational' then we will also need to reconsider the dialectic of rational, incredible and credible. Perhaps the dialectic that Gilkey is referring to is not properly described by such epistemological categories, but is better understood by reference to the symbolic language of creation, fall and redemption.

We have seen that Gilkey's reinterpretation of providence entails implications for our understanding of God. Some critical comments on his reinterpretation of God are, therefore, in order here.

c) God Revisited

Gilkey interprets modernity to be a culture that is suffused with the sense of contingency, relativity, temporality and autonomy. In this light it is interesting to note that while Gilkey attributes to God the first three of these characteristics of being under the categories of temporality and changeability, the fourth characteristic, autonomy, is cited as the primary reason for attributing to God another category, viz., self-limitation. Gilkey's argument is that if we really want to affirm the freedom of creatures, especially the human creature, then we must conceive of the self-limitation (and even the nonbeing!) of God. An omnipotent God must give room for freedom — omnipotence must be voluntarily limited.

This argument also seems out of place in Gilkey's corpus. One of his central complaints against process theology has been that such a theology attempts to understand and limit God in terms of ontological categories as one metaphysical factor among others. The reasoning behind this notion of self-limitation seems subject to the same critique. To say that the creation of a free being by an omnipotent God requires the self-limitation of that God is to assume that God is an external limit on human freedom *in the same sense* as other external things and beings limit freedom.[152] Such an assumption is ill-founded and contradicts what Gilkey has said in other places about God's transcendent distinctiveness in relation to creatures and the inappropriateness of understanding the divine in limited ontological terms. Indeed, in his arguments concerning God's temporality and changeability we noted that Gilkey insists that God's temporality and changeability is of a unique kind — neither dependent, contingent nor conditioned. A similar argument would apply to the relation of God and human freedom. The omnipotence of God is of a unique kind — it is the creative ground and conditioning norm of human freedom, not its external threat. In this light attributing self-limitation to God is unnecessary.

As I have suggested, Gilkey's discussion of the temporality and changeability of God is more helpful. If God is providentially and redemptively involved in history then it is necessary that we conceive of God in terms that include temporality and changeability. Gilkey is also right to note that such conceptions must somehow be formulated in such a way that will maintain God's aseity, eternality and unconditionedness. While I am not sure whether Gilkey's formulations have taken us beyond simply affirming that God is both temporal and eternal, changeable and unconditioned, I am sure that at least these polar conceptions are real problems that need to be reflectively addressed — self-limitation is not.

One further problem that arises in Gilkey's reinterpretation of God relates to the question of possibility and actuality. Gilkey's argument for both divine temporality and changeability includes the observation that the future, even for God, is possibility and not actuality. Yet we have also seen that the third stage of his argument for providence includes the conviction that all possibility must be related to actuality and that ultimately all future possibility must be related to an actuality of transcendent scope, viz., God. This is confusing. If God is the primordial actuality that grounds possibility then how could possibility still be possible for God? It would appear that Gilkey's argument for the rationality of envisioning providence contradicts an important feature of his reinterpretation of God.

This discussion of the relation of God to possibility and actuality leads me to my third, and most important, criticism of Gilkey's constructive theology.

d) Eschatology Revisited

Gilkey has convincingly argued that a viable theology for a culture in decline must both affirm human freedom in relation to destiny (over against historical fatedness) and offer that culture a hope in possibilities beyond its present nemesis. Only a theology which affirms the preserving, concurring and envisioning providence of God, takes seriously the estrangement that characterizes history, and discerns the redemptive significance of the Christ-event in its dialectical complexity, will be credible in such a time of troubles. We have also noted that Gilkey's understanding of that redemption is better characterized as a *theologia crucis* than a *theologia gloriae* and that his understanding of the atonement is characteristically Abelardian.

This understanding of redemption, combined with his care to reaffirm human freedom in history, leads Gilkey to speak of eschatology more in terms of open possibilities than final divine victories. The God who is self-limited by the freedom of the creature can only envision future possibilities in some form of a normative order, but that God cannot enact those possibilities. The suffering of the Christ is exemplary of divine love, but does not effect an atonement. The Kingdom of God represents a divine logos that lures us to future possibilities, but those possibilities are never realized because, in fact, the Kingdom presents us with possibilities beyond possibilities. I would suggest that such an understanding of redemption and eschatology is neither eidetically faithful to the tradition that Gilkey is here interpreting, reflectively coherent, nor existentially appropriate to our present cultural context.

It is undoubtedly the case that a Christian understanding of God's relation to human creatures in creation, providence, judgment and redemption is such that human freedom is grounded, affirmed, judged and redeemed. Determinism has no place in a Christian understanding of reality. Here Gilkey's constructive theology is faithful to the biblical and traditional witness. Yet it is just as equally the case that the Christian God is a God who, either through human freedom or in spite of the waywardness of that freedom, *enacts* the divine will. It is not clear that a God interpreted in Gilkeyian categories could do any such thing. Just as it was not such a large step from neo-orthodoxy's totally other God to radical theology's death of God, so also is it a small step from a radically self-limited God who can only lure human freedom to an impotent God. Such an impotent God can certainly not be the God of the Christian tradition.

Another way that I could voice my concern would be to say that Gilkey's affirmation of a *theologia crucis* is in fact not dialectical enough because insufficient attention is given to a non-triumphalistically conceived *theologia gloriae* in which the people of God are called to participate (indeed, through their sufferings) in a Kingdom that comes with power and certainty as the culmination of the redemptive ministry of the risen one. Gilkey's *theologia crucis* presents the Kingdom of God as a possibility beyond possibility, a radical principle of criticism, because it will never be realized.[153] Indeed, Gilkey says that the idea of a perfect society realized in the future contradicts the very structure of history: "If future history is thus continuous with past and present, then a perfect society denies the ontological structure of history, the continuation of sin within that structure and the permanence of the self-limitation of God."[154]

There are a number of problems with Gilkey's argument here. In the first instance, granting that there must be at least some continuity between future history and the past and present, why would a perfect society deny the ontological structure of history? The only answer that I can conceive of from Gilkey's thought is that such a society would not be the result of human freedom (which is estranged) but would be imposed on history, thus being discontinuous with past and present

260

and, thereby, denying human freedom. That such discontinuity is present in literally all eschatological imagery in Scripture seems clear enough. The Kingdom 'comes,' it is not 'erected' by human action. Moreover, its coming is surprising, overturning old patterns and establishing new ones. It is no less than a new heaven and a new earth — re-creation. Yet this is not a radical discontinuity. Indeed, it is precisely the ontological structure of history as destiny and freedom that is renewed and restored in the overcoming of fate and sin. Gilkey's own phenomenological disclosure of a normative dimension of ultimacy constitutive of both history and freedom should alert him to the fact that the establishment of the sovereign rule of God in the Kingdom is in no way contradictory of human freedom. Freedom is estranged in autonomous independence, it is fulfilled in obedient service of the Ultimate.

Secondly, Gilkey's suggestion that such a perfect society can never be realized because of the continuation of sin in the structure of history is in conflict with both the biblical witness and his own insistence that sin is not structurally necessary. In this sense his argument not only fails the test of eidetic fidelity, it is also reflectively incoherent. If sin is a warping of ontological structures then why could we not conceive of a restoration of those structures that would overcome even sin? Perhaps the Niebuhrian adage that sin is not necessary, though inevitable, is here shown to be an equivocation. While neither Gilkey nor Niebuhr want to ontologize sin as essential to the very fabric of existent being, this suggestion that freedom will inevitably fall into sin comes perilously close to doing precisely that — at least *de facto*, if not *a priori*. Biblical eschatology dares to imagine a Kingdom that is now only possible but will be actualized, in which freedom is enacted without sin. The incarnate one is not only an example to follow like a new law; the promise of his gospel is that human life will one day be like his — subject to the conditions of existence, free, and yet without sin.

It is interesting to note that while Gilkey's eschatology is preoccupied with human freedom, the one time that he actually gives content to that eschatology, he himself undermines that freedom. I am referring to his universalism. While universalism has not been addressed in this discussion of Gilkey's constructive theology, it has been criticized earlier in this book. I have argued that universalism is neither consistent with Gilkey's prolegomenon nor justified in terms of an eidetic analysis of the central biblical symbols that deal with judgment. Here I would argue further that universalism is also an affront to human freedom. Universalism offers something of a metaphysical guarantee that people cannot damn themselves. Yet I would suggest that the possibility of self-damnation seems to be a touchstone of freedom.[155] Universalism says that one's future is in fact fated. We are fated to a universal salvation (or pantheistic participation in God) regardless of whether such a fate is our choice. Universalism is fatalism precisely in Gilkey's sense of the word fate. It imposes an eternal future on one's personal history regardless of human freedom. The imperative of Jesus's preaching of the Kingdom makes clear that a choice is involved for both individuals and cultures, and that that choice is respected by the author of the coming Kingdom.

The final question that we need to ask of Gilkey's view of eschatology in the light of his theology of culture is whether it is an adequate response to the present cultural malaise. Gilkey argues that an existentially appropriate theology of culture in decline must both affirm human freedom in the face of fate, thereby opening up the future to new possibilities that freedom can actualize, and provide a sober estimation of freedom in terms of its fundamental spiritual estrangement. Gilkey's theology certainly attempts to do both of these things. But is this enough?

Any culture, and especially a culture in decline, can only creatively proceed and experience renewal if it has hope. In this sense the future must be open. Is it possible, however, for a culture to have hope if the only way in which the future is open is through the human freedom to enact future possibilities? If we find Gilkey's (and Niebuhr's) description of the inevitable waywardness of human freedom to be convincing, then how could such a future contain hope for us? Can a Kingdom that represents a possibility beyond possibility and, therefore, is never actualized, be any more than a radical principle of criticism for all past, present and future actualizations that attempt to appropriate it? Can a Kingdom that is ultimately unactualizable because of human freedom and its sinfulness really provide us hope in our time of troubles? Indeed, if we acknowledge that it is precisely the ambiguity of human freedom that created the present cultural crisis, is an envisioned Kingdom that can only lure that freedom really an adequate basis for cultural hope? Such questions would appear to be foundational both for a constructive theological interpretation of providence and eschatology and for any credible theology of culture in decline. Yet they are essentially unanswered by Gilkey.

For a culture to have hope in the face of a sober appreciation of the estranged character of human existence it must have a vision of a future Kingdom that comes both as a gift, not the work of human hands, and as the fulfillment, restoration and redemption of creaturely life in all of its fullness — including its freedom. Such a vision cannot be of a God who only lures history forward because the divine is self-limited by that freedom. Rather, this eschatological vision must be of a Kingdom that is now possible but will then be actualized. Only with such a vision, I would suggest, can the present crisis be faced with the kind of courage, serenity and hope that Gilkey calls for.

NOTES

1 *Message and Existence*, p. 2.

2 David Tracy, "Response to Gilkey," in "On Thinking about the Unthinkable," *The University of Chicago Magazine* 76, 1 (Fall 1983), p. 29.

3 *Catholicism*, p. 114.

4 Cf. chapter two, section 4 (e).

5 Cf. "Culture and Religious Belief," pp. 2, 12-14.

6 *Society and the Sacred*, pp. 64-65.

7 Cf. *Society and the Sacred*, pp. 47, 67-71; and *Reaping*, pp. 262-266.

8 *Message and Existence*, p. 182. Walter Brueggemann's discussion of psalms of orientation, disorientation and reorientation seems spiritually akin to Gilkey's analysis. Cf. Brueggemann's *The Message of the Psalms: A Theological Commentary* (Minneapolis: Augsburg, 1984). Other works by Brueggemann that would provide powerful biblical foundations to Gilkey's theological project are *The Prophetic Imagination* (Philadelphia: Fortress, 1978); *The Hopeful Imagination: Prophetic Voices in Exile* (Philadelphia: Fortress, 1986); and *Israel's Praise: Doxology against Idolatry and Ideology* (Philadelphia: Fortress, 1988).

9 Ibid.

10 Ibid, p. 183.

11 Ibid, p. 184.

12 Richard Middleton and I have discussed the relation of creation, fall and

redemption at greater length in *The Transforming Vision*, part II.

13 It is important to make two remarks qualifying my use of the term 'dialectic' in Gilkey's thought. Gilkey observes in both the biblical witness and in cultural history these kinds of dialectical patterns. He does not move from that observation to sweeping Hegelian (or Marxist) conclusions about the necessary structure of either being or history. Gilkey's dialectic is suffused with contingency. He is describing observable patterns, not prescribing universal structures.

The second remark follows from the first. Rather than following the Hegelian (and, more recently, deconstructionist) dialectic by describing the third moment as a double negation (negation of negation) or (more ambiguously) as *Aufhebung*, Gilkey uses the more simple (and more positive) term of reaffirmation.

For an example of a deconstructionist dialectic which is clearly in the tradition of Hegel, cf. Mark C. Taylor, *Deconstructing Theology*, American Academy of Religion Studies in Religion, 28 (New York: Crossroad, 1982). One might also consult the present author's review of this book in *Christian Scholar's Review* XIII, 3 (1984), pp. 284-286.

14 Cf. "The Understanding of Suffering," pp. 7-25. That Gilkey's understanding of dialectic is stamped by both Tillichian and Niebuhrian influences is evident in, "Tillich: Master of Mediation," pp. 32-34; and "Reinhold Niebuhr's Theology of History," p. 364.

15 Section 4 (c).

16 *Society and the Sacred*, p. 29.

17 Ibid.

18 Ibid, p. 28.

19 Ibid, p. 30.

20 *MH*, p. 3. It should be noted that while metaphysics is Gilkey's preferred term for this branch of philosophy in his earliest writings, his later writings increasingly refer to ontology. There seems to be little (if any) distinction between these terms in Gilkey's usage.

21 Ibid, p. 6.

22 Cf. *Maker*, pp. 292-293.

23 Cf. *Maker*, pp. 42, 133-138.

24 *Maker*, p. 193.

25 "Cosmology, Ontology and the Travail of Biblical Language," p. 203.

26 Cf. chapter one, section 3 (c).

27 Cf. "New Modes," p. 355.

28 *Naming*, p. 275.

29   Indeed, pp. 333-340 of *Naming* function as something of an ontological interlude in the prolegomenon.

30   Cf. chapter one, section 3 (d).

31   Cf. *Naming*, p. 463; and "New Modes," p. 369.

32   "The Role of the Theologian in Contemporary Society," p. 335. Cf. "Tillich: Master of Mediation," pp. 36-37. For Tillich, philosophy is primarily ontology. He says, "Philosophy asks the question of reality as a whole; it asks the question of the structure of being. And it answers in terms of categories, structural laws, and universal concepts. It must answer in ontological terms" (*Systematic Theology*, I, p. 20).

33   *Catholicism*, p. 124.

34   *Reaping*, p. 145. Wolfhart Pannenberg expresses his fundamental agreement with Gilkey on this matter in "Providence, God, and Eschatology," in *The Whirlwind in Culture*, p. 175.

35   *Catholicism*, p. 123, italics added. Earlier in this book he says that "theology for its own completion calls for the appropriation and use of contemporary philosophy if the symbols it expresses are to be reflectively alive, that is, meaningful and valid for us" (p. 103).

36   Ibid, p. 126. In this light it is significant that Gilkey's critique of Cobb's adoption of a Whiteheadian ontology is not just that the ontology lacks coherence but that it seriously deviates from the central tenets of the Christian tradition. Cf. "Review of *A Christian Natural Theology*."

37   Cf. *MH*, p. 27. Gilkey goes on to say that "the most intelligible metaphysics is that one which grows on Christian soil."

38   *Symbolism of Evil*, p. 348.

39   *Naming*, p. 434.

40   Cf. *Catholicism*, p. 103.

41   *Reaping*, p. 100.

42   Ibid, p. 119.

43   "Theology and the Future," pp. 250-251. Cf. *Catholicism*, p. 5: "Change is the basic reality of history; it is in some way the character of whatever being there is. The flux of becoming, not the changelessness of being, characterizes our existence and that of our world."

44   *Catholicism*, p. 148. Cf. p. 49.

45 *Reaping,* p. 301. Cf. *Message and Existence,* p. 72; *Naming,* p. 49; and *Creationism,* p. 13.

46 Ibid, p. 43.

47 *Message and Existence,* p. 75.

48 Cf. *Reaping,* p. 96.

49 Ibid, p. 44. Cf. p. 7. Referring to destiny as the "ground" of freedom is an unfortunate use of words for Gilkey. In the next subsection we will see that Gilkey argues that "concurring providence" is the "ground" of freedom. Perhaps it would have been more helpful if he distinguished more clearly between proximate and ultimate grounds.

50 *Society and the Sacred,* p. 59.

51 *Message and Existence,* p. 76.

52 Cf. *Systematic Theology,* I, pp. 168-171, 182-186.

53 *Reaping,* p. 49.

54 Cf. *Reaping,* pp. 50-51, 235. For Gilkey's discussion of Niebuhr's emphasis on freedom in history, cf. "Niebuhr's Theology of History," pp. 378-379.

55 Cf. "Theology for a Time of Troubles," p. 478.

56 Cf. *Reaping,* p. 119.

57 "Heilbroner's Vision of History," p. 232. Cf. "Religion and the Technological Future," pp. 11-12; and "Theology and the Future," p. 256.

58 *Reaping,* p. 247.

59 Ibid. Cf. "The Concept of Providence in Contemporary Theology," pp. 180-181.

60 "The Concept of Providence," p. 184. Gilkey also argues that, with reference to providence, "modern 'neo-Reformation' theology represents a very different position than does the Reformation, an interiorizing and privatizing of the Reformation vision that God rules in his mysterious way the entire course of events both 'subjective' and objective.'" *Reaping,* p. 403, n. 74.

61 Ibid, p. 185.

62 *Reaping,* p. 170.

63 Ibid, p. 122.

64 Gilkey refers to this argument as a natural theology in *Reaping,* pp. 127, 370-371, note 13; and *Society and the Sacred,* pp. 28, 30. His development of a natural theology is surprising (including to himself) in the light of his earlier critique of such an

enterprise in *Naming*, pp. 205-210; and his "Review of *A Christian Natural Theology*," p. 541.

65 *Reaping*, p. 302.

66 The argument is most clearly articulated in three places: *Reaping*, pp. 303-306; *Society and the Sacred*, pp. 31-33; and *Message and Existence*, pp. 78-81.

67 *Reaping*, p. 303. Cf. pp. 249-250: "The continuing effectiveness of finite events, themselves passing away, that makes all continuity and all becoming possible is itself dependent on that which does not pass, on a power of being which bears every achieved and objectified event beyond itself to become the destiny of the next event."

68 Ibid.

69 Ibid, p. 250. Gilkey also argued for the preserving power of God in *Maker*, p. 95. Commenting on the fundamental dependence of creatures, he says: "They *are*, then, only so long as God's creative act continues to give them being, for they do not generate their own power to be from themselves, but as the moments of their existence pass, they receive it continually from beyond themselves." He then adds: "If God were to cease to be in things, they would simply cease to be."

70 Ibid, p. 304. It should be noted that Gilkey's argument here is ontological, not merely anthropological. It is not just human creatures who are self-actualizing (though they may be the clearest example of this process), but all finite creatures. Gilkey follows Whitehead's conviction that "the world is 'self-creative' for in each occasion the universe actualizes itself anew" (cited in *Reaping*, p. 304).

71 *Message and Existence*, p. 80, italics added.

72 *Reaping*, p. 304.

73 Ibid, p. 305. Again, Gilkey's formulations are deeply influenced by Whitehead who also argues that for any possibility to be it "must be somewhere" related to actuality. Cf. *Society and the Sacred*, pp. 32-33; *Reaping*, p. 431, n. 15; and *Message and Existence*, p. 85, n. 1.

74 Cf. *Reaping*, p. 251: "Possibility must be related to an eternal, everlasting and encompassing actuality, some being that orders possibility for the whole process: God's providence. Thus the very possibility of openness and of the new in the future, far from denying the presence of God, requires it."

75 Section 1 (d).

76 *Reaping*, p. 252.

77 Ibid. Gilkey goes on to say: "Possibility enters history with a moral tone, as a claim on our integrity and responsibility."

78 It should be noted that this discussion of Gilkey's reinterpretation of God technically does not fall under the first stage of the dialectic of rational, incredible

and credible that I am using as a hermeneutic key to Gilkey's constructive theological reflections. The reason I include this discussion in the context of explicating Gilkey's arguments concerning the rationality of providence is that it is in that context that this reinterpretation occurs in his own work. In *Reaping* the argument for the rationality of providence (pp. 302-306) is immediately followed by a discussion of "New Elements in the Conception of God" (pp. 306-310).

79 Cf. *Message and Existence*, p. 93.

80 Cf. Wolfhart Pannenberg, "The God of Hope," and "The Question of God," in *Basic Questions in Theology*, vol. II, trans. by G. H. Kehm (Philadelphia: Fortress Press, 1972); "Speaking of God in the Face of Atheist Criticism," in *The Idea of God and Human Freedom*, trans. by R. A. Wilson (Philadelphia: Westminster Press, 1973); "Appearance as the Arrival of the Future," in *Theology and the Kingdom of God*, ed. by Richard J. Neuhaus (Philadelphia: Westminster Press, 1969); and Jürgen Moltmann, *Theology of Hope: On the Ground and Implications of Christian Eschatology*, trans. by J. W. Leitch (New York: Harper and Row, 1967); and *The Future of Hope: Theology as Eschatology*, ed. by P. Herzog (New York: Herder and Herder, 1970).
In Moltmann's more recent writings he has, similar to Gilkey, adopted the notion of God's self-limitation. Moltmann's understanding of self-limitation, however, is deeply influenced by Isaac Luria's kabbalistic concept of *zimsum* whereby God withdraws into himself in order to 'make room' for creation. Cf. *Trinity and the Kingdom*, trans. by M. Kohl (San Francisco: Harper and Row, 1981); and *God in Creation: An Ecological Doctrine of Creation*, trans. by M. Kohl (London: SCM Press, 1985). For a critical discussion of Moltmann's doctrine of creation, see the present author's "Theology of Hope and the Doctrine of Creation: An Appraisal of Jürgen Moltmann," *The Evangelical Quarterly* LIX, 1 (January 1987), pp. 52-76.

81 *Reaping*, p. 249.

82 Ibid, p. 235. Cf. "Pannenberg's *Basic Questions in Theology*," pp. 52-54; and "The Universal and Immediate Presence of God," p. 83.

83 Cf. *Message and Existence*, p. 92.

84 *Reaping*, p. 248. Cf. pp. 307-308; *Maker*, p. 229; and "Niebuhr's Theology of History," p. 379. Gilkey has advocated the notion of the self-limitation of God since his dissertation. Cf. *MH*, p. 485: "The paradox of creation depends for its intelligibility on the self-limitation of the creator so that his creation is independent and therefore real; such self-limitation is a personal act of freedom and can never be understood in impersonal metaphysical terms."

85 Cf. *Reaping*, p. 279. Again, Pannenberg has expressed his fundamental agreement with Gilkey's notion of self-limitation (though disliking the term itself) in "Providence, God, and Eschatology."

86 Cf. *Reaping*, pp. 303, 311; and "The New Being in Christology," p. 310.

87 *Society and the Sacred*, p. 135. Earlier in this article, "The Mystery of Being and Nonbeing," Gilkey says that the being/nonbeing relation is more profound than the being/becoming relation. Indeed, "we seem here to have reached a 'basement' question, one that supports and illuminates all else we have to say" (p. 45). We

might comment that while the being/nonbeing relation may well be of such foundational significance, Gilkey only began to address it late in his career and that his conclusions are far from conclusive. In fact, this article is the only significant discussion of the issue.

88 Cf. *Reaping*, pp. 201-202.

89 *Reaping*, pp. 308-309.

90 Ibid, p. 310.

91 Cf. *Reaping*, pp. 288, 292, 310.

92 *Message and Existence*, p. 93.

93 Perhaps this is one of the most significant ways in which Gilkey's later writings deviate from *Maker*. In that book the dialectic is between "God's transcendent eternity and the finite world of change and flux," not within God's being itself (p. 259). He also uses the characteristically neo-orthodox language of the "paradox" of the eternal at work in time (p. 279) and gives voice to the idea that by hearing the proclaimed Word human beings make contact with the eternity that has appeared in Jesus Christ (p. 252).

94 *Reaping*, p. 308, italics added.

95 Ibid, p. 249.

96 Ibid, pp. 312. Cf. pp. 303-304. For a similar formulation, cf. David Tracy's discussion of God's *bi-polarity* in *Blessed Rage for Order*, pp. 178ff.

97 Ibid, p. 308.

98 Ibid, pp. 309, 310. Cf. *Message and Existence*, p. 95: "God thus 'becomes' as the process becomes and in this becoming the actuality of God changes."

99 Gilkey's critique of John Cobb's process theology is that it loses the self-sufficiency and permanence of God in the process of activity and becoming. Cf. "Review of *A Christian Natural Theology*," pp. 542-544.

100 *Message and Existence*, p. 96.

101 Cf. *MH*, p. 604; *Maker*, pp. 95-96; "Theology in the Seventies," pp. 300-301; and *Catholicism*, pp. 59, 90. It is also interesting to note that one of Gilkey's criticisms of W. C. Smith's theology is its undialectical immanentism. Cf. "A Theological Voyage with Wilfred Cantwell Smith," pp. 304-305.

102 *Society and the Sacred*, p. 33.

103 Cf. *Maker*, p. 182. In the light of this view of evil Gilkey voices strong criticism in this book of any worldview that identifies evil with the very structure of creaturely finitude. Cf. pp. 58-61, 158, 183-184. See also *MH*, pp. 399f; and *Message and Existence*, p. 120.

104   *Maker*, p. 185.

105   Cf. Gilkey's description of Augustine's anthropological view of evil in *Reaping*, p. 167.

106   *Message and Existence*, p. 141. Earlier in this chapter Gilkey responds to the Buddhist view that "it is being a self in the world among other selves, and it is the attachment to the self, to others and to its world that constitutes the human problem" (p. 121). His difficulty with this Buddhist conception is that it does not seem to account for "the persistent appearance and reappearance ... both in others and in ourselves, of moral blame or moral condemnation whenever estrangement manifests itself" (p. 122). To be morally culpable means being free to engage or not to engage in certain acts, and it is because of this freedom that "the sense of guilt ... is all pervasive in human experience" (p. 122).

107   *Reaping*, p. 256. Cf. *Maker*, p. 186: "Since its seat is in freedom rather than essential structure, evil is historical rather than ontological in character."

108   Cf. *Reaping*, pp. 44, 152; *Message and Existence*, pp. 125, 215; and *Society and the Sacred*, p. 33.

109   Cf. *Reaping*, p. 257; *Maker*, pp. 187-185; *Society and the Sacred*, p. 33; and "Niebuhr's Theology of History," pp. 370-371.

110   *Reaping*, p. 49. Cf. pp. 55, 278; *Society and the Sacred*, pp. 49-51; and *Message and Existence*, pp. 154-155; 224-225.

111   *Reaping*, pp. 49-50.

112   Cf. *Naming*, pp. 323-327.

113   Cf. *Reaping*, p. 257.

114   Gilkey accepts Niebuhr's distinction between the "equality of sin" and the "inequality of guilt." While sin is the universal human condition, the sin of the person who has power has greater consequence (and therefore greater guilt) than the sin of someone who is powerless. Cf. "Niebuhr's Theology of History," pp. 380-381; and *Society and the Sacred*, p. 52; as well as Niebuhr, *Nature and Destiny of Man*, I, pp. 219-227.

115   *Reaping*, p. 51.

116   Cf. *Reaping*, pp. 55-56.

117   Cf. *Reaping*, pp. 90, 254; and *Maker*, pp. 217-218.

118   Cf. *Society and the Sacred*, p. 152.

119   *Reaping*, p. 236. Cf. Niebuhr, *Faith and History*, chapters 5 and 8.

120   Ibid.

121 *Society and the Sacred*, p. 36.

122 Cf. *Message and Existence*, p. 182.

123 *Reaping*, p. 127.

124 *Society and the Sacred*, p. 38. Cf. *Catholicism*, pp. 92-93. This concern that the expression of Christian faith must go beyond ontology is also foundational to Gilkey's critique of process theology. Cf. "Review of *A Christian Natural Theology*," pp. 536-538; and "Theology in Process: Schubert Ogden's Developing Theology," p. 453.

125 *Reaping*, p. 266. Cf. pp. 258, 315-316.

126 Cf. *Reaping*, p. 128; *Society and the Sacred*, pp. 29, 37-38; and "The New Being and Christology," p. 314.

127 "The Christian Understanding of Suffering," p. 23.

128 *Society and the Sacred*, p. 39.

129 *Reaping*, p. 297, italics added.

130 Cf. *MH*, p. 505; *Maker*, p. 211; *Reaping*, pp. 315-316; *Message and Existence*, pp. 173, 193; and "The Meaning of Jesus the Christ," pp. 3-4.

131 *Catholicism*, p. 189. Cf. p. 151; *Maker*, pp. 209-210; *Message and Existence*, p. 227; and "Symbols, Meaning and the Divine Presence," pp. 261-262. For a similar view of the relation of creation and redemption see Albert M. Wolters, *Creation Regained: Biblical Basics for a Reformational Worldview* (Grand Rapids, Mich.: Eerdmans, 1985).

132 *Message and Existence*, p. 171.

133 Ibid, p. 189. Cf. "The New Being and Christology," pp. 317-318; "Symbols, Meaning and the Divine Presence," p. 256; and "The Meaning of Jesus the Christ," pp. 5-6.

134 Tillich, *Systematic Theology*, II, p. 94. Cf. *Reaping*, pp. 280-282; and "Niebuhr's Theology of History," pp. 376-378.

135 *Message and Existence*, p. 183.

136 *Reaping*, p. 282. Cf. *Naming*, p. 409.

137 While Gilkey's understanding of atonement is primarily in terms of Abelardian 'exemplary' theory, he does, in one unpublished article, give at least some credence to the Anselmian 'substitutionary' view. Referring to this view as a "strange theory of transaction" he suggests that without at least some sense of the Christ as a 'savior' (which entails some notion of 'effective' atonement), "the new possibilities presented by Jesus as model and teacher remain only a new law misleading us to an illusory sense of virtue or condemning us to frustration" ("The Meaning of Jesus the Christ," p. 20).

271

138 Cf. *Maker*, pp. 214, 221-222; *Naming*, p. 408; *Message and Existence*, pp. 192-193; and "The Christian Understanding of Suffering," p. 26.

139 *Reaping*, pp. 283.

140 Cf. "Niebuhr's Theology of History," p. 380.

141 In this regard it is interesting to note that the resurrection is hardly mentioned in *Reaping*. It would appear that Christ's resurrection and the hope of a general resurrection are inconsequential themes for a Christian interpretation of history.

142 Cf. *Message and Existence*, p. 179.

143 Cf. *Message and Existence*, pp. 253-254.

144 "The Contribution of Culture to the Reign of God," p. 47. For further discussion of Gilkey's critique of Moltmann's view of the eschaton as a radical *creatio nova* which negates all previous actuality, see the present author's "Theology of Hope and the Doctrine of Creation," pp. 58ff.

145 Ibid, p. 53. Cf. *Catholicism*, pp. 144-147.

146 *Reaping*, p. 287.

147 Cf. *Reaping*, pp. 292-293.

148 *Message and Existence*, p. 233. Cf. *Reaping*, p. 288.

149 Ibid, p. 168.

150 Ibid, pp. 294-295.

151 *Reaping*, p. 303.

152 This is Robert C. Neville's argument against process theology in *Creativity and God: A Challenge to Process Theology*, A Crossroad Book (New York: Seabury Press, 1980), pp. 8-10.

153 Is it not the case that referring to the Kingdom of God in terms of a possibility beyond possibility is, in fact, saying that it is an impossibility?

154 *Reaping*, p. 280.

155 Cf. Neville, *Creativity and God*, p. 9.

CONCLUSION

Langdon Gilkey's theological project is broad in scope. This does not mean, however, that his thought is without focus. I have argued in this book that the overriding focus of his thought is the relation of Christian theology to the culture of modernity. He employs insights from historical, systematic and philosophical theology, anthropology, sociology, political theory, environmental studies, philosophy and philosophy of history, all in service of articulating the meaning of the Christian message in the context of modern existence. Acknowledging Gilkey's own methodological distinction of three stages or moments of theological reflection, I have endeavoured to understand the first two stages — prolegomenon and constructive theology — in terms of the third — theology of culture. The fruitfulness of this hermeneutical procedure is to be evaluated in the light of the illuminative power of this exposition of Gilkey's thought.

Throughout we have noted repeatedly how the three stages of Gilkey's project mutually reinforce each other. More specifically, I have attempted to demonstrate how central features of his theology of culture are grounded in elements of his prolegomenal analysis and constructive theological reflections. For example, a *theology* of culture is only a meaningful enterprise if it can be established that a dimension of ultimacy is a constitutive element of all cultural life. The success of Gilkey's prolegomenon, which attempts to demonstrate that such a dimension is present in the most apparently secular facets of culture, is foundational, therefore, to his theology of culture. Further, a theology of culture that wants to affirm human freedom and the openness of history will require both an ontological elucidation of the structure of historical passage which recognizes freedom as constitutive of that structure, and an understanding of God's providence as the ground of freedom and the envisionment of new possibilities in an open future. In this way Gilkey's constructive theological and ontological reflections are foundational to his theology of culture. Further,

273

his theological understanding of the fall of freedom into sin, and destiny into fate, provides him with a basis for a more realistic discernment of the distorting effects of estrangement in cultural history than the optimistic progressivism of modernity And his understanding of redemption and eschatology provides him with a foundation for cultural praxis which reveals the injustices of the present, opens new possibilities, and functions as a ground for radical criticism because the eschatological Kingdom transcends those who attempt to enact it.

Throughout this study I have also evaluated Gilkey's project. Often that evaluation has been positive. His theological method is creative and fruitful. The criteria of eidetic fidelity, reflective coherence and existential appropriateness or relevance would appear to summarize the standards by which theological reflection should be evaluated. I have used these criteria in my evaluation of Gilkey's own theology. The theoretical foundations that he proposes for theology of culture, together with his analysis and diagnosis of modernity, demonstrates both intellectual breadth and spiritual discernment. The crisis of modernity is indeed a spiritual crisis and therefore calls for theological analysis and religious response. We have already noted that such an analysis is rooted in a prolegomenal demonstration of the reality, necessity and legitimacy of a dimension of ultimacy. The evidence for such a dimension is presented and argued by Gilkey in a convincing way. Finally, his constructive theological reflections demonstrate a profound concern that the central tenets of a Christian worldview be reinterpreted in such a way that they are intelligible in the modern context.

I have also given voice to numerous criticisms of Gilkey's project, however. His theology of culture suffers from not taking serious enough account of the oppressive character (racist, classist and sexist) of the religious substance of modernity. His proposals also lack specificity with regard both to the foreground and background of culture. I have argued that his proposal (against fundamentalism) for a 'mixed economy' whereby we affirm our own particular religious vision as well as the general civil religion, is both inconsistent with his own understanding of the nature of the religious substance of culture and is internally incoherent. Further, his argument that we need to respond to the absolutism of fundamentalism with a dialectic of one part absolute and two parts relative (a relative absoluteness) does not get him off the horns of the relativism/absolutism dilemma.

The problem of relativism reappeared in our various discussions of Gilkey's view of the parity of religions and his concomitant universalism. I have attempted to demonstrate that his argument for universalism and his model of a covenant with other religions is neither eidetically faithful to the scriptural sources of the Christian tradition, nor reflectively coherent.

The difficulties inherent in Gilkey's universalism are compounded by problems in his prolegomenon. I have argued that it is a short step from the conflation the dimension of ultimacy and the Ultimate itself to universalism. That each culture has a dimension of ultimacy I do not doubt. Whether that dimension can be taken to be a positive manifestation of the sacred in that culture and to be evidence for universal salvation, I think is not argued soundly by Gilkey.

We have also seen that Gilkey's conflation of the dimension of ultimacy and the Ultimate is itself rooted in a confusion concerning the relation of a *dimension* of ultimacy to the *centre* of human life and the *transcendent* to which both refer. Therefore, my affirmation of Gilkey's argument for the reality of a dimension of ultimacy is tempered by a criticism of his phenomenological description of the central contours of this dimension and its relation both to the divine and the rest of life. This ambiguity in Gilkey's description of the dimension of ultimacy has further implications for his view of religious language, especially as that view is articulated in his critique of creation science. If his universalism displays certain *monistic* tendencies then his view of the science/religion relation (at least in the context of the creationist debate) tends to be *dualistic*. While such tendencies may be contradictory, I have argued that both are explicable in terms of the inherent problems in his description of the dimension of ultimacy. In the text I have also suggested a model that could bring some clarity to what appears to be Gilkey's confusion.

In the light of Gilkey's concern for a viable theology of culture it is not surprising that the weight of his constructive theological reflection has fallen upon a reinterpretation of providence. A theology of culture always includes, at a foundational level, a theology of history. Gilkey's argument that a theology of history is dialectical parallels both his dialectical interpretation of the career of modernity and the flow of the biblical worldview in terms of creation, fall and redemption. My question is whether this historical and symbolic dialectic is appropriately recast in the epistemological categories of rational, credible and incredible. I have argued that it is not. The central problem concerns the first stage — rationality. The natural theological argument that Gilkey proposes to establish the rationality of belief in providence is less than convincing. It is also out of place in Gilkey's corpus. Equally out of place is his argument for God's self-limitation. The argument appears to assume that an omnipotent God is an external limit of human freedom. Such an assumption, I have argued, reduces God to one ontological (or metaphysical) factor among others. Throughout his career Gilkey has argued against the viability of such a reduction.

The problem of divine self-limitation gives rise to an even more profound criticism, however. I have asked whether Gilkey's self-limited God who can only lure us with possibilities in an open future is not, in the end, an impotent God. Is this why Gilkey has emphasized a *theologia crucis*, together with an Abelardian understanding of atonement, at the expense of a sufficiently reinterpreted *theologia gloriae?* Can such a theology demonstrate fidelity to the eidetic meaning of the Kingdom of God that comes as an enactment of the divine will? Is Gilkey's argument that such a Kingdom could not be actualized historically because such actualization would deny the ontological structure of history and the continuation of sin in that structure, reflectively coherent? I think that it is not. Nor can such a view pass the test of existential relevance or adequacy. A culture in decline, I have argued, needs a vision of a Kingdom that comes as a gift that restores and redeems creaturely life in all of its fullness. Without such a vision a theology of culture lacks both power and a sure hope.

Langdon Gilkey's theological project, including his theology of culture, has numerous deficiencies. It also has profound strengths. In this book I have attempted to celebrate the strengths and criticize the deficiencies. With adequate attention to the problems I have noted, combined with a building upon the foundations that Gilkey has established, I believe that a theology of culture can be articulated that will offer spiritual discernment in our present cultural malaise and redirection for our culture in decline. A concern for such discernment and redirection has characterized Langdon Gilkey's life and has been the underlying *élan* of his thought.

276

BIBLIOGRAPHY

This bibliography is organized into three sections. The first section lists primary sources in terms of books, articles and unpublished materials. These entries are presented in chronological order. The second section lists critical studies pertaining to Gilkey. These entries are presented alphabetically. The third section identifies various secondary sources that have proven useful in the writing of this book. These entries are also presented alphabetically.

I. Primary Sources

A. Books by Langdon Gilkey

Maker of Heaven and Earth: A Study of the Christian Doctrine of Creation. New York: Doubleday, 1959. German edition: *Der Himmel und Erde gemacht hat.* Munich: Claudius Verlag, 1971.

How the Church can Minister to the World Without Losing Itself. New York: Harper and Row, 1964.

Shantung Compound: The Story of Men and Women under Pressure. New York: Harper and Row, 1966.

Naming the Whirlwind: The Renewal of God-Language. Indianapolis and New York: Bobbs-Merrill, 1969.

Religion and the Scientific Future. New York: Harper and Row, and London: SCM, 1970. Reprinted, Marcon, GA: Mercer University Press, 1981. Italian edition: *Il destino dell religione nell'era technologie.* Trans. by P. Prini. Rome: Armando Armando Editore, 1972.

Catholicism Confronts Modernity: A Protestant View. A Crossroad Book.

New York: Seabury Press, 1975.

Reaping the Whirlwind: A Christian Interpretation of History. A Crossroad Book. New York: Seabury Press, 1976.

Message and Existence: An Introduction to Christian Theology. New York: Seabury Press, 1981.

Society and the Sacred: Toward a Theology of Culture in Decline. A Crossroad Book. New York: Seabury Press, 1981.

Creationism on Trial: Evolution and God at Little Rock. Minneapolis, Mn.: Winston Press, 1985.

Gilkey on Tillich. New York; Crossroads, 1990

B. Articles, Reviews and Contributions to Books by Langdon Gilkey

"Academic Freedom and the Christian Faith." *Christianity and Crisis* 12 (Nov. 22, 1952), 171-173.

"Morality and the Cross." *Christianity and Crisis* 14 (Nov. 5, 1954), 35-38.

"A Christian Response to the World Crisis." *Christianity and Crisis* 15 (Aug. 8, 1955), 107-111.

"Great Good Sense." Review of Nathaniel Micklem's *Ultimate Questions. Christian Century* 72, 31 (August 3, 1955), 896.

"Christ and the City." *Motive* 17 (April 1957), 2, 3, 59.

"Neo-Orthodoxy." In *A Handbook of Christian Theology.* Edited by M. A. Halverson and A. Cohen. Cleveland: Living Age Books, 1958, 256-261.

"Biblical Theology and Historical Reality." *Encounter* 19 (Spring 1958), 214-218.

"The Imperative for Unity — A Re-Statement." In *Issues in Unity.* Indianapolis: Council on Christian Unity, 1958, 11-32.

"Calvin's Religious Thought." *Motive* 20 (February 1960), 5-6.

"Darwin and Christian Thought." *Christian Century* 77, 1 (January 6,1960), 7-11. Reprinted as part one of "Evolution and the Doctrine of Creation." In *Religion and Science.* Edited by Ian Barbour. New York: Harper and Row, 1968, 159-181.

"Cosmology, Ontology and the Travail of Biblical Language." *Journal of Religion* 41 (July 1961), 194-205. Reprinted in *Concordia Theological Monthly* 33 (March 1962), 143-54.

"The Concept of Providence in Contemporary Theology." *Journal of Religion* 43, 3 (July 1963), 128-136.

Review of G. H. Tavard's *Paul Tillich and the Christian Message.* Union *Seminary Quarterly Review* 18, 3 (March 1963), 283-284.

"Stewards of the Mysteries of God." *Criterion* 3 (Winter 1964), 29-31.

"A New Linguistic Madness." *Journal of Religion* 44, 3 (July 1964), 238-243. Reprinted in *New Theology II.* Edited by M. Marty and D. Peerman. New York: Macmillan, 1965, 39-49.

"Secularism's Impact on Contemporary Theology." *Christianity and Crisis* 25 (April 5, 1965), 64-67. Also published in *Witness to a Generation.* Edited by A. Roy Eckardt. New York: Harper and Row, 1968, 192-197; and in *Radical Theology: Phase Two.* Edited by C. W. Christian and G. R. Witting. Philadelphia and New York: J. B. Lippincott Co., 1967, 17-23.

"Holy, Holy, Holy." *The Baptist Student* 44 (1965), 24-27.

Review of A. J. McKelway's *The Systematic Theology of Paul Tillich.* *Foundations* 8 3 (July 1965), 262-265.

"Is God Dead?" Review of Daniel Jenkins' *The Christian Belief in God.* *Christian Century* 82, 1 (January 1965), 18-19.

"Dissolution and Reconstruction in Theology." *Christian Century* 82, 5 (February 3, 1965), 135-139. Reprinted in *Frontline Theology.* Edited by Dean Peerman. Richmond, Va.: John Knox Press, 1966, 29-38. Translated into German as "Abbau und Wiederaufbau in der Theologie."

In *Theologie im Umbruch.* München: Chr. Kaiser Verlag, 1968, 32-41.

"The Authority of the Bible." *Encounter* 27 (Spring 1966), 112-123.

Review of John Cobb's *A Christian Natural Theology. Theology Today* 22, 4 (January 1966), 530 -545.

"Seeds of Malaise." Review of Karl Lowith's *Nature, History and Existentialism. Christian Century* 83, 44 (November 2, 1966), 1341-1342.

"A Paganized Judaism." Review of Richard Rubenstein's *After Aushchwitz. Christian Century* 84, 19 (May 10, 1967), 627-628.

Review of J. L. Adams' *Paul Tillich's Philosophy of Culture. Theology Today* 23, 4 (January 1967), 565-569.

"If There is No God ..." *Criterion* 6 (Spring 1967), 5-7.

"New Modes of Empirical Theology." In *The Future of Empirical Theology.* Edited by Bernard Meland. Vol. VII of *Essays in Divinity.* Edited by Jerald C. Brauer. Chicago and London: University of Chicago Press, 1969, 345-370.

"Standing on the Promises." Review of J. Moltmann's *The Theology of Hope. Christian Century* 84, 51 (December 20, 1967), 1630-1632.

"Anatomy of Reconciliation." A review of Emil L. Fackenheim's *The Religious Dimension in Hegel's Thought. Christian Century* 86, 2 (January 8, 1969), 52-53.

"Social and Intellectual Sources of Contemporary Protestant Theology in America." *Daedelus* 96 (Winter 1967), 69-98. Reprinted in *Religion in America.* Edited by W. McLaughlin and R. Bellah. Boston: Beacon Press, 1968, 137-166.

"The Problem of God and the Study of Theology." *Criterion* 6 (Spring 1967), 5-7.

"Theology in Process: Schubert Ogden's Developing Theology." *Interpretation* 21 (October 1967), 447-459.

"Evolutionary Science and the Dilemma of Freedom and Determinism." *Christian Century* 84, 11 (1967), 339-343. Reprinted in *Changing Man: The Threat and the Promise.* Edited by K. Haseldon and P. Hefner. Garden City, N. J.: Doubleday, 1968, 63-76.

"Theology." In *The Great Ideas Today.* Edited by R. M. Hutchins and M. Adler. Chicago: Encyclopedia Britannica Inc., 1967, 238-70.

"The Integrity of History." Review of Philip Hefner's *Faith and the Vitalities of History. Una Sancta* 24, 2 (Pentecost 1967), 67-71.

"Modern Myth-Making and the Possibilities of Twentieth Century Theology." In *Theology of Renewal.* Vol. 1. Edited by L. K. Snook. Montreal: Palm Publishing, 1968, 238-312.

"American Policy and the Just War." *Criterion* 7 (Winter 1968), 9-16.

"Evolution and the Doctrine of Creation." In *Science and Religion.* Edited by Ian Barbour. New York: Harper and Row, 1968, 159-181.

"The Contribution of Culture to the Reign of God." In *The Future as the Presence of Shared Hope.* Edited by M. Muckenhirn. New York: Sheed and Ward, 1968, 34-58.

"Religion and the Secular University." *Dialog* 8 (Spring 1969), 109-115. Reprinted in *Religious Education,* 64, 6 (1969), 458-466

"Trends in Protestant Apologetics." In *The Development of Fundamental Theology.* Edited by J. B. Metz. *Concilium* New York: The Paulist Press, 1969, 127-157.

"Unbelief and the Secular Spirit." In *The Presence and Absence of God.* Edited by C. F. Mooney. New York: Fordham University Press, 1969, 50-69.

"Human Values in the Twenty-First Century." *Thesis Theology Cassettes* 1, 3 (1970).

"That Mysterious Sleeping Dragon." Review of *Understanding Modern China.* Edited by J. M. Kitagawa. *Christian Century* 87, 34 (August 26, 1970),1019-1020.

"Religious Dimensions of Scientific Inquiry." *Journal of Religion* 50 (July 1970), 245-267. A revised version of this article appears as chapter 2 of *Religion and the Scientific Future.*

"Theology in the Seventies." *Theology Today* 27 (1970), 292-301.

"The Universal and Immediate Presence of God." In *The Future of Hope.* New York: Herder and Herder, 1970, 81-109.

Review of Karl Rahner's *Spirit in the World." Journal of Ecumenical Studies* 7, 1 (1970), 138-144.

"Biblical Symbols in a Scientific Culture." In *Science and Human Values in the 21st Century.* Edited by R. W. Burhoe. Philadelphia:Westminster Press, 1971, 72-98.

"Ervaring en Interpretatie van de Religieuze Dimensie: een Reaktie. *Tijdschrift voor Theologie* 11 (1971), 292-302.

"Empirical Science and Theological Knowing." In *Foundations of Theology.* Papers from the International Lonergan Congress. Edited by Philip McShane. Notre Dame, Ind.: University of Notre Dame Press, 1972, 76-101.

"Pannenberg's *Basic Questions in Theology:* a review article." *Perspective* 14 (Spring 1973), 34-55.

"Idea of God Since 1800." *Dictionary of the History of Ideas.* Volume II. Edited by Philip Weiner. New York: Charles Scribner's Sons, 1973, 351-366.

"Addressing God in Faith." In *Liturgical Experience of Faith.* Edited by H. Schmidt and D. Power. Vol. 82 of *Concilium.* New York: Herder and Herder, 1973, 62-76.

"The Problem of God: A Programmatic Essay." In *Traces of God in a*

Secular Culture. Edited by G. F. McLean. New York: Alba House, 1973.

"Christian Theology." *Criterion* 13 (Winter 1974), 10-13.

"Response to C. Meyer and Z. Hayes article, "Being a Catholic: does it make a difference?" *Catholic Theological Society of America: Proceedings of the 29th Annual Convention.* Edited by L. Salm. New York: Catholic Theological Society of America, 1974.

"Reinhold Niebuhr's Theology of History." *Journal of Religion* 54, 4 (October 1974), 360-386. Also published in *The Legacy of Reinhold Neibuhr.* Edited by Nathan A. Scott Jr. Chicago: University of Chicago Press, 1975, 36-62.

"Religion and the Technological Future." *Criterion* 13 (Spring 1974), 9-14.

"Robert Heilbroner's Morality Play." *Worldview* 17 (August 1974), 51-55.

"Symbols, Meaning and the Divine Presence." *Theological Studies* 35 (June 1974), 249-267.

"The Spirit and the Discovery of Truth Through Dialogue." In *Experience of the Sacred.* Edited by P. Huizing and W. Bassett. Vol. 99 of *Concilium.* A Crossroad Book. New York: Seabury, 1974, 58-68. Also published in *Leven uit de Geest.* A Festschrift for Edward Schillebeeckx. Edited by Paul Brand. Hilversam, The Netherlands: Gooi en Sticht, 1974. Translated into French as "L'Espirit et la decouverte de la verité dans le dialogue." In *L'Experience de L'Espirit: Melanges E. Schillebeeckx.* Paris: Beauchesne, 1976, 225-240.

"The Structure of Academic Revolutions." In *The Nature of Scientific Discovery.* Edited by Owen Gingerich. Washington: Smithsonian Institute Press, 1975, 538-573.

"On Going to War Over Oil." *Christian Century* 92 (March 12, 1975), 259-260.

"Robert Heilbroner's Vision of History." *Zygon* 10 (September 1975), 215-233.

"God: Eternal Source of Newness." *Living With Changes, Experience and Faith.* Edited by F. A. Eigo. Villanova, Pa.: Villanova University Press, 1976, 151-166.

"Future of Science." In *The Future of Science.* Edited by T. C. L. Robinson. New York: John Wiley and Sons, 1977, 105-128. A revised version of this article is also published as chapter six of *Society and the Sacred.*

"The Covenant With The Chinese." In *China and Christianity: Historical and Future Encounter.* Edited by J. D. Whitehead. Notre Dame: Center for Pastoral and Social Ministry, 1977, 118-132. Also published as chapter ten of *Society and the Sacred.*

"Theology and the Future." *Andover Newton Quarterly* 17, 4 (March 1977), 250-257.

"Anathemas and Orthodoxy: A Reply to Avery Dulles." *Christian Century* 94, 36 (November 9, 1977), 1026-1029.

"A Covenant With the Chinese." *Dialog* 17 (1978), 181-187. A revised version of this article appears as chapter ten in *Society and the Sacred.*

"Responses to Berger." *Theological Studies* 39, 3 (September 1978), 486-507.

"Toward a Religious Criterion of Religions." In *Understanding the New Religions.* Edited by J. Needleman and G. Baker. New York: Seabury, 1978, 131-137.

"The Religious Dilemmas of a Scientific Culture: The Interface of Science, Technology and Religion." In *Being Human in a Technological Age.* Edited by D. M. Borchert and D. Stewart. Athens, Ohio: Ohio University Press, 1979, 73-88. Also published as chapter seven of *Society and the Sacred.*

"The Dialectic of Christian Belief: Rational, Incredible, Credible." In

Rationality and Religious Belief. Edited by C. Delaney. Notre Dame: University of Notre Dame Press, 1979, 65-83. Also published as chapter three of *Society and the Sacred.*

"The Political Dimensions of Theology." *Journal of Religion* 59 (April1979), 154-168. A revised version of this article appears as chapter four in *Society and the Sacred* and was also published in *The Challenge of Liberation Theology: A First World Response.* Edited by Brian Mahan and L. Dale Richesen. Maryknoll, N.Y.: Orbis Press, 113-126.

"The AAR and the Anxiety of Non-Being." *Journal of the American Academy of Religion* 48, 1 (March 1980), 5-18.

"The Roles of the 'Descriptive', or 'Historical' and the 'Normative' in our Work." *Criterion* 20 (Winter 1981), 10-17.

"Theology for a Time of Troubles: How My Mind Has Changed." *Christian Century* 98 (April 29, 1981), 474-480.

"A Theological Voyage with Wilfred Cantwell Smith." *Religious Studies Review* 7, 4 (October 1981), 298-305.

"Is Religious Faith Possible in an Age of Science?" In *Unfinished... Essays in Honor of Ray L. Hart.* Edited by Mark Taylor. *Journal of the American Academy of Religion,* 48 (1981), 31-44. Also published as chapter eight of *Society and the Sacred.*

"Can Art Fill the Vacuum?" *Criterion* 20 (Autumn 1981), 7-9. Also published in *Art, Creativity and the Sacred.* Edited by D. Apostolos-Cappadona. New York: Crossroad, 1984, 182-187.

"A New Watershed in Theology." *Soundings* 64 (Summer 1981), 118-131. A revised version of this article appears as chapter one in *Society and the Sacred.*

"The Creationist Controversy: The Interrelations of Inquiry and Belief." *Science, Technology and Human Values* 7 (Summer 1982), 67-71. Also published in *Creationism, Science and the Law.* Edited by M. La Follette. Cambridge, Mass.: MIT Press, 1983, 129-137.

287

"God." In *Christian Theology: An Introduction to its Traditions and Tasks.* Edited by Peter C. Hodgson and Robert H. King. Philadelphia: Fortress Press, 1982, 62-87.

"Tillich: Master of Mediation." In *The Theology of Paul Tillich.* 2nd ed. Edited by Charles W. Kegley. New York: The Pilgrim Press, 1982, 26-56. A revised version of this article appears in *Gilkey on Tillich*, 56-78

"On Thinking About the Unthinkable." *The University of Chicago Magazine* 76, 1 (Fall 1983), 4-9, 28.

"Response to Ross Reat's Article, 'Insiders and Outsiders in the Study of Religion'." *Journal of the American Academy of Religion* 51, 3 (1983), 484-488.

"The Political Meaning of Silence." *Philosophy Today* 27 (Summer 1983), 128-132.

"Creationism: The Roots of the Conflict." In *Is God a Creationist? The Religious Case Against Creationism.* Edited by R. Frye. New York: Charles Scribner's Sons, 1983, 56-67.

"The Creationist Issue: A Theologian's View." In *Cosmology and Theology.* Edited by David Tracy and Nicholas Nash. Vol. 166 of *Concilium: Religion in the Eighties.* Edinburgh: T. & T. Clark Ltd., and New York: Seabury, 1983, 55-69.

"Scripture, History and the Quest for Meaning." In *History and Historical Understanding.* Edited by C. T. McIntire and R. A. Wells. Grand Rapids, Mich.: Eerdmans, 1984, 3-16. This article is also published as chapter five of *Society and the Sacred* and in *Humanizing America's Iconic Book.* Edited by G. M. Tucker and D. A. Knight. Chico, California: Scholar's Press, 1982, 25-38.

"Theology of Culture and Christian Ethics." *The Annual of the Society of Christian Ethics* (1984), 341-364.

"Theology as the Interpretation of Faith for Church and World." In *The Vocation of the Theologian.* Edited by Theodore W. Jennings. Philadelphia: Fortress Press, 1985, 87-103.

BIBLIOGRAPHY

"Theological Frontiers: Implications for Bioethics." In *Theology and Bioethics.* Edited by E. E. Shelp. Dordrecht, The Netherlands: D. Reidel Publishing, 1985, 115-133.

"The Role of the Theologian in Contemporary Society." In *The Thought of Paul Tillich.* Edited by J. L. Adams, W. Pauck and R. L. Shinn. An American Academy of Arts and Sciences Book. New York: Harper and Row, 1985, 330-350. Reprinted in *Gilkey on Tillich,* 177-196.

"The New Being and Christology." In *The Thought of Paul Tillich.* Ibid, 307-329. Reprinted in *Gilkey on Tillich,* 138-157.

"Religion and Science in an Advanced Scientific Culture." In *Knowing Religiously.* Edited by Leroy S. Rouner. Boston: Boston University Studies in Philosophy and Religion, vol. 7, 1985, 166-176. Also reprinted in *Zygon* 22, 2 (June 1987), 165-178.

"Events, Meanings and the Current Tasks of Theology." *Journal of the American Academy of Religion* 53, 3 (1986), 717-734.

"An Appreciation of Karl Barth." In *How Karl Barth Changed My Mind.* Edited by Donald K. McKim. Grand Rapids, Mich.: Eerdmans, 1986, 150-155.

"Reinhold Niebuhr as Political Theologian." In *Reinhold Niebuhr and the Issues of Our Time.* Edited by Richard Harries. Grand Rapids, Mich.: Eerdmans, 1986, 157-182.

"Ordering the Soul: Augustine's Manifold Legacy." *Christian Century* 105 (April 27, 1988), 426-430

"Philosophy as Metanoetics: A Review Article." *Journal of Religion* 68 (July 1988), 435-445.

"Introduction: A Retrospective Glance at My Work." In *The Whirlwind in Culture: Frontiers in Theology — In Honor of Langdon Gilkey.* Edited by D. W. Musser and J. L. Price. Bloomington: IN: Meyer Stone Books, 1989), 1-35.

"Nature, Reality, and the Sacred: A Meditation in Science and

Religion." *Zygon* 24, 3 (September 1989), 283-298.

C. Unpublished Materials by Langdon Gilkey
i) Dissertation

Maker of Heaven and Earth: A Thesis on the relation between metaphysics and Christian Theology with Special Reference to the Problem of Creation as that Problem Appears in the Philosophies of F. H. Bradley and A. N. Whitehead and in the Historic Leaders of Christian Thought. Ph. D. Dissertation, New York, Columbia University, 1954.

ii) Essays and Addresses

"Some Problems in the Concept of Providence." University of Chicago, 1963.

"The Search for Meaning." Concordia College, December 3, 1976.

"Secularization." August, 1981.

"The Relevance of Luther Today." Carroll College, November 19, 1983.

"Religion and Science in an Advanced Scientific Culture." Boston University, November 30, 1983.

"The Christian Understanding of Suffering." Honolulu: Conference on Buddhist-Christian Dialogue, January 1983.

"The New Global Context for Missions." The World Mission Institute, April 12, 1984.

"The Meaning of Jesus the Christ." Middlebury College, September 1984.

"Culture and Religious Belief." 1984.

"The God is Dead Theology and the Possibility of God Language." No date.

"Religion and the American Future." No date.

"Science, Power, and the Ambiguities of History." Toronto: York University, Prospects for Mankind Conference, June 1987.

D. Other

"Interviews with Langdon Gilkey." Eight hours of taped interviews with Brian Walsh and Langdon Gilkey. Chicago: November 27 to December 7, 1984.

II. Critical Studies

E. Theses and Dissertations

Beaugh, M. B. *The Development of the Concept of Meaningful Existence in the Chicago Divinity School as Represented by Shailer Mathews, Henry Nelson Wieman and Langdon Gilkey.* Th. D. Dissertation, Southwestern Baptist Seminary, 1975.

Bihl, Hugh William. *Langdon Gilkey's Theology of Providence: An Interpretation for a Secular Culture.* Ph.D Dissertation, Fordham University, 1987.

Clifford, Anne Marie. *The Relation of Science and Religion/Theology in the Thought of Langdon Gilkey.* Ph.D. Dissertation, The Catholic University of America, 1988.

Davis, G. F. *Langdon Gilkey and Religious Language.* M.C.S. Thesis, Vancouver, Regent College, 1979.

Littlejohn, R. L. *An Analysis of Langdon Gilkey's Phenomenology of Ultimacy and Its Implications for Theology and Ethics.* Ph. D. Dissertation, Waco, Texas, Baylor University, 1979.

Marai, J. S. *The Problem of God-Language in the Theology of John Macquarrie and Langdon Gilkey.* M.A. Thesis, Toronto, University of St. Michael's College, 1975.

McElwee, W. R. *An Analysis of the Relationship Between Content Teleministry and the Church in the Light of Langdon Gilkey's Dialectic Between Transcendence and Relevance.* D. Min. Dissertation, Princeton Theological Seminary, 1975.

Sanders, Stephen Allen. *The Contribution of Phenomenology to Theology as Reflected in the Writings of Langdon Gilkey and Edward Farley.* Th.D. Dissertation, New Orleans Baptist Theological Seminary, 1987.

Shea, John. *Religious Language in a Secular Culture: A Study in the Theology of Langdon Gilkey.* Published S.T.D. Dissertation, Mundelin, Illinois, University of St. Mary of the Lake, 1976.

Stiver, D. R. *Converging Approaches to a Natural Awareness of God in Contemporary Theology.* Ph.D. Dissertation, Southern Baptist Theological Seminary, 1983.

F. Articles and Reviews

Berger, Peter. "Secular Theology and the Rejection of the Supernatural: Reflections on Recent Trends." *Theological Studies* 38, 1 (March 1977), 39-56.

Carr, Anne. "The God Who is Involved." *Theology Today* 38, 3 (October 1981), 314-328.

Clapp, Rodney. "Laboratories of the Soul: Testing God's New Creation in Two Japanese Prison Camps." *Christianity Today* 30, 4 (March 7, 1986), 23-26.

Driver, Tom. Review of *Naming the Whirlwind. Union Seminary Quarterly* 25, 3 (Spring 1970), 361-367.

Dulles, Avery. "Latent Heresy and Orthodoxy." *Christian Century* 94 (November 16, 1977), 1053-1054.

Elshtain, Jean Bethke. Review of *Society and the Sacred. Theology Today* 39, 4 (January 1983), 429-434.

Farley, Edward. Review of *Reaping the Whirlwind. Religious Studies Review* 4, 4 (October 1978), 233-237.

Ferré, Frederick. "A Renewal of God-Language?" *Journal of Religion* 52, 2 (July 1972), 286-304.

Gibbs, John. Review of *Naming the Whirlwind. Journal of the American Academy of Religion* 39, 2 (June 1971), 272-274.

"Gilkey, Langdon B." In *Contemporary Authors*. Edited by Ann Evory. New Revision Series. Detroit: Gale Research Co., 1982, 183-184.

Hosinski, Thomas E. "Experience and the Sacred: A Retrospective Review of Langdon Gilkey's Theology." *Religious Studies Review* 11, 3 (July 1985), 228 235.

Inbody, T. "Myth in Contemporary Theology." *Anglican Theological Review* 58, 1 (April 1976), 139-157.

Kane, G. Stanley. "God-Language and Secular Experience." *International Journal of Philosophy of Religion* 2, 1 (1971), 78-95.

Kaufman, Gordon. "The Christian and History: Structure or Process?" *Interpretation* 32, 2 (April 1978), 194-196.

Mueller, D. L. "Changing Conceptions of Christian Experience." *Perspectives in Religious Studies* 1 (Fall 1974), 165-186.

Noel, Daniel. "God-Language Grounded? A Review Article." *Anglican Theological Review* 53,1 (January 1971), 57-70.

Ommen, Thomas B. "Verification in Theology: A Tension in Revisionist Method." *The Thomist* 43, 3 (July 1979), 357-384.

Olson, Arthur L. "Why the Church?" *Dialog* 12 (1973), 206-212.

Outler, Albert C. Review of *Society and the Sacred. The Christian Century* 99, 14 (April 21, 1982), 489-490.

Peters, Ted. "The Whirlwind as yet Unnamed." *Journal of the American Academy of Religion* 42, 4 (December 1970), 699-709.

_____ "The Christian Realism of Langdon Gilkey." Unpublished, no date.

_____ "Langdon Gilkey: Theologian to the Modern Mind." *Dialog* 27 (Winter, 1988), 55-62

Robbins, J. Wesley. "Professor Gilkey and Alternative Methods of Theological Construction." *Journal of Religion* 52, 1 (1972), 84-101.

Schreurs, N. "Naar de basis van ons spreken over God: de weg van Langdon Gilkey." *Tijdschrift voor Theologie* 11, 3 (1971), 274-292.

Schussler Fiorenza, Francis. Review of *Reaping the Whirlwind. Religious Studies Review* 4, 4 (October 1978), 237-240.

Sheehan, Helena. Review of *Naming the Whirlwind. Journal of Ecumenical Studies* 7 (Fall 1970), 836-839.

Stinson, L. "Gilkey's *Reaping the Whirlwind*: a review article." *The Thomist* 42 (1978).

TeSelle, Eugene. "Being in History." *Journal of Religion* 58, 3 (July 1978), 303-308.

Thompson, William. "Theology's Method and Linguistic Analysis in the Thought of Langdon Gilkey." *The Thomist* 36 (July 1972), 363-394.

Van Buren, Paul. Review of *Naming the Whirlwind. Theology Today* 27 (July 1970), 226-228.

Walsh, Brian John. "The Dimension of Ultimacy and Theology of Culture: A Critical Discussion of Langdon Gilkey." *Calvin Theological Journal* 24, 1 (April 1989), 66-92.

_____ "Langdon B. Gilkey." In *Dictionary of Christianity in America.* Edited by D. G. Reid, R. D. Linder, B. L. Shelly and H. S. Stout. Downers Grove, Ill.: InterVarsity Press, 1990, 481-482.

Williamson, Clark M. "The Divine Mortuary Was Premature: A Review Article." *Encounter* 31 (Autumn 1970), 396-399.

G. Festschrift

The Whirlwind in Culture: Frontiers in Theology — In Honor of Langdon Gilkey. Edited by D. W. Musser and J. L. Price. Bloomington: IN: Meyer Stone Books, 1989).

III. Secondary Sources

Adams, James Luther. *Paul Tillich's Philosophy of Culture, Science and Religion.* New York: Harper and Row, 1965.

Altizer, Thomas J. J. *The Gospel of Christian Atheism.* Philadelphia: Westminster Press, 1966.

Altizer, Thomas J. J. and Hamilton, William. *Radical Theology and the Death of God.* Indianapolis: Bobbs Merril, 1966.

Bacon, Francis. "New Atlantis." In *Ideal Commonwealths.* Rev. ed. Edited by H. Morley. New York: Colonial Press, 1901.

_____ *The New Organon and Related Writings.* Edited by F. H. Anderson. New York: The Liberal Arts Press, 1960.

Baillie, John. *The Belief in Progress.* New York: Charles Scribner's Sons, 1951.

Barbour, Ian. *Issues in Science and Religion.* New York: Harper Torchbooks, 1971.

Becker, Carl Lotus. *The Heavenly City of the Eighteenth-Century Philosophers.* New Haven: Yale University Press, 1932.

Bell, Daniel. *The Cultural Contradictions of Capitalism.* 2nd ed. London: Heinman, 1979.

Berger, Peter and Luckmann, Thomas. *The Social Construction of Reality: A Treatise in the Sociology of Knowledge.* Garden City: Doubleday, 1966.

Bloom, Allan. *The Closing of the American Mind.* New York: Simon and Schuster,1987.

Bowles, Samuel and Gintis, Herbert. *Schooling in Capitalist America.* New York: Basic Books, 1976.

Brueggemann, Walter. *The Message of the Psalms: A Theological Commentary.* Minneapolis: Augsburg, 1984.

_____ *The Hopeful Imagination: Prophetic Voices in Exile.* Philadelphia: Fortress, 1986.

_____*Israel's Praise: Doxology against Idolatry and Ideology.* Philadelphia: Fortress, 1988.

_____*The Prophetic Imagination.* Philadelphia: Fortress, 1978.

Brummer, Vincent. *Theology and Philosophical Inquiry: An Introduction.* Philadelphia: Westminster, 1982.

Bury, J. B. *The Idea of Progress: An Inquiry into its Origin and Growth.* London: Macmillan, 1920.

Campolo, Anthony. *A Reasonable Faith: Responding to Secularism.* Waco, Texas: Word Books, 1983.

Collingwood, R. G. *The Idea of History.* Edited by T. M. Knox. New York: Oxford University Press, 1956.

Dawson, Christopher. *Progress and Religion: An Historical Inquiry.* New York: Sheed and Ward, 1938.

Dewey, John. *Intelligence in the Modern World.* Edited by J. Ratner. New York: Random House, 1939.

_____ *Reconstruction in Philosophy.* New York: Henry Holt and Co., 1929.

Dooyeweerd, Herman. *A New Critique of Theoretical Thought.* Volumes I, II, III and IV. Translated by D. H. Freeman and W. S. Young.

Philadelphia: Presbyterian and Reformed, 1953-1958.

_____ *In the Twilight of Western Thought.* Nutley, N. J.: The Craig Press, 1972.

_____ *Roots of Western Culture.* Translated by John Kraay. Edited by Mark Vander Vennen and Bernard Zylstra. Toronto: Wedge Publishing, 1979.

_____ *The Secularization of Science.* Translated by Robert Knudsen. Memphis: Christian Studies Center, 1954.

Dulles, Avery. "Method in Fundamental Theology: Reflections on David Tracy's *Blessed Rage for Order.*" *Theological Studies* 37 (June 1976), 304-316.

_____ *The Resilient Church.* New York: Doubleday, 1974.

Edie, J., ed. *An Invitation to Phenomenology: Studies in the Philosophy of Experience.* Chicago: Quadrangle Books, 1965.

Ellul, Jacques. *The Technological Society.* Translated by J. Wilkinson. New York: Alfred A. Knopf, 1964.

Farley, Edward. *Ecclesial Man: A Social Phenomenology of Faith and Reality.* Philadelphia: Fortress Press, 1975.

Feather, Frank, ed. *Through the 80's: Thinking Globally, Acting Locally.* Washington: World Futures Society, 1980.

Ferkiss, Victor. *Technological Man: The Myth and the Reality.* New York: George Braziler, 1969.

Fernhout, J. Harry and Boyd, Dwight. "Faith in Autonomy: Development in Kohlberg's Perspectives on Religion and Morality." *Religious Education* 80, 2 (Spring 1985), 287-307.

Fernhout, J. Harry and Malcolm, Tom. *Education and the Public Purpose.* Toronto: Curriculum Development Centre, 1979.

Fernhout, J. Harry. *The Relation of Religion or Faith to Morality According* to *Lawrence Kohlberg and James Fowler.* M.A. Thesis, University of Toronto, 1982.

Gadamer, Hans-Georg. *Truth and Method.* Translated by G. Barden and J. Cumming. A Continuum Book. New York: Seabury Press, 1975.

Galbraith, John Kenneth. *The New Industrial State.* Boston: Houghton Mifflin, 1967.

Gay, Peter. *The Enlightenment: An Interpretation.* Two Volumes. New York: Alfred A. Knopf, 1966 and 1969.

Geertz, Clifford. *The Interpretation of Cultures.* New York: Basic Books, 1973.

_____ "Religion as a Cultural System." In *Reader in Comparative Religion: An Anthropological Approach.* 3rd ed. Edited by W. A. Lessa and E. Z. Vogt. New York: Harper and Row, 1972.

Gendlin, Eugene T. *Experiencing and the Creation of Meaning.* Glencoe, Ill.: The Free Press, 1962.

Glacken, Clarence J. *Traces on the Rhodian Shore: Nature and Culture in Western Thought from Ancient Times to the End of the Enlightenment.* Berkeley: University of California Press, 1976.

Goudzwaard, Bob. *Aid for the Overdeveloped West.* Toronto: Wedge, 1975.

_____ *Capitalism and Progress: A Diagnosis of Western Society.* Translated and edited by Josina Van Nuis Zylstra. Toronto: Wedge, and Grand Rapids: Eerdmans, 1979.

_____ *Idols of Our Time.* Translated by Mark Vander Vennen. Downers Grove, Ill.: InterVarsity Press, 1984.

Gouldner, Alvin. *The Dialectic of Ideology and Technology: The Origins, Grammar and Future of Ideology.* A Continuum Book. New York: Seabury Press, 1976.

Grant, George. *Technology and Empire: Perspectives on North America.*

Toronto: Anansi Press, 1969.

Guiness, Os. *The Gravedigger File: Papers on the Subversion of the Modern Church.* Downers Grove, Ill: InterVarsity Press, 1983.
Gutiérrez, Gustavo. *A Theology of Liberation.* Translated and edited by Caridad Inda and John Eagleson. Maryknoll, N.Y.: Orbis Books, 1973.

Hamilton, William. *The New Essence of Christianity.* New York: Association Press, 1961.

Hanson, N. R. *Patterns of Discovery.* Cambridge: Cambridge University Press, 1965.

Hart, Hendrik. *Understanding Our World: Toward an Integral Ontology.* Christian Studies Today Series. Lanham, MD: University Press of America, 1984.

Harvey, Van A. "The Pathos of Liberal Theology," *Journal of Religion* 56, 4 (October 1976), 382-391.

Heilbroner, Robert. *An Inquiry into the Human Prospect.* New York: W. W. Norton, 1974.

_____ *The Making of Economic Society.* Rev. ed. Englewood Cliffs, NJ: Prentice-Hall, 1968.

_____ *The Worldly Philosophers.* 4th ed. New York: Simon and Schuster, 1972.

Holmes, Arthur F. *Contours of a Worldview.* Grand Rapids: Eerdmans, 1983.

Hooykaas, R. *Religion and the Rise of Modern Science.* Grand Rapids: Eerdmans, 1972.

Husserl, Edmund. *The Crisis of European Sciences and Transcendental Phenomenology.* Translated by David Carr. Evanston: Northwestern University Press, 1970.

_____ *Ideas: General Introduction to Pure Phenomenology.* Translated by W. R. Boyce-Gibson. New York: Collier Books, 1967.

Inge, W. R. *The Idea of Progress.* Oxford: Clarendon Press, 1920.

Joldersma, Clarence. *Beliefs and Scientific Enterprise: A Framework Model Based Upon Kuhn's Paradigms, Polanyi's Commitment Framework, and Radnitzky's Internal Steering Fields.* Published M.Phil. Thesis. Toronto: Institute for Christian Studies, 1982.

Kalsbeek, L. *Contours of a Christian Philosophy.* Edited by Bernard and Josina Zylstra. Toronto: Wedge, 1975.

Kant, Immanuel. "What is Enlightenment?" In *On History.* Edited by L. W. Beck. Translated by L. W. Beck, R. E. Anchor and E. L. Fackenheim. The Library of Liberal Arts. New York: Bobbs-Merrill, 1963.

Kaufman, Gordon. *An Essay on Theological Method.* Rev. ed. Number 11 of American Academy of Religion Studies in Religion. Edited by C. C. Cherry. Missoula, Montana: Scholars Press, 1979.

_____ *God the Problem.* Cambridge: Harvard University Press, 1971.

Kavanaugh, J. F. *Following Christ in a Consumer Society: The Spirituality of Cultural Resistance.* Maryknoll, NY: Orbis Books, 1981.

Kegley, Charles W., editor. *The Theology of Paul Tillich.* Rev. ed. New York: Pilgrim Press, 1982.

Klapwijk, Jacob. "Dooyeweerd's Christian Philosophy: Antithesis and Critique." *Reformed Journal* 30, 3 (March 1980), 20-24.

_____ "The Struggle for a Christian Philosophy: Another Look at Dooyeweerd." *Reformed Journal* 30, 2 (February 1980), 12-15.

Kozol, Jonathon. *The Night is Dark and I am Far from Home.* Boston: Houghton Mifflin, 1975.

Kraay, John and Tol, Anthony, eds. *Hearing and Doing: Philosophical Essays Dedicated to H. Evan Runner.* Toronto: Wedge, 1979.

Kuhn, Thomas. *The Structure of Scientific Revolutions*. Rev. ed. Chicago: University of Chicago Press, 1962.

Küng, Hans. *Does God Exist? An Answer for Today*. Translated by E. Quinn. Garden City, NY: Doubleday, 1980.

Lonergan, Bernard. *Insight: A Study of Human Understanding*. London: Longmans, 1964.

_____ *Method in Theology*. New York: Seabury Press, 1974.

Löwith, Karl. *Meaning in History*. Chicago: University of Chicago Press, 1964.

_____ *Nature, History and Existentialism*. Edited by Arnold Levison. Evanston: Northwestern University Press, 1966.

Lyon, David. "Secularization: The Fate of Faith in Modern Society." *Themelios* 10, 1 (September 1984), 14-22.

Maddox, Randy L. *Toward an Ecumenical Fundamental Theology*. Number 47 of American Academy of Religion Academy Series. Edited by C. A. Raschke. Chico, CA: Scholars Press, 1984.

Manuel, Frank E. and Manuel, Fritzie P. *Utopian Thought in the Western World*. Cambridge: Belknop Press of Harvard University Press, 1979.

Marshall, Paul; Griffioen, Sander and Mouw, Richard, eds. *Stained Glass: Worldviews and Social Science*. Christian Studies Today Series. Lanham: MD: University Press of America, 1989.

Marshall, Paul. *Thine is the Kingdom: A Biblical Perspective on Government and Politics Today*. London: Marshall, Morgan and Scott, 1984.

McIntire, C. Thomas, ed. *God, History and Historians*. New York: Oxford University Press, 1977.

Merleau-Ponty, Maurice. "What is Phenomenology?" In *Phenomenology of Religion*. Edited by Joseph Bettis. New York: Harper and Row, 1969.

Moltmann, Jürgen. *The Future of Hope: Theology as Eschatology.* Edited by P. Herzog. New York: Herder and Herder, 1970.

_____ *God in Creation: An Ecological Doctrine of Creation.* Translated by Margaret Kohl. London: SCM Press, 1985.

_____ *Theology of Hope: On the Ground and Implications of Christian Eschatology.* Translated by J. W. Leitch. New York: Harper and Row, 1967.

_____ *Trinity and the Kingdom.* Translated by Margaret Kohl. San Francisco: Harper and Row, 1981.

Monsma, Stephen V., ed. *Responsible Technology.* Grand Rapids: Eerdmans, 1986.

Nathanson, Paul. "Religion and Secularity: A Methodological Inquiry." Unpublished essay. Montreal, McGill University, Faculty of Religious Studies, 1986.

Neville, Robert C. *Creativity and God: A Challenge to Process Theology.* A Crossroad Book. New York: Seabury Press, 1980.

Newbigin, Lesslie. *Foolishness to the Greeks: The Gospel and Western Culture.* Grand Rapids, Mich.: Eerdmans, 1986.

_____ *The Gospel in a Pluralist Society.* Grand Rapids, Mich. and Geneva: Eerdmans and WCC, 1989.

Niebuhr, H. Richard. *Christ and Culture.* New York: Harper and Row, 1951.

Niebuhr, Reinhold. *Faith and History.* New York: Charles Scribner's Sons, 1949.

_____ *The Interpretation of Christian Ethics.* New York: Harper and Bros., 1935.

_____ *The Irony of American History.* London: Nisbet and Co., 1952.

_____ *The Nature and Destiny of Man.* Volume I: *Human Nature.* New

York: Charles Scribner's Sons, 1941.

_____ *The Nature and Destiny of Man.* Volume II: *Human Destiny.* New York: Charles Scribner's Sons, 1943.

_____ *Reflections on the End of an Era.* New York and London: Charles Scribner's Sons, 1934.

Nisbett, Robert. *The Sociological Tradition.* New York: Basic Books, 1966.

Ogden, Schubert. *The Reality of God.* New York: Harper and Row, 1966.

Olthuis, James H., et al. *A Hermeneutics of Ultimacy: Peril or Promise?* Christian Studies Today Series. Lanham, MD: University Press of America, 1986.

Olthuis, James H. "Faith Development in the Adult Life Span." *Studies in Religion/ Sciences Religieuses* 14, 4 (1985), 497-509.

_____ "Must the Church Become Secular?" In *Out of Concern for the Church.* Toronto: Wedge Publishing, 1970, ch. 5.

_____ "On the Nature of Religion: Faith, Vision of Life and Praxis." Unpublished paper. Toronto, Institute for Christian Studies, no date.

_____ "On Worldviews." *Christian Scholar's Review* XIV, 2 (1985), 153-164.

_____ "Straddling the Boundaries Between Theology and Psychology: the Faith-Feeling Interface." *Journal of Psychology and Christianity* 4, 1 (Spring 1985), 6-15.

Pannenberg, Wolfhart. *Anthropology in Theological Perspective.* Translated by M. J. O'Connell. Philadelphia: Westminster Press, 1984.

_____ *Basic Questions in Theology.* Volumes 1 and 2. Translated by G. H. Kehm. Philadelphia: Fortress Press, 1971 and 1972.

_____ *Faith and Reality.* Translated by John Maxwell. Philadelphia: Westminster Press, 1977.

_____ *The Idea of God and Human Freedom.* Translated by R. A. Wilson. Philadelphia: Westminster Press, 1973.

_____ *Theology and the Kingdom of God.* Edited by Richard J. Neuhaus. Philadelphia: Westminster Press, 1969.

_____ *Theology and the Philosophy of Science.* Translated by Francis McDonagh. Philadelphia: Westminster Press, 1976.

Passmore, John. *Man's Responsibility for Nature: Ecological Problems and Western Traditions.* London: Gerald Duckworth, 1974.

Pico, Giovanni della Mirandola. *Oration on the Dignity of Man.* Translated by A. R. Caponigni. Chicago: Henry Regnery, 1965.

Polanyi, Michael. *Personal Knowledge: Toward a Post-Critical Philosophy.* Chicago: University of Chicago Press, 1958.

_____ *Science, Faith and Reality.* Chicago: University of Chicago Press, 1964.

_____ "The Scientific Revolution." In *Christians in a Technological Age.* Edited by H. White. New York: Seabury Press, 1967.

_____ *The Tacit Dimension.* Garden City: Doubleday, 1966.

Price, David, et al. *Teaching Science in a Climate of Controversy.* Ipswich, MA: American Scientific Affiliation, 1986.

Quinney, Richard. "The Theology of Culture: Marx, Tillich and the Prophetic Tradition in the Reconstruction of Social and Moral Order." *Union Seminary Quarterly Review* 34, 4 (Summer 1979), 203-214.

Rahner, Karl. *Hearers of the Word.* Translated by M. Richards. Montreal: Palm Publishers, 1969.

_____ *Spirit in the World.* Translated by William Dych. New York: Herder and Herder, 1968.

Rasmussen, David R. *Mythic-Symbolic Language: A Constructive Interpretation of the Thought of Paul Ricoeur.* The Hague: Martinus Nijhof, 1971.

Ricoeur, Paul. *The Conflict of Interpretations: Essays in Hermeneutics.* Translated by C. Freilich. Edited by D. Ihde. Evanston: Northwestern University Press, 1974.

_____ *Fallible Man: Philosophy of the Will.* Translated by Charles Kelby. Chicago: Henry Regnery Press, 1965.

_____ *Hermeneutics and the Human Sciences.* Edited and translated by John B. Thompson. Cambridge: Cambridge University Press, 1981.

_____ *The Philosophy of Paul Ricoeur: An Anthology of His Work.* Edited by C. E. Reagon and D. Stewart. Boston: Beacon Press, 1978.

_____ *The Symbolism of Evil.* Translated by Emerson Buchanan. Boston: Beacon Press, 1967.

Rifkin, Jeremy. *The Emerging Order: God in the Age of Scarcity.* New York: G. P. Putnam's Sons, 1979.

Ruether, Rosemary. *Liberation Theology: Human Hope Confronts Christian History and American Power.* New York and Toronto: Paulist Press, 1972.

_____ *Sexism and God-talk: Toward a Feminist Theology.* Boston: Beacon Press, 1983.

_____ *To Change the World: Christology and Cultural Criticism.* New York: Crossroad Press, 1983.

Ryan, M. D., ed. *The Contemporary Explosion in Theology: Ecumenical Studies in Theology.* Meutchen, NJ: Scarecrow Press, 1975.

Schell, Jonathan. *The Fate of the Earth.* New York: Alfred Knopf, 1982.

Schumacher, E. F. *Small is Beautiful: Economics as if People Mattered.* London: Abacus Books, 1974.

Schuurman, Egbert. *Reflections on the Technological Society*. Translated by H. Van Dyke and L. Teneyenhuis. Toronto: Wedge Publishing, 1977.

Scriven, Charles. *The Transformation of Culture: Christian Social Ethics after H. Richard Niebuhr*. Scottdale, Penn.: Herald Press, 1988.

Smart, Ninian. *Worldviews: Crosscultural Explorations of Human Beliefs*. New York: Charles Scribner's Sons, 1983.

Smith, Wilfred Cantwell. *Faith and Belief*. Princeton: Princeton University Press, 1979.

_____ *The Meaning and End of Religion*. Toronto: Mentor Books, 1964.

Sontag, Frederick and Roth, John K. "The Premise of all Criticism." *Andover Newton Quarterly* 17, 3 (January 1977), 195-200.

Spiro, M. "Religion: Problems of Definition and Explanation." In *Anthropological Approaches to the Study of Religion*. Edited by M. Banton. London: Tavistock Publications, 1966.

Stevenson, Leslie. *Seven Theories of Human Nature*. New York and Oxford: Oxford University Press, 1974.

Storkey, Alan. *A Christian Social Perspective*. Leicester, England: InterVarsity Press, 1979.

Taylor, Mark C. *Deconstructing Theology*. Number 28 of American Academy of Religion Studies in Religion. New York: Crossroad Press, 1982.

Tillich, Paul. *The Courage to Be*. The Fontana Library. London and Glasgow: Collins, 1962.

_____ *Dynamics of Faith*. New York: Harper Torchbooks, 1958.

_____ *The Protestant Era*. Abridged edition. Phoenix Books. Chicago: University of Chicago Press, 1957.

_____ *The Religious Situation.* Translated by H. Richard Niebuhr. Meridian Books. Cleveland and New York: World Publishing Co., 1956.

_____ *Systematic Theology.* Volumes I, II and III. Chicago: University of Chicago Press, 1951, 1957, 1963.

_____ *Theology of Culture.* London, Oxford and New York: Oxford University Press, 1959.

Thiselton, Anthony C. "Knowledge, Myth and Corporate Memory." In *Believing in the Church: The Corporate Nature of Faith.* A Report of the Church of England Doctrine Commission. London: S.P.C.K., 1981.

_____ *The Two Horizons: New Testament Hermeneutics and Philosophical Description.* Grand Rapids: Eerdmans, 1980.

Toulmin, Stephen. *An Examination of the Place of Reason in Ethics.* Cambridge: Cambridge University Press, 1961.

_____ *Foresight and Understanding.* New York: Harper Torchbooks, 1961.

Toynbee, Arnold. *A Study of History.* Volumes I and IV. London: Oxford University Press, 1934 and 1939.

Tracy, David. *The Analogical Imagination: Christian Theology and the Culture of Pluralism.* New York: Crossroad, 1981.

_____ *Blessed Rage for Order: The New Pluralism in Theology.* New York: Seabury Press, 1975.

_____ "Response to Gilkey." *The University of Chicago Magazine* 76, 1 (Fall 1983), 14.

Turner, Victor. *Dramas, Fields and Metaphors: Symbolic Action in Human Society.* New York: Cornell University Press, 1974.

van Buren, Paul. *The Secular Meaning of the Gospel.* New York: Macmillan, 1963.

VanderMarck, William. "Fundamental Theology: A Bibliographical and Critical Survey." *Religious Studies Review* 8, 3 (July 1982), 244-253.

van Peursen, C. A. "Life-World and Structures." In *Patterns of the Life-World: Essays in Honor of John Wild.* Edited by J. M. Edie, F. H. Parker and C. O. Schrag. Evanston: Northwestern University Press, 1970, 139-153.

Voegelin, Eric. "The Religion of Humanity and the French Revolution." In *From Enlightenment to Revolution.* Edited by J. H. Hallowell. Durham: Duke University Press, 1975, 160-194.

Walsh, Brian J. and Middleton, J. Richard. *The Transforming Vision: Shaping a Christian Worldview.* Downers Grove, Ill.: InterVarsity Press, 1984.

Walsh, Brian J. and Chaplin, Jon. "Dooyeweerd's Contribution to a Christian Philosophical Paradigm." *Crux* XIX, 1 (March 1983), 8-22.

Walsh, Brian J. "A Critical Review of Pannenberg's *Anthropology in Theological Perspective.*" *Christian Scholar's Review* 15, 3 (1986), 247-259.

_____ "Anthony Thiselton's Contribution to Biblical Hermeneutics." *Christian Scholar's Review* 14, 3 (1985), 224-235.

_____ "End-times Theology Offers No Hope." *Catalyst* 9, 7 (June/July 1986), 7.

_____ *Futurity and Creation: Explorations in the Eschatological Theology of Wolfhart Pannenberg.* Published M.Phil. thesis. Toronto: Institute for Christian Studies, 1979.

_____ "Pannenberg's Eschatological Ontology." *Christian Scholar's Review* 11, 3 (1982), 229-249.

_____ Review of *Deconstructing Theology. Christian Scholar's Review* 13, 3 (1984), 284-286.

_____ *Subversive Christianity.* Bristol, U.K.: Regius Press, 1991.

_____ "Theology of Hope and the Doctrine of Creation: An Appraisal of Jürgen Moltmann." *Evangelical Quarterly* LIX, 1 (January 1987).

_____ "*The Transformation of Culture:* A Review Essay." *Conrad Grebel Review* (Spring 1990).

_____ *Who Turned Out the Lights? The Light of the Gospel in a Post-Enlightenment Culture.* An Inaugural address. Toronto: Institute for Christian Studies, 1990.

Whitehead, Alfred North. *Modes of Thought.* New York: Macmillan, 1938.

_____ *Process and Reality: An Essay in Cosmology.* Corrected edition. Edited by David Ray Griffin and Donald W. Sherburne. New York: The Free Press, 1978.

_____ *Science and the Modern World.* New York: Macmillan, 1948.

Wiebe, Donald. "The Failure of Nerve in the Academic Study of Religion." *Studies in Religion/Sciences Religieuses* 13, 4 (1984), 401-423.

Wild, John. *Existence and the World of Freedom.* Englewood Cliffs, NJ: Prentice-Hall, 1963.

Wilkenson, Loren, ed. *Earthkeeping: Christian Stewardship of Natural Resources.* Grand Rapids: Eerdmans, 1980.

Wink, Walter. "Unmasking the Powers: A Biblical View of Roman and American Economics." *Sojourners* 7, 10 (October 1978), 9-15.

Winquist, Charles E. "Theology, Deconstruction, and Ritual Process." *Zygon* 18, 3 (September 1983), 295-309.

Wittgenstein, Ludwig. *Philosophical Investigations.* Oxford: Blackwells, 1967.

Wolters, Albert M. *Creation Regained: Biblical Basics for a Reformational Worldview.* Grand Rapids: Eerdmans, 1985.

Wolterstorff, Nicholas. *Reason Within the Bounds of Religion.* Grand Rapids: Eerdmans, 1976.

_____ *Until Justice and Peace Embrace.* Grand Rapids: Eerdmans, 1984.

Yoder, John Howard. *The Politics of Jesus.* Grand Rapids: Eerdmans, 1972.

Zylstra, Bernard. "A Neo-Conservative Critique of Modernity: Daniel Bell's Appraisal." *Christian Scholar's Review* 7, 4 (1978), 337-355.

_____ "Modernity and the American Empire." *International Reformed Bulletin* 68 (1977), 3-19.

Colophon

*This book was typeset in
New Baskerville with
Optima chapter headings
by Willem Hart on a
Macintosh SE using the
Pagemaker layout program.
Body copy is 11/13 point,
quotes are 10/11 point
and footnotes are 9/10 point.
Final printout was
produced on a
LaserWriter Plus*